European Economic Governance after the Eurozone and COVID-19 Crises

European Economic Governance after the Eurozone and COVID-19 Crises

Edited by

Ioannis Papadopoulos

Cambridge Scholars Publishing

European Economic Governance after the Eurozone and COVID-19 Crises

Edited by Ioannis Papadopoulos

This book first published 2022

Cambridge Scholars Publishing

Lady Stephenson Library, Newcastle upon Tyne, NE6 2PA, UK

British Library Cataloguing in Publication Data
A catalogue record for this book is available from the British Library

ISBN (10): 1-5275-7774-0
ISBN (13): 978-1-5275-7774-9

With the support of the Erasmus+ Programme of the European Union

TABLE OF CONTENTS

Part C: EU Banking Union

Part D: The Legal and Economic Dimension of Credit Rating Agencies

ACKNOWLEDGMENTS

ABOUT THE JEAN MONNET CENTRE OF EXCELLENCE

In the present book, the Jean Monnet Centre of Excellence "Research on Crucial Issues of European Integration" of the University of Macedonia presents the results of two scientific conferences and a roundtable discussion, as well as the research carried out within the framework of the Centre's 2nd Research Axis entitled "European Economic Governance", under the direction of its thematic coordinator, Associate Professor Ioannis Papadopoulos.

The Jean Monnet Centre of Excellence "Research on Crucial Issues of European Integration" was established in 2015 after having been selected for co-funding by the ERASMUS+ Jean Monnet Action Programme. It was hosted within the Institute of International Relations and European Integration (IDEA) of the Department of International and European Studies at the University of Macedonia (Greece) directed by the Head of the Department, Professor Ilias Kouskouvelis.

The main purpose of the Centre was to conduct research on topical and crucial issues of European integration in five research axes: a) The European Union in the International System: Security and Defence; b) European Economic Governance; c) The Development of the European Union; d) Constitutional Values, Rights and Citizenship in the European Union; and e) Research, Education and Youth Policies in the European Union. Each axis had three research projects. Overall, 38 researchers participated in the 15 research projects from the University of Macedonia, from the Aristotle University of Thessaloniki, as well as from other universities and research centres in Greece and abroad. The Centre organised 18 conferences and roundtable discussions on the above topics, as well as research visits abroad by the researchers, e.g. in the European Central Bank and the European Securities and Markets Authority.

The Centre also organised 3 summer academies on the EU Area of Freedom, Security and Justice, a seminar and a webinar on hate speech, and established the "Observatory of EU Constitutional Values", with its main aim being to report and comment on relevant EU legislation and case law.

As academic coordinator, I would like to thank everyone, the distinguished speakers and contributors in this volume, and all those who supported the Centre of Excellence in organising the conferences and events. Most of all, I would like to thank Professor Aristidis Bitzenis for hosting our roundtable discussions and panels in the framework of the annual International Conference for International Business (ICIB) of the University of Macedonia, in which Prof. Bitzenis serves as Academic Coordinator and Assoc. Professor Papadopoulos serves as member of the organising committee.

I would like to express my appreciation for, and acknowledge, the voluntary work of: a) the interns at the Jean Monnet Centre of Excellence, i.e., students from the Department of International and European Studies of the University of Macedonia, the Law School, and the Department of Political Sciences of the Aristotle University of Thessaloniki, who were selected to assist in compiling this volume, to conduct relevant research, and to prepare the notebooks of the 2nd Research Axis that are posted on our website "jmcexcellence.uom.gr" (in alphabetical order): Maria Kilinkaridou, Fotis Kokkinis, Panagiotis Moumtsidis, Aggeliki Roussou, Evlampia Stogianni, and Kornilia Vikelidou. Dr. Vikelidou also prepared a lexicon of the relevant terms; b) the undergraduate students (in alphabetical order) Aliki Chapsanidou and Christos Zois, who reviewed the transcripts of certain presentations in order to assist the contributors in the preparation of their chapters; and c) the undergraduate student Despoina Damianidou and the postgraduate student Antonia Koumpoti (experts and interns/researchers of the Centre for Research on Democracy and Law, directed by Assoc. Prof. Papadopoulos), for assisting in checking the use of the Chicago referencing system and in correcting the text format.

My acknowledgments are also addressed to the PhD candidates (in alphabetical order) Chrysothea Bassia, Theofano Mantzari and Afentoula (Fenia) Palla (University of Macedonia), who assisted the thematic coordinator and me in organising the events of the 2nd Research Axis, as well as Ms. Antonia Koumpoti for her voluntary assistance to complete the necessary paperwork in the later stages of the Jean Monnet Centre administrative procedures.

I would like to thank Associate Professor Ioannis Papadopoulos, who undertook the challenging and complex task of editing this research volume, which combines academic research with practice, as well as his PhD Researcher, Dr. Alexandros Kyriakidis, for his valuable contribution in coordinating the editing process and for his diligent work in the proofreading of the volume. I would also like to thank Ms. Dionysia Tsolaki, PhD researcher at the Department of International and European Studies of the University of Macedonia, native speaker and teacher of the English language, for her outstanding work in reviewing the correct use of English terminology and the homogeneity of the whole text.

Finally, I would like to express my gratitude to the Jean Monnet Team in the European Education and Culture Executive Agency (EACEA) and most of all, the project officer Ms. Alexandra Campos Bray, for her valuable advice and support during the Jean Monnet Centre of Excellence project.

None of this would have been possible without the Erasmus+/Jean Monnet Action co-funding arrangements, which contributed significantly to the extroversion and cross-fertilisation of our research.

Thessaloniki, October 29, 2021

Despoina Anagnostopoulou
Associate Professor
Department of International and European Studies
Jean Monnet Chair
Former Academic Coordinator of the Jean Monnet Centre of Excellence
University of Macedonia

INTRODUCTION

THE CHALLENGE OF THE COVID-19 PANDEMIC FOR EUROPEAN ECONOMIC GOVERNANCE

IOANNIS PAPADOPOULOS*

Increasing structural divergences in Europe due to the pandemic

The Covid-19 health crisis came as a tremendous shock to the world, and to the European Union (hereinafter EU) more particularly, only a few years after the Eurozone crisis. The fact is that EU member states were not affected to the same degree, at least in terms of the economic impact, by the Covid-19 crisis; on the contrary, the asymmetrical nature of this crisis confirmed the already existing disequilibrium between them. The most evident source of this asymmetry is that the southern countries of the EU (Portugal, Spain, Italy, Malta, Greece and Cyprus) are very dependent on tourism, which is one of the sectors that were most hit by the Covid-19 pandemic. But that is only the tip of the iceberg. More profoundly, the pandemic exacerbated the old structural differences in the economic growth models between the South and the North of Europe. The South mostly relies on internal demand and the services sector, whereas the North on exports and a robust industrial basis. Yet it so happens that the Covid-19 pandemic, by its nature, struck services much more than industry, because the services sector is to an important extent dependent on the interpersonal element, which was put in brackets due to the confinement measures.

But even the industrial products produced in the South are more mid-range market than in the North; the South has no real presence in the

* Associate Professor and Director, Centre for Research on Democracy and Law, Department of International and European Studies, University of Macedonia (Thessaloniki, Greece).

Artificial Intelligence sector yet, which seems to be the driving force behind the new, fourth, wave of industrialisation (known as "Industry 4.0") currently unfolding. Moreover, the institutions in the South tend to be weaker and less impervious to partisan pressures than in the North; this inevitably produces less efficiency in public services. Finally, the education and training systems of the Northern countries are better adapted to the needs of the market and closely fit the local and regional productive fabric, as is the case of the famous "dual learning" system in Germany, which revolves around the industrial enterprises of the country and is flexible enough to stick to the changes in international demand (Bosch 2010).

The cause of this structural divergence can be traced back to the first two industrial revolutions between the mid-18th and the beginning of the 20th centuries, when industrial plants were primarily concentrated in the area between the Northern Sea and the north of Italy, leaving outside the periphery of the continent. The fundamental lack of territorial cohesion in Europe is due foremost to economic history (Crescenzi et al. 2020). This is the reason for the establishment of EU cohesion policy in the end of the 1980s. Nevertheless, the creation of the euro area accentuated the pattern of divergence, since the removal of the foreign exchange risk directed more resources towards the specialised structures of production, i.e., services in the South and industry in the North. The austerity policies that took hold after the eruption of the Eurozone crisis stressed even more the fundamental structural divergence between the South and the North. The heterogeneity of the euro area became entrenched, even though the internal devaluation measures, the reforms that promoted competitiveness, and the extremely accommodating monetary policy of the European Central Bank (hereinafter ECB) had gradually allowed the South to recover by the mid-2010s despite the grave problems in the policy mix that was adopted and the generally low institutional quality of the involved countries (Pelagidis & Moutsopoulos 2021).

The Covid-19 pandemic made its deleterious appearance shortly after the Eurozone crisis had started to heal. Only this time, the response of the EU was of a completely different nature than in the 2010s. An impressive array of fiscal and monetary policy instruments was mobilised to counteract the pandemic shock and to restore confidence in a time of panic. The foundations of a true Transfer Union made their appearance with the 750 billion euro EU Recovery Plan, the launching of a form of jointly issued debt (Eurobonds) for the very first time in the history of European integration, and the creation of new own resources for the EU budget. A federal-type Fiscal Union has thus been watermarked. We can notice it when we take a comprehensive look at the full panoply of measures that the European institutions decided to espouse in the midst of the worst crisis since World War II.

Conditions for optimism

Consequently, there is reason to be optimistic despite the ravages of the Covid-19 pandemic. Compared to the Eurozone crisis in the 2010s, this new challenge has brought about a breakthrough in the European economic governance with innovative financial tools and new procedures for their use. And it seems by now that even though there will be negative economic consequences from this pandemic crisis, these will be shallower and more short-lived than the wounds that the Eurozone crisis left behind.[1] Contrary to the double —public and current account— deficit that we had witnessed just before the outbreak of the Eurozone crisis, the situation now is very different: we never experienced a downfall in aggregate demand, since public deficit spending by the EU member states after the suspension of the Stability and Growth Pact in 2020 has been compensated by surplus savings of households and businesses.[2] This state of affairs prefigures a situation in which private sector expenditure will rise at the same time that the public sector will start spending less to support the economy. There is, thus, a sort of internal equilibrium that will certainly smooth the transition to normality, provided that state aid will not be withdrawn abruptly for the sake of fiscal consolidation, as had happened during the Eurozone crisis in 2011.

The European Commission confirms this perspective. In its Spring 2021 Economic Forecast, the Commission projects that the EU economy will expand by 4.2% in 2021 and by 4.4% in 2022, after a contraction of 6.1% in 2020, and also that public investment, as a proportion of GDP, is set to reach its highest level in more than a decade in 2022, and that this will be driven by the Recovery and Resilience Facility, the key instrument at the heart of the EU initiative NextGenerationEU (EC 2021). In such circumstances, all EU member states should see their economies return to pre-crisis levels by the end of 2022. Yet, the ratio of public debt to GDP is

---

[1] A recent International Monetary Fund working paper has estimated that there will be significant negative impacts in economic performance and income distribution, as well as an increase in poverty until 2025, but only if more effective policy responses than those in the past are not adopted (Emmerling et al. 2021).

[2] Indeed, in America the recession caused by the Covid-19 pandemic only lasted two months, which makes it the shortest US recession on record (NBER 2021).

forecast to peak at 94% this year before decreasing slightly in 2022, while aggregate general government deficit is set to rise by about half a percentage point to 7.5% of GDP in the EU this year before halving to just below 4% by 2022 (EC 2021).

The European Commission prudently notes that "[t]he risks surrounding the GDP forecast are high and will remain so as long as the pandemic hangs over the economy. On the epidemiological front, developments concerning the pandemic and the efficiency and effectiveness of vaccination programmes could turn out better or worse than assumed in the central scenario of this forecast. On the economic side, this forecast may underestimate the propensity of households to spend, or, on the opposite, consumers' desire to maintain high levels of precautionary savings. […] Another risk to the outlook is the timing of policy support withdrawal, which if premature could jeopardise the recovery. On the downside, the impact of corporate distress on the labour market and the financial sector could prove worse than anticipated" (EC 2021). In truth, even though the epidemiological and macroeconomic conditions play a very important role as to the future direction of the European economy, the American Recovery Plan instigated by President Joe Biden highlights the potential that could be unleashed also in Europe if the EU —or at least the Eurozone— shared a stronger common approach to fiscal policies, as the Chief Economist of the ECB Philip Lane says in an interview for the French journal *Le Monde* (Albert & Charrel 2021). In the United States of America (hereinafter US), there has been little doubt as to the capacity of the federal state to finance public deficits of any size. If a full-blown Fiscal Union had been established in the EU by now, the economic actors —and foremost the governments that will have to borrow to finance their national recovery and investment plans— would have been less apprehensive about the economic outlook.

To the advancement of a Fiscal Union, we could also add the establishment of a common European Industrial Policy, which would place emphasis on building clusters of innovation and joint technology initiatives at European level for the promotion of investments in cutting-edge sectors such as the hydrogen economy or the manufacturing of electrical batteries. With the Covid-19 health crisis, it became evident that the European industry stakeholders —industrial enterprises, research institutions and educational systems, corporate finance, national and regional governments— should collaborate more closely so as to restructure the supply and logistic chains and to bring productive plants closer to the product users. In some strategic sectors it is of good economic logic to construct European industrial champions capable of withstanding international competition and of providing security of supply to the Europeans, especially in troubled times such as these. In summary, a more coherent and demanding European fiscal framework together with a dedicated European industrial policy could turn out to be the real game changers for European economic governance and for the process of European integration more broadly.

Structure of the book

The title of this collective volume refers to the economic governance of the EU after the economic crisis of 2007-08 and during the Covid-19 pandemic crisis, and to the challenge of sustainability in its growth model.

The chapters are organised in four parts. The first part of the book *Where is Europe heading?* contains ideas on the future of Europe and on the reorganisation of European economic governance from two renowned European economists, Michel Aglietta and Karl Aiginger. The second part *EU Fiscal and Monetary Union* analyses the two basic policy tools used by the EU to tackle the subsequent Eurozone and Covid-19 pandemic crises, i.e., the Stability and Growth Pact and the EU Recovery Initiative, commonly known as "NextGenerationEU". The third part *EU Banking Union* discusses several legal aspects of the EU Banking Union —notably the combination and balancing of various EU competences with member states' powers—, a case study on the implementation and shortfalls of the EU Banking Union, and a possible structural reform of the banking sector both in the US and in the EU aiming towards some form of separation between commercial and investment banking. The fourth and last part of the book *The Legal and Economic Dimension of Credit Rating Agencies* critically examines Credit Rating Agencies (hereinafter CRAs), especially their legal dimension and their efficiency as tools of economic prediction, develops some thoughts on the impact of credit rates on the efficiency and resilience of the economy, and expounds an alternative model of Independent Credit Rating Agencies (hereinafter ICRAs).

The opening chapter of the first part is an across-the-board interview of the French economist *Michel Aglietta*, Professor Emeritus at the University of Paris X Nanterre and scientific advisor to CEPII and to France Stratégie, by the editor Ioannis Papadopoulos. Professor Aglietta explains why he thinks the Stability and Growth Pact is not sufficient and capable of leading to a real Fiscal Union in Europe, since it was not designed with foresight. The source of the problem is that the disruption of the growth regime of financial capitalism that we are experiencing after 2008 has not been well understood. The endogenous dynamic of finance expresses a logic of momentum and radical uncertainty, whereas the neoclassical conception of efficiency, which is the basic macroeconomic assumption in Western countries, eliminates temporality and uncertainty. According to Aglietta, the most fundamental element that needs to be put in place is a common European long-term investment and industrial policy. This policy must be founded on the presupposition that the new growth regime is a new form of globalisation based on common goods such as the climate. It is the idea of European added value that will help us define a long-term investment programme by transforming finance. We need a restructuring of the European budget on the fiscal revenue side, with new own resources related to the European common goods, particularly a tax on digital data, a tax on financial transactions, and a carbon tax. The new EU budget, and the common investment and industrial policy that it will support, can play a countercyclical stabilisation role and at the same time create a sense of European belonging for the citizens.

Michel Aglietta also expounds his conception of a public-private partnership financial system. Such a system needs to promote a European network of national promotional banks. It also needs to encourage the issuance of European bonds linked to low-carbon investments, which are capable of boosting production and income in the long run. Aglietta explains the price mechanism that can lead to carbon neutrality. In a context in which deflationary pressures must be prevented from turning into stagnation equilibrium, the European Central Bank's mission must change; since money is a fundamental public good that is global and climate is a global public good, we need a money-climate link. Structural change can come from new incentives induced by the evolution of consumption patterns. Furthermore, a new European paradigm needs to avoid restrictive fiscal policies and to impose some countercyclical action for the euro area as a whole. This will need an institutional reform comprising a European finance minister and democratic control of the European economic governance. Finally, Aglietta reflects on Europe's demographic deficit as a long-term structural challenge that can pave the way for an understanding of social protection as a universal right of citizenship.

The second chapter of the first part has been written by *Karl Aiginger*, Director of the Policy Crossover Centre Vienna-Brussels and

Professor Emeritus of Economics at the Viennese University of Economics and Business (WU Wien). It contains an all-embracing vision for a stronger and larger Europe, lighthouse of sustainable growth and reforms mentor for its vicinity. In Aiginger's view, the European unification project has met with tremendous success, but it also faces problems on the road to the future. The increasingly irrational competitive advantage of the US dollar has to be addressed by a new European strategy, part of which would be the issuance of European safe bonds and the denomination of more international contracts in euros so as to enhance European economic power in the globalising world. The author argues that it is extremely important to develop synergies between public sector reforms and an improved European budget, climate policy, and stimulus packages to counteract the crisis.

In this context, he carves out four basic policy choices that may determine strategies for the Union and its member states: a high road strategy focusing on innovation and skills, raising energy or resource productivity, and fostering new firms and technologies, instead of seeking low costs only; a counterstrategy against populism that rejects pessimism and the narrative that everything was better in the past by placing emphasis on future-oriented reforms; a boost for energy efficiency and a shift of energy use from fossil fuels to clean energy; and a future-oriented industrial policy driven by societal goals such as climate change, health, poverty prevention, and the reduction of inequality. Professor Aiginger also develops some interesting ideas on the improvement of European governance: a combination of top-down common goals set by the EU and bottom-up preferences and innovations pursued by member states; a streamlining of EU decisions; a strengthening of European financial stability; and a delegation of decision-making on migration to regions or cities as well as a combination of the acceptance for migrants with financial incentives.

He also argues forcefully in favour of both an enlargement of the EU to the Western Balkans and a European outward strategy striving for new partnerships with its dynamic yet unstable neighbourhood, especially with Africa. Southern Europe can serve as a bridge to the southern and eastern non-European neighbours and can make Europe as a whole stronger and more capable of shaping globalisation in a responsible, welfare-increasing way. Putting everything into perspective, Professor Aiginger maintains that the European Green Deal, accompanied by a Social Europe that leaves no person or region behind, can provide a new narrative that will mobilise European citizens, and concludes with some intriguing ideas on how to combine measures to limit climate change and inequality with the large stimulus programmes due to Covid-19.

The second part of the book opens with a chapter by *Dimitrios Skiadas*, Professor at the University of Macedonia. The chapter focuses on a more technical aspect of the establishment of a Fiscal Union within the EU, namely the importance of the Excessive Deficit Procedure (hereinafter EDP) under the current fiscal governance scheme of the Economic and Monetary Union (hereinafter EMU) as a means of safeguarding and improving the coordination of the national economic policies of the EU member states. The author first presents the basic rationale of the Stability and Growth Pact (hereinafter SGP) as well as the controversies as to its legal nature and economic efficacy. He then develops the central part of the chapter, which is devoted to the European Court of Auditors' (hereinafter ECA) proposals to tackle the weaknesses of the SGP's functioning that have been diagnosed during the Eurozone financial crisis. The main problem identified by the ECA is the underperformance of the European Commission in its mission to monitor the implementation of the SGP preventive arm —as it was reinforced by the establishment of a Macroeconomic Imbalance Procedure in 2011— and to ensure the interaction of the latter with the SGP corrective arm.

As a consequence, the credibility of the SGP has been seriously undermined, sending thus an implicit political message to the EU member states that they should not be overly concerned neither with their slow pace of convergence to their medium-term fiscal objectives nor with their capacity to tackle another recession in the future. A complementary problem identified by the ECA is that the examination of data by Eurostat does not adequately assess EU member states' control systems, thus leaving them leeway to get around the fiscal and macroeconomic standards set up by the reformed SGP. In a broad way, more transparency and clarity are needed, since the SGP mechanisms have become more complicated due to the several strata of reforms that have been adopted. Overall, if the EDP is to be the instrument for enforcing the fiscal rules decided by the EU in the course of eventually establishing a Fiscal Union, the improvement of its use is imperative.

The second chapter of the second part has been written by *Ioannis Papadopoulos*, Associate Professor at the University of Macedonia and Director of the Centre for Research on Democracy and Law. The chapter concerns the EU Recovery Initiative, commonly known as "NextGenerationEU", that was adopted in the midst of the Covid-19 pandemic. Under the pressure of an unprecedented health and economic crisis, the EU established an innovative EU Recovery Instrument (hereinafter EURI) —official name of the initiative— as a dedicated instrument designed to tackle the adverse effects of the pandemic crisis and to support investment, speed up the recovery, strengthen cohesion among member states, and reinforce the long-term growth potential by focusing on the green and digital transition of the European economy.

This chapter first recounts the path towards a difficult European coordination in front of a crisis both symmetrical and asymmetrical, and presents a narrative of the events and the basic points of the discussion that accompanied the endorsement of NextGenerationEU, which it considers as a game changer for Europe. It then goes on to analyse five aspects of the initiative that stand out: the massive use of a form of Eurobonds; the onset of a Transfer Union; the substantial redistributive effects of the EURI; the National Recovery and Resilience Plans as guarantees of good governance; and the necessary expansion of the EU's own resources. The author proceeds to a thorough critical presentation of the Recovery and Resilience Facility, which was received positively both by the main European actors themselves and by scholars, and surely is the centrepiece of the EU fiscal policy response to the Covid-19 pandemic crisis. The main thesis of the chapter is that the NextGenerationEU initiative seems to be a European success story, since it has created a European budgetary capacity and new own resources, it has opened the way for direct transfers at unprecedented amounts, and most importantly, it has provided Europe with a strategic sense of orientation for the future.

The third part opens with a chapter by *Iosif Ktenidis*, Associate Professor at the Aristotle University of Thessaloniki, on the legal aspects of the Banking Union. The author argues that the legal novelty of the Banking Union is that its gradual establishment has required an extraordinary combination and balancing of various EU competences, in different policy areas, with member states' powers, and that this legal exercise resulted in the introduction of different legal instruments that, when examined together, constitute the Banking Union as a unique cross-policy legal structure. Ktenidis shows convincingly, by a combined reading of the Treaty and of relevant case-law, that in the area of prudential supervision (the Single Supervisory Mechanism, hereinafter SSM, which is the first pillar of the Banking Union), the EU does not have a monetary, but rather an internal market competence shared with the member states. He also shows that the Treaty has established a bridge between monetary policy, the internal market, and the stability of the financial system (which is an economic policy objective), and that implementing powers in the area of prudential supervision have been exceptionally conferred on the ECB.

As to the second pillar of the Banking Union (the Single Resolution Mechanism, hereinafter SRM), this is interwoven with, and supplements, banking supervision, since the latter can never rule out the possibility of failure of individual credit institutions; in such case, resort to a set of credible resolution tools is crucial so as to guarantee the continuity of the failing institution's critical financial and economic functions. Therefore, the centralisation of supervisory tasks at the EU level necessitates also a centralisation of resolution procedures for the institutions subject to the ECB's supervision. The author retraces the appropriate internal market legal basis for the establishment of the SRM, analyses the normative differences between the SRM and the SSM Regulations, and explains the reason for the limited role of the ECB in the SRM. He shows that the SRM is not only a mechanism of the EU internal market; it also serves the economic policy objective of financial stability, since its operation should release member states' economic policies and EU coordinating economic powers from the task of addressing the problems of bank failures that have not been prevented by the operation of the SSM. Ktenidis concludes by pointing out the importance of the internal market not only as an autonomous EU objective, but also as an instrument which serves the objectives of the EMU. Indeed, as the Eurozone crisis showed, the introduction of the EMU necessitated the remobilisation of EU internal market powers in the banking activity in order to avoid fragmentation of the internal market attributable to EMU asymmetries.

The second chapter of the third part has been written by *Ioannis Papadopoulos*, Associate Professor at the University of Macedonia and Director of the Centre for Research on Democracy and Law, *Apostolos Kiohos*, Associate Professor at the University of Macedonia, and *Nikolaos Stoupos*, Post-Doctoral Research Fellow at the University of Macedonia, and concerns the EU's effort to restructure its banking sector by introducing a type of separation between commercial and investment banking so as to minimise risks to financial stability from Too-Big-To-Fail phenomena. The authors first make a comparative assessment of the European Commission's policy scenarios concerning the scope and strength of the proposed structural separation between commercial and investment banking. They then propose a reading of the available materials that is alternative to the Commission's, the preferred models of which are either an enhanced functional separation (Subsidiarisation model) or a light ownership separation (Volcker Rule).

By placing emphasis on the reduction of moral hazard and of capital and resources misallocation, balanced against the losses in economies of scope, the authors tentatively conclude in favour of a very strong ownership separation (the Glass-Steagall model), that was meant to function as a prophylactic measure against the structural tendency towards excessive security loans and over-investment in securities of all kinds, produced by the integration of commercial and investment activities under one single banking group. This tentative conclusion is then closely tested against an extensive analysis of the original purposes of the Glass-Steagall Act in the US and of the problems brought about by a series of legislative interpretations over the years, which shows that both the original Glass-Steagall model and the subsequent Volcker Rule that took hold in the US were proven quite impracticable, since they were riddled with many definitional and practical conundrums.

This leads the authors to shift the perspective by examining a new model of structural banking reform based on the regulation of traders' pecuniary motivation in their specialised labour market, instead of threatening integrated banking groups with sanctions for lack of compliance with a ban on risky investment activities (most notably proprietary trading). In plain language, this new model would concern traders' compensation arrangements: if a trader were to engage in any kind of proprietary trading activities, he would not be allowed to participate in any profits made from this trade. The chapter concludes that as a matter of public policy, such a model seems preferable for a future EU structural banking reform since it does not rely on complicated supervisory and corrective requirements, but rather on rational motivational mechanisms underlying traders' risky behaviour and on the capacity of banking management to be incentivised by policy signals.

The third chapter of the third part has been written by Dr. *Kornilia Vikelidou* (University of Macedonia), and presents a case study on the EU Banking Union: the Italian Bank Monte dei Paschi di Siena (hereinafter BMPS) and its big capital shortfalls. This chapter critically examines the extent to which the ongoing situation of this bank interacts with the implementation and the progress concerning the still incomplete Banking Union framework. The aim of the chapter is to provide an insight into the extent to which the Banking Union framework has been implemented so far, to shed light on the missing elements, and to draw some tentative conclusions.

The main issue, as was exemplified in the BMPS case, was the unwillingness of resolution authorities to impose a bail-in, i.e., losses on shareholders, creditors and uninsured depositors of non-viable banks, since this would provoke chain reactions that the Italian political system could not manage: the fear of a potential panic made taxpayers' help seem safer than the implementation of a bail-in, even though this cannot be a long-term solution and raises serious issues of moral hazard. The case of BMPS is considered to be the first big test of how the Banking Union functions in practice. What the case study shows is that the two already established pillars of the Banking Union, i.e., the SSM and the SRM, have still not been effective enough to build the necessary confidence that would make participating countries more receptive regarding the implementation of the new banking resolution tools. Furthermore, the case of BMPS has shed light on the inefficiency of the key supervisory tools at the EU level to prevent the development of new non-performing loans. This chapter attempts to advance some proposals that could make a positive contribution to EU policies towards an effective Banking Union. The main conclusion is that the establishment of a European Deposit Insurance Scheme (EDIS) as the third pillar of the Banking Union, and of a fiscal backstop under the Banking Union framework, are an indispensable complement to moving supervision to the ECB, since these mechanisms would ensure the stability of the new integrated European banking system. It is thus clear that further harmonisation is needed at EU level through an adequate legal framework in order for viable debt to remain serviced and non-viable debt to get timely resolved, and also in order to prevent diverging national requirements from annulling the rules needed for the effectiveness and completion of the Banking Union.

The EU Banking Union is also the theme of the final chapter of the third part written by Dr. *Martha Kavvatha*, Attorney at law with the Bank of Greece. More specifically, the author analyses the complicated legal relation between the ECB and the so-called National Competent Authorities (hereinafter NCAs) regarding prudential supervision of Significant credit Institutions (hereinafter SIs) and Less Significant credit Institutions (hereinafter LSIs), and expounds the tasks and powers of the Bank of Greece (hereinafter BoG) in its quality as NCA and in correlation to those conferred on the ECB. The functioning of the SSM relies on the obligation of cooperation in good faith and of exchange of information between the European (ECB) and the national (NCAs) levels of supervision. The SSM, established in the aftermath of the financial crisis, results in a transfer of powers from national competent authorities to an EU institution (namely the ECB) in relation to banking supervision. The centralisation of decision-making at the European level is indisputable: the ECB remains ultimately responsible for the effective and consistent functioning of the entire mechanism and holds, to this end, important coordinating powers. Thus, micro-prudential supervision of SIs falls within the remit of the ECB. However, the NCAs retain important tasks and powers, while cooperation and coordination between the national and the European levels is deemed crucial for the fulfilment of the objectives of the SSM. Thus, the micro-prudential supervision of LSIs falls under the direct supervision of the BoG, and in exercising its tasks in relation to SIs established in Greece, the ECB cooperates closely with the BoG because EU law acknowledges the important and long-established expertise of national supervisors in the supervision of credit institutions within their territory, and their economic, organisational and cultural specificities.

As to macro-prudential supervision aimed at addressing systemic risks, the ECB shares powers with the NCAs, which remain primarily responsible for the application of macro-prudential tools in their jurisdictions. Finally, a good example of the complicated delineation of powers between the European and the national levels explained by the author are the enforcement and sanctioning powers: the ECB retains such powers only regarding SIs, while the BoG not only remains competent for sanctions vis-à-vis LSIs, but also reserves important sanctioning powers in regard to SIs as well, but only following a request of the ECB. The general conclusion is that of a unique institutional set-up of the SSM, in which the NCAs formally retain certain powers, which nonetheless can no longer be autonomously exercised for the purpose of carrying out tasks that have been attributed to the ECB.

The fourth and last part of the book opens with a chapter by *Periklis Gogas*, Professor at the Democritus University of Thrace, *Theophilos Papadimitriou*, Professor at the Democritus University of Thrace, *Athanasia Dimitriadou*, PhD Candidate, University of Derby, and *Anna Agrapetidou*, PhD, Democritus University of Thrace, expounding an alternative model of ICRAs. The chapter presents the history and evolution of CRAs. In the years following the US stock market crash in 1929, we have been seeing a growing reliance of investors and other markets participants on CRAs' ratings, to such a point that they have become the quasi-official arbitrators of credit risk throughout the global financial system. But after the 2008 financial crisis, CRAs have faced intense criticism, obviously because they failed to signal financial (default) risk. The basic structural problem underlying the CRAs' operation is the inherent conflict of interest due to the "issuer-pays system", since CRAs are paid by the issuers of the debt instruments, and they therefore have a strong incentive to assign the highest possible ratings. This structural problem is complemented by the relatively loose regulatory oversight from government agencies.

In recent years, new regulations, the abundance of economic and financial data, and the availability of powerful new methodologies and inexpensive computing power, have brought us to a new era of ratings that can be produced by non-market, not-for-profit ICRAs, which can either compete with CRAs or be used as an auxiliary risk-gauging mechanism by market participants. The authors show that these independent ratings are free from the problems inherent in traditional CRAs. They then present two relevant forecasting models with their methodologies, one for bank credit ratings and one for bank failures. These models, based only on quantitative and publicly available information, can be used by an ICRA to assign credit risk ratings to banking institutions and/or produce probabilities of default, with a very good overall accuracy level. The authors conclude that since public disclosure is now mandatory for transparency reasons, ICRAs must come into play. ICRAs do not suffer from the issuer-payer conflict of interest, they come with full transparency in the ratings procedure, they increase competition, thus minimising the oligopolistic power of the existing CRAs in information gathering and processing, and they are subject to market discipline or market rewards depending on the accuracy and fairness of the ratings they provide.

The second chapter of the fourth part, written by *Despoina Anagnostopoulou*, Associate Professor at the University of Macedonia, and Dr. *Kornilia Vikelidou* (University of Macedonia), contains a legal analysis and evaluation of the EU regulatory framework on CRAs in order to assess its role in the restoration of market confidence and the enhancement of investor protection. Everybody recognises that the ratings of CRAs play an important role in credit assessment. However, their use should not be mechanistic nor lessen a debtor's responsibility to ensure that its credit exposures are based on sound risk assessments. The chapter first presents the development of the EU regulatory framework on CRAs since 2009, which established the European Securities and Markets Authority (hereinafter ESMA) as supervisor and attempted to reduce the regulatory role of CRAs by obliging financial institutions to make their own credit risk assessments. It then proceeds to an evaluation of the EU regulatory framework in its multiple facets: registration and quality of the rating process, conflicts of interests, and rules on transparency. The supervision of registered CRAs by ESMA is explained in its details.

Special attention is given to competition issues raised by the oligopoly of the so-called “Big Three” CRAs (Moody’s, S&P, and Fitch), which constitutes a risk for financial stability: both the US and the EU authorities have investigated probable concerted practices and abuse of dominant position in the market, but these have proven difficult to confirm in the EU case. As to the possible civil liability of CRAs because of mishandled ratings, the authors depict the rise of the willingness to treat CRAs like other gatekeepers, e.g., banks, accountants, and lawyers, after the 2008 financial crisis, since reputational capital by itself does not seem to provide sufficient incentives for accurate ratings. In the EU, even though the CRA Regulation opened the possibility of claims against CRAs both by the issuers (contracting parties) and by the investors (third parties) in relation to infringements of the Regulation committed intentionally or with gross negligence, EU law refers all relevant aspects of civil law damage claims to the national laws; since there is a wide diversity of civil liability regimes in the member states, the authors are of the opinion that harmonisation is needed.

The authors conclude that although the EU regulatory framework constitutes a significant first step towards mitigating the adverse influence that CRAs were found to have, hardly can this regime be considered effective enough to satisfy the aim of independent, objective, and adequate quality ratings. The emerging Banking Union and Capital Markets Union could mitigate the pro-cyclical impact of credit ratings, while enhancing vigorous competition in a level playing field.

The last chapter of the fourth part, written by *Emmanouil Vlachogiannis*, First Vice-President of the Thessaloniki Chamber of Commerce and Industry, is an economic analysis of the contribution of credit ratings to market efficiency and/or resilience. In neoclassical economics, where the idea of equilibrium price is all-important, credit ratings are supposed to improve market efficiency by allowing supply and demand to define interest rates and to incorporate the underlying risks in the sense that they provide investors with information about the credibility of bonds. The chapter investigates the validity of this neoclassical assumption. In order to do this, the author examines the microeconomic conditions under which credit ratings are produced. Credit ratings are costly endeavours. In the case of sovereign debt, the source of financial compensation for CRAs is unknown. The temptation to manipulate credit rating outcomes is inherent in this system of privately produced, "condensed or compiled" information, which is broadcasted and made available to the general public. The author assumes that investors form their expectations around a statistical measure of the past that might be a median or an average of default risks, and also that when credit ratings suggest that the default risk is below the median, debt with lower interest rates will be issued, and on the contrary, when credit ratings suggest that the default risk is above the median, funding can be attracted under only significantly higher interest rates.

The consequence is that credit ratings, which aim to be an instrument of information, rather transform themselves into instruments of giving bonuses or maluses, and therefore inevitably spell a kind of political judgment. If we visualise these assumptions in a traditional market setting with supply (the willingness of investors to engage in funding with varying amounts regarding interest rates) and demand (the need of debtors for funds in varying amounts, depending on interest rates) curves and we suppose that a perceived supply curve intersects with the perceived demand curve in a price/quantity point that corresponds to the median default risk, we will notice that the elasticity of both supply and demand will increase due to credit ratings. That might be a problem for market efficiency, as both curves will intersect and create a new equilibrium, where interest rates will reflect increasing risk intolerance as market participants become more informed. The result is that interest rates will not always correspond to risk, so market efficiency, i.e., a stable relation between interest rates and inherent risks, is questioned. As to the impact of credit ratings on market resilience, experience has shown that the latter will receive a severe blow when bond markets with settings prone to divergence are confronted with contracting liquidity. And the fact that credit ratings try to anticipate market reactions aggravates the problem. Overall, credit ratings seem to contribute to an unintended instability of financial markets instead of improving market resilience. This is not a Pareto Efficient Equilibrium world; this is a Minsky Financial Market Instability world.

References

Albert, Eric & Marie Charrel. 2021. "Philip Lane: «Le chemin de la reprise sera long» dans la zone euro", Le Monde, 11 May 2021, https://www.lemonde.fr/economie/article/2021/05/10/le-chemin-de-la-reprise-sera-long-en-zone-euro_6079701_3234.html (accessed August 31, 2021).

Bosch, Gerhard. 2010. "The Revitalization of the Dual System of Vocational Training in Germany". In *Vocational Training: International Perspectives.* Edited by Gerhrd Bosch and Jean Charest, New York & London: Routledge.

Crescenzi, Riccardo, Simona Iammarino, Carolin Ioramashvili, Andrés Rodríguez-Pose & Michael Storper. 2020. "The Geography of Innovation and Development: global spread and local hotspots," LSE Paper in Economic Geography and Spatial Economics no. 4, (June), http://eprints.lse.ac.uk/105116/1/Crescenzi_geography_of_innovation_and_development_published.pdf (accessed August 31, 2021).

EC. 2021. "Spring 2021 Economic Forecast: Rolling up sleeves," Press release, 12 May, https://ec.europa.eu/commission/presscorner/detail/en/ip_21_2351 (accessed August 30, 2021).

Emmerling, Johannes, Davide Furceri, Francisco Libano Monteiro, Prakash Loungani, Jonathan D. Ostry, Pietro Pizzuto & Massimo Tavoni. 2021. "Will the Economic Impact of COVID-19 Persist? Prognosis from 21st Century Pandemics," IMF Working Paper WP/21/119, April, https://www.imf.org/en/Publications/WP/Issues/2021/04/30/Will-the-Economic-Impact-of-COVID-19-Persist-Prognosis-from-21st-Century-Pandemics-50288 (accessed August 30, 2021).

NBER (National Bureau of Economic Research). 2021. "Determination of the April 2020 Trough in US Economic Activity," Business Cycle Dating Committee Announcement, July 19, https://www.nber.org/news/business-cycle-dating-committee-announcement-july-19-2021 (accessed August 30, 2021).

Pelagidis, Theodore & Michael Moutsopoulos. 2021. *Who's to Blame for Greece? Life After Bankruptcy: Between Optimism and Substandard Growth*. Cham: Palgrave Macmillan.

PART A:

WHERE IS EUROPE HEADING?

CHAPTER 1

INTERVIEW WITH MICHEL AGLIETTA: THE CHALLENGES FACING THE EU IN FRONT OF THE CHANGES IN CAPITALISM

Ioannis Papadopoulos: Good morning.

Michel Aglietta: Good morning.

Ioannis Papadopoulos: So, I'm very happy, delighted even, to be with you at the CEPII (Centre d'études prospective et d'informations internationales) in Paris, where you also happen to have your office. First of all, I would like you to formally introduce yourself to us, and then we will start discussing the Fiscal Union.

Michel Aglietta: I am Michel Aglietta. I am professor emeritus at the University of Paris X Nanterre, and I am also a scientific advisor to the international economics research organisation called CEPII and to France Stratégie, the former Commissariat du plan (Plan Commission), which is somewhat of a public body of foresight for the French economy and its position vis-à-vis Europe and the world.

Ioannis Papadopoulos: So, we're going to try to talk about the Fiscal Union first. I will ask you a few questions, then you will position yourself freely, and afterwards the discussion can take us elsewhere. I don't want you to feel constrained to follow any strict conversation guidelines. You can also talk about growth issues, which I know are dear to you since I follow your work.

So, the first question is quite broad, of course. In your opinion, and considering its macroeconomic assumptions, is the Stability and Growth Pact an institutional framework that is sufficient and capable of leading us to a real Fiscal Union in Europe, in the European Union, or rather, in the euro area? Is this the case or not?

Michel Aglietta: I don't think it is enough. You can see the conditions under which it was put in place. It was set up in conditions of an ongoing crisis, of emergency, and it was essentially designed to safeguard the euro. It was not designed for the future. It was not designed with foresight, since it doesn't seem to realise what is constantly said: "Europe must become ever more united". It seems to me that the main reason is quite profound: there is an underlying theoretical view in Europe, which is pretty strong and came about as the result of the Anglo-Saxon neo-liberalism of the last thirty years; this began in the 1980s with Reagan and Thatcher, and then mixed with German ordo-liberalism. The overriding assumption of neo-liberalism is that the state is the problem and that everything goes through the market, which therefore gives rise to this notion of exclusive supply-side policy. The presupposition of ordo-liberalism is the idea that it is important to have a framework of stability, that this framework of stability implies that rules and discretion are in a hierarchical relationship, and accordingly, that under difficult conditions of lack of trust between governments, the rules must prevail. The Fiscal Compact of 2012[1] was designed to tighten, complicate, and multiply the rules, and at the same time, remove them from the political process of managing the economic cycle and of managing growth based on political choices, i.e., discretionary decisions. To overcome this contradiction, the notion of constrained discretion would have to be introduced. Rules and discretion lie at different logical levels. The set of possible scenarios that governments may have to choose from must be put in place within a framework of rules that allow for the possibility of action —since we are talking about an economic dynamic managed, regulated and directed by the public authorities— instead of blocking it.

Why is that the case? We never think about the nature of the crisis we are plunged into. We are in the midst of a transformation of the growth regime and of the disruption with the growth regime of financial capitalism. The 2008 financial crisis was the inaugural event of this transformation. The subsequent Eurozone crisis showed the inability of the arrangement of rigid rules governing the Eurozone to protect the Union. After all, periods of disruption are times when growth regimes deteriorate irreversibly, as they have exhausted their capacity for progress. Capitalism must be thought of as a historical succession of growth regimes, separated by phases of disruption. Therefore, we will have to think of the policies to

[1] The Treaty on Stability, Coordination and Governance in the Economic and Monetary Union (TSCG), containing the Fiscal Compact in its Title III, was formally concluded on 2 March 2012, and entered into force on 1 January 2013.

be carried out in Europe in relation to a long-term perspective on the transformations of contemporary capitalism.

The key issue today is that there are two types of forces that seem to be the elements of destruction of the growth regime. One is geopolitical, and it has accelerated recently: the weakening of the American hegemony and the order in which Europe was inserted as a cocoon. That is to say, Europe did not have certain strategic decisions to make because it was under the American hegemony. In this geopolitical dimension, our weakness is that we have not thought of Europe politically as a public power capable of existing autonomously. This lack comes back to us today as an emergency.

The second element is the financial nature of the crisis. It is necessary to reject any idea of financial efficiency, the fundamental value of assets, and the perfect knowledge of a financial future equilibrium of future prices. We need to think of finance in a totally different manner: as a complex system, in which there are interactions that can be stabilising if they are designed according to complementarity, interconnection, and relatively limited relations, but that can also become factors of the spread of destruction, and thus of cumulative chaotic phenomena if the interconnection of finance is pushed too far. And this is what happened in the late 1990s mainly because of the financial innovations introduced then in the derivatives markets: the disappearance of regulation, especially in the United States, as well as the abandonment of any regulation whatsoever in Europe.

This endogenous dynamic of finance leads to the concept of a financial cycle that is produced by an interaction between debt and asset prices. The financial cycle is known for expressing a logic opposed to the fundamental logic of equilibrium; a logic of momentum. This means — and here I enter into Keynesian theory— that finance is essentially confronted with radical uncertainty. The anticipations of future prices in financial markets are nothing but the formation of a collective belief through the mimetic interaction of the individual beliefs of financial actors. The decisions on asset allocation based on these beliefs produce the financial cycle of a periodicity of 15 to 20 years in five phases: boom, euphoria, reversal crisis, asset deflation, deleveraging, and balance sheet restructuring. On the contrary, the conception of efficiency is a conception that eliminates time. It assumes that there is an eternal present, since financial and economic actors in general have a perfect knowledge to the infinite of future prices of assets by their supposedly rational anticipations.

Therefore, they know in probability all possible scenarios since uncertainty is eliminated. The world of uncertainty is one of the heterogeneity of finance, and the heterogeneity of finance leads to what Mark Carney has defined as "the tragedy of the horizon" (Carney 2015). Therefore, if Europe wants to get out of the situation it is in, it must break the tragedy of the horizon.

So, the problem of the Fiscal Union for me is first and foremost a long-term problem. That is to say, the most fundamental element that needs to be put in place right away is a common long-term investment policy. What justifies a common long-term investment policy? Here I am relying on the Monti report on common structural policies (Monti 2009) and also on the question of the nature of a European budget. Considering that a long-term investment structure is of essence, the question is: What kind of investments? The only positive innovation at the budgetary level in this direction, from the start of the Eurozone crisis, has been the Juncker Plan.[2] What is wrong with the Juncker Plan? The first and most technical but least fundamental element, is that it provides for too much leverage and not enough capital by the European Investment Bank (EIB) together with the backing by a budget, which is not there to guarantee, or does guarantee very little. And the other most important thing is that it does not provide a direction, the nature of an "industrial policy", if you may, that allows us to define what investments to make.

There are things in the Monti report that I had added in my own book with Nicolas Leron, *Dual Democracy* (Aglietta and Leron 2017). The crucial concept is European added value. That is to say, we must promote investments that give a greater social utility than what could be obtained by the principle of subsidiarity. This allows you to define investment classes. And why are these investment classes important? Because the new growth regime, in my opinion, is a new form of globalisation based on the common goods. The main common good, the one that is most threatening if it is not taken into account, is the climate. The interaction of ecology and economy has sharply deteriorated, and therefore, we need to rethink all the problems of investment in ecosystems.

[2] A new boost for jobs, growth and investment was the number one priority of the President of the European Commission Jean-Claude Juncker. In November 2014, just three weeks into his mandate, President Juncker launched the Investment Plan for Europe, also called the "Juncker Plan", with the European Fund for Strategic Investments (EFSI) as its main pillar (Regulation 2015/1017).

There is also the problem of digital networks. These networks are very dangerous because they bring enormous concentration in the private sector, as a result of the withdrawal of the public sector. The big technology companies like Google, Facebook, Amazon etc., but also the Chinese "giants", are threatening in the same way that the giant companies of heavy industry were at the end of the 19th century. At that time, there was an extremely strong threat to democracy that came from heavy industry, raw materials, oil etc. Antitrust laws in the United States were the democratic responses to this threat. And that is crucial today as well. It is absolutely necessary to break these monopolies. These things are part of the market environment. If we really want a market environment that is capable of carrying a positive dynamic on a set of investments that are formed around digital networks, which are crucial because they interact, especially with energy, and therefore manufacture a new growth regime, we must put under social control these monopolies that are taking hold of e-commerce networks.

The other essential element, therefore, is the idea of European added value. In my opinion, this idea helps to define a long-term investment programme to be carried out today, because of the very strong inertia, in particular with regard to the environmental issue. Contrary to fashionable ideas among radical ecologists, it is a question of transforming the growth regime, so that political ecology is closely associated with social justice. Since the Organisation for Economic Co-operation and Development (hereinafter OECD) had already announced the possibility of a global recession in the autumn of 2019, followed by a long period of "secular" stagnation in a world plagued by social inequalities that have become unbearable, inclusive and sustainable growth has become absolutely vital.

This is why long-term investments are imperative and their choice is crucial. They need public guarantees and they need a transformation of finance. It is not a matter of doing a green finance next to the existing finance. It is about transforming all of finance to meet long-term goals.

The investment budget first. It is clear that the budget is European and that the climate is European as a whole. The Juncker Plan is also European as a whole. This budget must have its own resources. Indeed, the question today is not to make the European Parliament a public authority capable of issuing debt and raising taxes, which would be tantamount to a real public power. This is for a later, more distant stage. But you have to find your own resources. The Monti Committee, which I mentioned, proposes to extend the resources of the European budget that are directly allocated to the European Union, as are tariffs on trade with the rest of the world. There would therefore be a restructuring of the European budget on the fiscal revenue side. Thus, customs duties are collected by member states because there is no European administration, but they belong to the European Union. Since other taxes are needed to raise a long-term investment guarantee budget to a sufficient level, these taxes must be on the same level as tariffs, i.e., own resources. Since climate is a common good, investments in energy for a European energy policy in order to reduce fossil fuels and to develop electricity in road transport and rail in trans-European transport require a carbon tax as a new resource, depending on the nature of the investment projects. This carbon tax will have to be Europe's own resource to finance investments. We will see how France will play on the nuclear problem, what transition period it will indicate, and what choice it will make, but we must move towards a common energy policy that requires a much more sophisticated electricity distribution system (European smart grid).

Think of Greece. We need solar energy. It is clear that what is needed is not to give money to increase Greece's debt; it is to invest in Greece on solar energy, rather than doing it on the Baltic. One can see very well the need for a common investment policy. The advantage this would have, in my opinion, is that it would create a sense of European belonging for the citizens, which would occur, as they see the benefit, by the effects it would have. From these advances, we could go further towards building a European public power. We must be able to create a common sense of belonging, and this structuring can only happen through a new growth regime, by these investments.

The fact that this new common industrial policy would support potential growth would reduce the pressures that result from the distortions that exist between countries within the macroeconomic conjuncture. It is the idea of raising the water level for all boats at once. That is an important thing, but there is something even better than that. If we say that this investment programme must be acyclical, since it must break the tragedy of the horizon, on the contrary the taxation that comes with it will be procyclical, since it stems from Gross Domestic Product (hereinafter GDP). So, in times when European GDP is lower, the taxation proceeds will simply be lower. Therefore, the funding will be countercyclical as the investment program is being carried out. And we will create more debt in times of slowdown, since the investment budget is designed over the long term. Thus, this budget itself can play a countercyclical stabilisation role.

Ioannis Papadopoulos: This is very interesting. While I was listening to you, I had the impression that what is missing from the debate on the Fiscal Union is the long-term strategic direction of investment, the very structuring of the future, a new form of citizenship itself that is completely lost in sight by the institutional instruments that we have on the ground today because of the ordo-liberalism that you mentioned at the beginning, which has a fairly limited horizon...

Michel Aglietta: Western democracies have electoral political horizons, but the idea of "long term" goes beyond democratic choices. This is the tragedy of the horizon.

Ioannis Papadopoulos: I would just like to bounce back from that. Here you have been describing a situation in which we need new instruments that give us an extension of the Union's fiscal base and its long-term strategic projects, as well as of the economic, financial, energy, and other transitions. But at the same time, because of intergovernmentalism and what it entails, there is a lot of resistance at national level. For example, with respect to the carbon tax and the financial transaction tax, there is still a core of states that want to move forward, but quite a few other states are very wary. As a result, Europe is reorienting itself towards a kind of variable geometry, which makes us lose visionary, political, and governance power relating to what we must do with our common future.

How can this contradiction be resolved? Is there some kind of institutional impasse in the Treaty? The Treaty is quite restrictive in terms of the budget. The budget must be balanced. The European budget must never have a deficit, not even for countercyclical reasons, and our own resources can never reach beyond 1.20% of European Gross National Income (hereinafter GNI), which is obviously not enough to do the right thing. How do we get out of this impasse? Should we make a paradigm shift?

Michel Aglietta: The paradigm we are talking about has already undergone a structural change; it must also undergo a political change. United Europe started with a club. It is very possible that we will be forced to function as a gathering of countries with variable geometry, depending on the nature of the advances in structural changes. The slogan of an "ever closer union" should be replaced if the investment budget is not the EU budget. This can be done simply through a specific budget line within the framework of the European budget. The control of the guarantee provided by this budget to investors who would finance the projects under the investment programme concerned would be carried out by all MEPs who originate from the countries concerned by the programme. The key idea is: European added value and own resources. Therefore, the possibility of an open club that attracts others because of its success seems to be a path that is essential to move forward.

Ioannis Papadopoulos: So, let's go back to the Juncker Plan. I was intrigued because you said that the Juncker Plan, in the end, is not a public investment plan, but a plan that is based on securitisation to achieve more leverage so as to attract private investment...

Michel Aglietta: Of course, there is a lot of private investment. The question is how to transform a growth regime through investments of all kinds. There is probably a public base of public goods that need to be produced and that involve a lot of private investment, for example when you are going to do a transformation of urban planning with development, say a housing renovation. This leads to carbon investment at the microeconomic level, which is a crucial dimension. All growth regimes are transformed by cities, by transport. That means you have to crowd in the private sector, of course. That is why I was talking about public guarantees and a public-private partnership financial system.

The public-private partnership financial system that I am thinking of should have three types of players crowding in everyone, that is, banks, financial and standard intermediaries. These are the national promotional banks.[3] There is one European advantage, which is that there is a network of national promotional banks. They are everywhere, in almost every country. However, these national promotional banks are not organised in a network. And now, this should happen.

So, the idea is the following: for the European Fund for Strategic Investments (hereinafter EFSI) —the body that would drive these investment choices— to give the heavy investments crowding in other complementary investments or, if you will, provide them with fundamental innovation so as to lead to incremental innovation, it should, in my opinion, have as

[3] National promotional banks are legal entities carrying out financial, development and promotional activities on a professional basis, which are given a mandate by an EU member state at central, regional or local level. National promotional banks act as financial intermediaries for EIB Group investments directed to small-scale projects. They channel EIB loans to businesses and local authorities in their home countries and collaborate with the European Investment Fund (EIF) in the implementation of its guarantee or equity mandates (EIB n.d.).

shareholders all of Europe's national promotional banks and not just the EIB. The national promotional banks have the ability to make long-term choices, as they have no liquidity constraints or shareholder pressure, since they are under public ownership. There would thus be a fairly large base of investment that would be sufficient. So a network of national promotional banks in the case of the EFSI, coordinated by the EIB and secured by the EU public guarantee fund, can leverage responsible institutional investors whose liabilities are long-term commitments.

In addition to this, the Commission's proposal to create a European sovereign wealth fund co-funded by member states would encourage the issuance of European bonds linked to European investments; investments that create production and income and that are self-financed in a longer temporality than we usually know. Hence there is a need to find relays to take over. What are these relays? Bonds must be issued hence actors who are capable of acquiring them are needed. These are the responsible institutional investors. What makes them responsible? These institutional investors have no liquidity constraints since they collect retirement savings, and therefore have long commitments. Consequently, these investors must think that the financial return at 15-20 years depends on the possibility of having avoided environmental degradation. But negative interest rates in Europe show that the rate of return on capital is falling. So, they start to wonder: how am I going to find my own financial return to pay my pensions if there is no sufficient social return on capital? If they band together in a group so as to move from a market portfolio to a 2°C portfolio,[4] there will be the opportunity to buy the bonds issued by the national promotional banks to finance low-carbon investments, with or without securitisation, depending on the nature of the credit flows requested by project owners.

For the carbon recovery, on which the valorisation of investments to reduce the emitted carbon depends, we must distinguish between two kinds of prices: the carbon tax, on the one hand, which is a malus intended to discourage polluters, and the price, on the other hand, which is a bonus intended to encourage new actors-entrepreneurs who want to embark on low-carbon investments. The latter is a price for the future, it is a notional price; it is not a market price today. It is therefore necessary to differentiate between a carbon tax that should rise slowly and an already

[4] Investors and policymakers strive to translate the high-level climate policy goal of limiting global warming to 2°C into a benchmark that can inform portfolio allocation targets (2° Investing Initiative 2015).

high notional price to render profitable the essential component of future social return for the entrepreneur. The states participating in the InvestEU project (European Commission 2020), which follows on from the Juncker Plan, should establish a common carbon reference value set by the European Commission for climate-related investment choices, in order to achieve carbon neutrality beyond 2050.

So, the idea is this: We need to develop a green production structure and eliminate the brown production structure, but we know that if we destroy too quickly brown fixed capital, we will devalue the existing capital far too much, and we will drag the economy into recession, which will disadvantage new investment; hence the need to disconnect the incentive to invest in green production structures from the shrinking of brown industries. This is the reason why during the transition phase, the market price of carbon is below the notional value, which drives the calculation of the returns of new green investments. But the two prices must gradually converge on the single price for carbon neutrality. It is therefore essential that governments not only agree at the European level, at least for the group of countries that are seriously involved in the energy transition, but that they stick to the policies announced, so that private companies and financiers agree to play the game. This is how the tragedy of the horizon can be overcome.

This long-term industrial strategy would put the banking system in play. A certification process is still needed to avoid the formation of a carbon bubble that will ensue if an avalanche of failed investment projects is triggered to take advantage of the attractive returns associated with the high value of emission allowances. So, we have to establish certification bodies, a new profession of sorts, which will be independent. Such bodies are beginning to appear; they need to be developed and oriented towards the climate issue.

Then, there is the new integration of the financial system. This is new compared to the neoliberal era, since public actors are the spearhead now. Institutional investors would finally have long-term strategies, and could finally guide long-term savings on investments that bring social well-being through new European financial securities.

In my opinion, we need one last player: the Central Bank, which would imply a profound change in attitudes towards money. Indeed, the Central Bank should regulate the market price of carbon bonds on the notional price of the reduction of carbon emissions.

Ioannis Papadopoulos: That is a revolutionary idea. You know that is way beyond their horizon now.

Michel Aglietta: The monetary system, both European and international, needs to change profoundly. It is not going back to what it was. That is to say the aberration of monetarism, given what happened after the great financial crisis. Central banks have made $6 trillion of liquidity available to the world, only to reach $16 trillion of negative-interest rate bonds ten years later and an inability to meet their inflation targets in all advanced economies.

Ioannis Papadopoulos: Is the famous transmission belt of monetary choices not what it used to be?

Michel Aglietta: The neoliberal monetary doctrine will have to be transformed. And indeed, the Central Bank will have a role, not a certain type of independence, but it will be engaged in a dialogue with other actors, without questioning its institutional independence. The neoliberal doctrine stems from the effects of the great inflation of the 1970s. On the contrary, we live in a time of prolonged low inflation. But there is a profound theoretical error. There is an asymmetry in the process of transmitting monetary policy, depending on whether one is in a macroeconomic context in which the Central Bank's mission is to contain a divergent inflationary spiral, or in a context in which deflationary pressures are to be prevented from turning into stagnation equilibrium. In the first case, the inflation target and the Central Bank's exclusive mission to anchor expectations are justified because expectations are driving the inflationary process, as Milton Friedman argued. In the second case, the sole monetary policy cannot overcome the excess of the desired savings on the intentions to invest, as Keynes had clearly shown. The Central Bank must support fiscal policy and must be concerned about the vulnerability of debt in the financial cycle. It must therefore closely integrate monetary and macro-prudential policy.

This is why a thought-provoking work on money is essential. Money is a fundamental public good that is global. Climate is a global public good. We need a money-climate link. As a result, the Central Bank could hold carbon assets and therefore, instead of buying assets that already exist and that do not create any income, it would buy assets that generate new income.

Ioannis Papadopoulos: Exactly. On this point, it is very interesting that the European Central Bank, with its Quantitative Easing programme, buys a lot of securitised assets, mortgage loans, and of course, government bonds. But it would also have to consider buying new securities, green or transition securities, and to eliminate, or at least narrow, the gap between the notional element, i.e., the horizon we are seeking, and the cost of restructuring, that is to be incurred immediately, in the short term.

This is precisely the question I would really like to ask you: the question of demand, and more specifically of structural changes that are demand-driven. From the great crash of 1929 onwards, the Americans have always had this idea that demand can lead to a change of mentalities, and can turn —obviously without a kind of invisible hand and without too much regulation either— economic structures into being more efficient. Then, you also have to go beyond efficiency to move towards something new.

So, could we consider a mechanism, such as the European Central Bank, to stimulate green growth through demand for such types of products, including financial products, in portfolios supporting this long-term activity? What could we expect if this is the case? Would public policy at European level have a role in this, or is it just a question of the European Investment Bank and the network of promotional banks, in other words of banks at national level?

Michel Aglietta: This is the current idea of the Green New Deal that young Democrats pushed in the 2020 presidential campaign. When I studied the regulation of capitalism, I understood that the transformation of consumption patterns is the essential vector that links supply and demand. There is structural change in the evolution of consumption patterns. An important part of drivers lies in the structure of investments that induce changes in consumer behaviour and that reveal incremental innovations to diversify new patterns of consumption. When the automobile developed, the very notion of mobility, and thus the development of the territories, was transformed. Today, by changing some fundamental notions about the environment, we can encourage a change in attitude towards different lifestyles.

Therefore, we need incentives. That's why I said that the transformation of cities is important. Simulations in Paris have shown that to withstand the heat waves of 2050, which will be well above those of today, it will take 20% more green space. Urban transformations are thus crucial. What I think is important is that here democracy is at stake. Participatory, and not only representative, democracy should emerge, so as for civil society collectives to fight for the restoration of the common goods from the local to the global. After all, environmental problems exist across all levels; hence the importance of local and regional levels of public power that can make decisions that have as foundation citizens' deliberations. So, we have to follow through with this kind of transformation right now.

Ioannis Papadopoulos: This is the question of ownership, of appropriation. That is, people have to get involved in their own lives. The more local and regional the level of decision-makers, the stronger the ownership.

Michel Aglietta: I think these attitudes are emerging. Political impetus should do everything to promote them.

Ioannis Papadopoulos: Can the European Union do anything about it?

Michel Aglietta: The European level in relation to these levels?

Ioannis Papadopoulos: Because you can look at something strategically in the long term.

Michel Aglietta: In any case, there is something that should be done right now: this is to change the meaning of the European elections. That is to say, we want to move in this direction, even if we remain in the legal institutions as they are. There is absolutely nothing "European" about the European elections because people cannot see the use of them. If we manage to connect long-term investments with a guarantee of the European budget, at least in the countries that are starting to commit, and given that this is a very important issue for each country (let us not forget the notion of European added value), then we could have the formation of European political parties, or at least the development of a serious European political dimension in the national political parties, so that European elections become elections where people understand what the European issues are. Therefore, the nature of the European elections must change profoundly. That is my way of answering.

Ioannis Papadopoulos: But can we do that, which is perfectly desirable, at least with the Treaty we have? Because I think —and I have expressed this in several writings— that macroeconomic assumptions, such as ordo-liberalism and monetarism, have been constitutionalised at the European level. As a result, the European elections are not seen as giving a sufficient margin of political choice for citizens in order for them to really engage. In other words, European citizens still have a diffuse and intuitive, but still fair, conscience of not being able to change much with their vote.

Michel Aglietta: Yes, that is why I focused on that earlier.

Ioannis Papadopoulos: Perhaps it should be done as in America after the New Deal: deconstitutionalise the macroeconomic basis of the assumptions on which choices are made. And then, of course, little by little, as you said, start building institutional relays to get somewhere. But that obviously we cannot do as if we had a federal union; that is clear. We can still do it gradually though. So, the problem is that there is still a shackle that prevents us from doing so, and it is constitutionalised by the Treaty.

Michel Aglietta: The problem is the whole of Europe's legalism. In our book *Dual Democracy* (Aglietta and Leron 2017), we have shown that it is absolutely necessary to exit legalism. The new event is the serious crisis in which Germany has entered. The German industrial machine is profoundly and structurally affected by the major geopolitical changes that are taking place. Global value chains, from which Germany has benefited so much with the mediation of intensive accumulation in China, are unraveling. This is due not only to the Sino-American trade war, but more deeply to the new era of Chinese reform. Through the "Made in China 2025" plan, China has entered the so-called phase of "socialist modernisation", the aim of which is the complementarity between the reduction of inequality and the improvement of the environment, i.e., the transition from quantitative to qualitative growth by moving innovations towards the technological frontier. Growth will slow down and will be driven by the increase in the overall factor productivity. That is why the huge German trade surplus, on which full employment was based, will be reduced irretrievably. In addition, Germany has been particularly lagging behind in the implementation of the energy and climate transition, with its brutal and unilateral decision to give up nuclear power. As a result, the German model will have to transform itself by prioritising domestic demand, especially as public infrastructures are deteriorating by years of lack of maintenance.

Ioannis Papadopoulos: We still need to get rid of this legalism. Do you think we know how to do it?

Michel Aglietta: Several developments could converge in the right direction to return to the path of a budget-supported industrial policy: the change of direction in Germany for the abovementioned reasons, the implementation of the InvestEU Plan under the impetus of the Commission, which is developing a taxonomy of priority sectors of activity in the face of climate risk, and finally, the very deep recession in the global economy because of the Covid-19 pandemic.

Ioannis Papadopoulos: You have to make the fiscal base more flexible to be able to do something. And then the EU's own resources are still too limited. We cannot exceed 1.20% and, in reality, less than 1% of European GNI as resources.

Michel Aglietta: You can have an important lever for a European industrial policy by reforming the financial system following the paths I proposed above. However, there should be an increase in own resources through three categories of taxes: a tax on digital data, based on the conclusion of the upcoming OECD report on giant Internet companies, a tax on financial transactions related to the establishment of the unified capital market, and a carbon tax that is part of the change in the growth regime explained above. This may require a European budget of 3 to 3.5% of GDP for the period 2021-27, thus well above the ceiling of the current European budget. Hence the idea that was put forward: would it be a budget of a group of leading countries, inserted into the EU budget with a specific budget line? This is a problem that needs to be debated politically.

Ioannis Papadopoulos: I would like you to position yourself in relation to the Macron proposals in favour of a kind of European budget that is not a stabilisation, but rather a recovery or growth budget.

Michel Aglietta: The problem with Macron's proposals is those famous internal structural policies that, in my opinion, are not yet sufficiently well-defined. One thing is certain, and that is that he wants to get out of the corporative system. France imposes a considerable cost on production by the way it finances its social protection. The problem is that there is a possible opening: either towards the Anglo-Saxon system, and therefore towards a deterioration of social protection, or towards the Scandinavian system that takes seriously the notion of flexicurity.

To do that, we need a restructuring of the budget. By studying the Scandinavian crisis of 1991 and the way it was resolved, we see that the budget was not reduced, but it was completely transformed. There was both a reduction in transfers and a massive development of an investment budget for education, lifelong learning, and research and development. Scandinavian governments wanted to be at the forefront of information technology; hence the increase in research and development. To accompany this structural policy, they had the autonomy of the exchange rate, and therefore of external demand, in the transitional period. The problem is that the Eurozone member states did not take advantage of the economic rebound of 2016-18 to launch these reforms.

In addition to the transformation of the Juncker Plan, the European Semester should be reformed. But how? We have to solve two problems, which are not independent. The first is the absence of a countercyclical policy in the euro area. And the second is the polarisation between creditor and debtor countries, because we do not have instruments at the euro area level to regulate demand, even if the European Commission still wants to do that.

First, we need to avoid restrictive fiscal policies in the midst of a recession, as in 2011-13. At that time, the interdependencies that exist in a monetary area were not taken into account in the recommendations that the Commission made to each government.

The second element is that the potential growth on which we were counting was systematically overestimated, since we had not understood that we were in a financial recession and that a financial recession has much longer hysteresis effects[5] than a standard business cycle recession. There was, therefore, no countercyclical action for the euro area as a whole. To break this impasse, we must look at the macroeconomic situation in the euro area in light of the global situation, which is worrying for the period 2020-21. Drawing from this estimation, the Commission must prepare possible scenarios for the euro area growth over this period.

A budget authority should do this technical work, but this technical work must also be politically validated. This is where institutional reform that does not involve treaty change could take place: a European

[5] As Bluedorn and Leigh (2019) highlight, “the term hysteresis usually denotes the notion that recessions have permanent negative effects on the supply-side of the economy” (3).

finance minister and democratic control. Does it have to come from a European Parliament in a Eurozone Committee? Does it have to come from a committee set up by national parliaments? The idea is that democracy, which is absent from Europe, should be installed at a time when we are looking for a budget that affects everyone. That level is crucial. It has to be countercyclical, indeed. The Germans, in my opinion, do not have anything to fear, since we are in the term of a common assessment policy to be able to define a countercyclical action for the whole euro area.

The next operational question is the sharing of countercyclical action between the member states if there is no explicit budget for the euro area. It is the aggregate budget of the countries, conceived in a common macroeconomic policy aimed at stabilising the euro area that would be the tool of a countercyclical policy.

In this type of organisation, one cannot continue to think of the budget of each member state independently of the macro-economy of the area as a whole. We then stumble upon asymmetries incompatible with a countercyclical policy. So, let us be clear; the external balances of the countries, the current account balance, must be part of the diagnosis of the budget proposal. They must be tied to these balances. We can then see that in fact, the necessary symmetry of adjustments is not possible under the current conditions and that the rule that one must not exceed a certain amount of current balances must be activated. This is why the problems faced by the German economy could have a positive effect on intergovernmental consultation.

Ioannis Papadopoulos: On this asymmetry: on the one hand, there is still a very strict and one-size-fits-all fiscal framework for managing excessive deficits. But, on the other hand, the management of budget surpluses and, more importantly, of balance of payments surpluses, is not binding at all and is completely left to the discretion of the states, so the Germans do not want to make an effort. Thus, there certainly is an asymmetry.

I would also like to ask you a question about moral hazard. The only valid justification for the continuation of this state of affairs, which is obviously unsatisfactory, is moral hazard, or rather the strategic use, the instrumentalisation, of moral hazard, for example by the German government and others, in order not to do the right thing in terms of adjustment and reduction of asymmetries. We have transposed this notion of game theory to the strategic behaviour of actors in a framework that is quite different. As I was listening to you, I understood that we need an investment framework that is both acyclical and cyclical, that deals with the future, the long term, and that is quite different from the strategic behaviour of the players in game theory. So, is this transposition of moral hazard in this context always justified, or should we overcome it? If it is to be overcome, how can we thwart and deconstruct the strategic use, i.e., the instrumentalisation of moral hazard in these conditions? It seems that we are always stumbling upon this problem. Because you said it right: the Germans actually have nothing to fear.

Michel Aglietta: Let us look at what happened in Germany. Looking at the long-term evolution of capital accumulation rates, not just the gross investment-to-GDP ratio but net rates, we can see that Germany stopped investing much earlier than others, as early as the early 2000s, whereas the collapse of investment happened together with the crisis in the other EU member states. So, Germany's lack of investment has been very significant. On the other hand, we have said that everything is happening within the framework of a long-term policy. If there is no long-term policy, I do not think we can move forward. The long-term policy will lead the Germans to invest more at the turn of the decade.

If we commit to long-term investment under the conditions specified above, countries will participate. So, the rate of investment is expected to increase across Europe. This means that the very strong asymmetry that exists should be reduced. It will have to be reduced, if only because global macroeconomics has become a brake rather than a facilitator. That is to say that Europe as a whole, which was in balance until 2010, has risen in systematic surplus mainly because of Germany. Europe should return, with this type of policy, to a more balanced situation overall.

If Germany is driven to invest more, this by itself solves part of the problem. The long term gains over the short term. The other important element is the establishment of a European procedure. In my opinion, as soon as the Germans accept the idea of a European finance minister, this will reduce the fear of moral hazard.

Ioannis Papadopoulos: But the problem is that the Germans are very suspicious of the Commission to play this role of a Ministry of Finance, and they prefer something modeled on the ESM, that is, an intergovernmental mechanism, with a treaty establishing it outside the community acquis and outside the EU institutions.

Michel Aglietta: That is the other extreme position. I think that what is most reasonable —I believe the European Parliament has made this proposal— is an association. It seems to me that the Commission's presence is absolutely inescapable because there are technical aspects to this research, so it has to be present. But the Commission must be present in association with the Eurogroup; the Commission and the Eurogroup must jointly constitute what I have called a "European Budget Agency", or something of that kind. But, indeed, this European Budget Agency is an institutional entity that has a political mandate which —that is what is important— is provided to it by the European Council, of course. We need a basic policy; then this basic policy can choose the best scenario. Finally, the last word will be that of the European Council, but from a very different procedure than the one that exists today.

Ioannis Papadopoulos: What is paradoxical is that this institutional framework was already legislated in 2011 for the first time, in terms of preventing and correcting macroeconomic instabilities, with the famous "Six Pack".[6] However, this legislation is not really being applied, in the sense, once again, that we cannot force the Germans or the Dutch, in particular, to stimulate their investments so as to reduce their excessive surpluses.

Michel Aglietta: That is why we have to do the opposite, that is, we need to define the investment program for fundamental reasons —we talked about it at the beginning— and so we change the growth regime to make it sustainable and inclusive.

Ioannis Papadopoulos: So, this is the way out: through the long term.

Michel Aglietta: Yes. That is why I put a lot of emphasis on the long term before the short term, because there is a growing realisation that the neoliberal growth regime is no longer sustainable. In periods of disruption, social contradictions are exacerbated, and political changes result in institutional consequences.

[6] The so-called "Six-Pack" consists of five EU regulations and one EU directive: Regulation 1173/2011, Regulation 1175/2011, Regulation 1177/2011, and Directive 2011/85 as to fiscal policy, and Regulation 1174/2011 and Regulation 1176/2011 as to macroeconomic imbalances.

Ioannis Papadopoulos: There is also a change in the mindsets...

Michel Aglietta: The idea is to change the mindsets, yes.

Ioannis Papadopoulos: And the world of finance told us that even central banks will be involved.

I have no other questions; you are free to add anything complementary to our discussion so far, or something else that has not already been said.

Michel Aglietta: It is clear that there are things that can go in the right direction as a matter of political choice, indicating that among the common needs that will lead to certain types of investments, there are also security concerns and a common defence. These elements make us think straight away, of course, of growth regime issues.

Ioannis Papadopoulos: There is a window of opportunity, in my opinion. I fully agree with you. I wanted to ask you one last question that I omitted. There is a lot of discussion about the long term, the restructuring of demand, and even about the radical reorientation of the economy because of this crisis of capitalism (in that sense, this crisis will have somehow shown its usefulness). But we haven't talked about demographics at all, and that is one last thing I wanted you to comment on. Because when we talk about long-term structural problems, perhaps *the* basic problem is still Europe's demographic deficit. With the exception of France and Ireland, I think, no other European country has the population-replacement ratio to simply remain viable. How is the issue of demographics, which is absolutely strategic in the long term, integrated into your model?

Michel Aglietta: For me, it is part of the transformation of the way of life. That is to say, on this issue, the Anglo-Saxons may be ahead of us, even though the conditions in which they do so are not ideal. We have not made much progress on universal income yet, but we feel that there is something behind it. There is the issue of fundamental social rights, which are citizens' rights and are no longer linked to the positions that each one has in the economy. Obviously, we have to be able to fund them, which is why the health care system is going to be transformed, in my opinion. There is the idea of the possibility of individuals to define themselves the age at which they will stop their participation in work, with an intermediate period, where there will be people who will work a little less than they did before. But that means, of course, that this lifelong learning issue is really taken seriously. Because there are conversions that could be done at ages over 60.

You have to think about things like that. There is, if you will, very strong cognitive capital in people over 60. On the other hand, there are, in fact, professions where work cannot continue, because these are professions that have worn people down physically. That said, there may be fewer than before, given the transformation of production. That is why Scandinavians seem to me to be in a better position, as social protection is not seen as something that is linked to jobs, but is a right of citizenship.

Ioannis Papadopoulos: A universal right.

Michel Aglietta: It is a universal citizens' right. And so, to avoid an absolutely huge cost, you have to say: "That's it, you're given more freedoms, you have these rights, everyone has them, but obviously, if you have more work income because you want to keep working, you will modulate the payment of retirement in relation to that, so that it is the overall income of people that guarantees their integration into society".

Ioannis Papadopoulos: This resembles the idea of capability, after all, doesn't it?

Michel Aglietta: Yes, I think it is very important. Amartya Sen, with his concept of "capability" to pursue the development of life that we have reasons to value (Sen 1989), sheds light on what real freedoms are and therefore, on the social infrastructure that makes them possible.

Ioannis Papadopoulos: I was thinking about that while I was listening to you. To put an end, if you will, to this issue, which could turn into a very long discussion, we can say that the Scandinavians really had the right intuition in the end, because they gave a lot of flexibility to the basic financing of social security, and also at the level of the labour market, while combining that with a longer-term vision, which was the case with the radical restructuring of economies after the crisis of 1991. We have seen an entire society move towards another growth model that was really far ahead of its time and which was ultimately prophetic. It all ended very well. We see this in terms of development, standard of living, and even happiness of these countries today... All the evidence shows that.

In the end, all this is based on a model of consensus and strong political legitimacy, because it cannot be removed from political legitimacy. However, I keep having the impression that the problem in

Latin countries is that there is still a lack of political legitimacy for all of this. Just look at the low voter turnout and the prominence of the so-called "anti-systemic parties". I always come up against this problem, in the sense that if we had a more "Scandinavian" mentality, we could move things forward in the direction you are describing. But perhaps we also have a cultural problem, in the end, which is a heavier trend. We need to accomplish a much slower transformation than would be desirable, for cultural reasons. We lack the flexibility to do that.

Michel Aglietta: It is happening in France. It is interesting, because the antagonism of the political parties has disappeared. For the time being, we have the impression, keeping the same logic of the past, that it is a centrist magma of which we do not know what it is, but it may be another way of thinking about politics that appears, given the importance of people who are not, if you will, professionals in politics, but who have been elected Members of Parliament (MPs).

Ioannis Papadopoulos: Half of the French MPs are like that.

Michel Aglietta: Absolutely... This is an extraordinary phenomenon for France. We had never thought about it before.

References

2° Investing Initiative. 2015. "Assessing the alignment of portfolios with climate goals: Climate scenarios translated into a 2° benchmark," October, https://2degrees-investing.org/wp-content/uploads/2015/10/2dportfolio_v0_small.pdf (accessed April 10, 2021).

Aglietta, Michel, and Nicolas Leron. 2017. *La double démocratie : Une Europe politique pour la croissance* [*Dual Democracy: A Political Europe for Growth]*. Paris: Seuil.

Bluedorn, John C., and Daniel Leigh. 2019. "Hysteresis in Labor Markets? Evidence from Professional Long-Term Forecasts," May, https://www.imf.org/en/Publications/WP/Issues/2019/05/23/Hysteresis-in-Labor-Markets-Evidence-from-Professional-Long-Term-Forecasts-46908 (accessed April 10, 2021).

Carney, Mark. 2015. "Breaking the Tragedy of the Horizon – climate change and financial stability," 29 September, https://www.bankofengland.co.uk/-/media/boe/files/speech/2015/breaking-the-tragedy-of-the-horizon-climate-change-and-financial-stability.pdf?la=en&hash=7C67E785651862457D99511147C7424FF5EA0C1A (accessed April 2, 2021).

Directive 2011/85/EU of the Council of 8 November 2011 on requirements for budgetary frameworks of the Member States. 2011. OJ L 306: 41–47.

EIB. n.d. "National promotional banks and institutions," https://www.eib.org/en/about/partners/npbis/index.htm (accessed April 10, 2021).

European Commission. 2020. "Proposal for a Regulation of the European Parliament and of the Council establishing the InvestEU Programme," 29 May, https://eur-lex.europa.eu/legal-content/EN/TXT/?uri=CELEX%3A52020PC0403 (accessed April 2, 2021).

Monti, Mario. 2009. "A new Strategy for the Single Market for the European Economy and Society," 9 May, https://ec.europa.eu/docsroom/documents/15501/attachments/1/translations/en/renditions/pdf (accessed April 2, 2021).

Regulation (EU) 2015/1017 of the European Parliament and of the Council of 25 June 2015 on the European Fund for Strategic Investments, the European Investment Advisory Hub and the European Investment Project Portal and amending Regulations (EU) No 1291/2013 and (EU) No 1316/2013 — the European Fund for Strategic Investments. 2015. OJ L 169: 1–38.

Regulation (EU) No 1177/2011 of the Council of 8 November 2011 amending Regulation (EC) No 1467/97 on speeding up and clarifying the implementation of the excessive deficit procedure. 2011. OJ L 306: 33–40.

Regulation (EU) No 1176/2011 of the European Parliament and of the Council of 16 November 2011 on the prevention and correction of macroeconomic imbalances. 2011. OJ L 306: 25–32.

Regulation (EU) No 1175/2011 of the European Parliament and of the Council of 16 November 2011 amending Council Regulation (EC) No 1466/97 on the strengthening of the surveillance of budgetary positions and the surveillance and coordination of economic policies. 2011. OJ L 306: 12–24.

Regulation (EU) No 1174/2011 of the European Parliament and of the Council of 16 November 2011 on enforcement measures to correct excessive macroeconomic imbalances in the euro area. 2011. OJ L 306: 8–11.

Regulation (EU) No 1173/2011 of the European Parliament and of the Council of 16 November 2011 on the effective enforcement of budgetary surveillance in the euro area. 2011. OJ L 306: 1–7.

Sen, Amartya. 1989. Development as capability expansion. *Journal of Development Planning* 19, no.1: 41–58.

Treaty on Stability, Coordination and Governance in the Economic and Monetary Union, Brussels, 2 March 2012, https://eur-lex.europa.eu/legal-content/EN/TXT/PDF/?uri=CELEX:42012A0302(01)&from=EN (accessed April 3, 2021).

CHAPTER 2

TOWARDS A STRONGER AND LARGER EUROPE

KARL AIGINGER*

Combining crisis mitigation with reforms

The goal of this chapter is to analyse the status of the European unification project: its tremendous success, but also the problems it faces on the road to the future. We present crossroads for European Union (hereinafter EU) member states and Europe, as well as ways through which governance has to be improved. Particular emphasis is placed on Southern Europe and its forfeited chances to serve as a bridge to the southern and eastern non-European neighbours, or as a spearhead of renewable energy.

The European Commission has presented its vision of a "European Green Deal" combined with a Social Europe (European Commission 2019). This could be a narrative uniting Europeans and allowing the EU to play a broader geopolitical role. Nevertheless, the road is "bumpy" due to internal opposition from populist leaders in several countries longing for a past glory that never actually existed, and due to the external influence of former President Trump and current President Putin, who both sought, and the latter still seeks, to weaken Europe. Another problem is that high levels of already existing debt in some member states, plus heavy investments needed for achieving climate neutrality, and finally, the deep recession caused by the Covid-19 pandemic, all require big spending. If this later leads to substantial tax increases, recovery will come late and will be weak. It is all-important to develop synergies between (i) public sector reforms and an improved European budget (Multiannual Financial Framework - MFF), (ii) climate policy, and (iii) stimulus packages against

* Director of the Policy Crossover Center Vienna-Brussels (www.querdenkereuropa.at) and Professor Emeritus of Economics at the Viennese University of Economics and Business (WU Wien).

the crisis. I conclude that the enlargement of the EU to the Western Balkans and relevant partnerships with neighbouring countries can make Europe stronger and more capable of shaping globalisation.

The deepest recession of the past 70 years

European countries have decided to spend large amounts of money in order to mitigate the Covid-19 pandemic consequences. The planned programmes of the 27 EU member states are larger in relation to the economic output (Gross National Income - GNI) than in the United States of America (hereinafter US), and they are further topped by the EU itself. The stimulus started earlier than in the US and more quickly than the expansionist policy after the financial crisis.

This was no easy task and was not a matter of course. The goal of zero deficits had not yet been reached, and some countries like France, Italy and Greece still had high debts relative to their annual economic output at the start of 2020. The rules of the Fiscal Compact and the excessive deficit procedure adopted in the wake of the financial crisis would have demanded further debt cuts. However, after the last crisis, Europe has also created facilities for financing new expenditures in the case of new crises. The European Stability Mechanism (hereinafter ESM) has been installed, as well as the European Fund for Strategic Investment (EFSI), both separated from national budgets and leveraging small capital inputs into large facilities via the European Investment Bank (hereinafter EIB). The European Central Bank (hereinafter ECB) has increased money supply, inter alia by buying bonds from governments and even large firms.

In the midst of the Covid-19 crisis, the enactment of the Recovery and Resilience Facility (hereinafter RRF) by the EU has made it the centrepiece of NextGenerationEU, a temporary recovery instrument that allows the European Commission to raise funds to help repair the immediate economic and social damage brought about by the Covid-19 pandemic. The RRF will make €672.5 billion in loans and grants available to support reforms and investments undertaken by member states. Thus, the use of a form of Eurobonds has been made possible. Moreover, additional expenditures have been by now authorised by the EU without penalties by financial markets for countries with large debt. The question of how much conditionality can or should be added to EU financial aid remains important.

If we compare the reaction in Europe with that in the US, we see that the US entered the Covid-19 crisis with a larger budget deficit and reacted later. After first criticising China for being the origin of the problem, a rather high stimulus was eventually planned. This is needed even more in the US due to an expensive health sector that is not accessible to less privileged people, such as migrants and those of African descent. New expenditures, even on top of very large deficits and debts, are easier in the US due to the privilege of the dollar as an informal reserve capacity. This increasingly irrational competitive advantage has to be addressed in a new European strategy, perhaps in cooperation with China and other large net investors. European safe bonds and the denomination of more international contracts in euros would be part of a strategy to enhance European economic power in the globalising world and guarantee low-interest rates without the current efforts of the ECB.

Europe as a success model in midlife crisis

In historical comparison, the EU has become a firmly established success model. It started with six member states and now has twenty-seven, developing from a free trade agreement (initially restricted to coal and steel) to a common market. The majority of the EU member states use a common currency, which —despite short-run crises in its first decade— is now much more stable than during its initial adoption, challenging the dominance of the US dollar. On a formerly conflict-ridden continent, no military conflict has taken place between the member states for over seventy years. The rule of law, as well as conflict management, is extended to countries applying for membership. The former socialist countries have been integrated in a shorter time than any other transformation in history; for this, the EU has been lauded as an integration machine by the World Bank (Gill and Raiser 2012). Europe is called a soft power by leading US scholar Jeremy Rifkin (Rifkin 2004) and has been awarded the Nobel Peace Prize.

However, new problems have arisen and have led to a kind of "midlife" crisis. Economic dynamics are low, inequality is rising, and youth unemployment is irresponsibly high. Development is not even across countries and, over time, progress is often not interpreted as a European achievement, while "Brussels" is held responsible for many problems. Reforms in Southern Europe have not been implemented quickly enough, as a substantial part of production has been transferred to low-wage countries. No clusters of new firms or sophisticated industries are substituting the loss of some capital as well as labour-intensive industries (Aiginger et al. 2013). Each smaller crisis has been covered by ever-higher public expenditures, without focusing on innovation and future competitiveness. Now, East-West divides, as well as North-South splits, are endangering the consensus among countries.

Europe currently lacks a new narrative, since the peace mission is considered —erroneously— to have been fulfilled. Citizens no longer support the "ever-deeper integration", even if problems that could be more successfully answered through joint efforts are on the rise. As an outside challenge, Europe was confronted in the last four years with a US administration that intended to weaken it. This is also the intention of President Vladimir Putin, who seeks to regain political dominance in Central and Eastern Europe and the Western Balkans. China is trying to fulfil the investment needs in Southern Europe and the eastern and southern non-European neighbourhood, while, to a large extent, aiming at its own advantage, at the cost of the environment and of local workforce.

Crossroads available in the decisive year 2021

The situation is challenging, but pessimism need not be the consequence. Hereinafter I carve out four crossroads that may determine strategies for the Union and its member states. Not all countries must follow the same principles, but should at least consider the following choices.

Going for the high road vs. seeking low costs only

On a low road path, wages are cut, and social and ecological standards are declared to be too expensive. A high road strategy focuses on innovation and skills, raising energy or resource productivity, and fostering new firms and technologies. On the low road path, subsidies are needed to shelter inefficient firms from competition, while the high road path promotes change to better jobs and the production of cleaner, more customised products.

The high road path focuses on improving education, ranging from preschool to apprenticeship and technical universities, and on bolstering innovation. This is encouraged by a new definition of competitiveness, which is defined as the ability of a region or country to deliver societal goals (Aiginger 2018; Aiginger and Rodrik 2020). This leads to very different policy conclusions than defining competitiveness as the presence of cheap labour and low social standards. Firms have indirectly promoted this redefinition; when they sell shares at the stock market, they never claim to have found a niche of low-cost inputs, but instead persuade the buyers by marketing their outstanding competence to solve future needs with their products.

Calling back the past vs. future-oriented reforms

Populist movements led to Brexit and appear in many countries in different political constellations. Their common feature is creating a division between a virtuous "us" and a corrupt "them". They call for illiberal democracies and a return to past glory (Aiginger 2020). In Italy and Austria, populists have come into government, but have been ousted by different coalitions. In France, a populist party had taken the lead in opinion polls for several years, but has finally been defeated by a young President founding a new party. In Hungary and Poland, autocratic regimes dominate the government. After gaining power, populist regimes change the rules of voting so that a minority of voters is converted into a majority in the legislature. Furthermore, they dismantle the division of power between the parliament, the government, and the judicial branch. They fight against migration, even if they essentially need immigration since they are depopulating. Reasons for the success of populism are economic and cultural, but also related to regional distress and deindustrialisation in rust belts. Policy failures and a fear of "population exchange" through the mass migration of people from different cultures support the political gains of populists.

A counterstrategy consists of four stages (Aiginger 2020). It starts with an open discussion of the problems, but also rejects pessimism and the narrative that everything was better in the past. Then, a vision is to be offered of where a country or region wants to be in 2030. Furthermore, if citizens approve of the vision, the issues of which instrument will be used and which cooperation with other countries or international organisations might help are considered. Future-oriented reforms are based on education, training and innovation, and not on an idealisation of the past.

Cheap fossil energy vs. efficiency plus renewables

In the past, cheap oil or coal formed the basis of efforts to catch up and strive for high growth. As oil and coal reserves became smaller relative to demand, new imports and expensive and environmentally detrimental methods (deep-ocean or horizontal drilling) became necessary, and fossil energy had to be subsidised. Currently, subsidies for fossil energy are much higher than those for clean energy. The US returned to this path under the Trump administration, starting from a level where energy efficiency is one third of that of Switzerland and half of the European average.

Europe can follow this path or alternately try to boost energy efficiency and shift energy use from fossil fuels to clean energy. Modal shifts in transport and traffic are possible, and electric cars are already cheaper than diesel or gasoline-driven ones if the life cycle costs are calculated instead of the purchasing price and if firms are prevented from offering luxury electrical vehicles with high power and speeds not allowed on highways, let alone cities. Efficient European battery production could reduce the cost of electric cars, in addition to the reuse of old batteries for storing renewable energy. Change can be accelerated through a double strategy of subsidies for the purchase and taxing of emissions. Employees and today's workers in the production and repair of combustion-driven cars have to be retrained to be able to switch to digitalised jobs or the construction of zero or positive energy houses; otherwise, they are taken hostage by lobbies to prevent decarbonisation.

Industrial policy for ailing champions vs. support of societal goals

There are not many examples of success among countries pursuing an industrial policy. Specifically, countries supporting their own large firms through public procurement, subsidies or protection tend to experience a strong decline in the share of manufacturing, leading to a trade deficit. European industrial policy did not follow this path and has stressed horizontal policy measures.

A future-oriented industrial policy should be driven by societal goals. Correcting market failures is important, but the goals of industrial policy are wider; they include market shaping, mission orientation, and the provision of new basic technologies. Governments should only intervene if there are long-run interests, not for the short term. Their goals and instruments should be communicated with citizens, since the success and demise of industrial policy leads to successful clusters or forgotten regions respectively. Regions with decreasing populations and underinvestment in infrastructure constitute hotspots for populism and a threat to liberal democracy. Societal goals in a new systemic industrial policy include climate change, health, poverty prevention, and the reduction of inequality (Aiginger and Rodrik 2020).

Towards a governance fitter for the European future

European governance is a compromise between designing a common policy and respecting differences in the priorities of independent member states. With the enlargement of the EU to peripheral countries and the deepening from a Free Trade Area to a Currency Union for the majority of its member states, along with new challenges due to globalisation, migration, and the financial crisis, the decision processes have become even more complicated.

Combining top-down goals with bottom-up preferences and innovations

Global challenges call for common European solutions. Yet, several member states and a substantial share of citizens are requesting less intervention by "Brussels". The solution for this dichotomy is that the EU sets common goals and empowers or obliges member states to choose implementation according to their own preferences and abilities (Aiginger 2017). This technique is well applied in the climate question. The Paris Treaty, which all member states and the EU have signed, sets the goal of limiting global warming to less than 2 degrees Celsius. Each member state can then decide which instruments it will use and which innovations it will develop. The national strategy must be elaborated and developed in the form of an annual climate plan, which is then judged by experts from the Commission. If an inadequate plan must be improved, which is usually the case, further monitoring of the adherence of national policy to the more ambitious reform plan is necessary. If more coordination reduces costs or increases effectiveness, norms and standards can be set at the global level during the annual or biannual climate conferences that are organised by the UN in different countries, so as to increase national commitment.

Combining top-down necessities with bottom-up choices also applies for the Fiscal Compact and financial stability. The Europe 2020 Strategy sets goals for Research and Development (R&D), and then member states can choose national targets, while labour market indicators are closely watched and compared, as is social coherence in the European Pillar of Social Rights that was added recently. Economic performance, as well as the adherence to broader goals, is then summarised in the European Semester. This procedure starts with a growth projection and general priorities set by the European Commission. Then, each member state must report measures for implementation, and finally, the European Commission evaluates them by offering "country-specific recommendations". This process is in principle a good mix of top-down and bottom-up policy, but should be made more binding, while climate goals, tax structures, and regulatory burdens should gain larger attention. The citizens of each member state should be informed about priorities and deficits in a dialogue.

Streamlining decisions

Decisions by the EU tend to go in the right direction in the medium and long run, but slowly, and generally after some negative events reveal deficits. Non-adherence to the conditions set for entering the Eurozone led to the huge debt of Greece. Low R&D expenditures, along with insufficient educational systems and vocational training, have led to deficits in budget and trade in other countries, including the founding members and former manufacturing strongholds of Italy and France. Reluctant adoption of the tasks of the ECB, ranging from a single focus on price stability to the dampening of high interest rates for individual countries and still later the support of investment, caused a sluggish recovery after the financial crisis and a period of instability for the euro. To some extent, this is the result of the fact that Europe is only slowly changing from an economic to a political Union. Maybe even more so, this is the result of a very sophisticated and complex distribution of tasks between the institutions, namely the European Commission, the European Council, the Council of the European Union, and the European Parliament. The governance design should not be that of a strong European executive, able to overrule the interest of member states and even more of small member states. Even if the model of the "United States of Europe" is not supported by many experts and political groups, there is an overwhelming consensus to strengthen the role of the European Parliament by giving it the right for legislative initiatives, abolish the unanimity requirement (perhaps with some exceptions) in the Council of the EU, and facilitate the existing instrument of enhanced cooperation (in which a subgroup of member states go ahead in a policy field).

Making Europe a financially stable region

European financial stability has been strengthened after the financial crisis and the Eurozone crisis through the creation of the ESM and a European banking surveillance structure. Capital requirements are set, and stability will increase even more in the upcoming Banking Union. One goal is that the money of European citizens should never again be used for bailouts. The success of the new policy is shown by a smaller variance in the interest rates of government bonds between member states.

Connecting migration with ageing and depopulation

As far as immigration is concerned, there is still no system that, on the one hand, is compatible with humanitarian law and, on the other hand, respects the problems of the country of entry, not least the needs of depopulating regions and industries with a short supply of labour. The Dublin process looked well-designed but was not enough to handle disruptive immigration waves concurring with populist opposition to needed migration. Quotas for member states according to income and employment would be rational but are rejected at least by many member states. A solution could be to delegate the decision to regions or cities and to combine the acceptance for migrants with financial incentives. If a region loses population and does not want to go into cumulative depopulation and deindustrialisation, it can apply for migrants and get funds for investing in new firms, better schools and infrastructure. This would reduce regional distress and, at the same time, lower the burden for the country of entry. Refugee camps could become less crowded and inhumane and migrants could be directed towards locations where they are welcomed, needed, and integrated.

Table 2-1 Population - fewer young people, doubling of 65 (plus)

	1990/ 2000	2000/ 2020	2000/ 2050	1990/ 2000	2000/ 2020	2000/ 2050	1990/ 2000	2000/ 2020	2000/ 2050
	Total			**1 to 19 year olds**			**20 to 29 year olds**		
EU27	2.6	4.5	5.1	-11.2	-8.7	-15.3	-5.2	-16.3	-21.2
EU – East	-1.9	-5.7	-15.3	-16.8	-27.3	-39.0	11.2	-31.5	-45.0
EU – South	2.5	8.0	6.5	-20.0	-2.6	-17.3	-1.1	-28.3	-33.2
Greece	6.8	-2.3	-17.5	-15.7	-10.4	-27.2	15.7	-36.6	-52.7
Spain	4.4	14.8	21.4	-22.4	6.5	-1.4	7.6	-31.3	-22.9
Italy	0.4	6.6	3.6	-19.3	-4.5	-22.9	-10.7	-23.7	-34.5
	30 to 64 year olds			**65 (plus)**					
EU27	8.4	6.9	-8.6	19.5	35.3	98.5			
EU – East	-0.4	3.8	-22.3	17.9	36.0	91.1			
EU – South	9.6	14.4	-10.9	27.3	35.4	115.7			
Greece	8.1	4.0	-30.3	37.4	22.5	59.3			
Spain	13.4	27.4	-2.3	30.3	37.4	158.9			
Italy	7.6	8.7	-11.7	23.8	36.9	102.4			

Source: Eurostat, EU-South: Greece, Italy, Spain, Portugal. EU-East: Bulgaria, Czech Republic, Estonia, Latvia, Lithuania, Hungary, Poland, Romania, Slovenia, Slovak Republic.

Partnership with neighbours

Europe is currently the largest economic region in the world and enjoys the highest standard of living, as defined by economic, social and ecological criteria. Life expectancy is high and increasing, while in the US and in Russia it is decreasing. However, in order to remain an important international player, Europe must begin implementing ambitious internal reforms and engage in a new partnership with its dynamic neighbourhood. The alternative would be to become an isolated region of less than 10% of world output and 5% of population, lower than the shares of India and South Africa. A small, ageing and shrinking Europe would be surrounded by a "ring of fire" and countries longing for a "past glory" that never existed. New hegemonies, which are often governed by autocratic regimes like Russia, Turkey, or Iran, are seeking past glory and may not refrain from requesting border changes to remain popular with their own people despite economic distress.

An inward-looking strategy calls for protection and European military buildup. A European outward strategy strives for a new partnership with its dynamic yet unstable neighbourhood. The European neighbourhood —post-Soviet and Black Sea countries, the Arab world and rising Africa— could become a driver for European exports. A new partnership policy could fight poverty and desertification, two of the root causes of disruptive migration. Shifting the focus of the military sector from potential conflicts between member countries to monitoring frontiers and helping to stabilise conflicts is needed, not least after the US retreat from its unlucky role of international interventions, leading to political chaos thereafter.

Sheltering responsible globalisation

If the EU solves its internal problems and extends to the countries of the Western Balkans, it could remain —together with its neighbours and on par with China— the largest economic power. Then, it can offer its high social and ecological standards to other countries and shape globalisation in a responsible, welfare-increasing process. Europe can support human rights and the rule of law. A sound financial sector must serve the real economy and European citizens. The euro can become one of the world's reserve capacities, dethroning the dollar. Interest rates for European government bonds will then be lower than in the US, with its much higher debt. Globalisation can step by step harmonise social and ecological standards, this time upwards.

Game changers needed in Southern Europe

Southern Europe deserves special attention. Productivity and per capita income have been low in the South in "modern times", although Greece, Italy, Spain and Portugal have historically been leading cultures, starting globalisation and spreading their values globally, even if sometimes through force or to their asymmetric economic advantage. Up to the outburst of the financial crisis, Southern European countries managed to catch up and approach the European average at a remaining difference of ten or twenty percent. However, since the financial crisis in 2009, the catching up process has been stopped, and incomes have declined in Southern Europe. Greece, Spain, and Portugal have needed rescue programs paid for by European partners.

We cannot analyse all problems of the South here; this is done in Aiginger et al. 2013. Among these new problems, there is the double loss of capital-intensive industries (such as steel and chemicals), which have shifted to locations nearer to those of the raw materials, and those of low-cost textile industries relocated into former socialist or emerging countries. The education and innovation systems in the European South are unfit for firms competing internationally. The education system never supported practical skills, and innovation centres or clusters for high-end products were never created. Church, military systems, rich families, and ship owners, as well as the mafia, are de facto exempt from paying taxes, while a large public sector offers lifelong employment for the elite and their children. Money is transferred into tax shelters. What we can do here is list a few game changers that were developed for Greece, but many of which are also fit for other southern regions of Europe. In general, they shift the attention from the past to the future.

Creating industrial zones and clusters for innovation

Innovation zones or clusters could attract international firms that currently do not invest in Greece because of burdensome procedures and the length of legal disputes. Start-up centres may supply computer facilities, office space, meeting rooms, and joint secretarial services for new businesses starting as single-person firms. Rents, electricity costs, and taxes could be waived for young firms in such centres for one year.

Youth reform boards

Greece is still dominated by old boys' networks; it finances a large government, an expensive military, and tax-exempt ship owners. Young people have excellent command of ICT technology, but today do not find work and, if they do, they are not paid adequately, while they are underrepresented in the political process, especially young females. Given the high youth unemployment, young people tend to stay with their parents since they cannot afford to live without work in Athens and neither in the regional centres, which would be even better.

A competition for the best ideas on how to improve the chances for young people should be organised via social networks, and the best proposals could be presented in a televised event. Young people, including the winners of the contest, could then build an advisory reform board for the government, e.g., providing a "youth test" for all reforms.

Private funds managed by the Diaspora

Government funding for reforms will be limited for some time, but private funding is in principle abundant, given the uneven distribution of incomes and property, as well as the capital that is hidden tax-free in foreign banks. The foreign bank accounts should be incentivised to be returned at a lump sum payment of 25%, combined with a tax amnesty. On the other hand, if foreign accounts are not reported within a year, the full penalties by law should be applied.

Successful Greek expatriates could support their home country and monitor the use of repatriated money for reforms and new firms. Investment bonds bought by Greek expatriates or other wealthy Greeks could be managed by a Greek investment fund, managed by expatriates and the ECB. If expatriates engage more in the reform process, this can substitute the necessity for European agencies to supervise economic reforms, which is unpopular, not just because Germans are the spearheads of a tough policy for the frivolous Greeks, but also because they are reminded by left-leaning Greeks that they have not honoured their obligation for restoration payments after World War II.

Making use of the qualifications of migrants

Greece is one of the entry "havens" for immigrants looking for shelter and life chances. Migrants are forced into refugee camps or islands, where they experience hunger, unhygienic conditions, and often molestation by other refugees. Many kids lose the ability to learn and prepare for real life, if they ever manage to leave the camps. Unaccompanied children or those with only one parent suffer the most.

Quasi-governmental institutions could be set up to foster the integration of immigrants into the Greek economy and of their children into the system of preschool care. Practical skills and the entrepreneurial spirit of immigrants are needed in Greece, as service quality is often low and construction work is done by Albanians or Bulgarians. Renting boats or getting refreshments at the beach is often not possible outside the large tourism centres. The share of Greeks between 20 and 30 years old in the total population is already decreasing due to emigration, and is forecasted to be cut in half between 2000 and 2050.

Bridge to a vibrant and dynamic neighbourhood and a rising Africa

Greece has a specific geographical position compared to all other European countries. It is the closest one to the Black Sea region, the Middle East and North Africa. The distance from Athens to Cairo is 1,200 km and to Kiev 1,500 km. This is much less than the distance to Berlin, Paris, or Brussels (all more than 3,000 flight kilometers away). Historically, this location between Asia, Europe and Africa was the reason why civilisation took hold early in this region; Greek merchants took the lead in trade and Greek ideas enriched philosophy and science.

Greece could become a hub for production, exports, and trade in a dynamic geographical region. The Greek neighbouring countries are growing fast, whenever there is peace. This holds for Turkey, the Arab countries, North Africa, and even more for Sub-Saharan Africa, and to a lesser degree, for former Soviet Union countries and the Western Balkans.

Regional leader in decarbonisation

Greece is an energy- and resource-intensive society with a high input of coal, oil, and gas. Imports of fossil energy are large and have turned the trade balance into the negative. Large subsidies for fossil energy are maintained, preventing energy-saving technologies and the inroads of alternative energy. They are also a heavy burden for public budgets.

Greece should try to become the first decarbonised society or climate-neutral economy in Europe. Energy savings and renewable energy using the wind and the sun should become the top priority. Cars using combustion technology should step by step be forbidden until 2025. Efficient loading infrastructure must be provided in all homes and offices, traditional gasoline stations, and public buildings. As the first decarbonised society, Greece could improve and export clean technologies to neighbouring countries in the Black Sea region, the Western Balkans, and North Africa.

Cutting debt in three stages

In the last decade, Greece has made an ambitious switch toward fiscal stability. The fiscal balance had yielded a surplus before the Covid-19 pandemic, even if this is not enough to reduce the high debt to a significant degree. Moreover, Covid-19 presents another very big challenge. The most important driver of a late recovery, tourism, has suffered considerably. Whether foreign tourists will be able to travel to Southern Europe in the winter of 2022 remains open. Many new establishments will not survive without large support. The burden of refugees not allowed to travel towards richer countries like Austria or Germany and, at the same time, not able to be integrated into stagnant economies will be felt. Finally, there is the danger that Covid-19 will break out in refugee camps and that hospitals and emergency units will be overcrowded. The new credit and support facilities provided by the EU in April 2021 will mitigate some problems, but Greek debt will rise again, and this cannot be tackled by even more austerity.

Debt should be cut if Greece develops a vision and sticks to it. This could be done in three stages: one third should be cut directly through decisions made by the EU and its member states, another third should be paid back but at a very low interest rate, subsidised by institutions connected with the EIB, and a final third should be handled through the repatriation of Greek capital currently stored at foreign banks. Such a plan is now more pressing than before the health crisis, and the EU must cut Greece's debt.

A new narrative challenged by Covid-19

The new President of the European Commission has realised that Europe needs a new narrative, which will streamline the needed reforms into a unifying concept. Ursula von der Leyen has chosen the vision of a

"Green Deal", in which Europe takes the lead in fighting climate change and becomes the first major region in the world achieving climate neutrality until 2050. The European Green Deal should be accompanied by a Social Europe that leaves no person or region behind. One of the proposals included is to raise the minimum wages in member states. The Green Deal, as well as a Social Europe, should be incorporated into a strategy aiming at a larger role for the EU in the world, made possible by a "Geopolitical Commission". In general, Ursula von der Leyen encourages the EU to "strive for more", and this could mobilise resources, enthusiasm, and a new self-awareness among countries and citizens.

The new narrative is welcomed by the member states. However, the proof of the pudding will be in its operationalisation, and proceeding in small steps. The new strategy requires money and commitment at the European as well as the national level, the engagement of experts, investment, and the use of radical new technologies. The financial requirement is estimated to amount to one trillion euro up to 2030, which amounts to 100 billion euro per annum. This sounds like a lot, but must be compared to the money spent for subsidies in fossil energy and those for large agricultural units, plus expenditures for inward-oriented military systems and the purchase of weapons and military aircrafts (in some countries mainly used for airshows). Tax avoidance due to tax loopholes and evasion by internet platforms and multinational conglomerates could be stopped, or an overdue tax on short-run financial speculation could be installed. All this would mobilise more than the necessary 100 billion euro per year. Knowing that Europe is currently suffering an investment trough and that the leader in fighting climate change will have the advantage (while the laggard will have the burden), this investment is, indeed, feasible and profitable, as the rewards are higher than the costs.

However, we must emphasise that this extra spending should not take place on top of current public expenditures. Taxes and public commitments are already very high in Europe. If we aggregate the national budgets plus that of the EU (including its leveraging by external funds), more than half of the economic output is spent by the public sector. The all-important task is to cut unproductive public expenditures for the 27 national bureaucracies. These comprise state, regional, and community budgets, often blown up by overlapping competencies. Since tasks have been shifted to the European level, costs at the national level should decrease. Old regulations should be substituted, and not complemented, by European rules. The costs and time needed for starting new firms should be reduced, while public sector management and learning from the best performers should be made obligatory. The overall public expenditures (European plus national) should not increase, but rather decrease in the region with the highest taxation and the tightest regulations of the world.

The need to complement the Green Deal with cost-cutting is becoming ever more evident due to the Covid-19 health crisis. The member states and the European Commission have reacted faster than during the financial crisis by starting large expansionary programs, amounting again to additional expenditures of 750 billion euro. Since these funds should be mobilised within the next 1-3 years, this is per annum more than the amount planned for the Green Deal. This is positive and great. However, the question arises as to whether this necessity will substitute, or add to, the expenses for the Green Deal. The expenses for Covid-19 definitely cannot be made in addition to the Green Deal, if the Green Deal must be financed on top of current expenditures. Even creative tricks can only be applied once.

The problem, therefore, lies in combining long-term prudence with short-term crisis mitigation and investment into climate neutrality. This is a tough requirement, but it is not impossible since the problems of climate change, the spread of diseases, and social distress are more interrelated than we realise. Moreover, an optimist might believe that with red ink for past privileges, Europe could raise the money needed for climate and Covid-19 consequences without overburdening taxpayers and the economy later.

Closely connected problems call for systemic answers

There exists no empirical evidence so far on the degree to which the new health crises, the problems of social inequality, and climate impairments (affected by pollution) are connected. However, there is evidence that there exist feedbacks and cross effects at the personal, as well as societal, level. This is first and foremost a problem, but on the other hand, also offers a chance to look for solutions that support each other and limit the overall cost of fighting climate change, inequality, and the negative consequences of Covid-19.

Interrelated causes

It is proven that inequality decreases life expectancy and impairs health. If health problems arise, whether from smoking, obesity, or infection, poor people and the less educated do not tend to see a doctor, do not restrict smoking or drinking nor do they seek alternative health-improving measures such as exercise or yoga. Therefore, pulmonary diseases, obesity, and heart deficiencies are more likely to affect individuals with lower income. Past health problems —even if treated— are known to relate to the severity and death toll of Covid-19.

There is also evidence that pollution reduces life expectancy, with the extreme conclusion that the death toll due to air pollution is higher than that of traffic casualties. Since smog and air particles are heavier in large cities (and the crowded districts within them), this is another bridge between poverty, health problems, and the likelihood of being impaired by Covid-19.

Poor people live in districts with lower air quality or along high-traffic roads and intra-city highways. They have fewer parks or woods nearby and take fewer vacations. They go to work even when they are sick, fearing to lose their jobs, and informal contracts tend not to offer paid leaves for illness. Poor people must sometimes enter short-term contracts or look for daily opportunities.

They also necessarily crowd together in small flats, and therefore have close personal contacts and little private space, in addition to seldom possessing a separate working desk or laptop. It is more difficult to keep social distance, so the probability of infection, as well as the likelihood of propagating infection, is larger. Migrants and homeless people are subject to all the aforementioned problems.

Searching for synergies

Emissions, the size and power of cars, waste and garbage increase with income and affluence. On the other hand, higher financial leverage enables to switch to more sustainable consumption. Houses can be insulated, energy systems can be changed from fossil to alternative sources, and photovoltaics can be added. Electric cars, with their high purchasing price, can be bought and reloaded in a private, one-family house more easily than in big houses with many small flats. Enabling a similar switch for poorer households requires substantial incentives. Pricing emissions and taxing gasoline or diesel cars must be combined with a tax bonus for low incomes. The latter must not be too small, given the higher personal discount rate and status quo bias of low-income earners and older people.

Since the under-privileged suffer over-proportionately from pollution, poor people would profit from the Green Deal through better health, improved living conditions, and less exposure to smog and particles. Emissions are over-proportionally caused by the affluent strata, and taxes lower than the negative external effects of large cars or untaxed kerosene for air traffic are socially and environmentally unjustified. The Green Deal would mitigate this problem, but must respect the distributional consequences mentioned above.

Covid-19 increases inequality and presents a different burden for different groups. People with higher education and incomes have better opportunities to continue working from home and their children have laptops, while the children of low-income earners or migrants may lose contact with their teachers. High-income people are more experienced in the use of digital deliveries and internet services, as well as in making use of digital problem-solving, including guidance in case of upcoming health problems. Staying at home is more convenient, and first steps outside in crowded hardware stores or supermarkets are less needed due to digital deliveries. Public traffic is used less frequently, and teleworking will be possible at least on some weekdays. Less crowding was already the case at the time when the infectious disease was not yet known so that the infection rate could be income-dependent: higher for the less privileged.

No evidence is available on this, with the exception that in the US the African-American population is infected to a greater extent and has a higher death toll (Hermann 2020; Richter 2020). Rather marginal contrary evidence shows that the virus has spread specifically in tourist areas in western Austria, in which high-income people sought sport and entertainment. Racial prejudices came up as European firms announced they would test vaccines in Africa first, and as agencies reported that African-Chinese people had been forced to be tested to a higher degree, and had also been forced to leave their homes in Guangzhou (Economist 2020).

Conditioning crisis support on investment in the future

If we look at how measures to limit climate change and inequality could be combined with the large stimulus programmes due to Covid-19, we could think of making the application of firms' emergency support credits or short-time work for many employees conditional on their offer to support retraining or upgrading of their workforce skills. Firms could be incentivised to offer laptops or internet training to the employees they send into short-time work or temporary layoffs.

Firms that suffer from the crisis and apply for public subsidies should supply a programme in which they define steps towards becoming climate-neutral, saving energy and reducing emissions, precisely at a time in which demand is weak. If some of these programmes start during the crisis, which may be even easier since offices are empty, this could boost demand when it will be most needed.

We know today, with hindsight, that subsidies for firms as well as individuals during the financial crisis supported investment in fossil energy, e.g. due to the scrapping of old cars or the buying of new diesel or petrol cars (Koundouri 2020). This time, subsidies for firms, as well as income substitutes for individuals, should be conditional upon climate compatibility or upgrading of qualifications.

A quick start for investment leading to decarbonisation could support employment as well as climate neutrality. Incentives for better insulation or a change in heating systems will have double benefits if we also support households with low income; we may even get a triple benefit: higher employment, lower emissions, and stronger support for the underprivileged. If these three goals are targeted simultaneously, the short-run budgetary cost will be much smaller.

A stronger and larger Europe may shape globalisation

We have carved out crossroads. Europe could stay small and unable to shape globalisation and climate policy. In this case, it would suffer from low dynamics, high and rising inequality, and further inroads from the populist call for a return to past national policies. Alternatively, Europe could become larger, stronger, and better connected with neighbours to the East and the South outside geographical Europe, and could become a role model for a rich welfare- and choice-providing society.

The new President of the European Commission proposed the more ambitious road of the two. Europe should "strive for more" and play a geopolitical role, an especially important statement considering that, at that time, the US was retreating from multinationalism and human rights, as well as the Climate Treaty, and eventually also from the International Monetary Fund (IMF), the World Bank, and the World Health Organisation

(WHO). China is on its way to becoming the largest economic power, with Sino-centric ambitions, as well as low environmental concerns in its external investment. Nevertheless, it is still ruled by one party and rejects Western democratic rules of power-sharing. It defies individual as well as minority rights and remains open to racial discrimination. In the non-European neighbourhood, new hegemonies like Russia, Turkey or Iran want to restore their former territorial authority and perhaps also borders, thereby destabilising the Western Balkans and North Africa.

The proactive European strategy requires governance reforms within the EU, a stronger European Parliament, fewer unanimity requirements in the Council, and a better combination of top-down and bottom-up policies. Europe has to accelerate memberships for the countries of the Western Balkans, which are lured by Russian politicians and Chinese investment. The European Green Deal is a narrative that demands huge investment and coordinated regulatory rules, and that has to be based on new technology and the redirecting of technical progress from primarily saving labour to saving energy and resources. Social Europe needs strategies for deindustrialising regions, which lose a large part of their young population through emigration to Western countries. Europe needs immigration due to its ageing population, but immigrants also have to be welcomed, integrated and steered into regions where their qualifications are needed the most and where they are welcomed.

The Covid-19 crisis must not reduce investments in decarbonisation or the quest for an empowering Social Europe. This danger exists, given the huge amount of money needed, and fortunately mobilised, to limit the economic crisis following the pandemic. Measures to fight the economic consequences of the health crisis have to be combined with the instruments needed to fight climate change and reduce inequality. Education, training and innovation can, at the same time, reduce economic volatility, the unemployment rate, and the spread of incomes. If expenditures are raised under a silo mentality, the costs of fighting climate change plus those for mitigating the economic downturn would become too high. And it is all-important that new spending does not happen on top of the current large expenditures, specifically in countries with a large debt. Counterproductive and welfare-reducing expenditures have to be curbed, whether they are subsidies for fossil energy or for large-scale, heavy fertilising and polluting agriculture, for expensive inward-oriented military systems, and the existing quadruple bureaucracy. The Multiannual Financial Framework (EU budget for 2021-27) must follow new priorities and the country-specific recommendations. Furthermore, a reformed European Semester should monitor ambitious cuts in national expenditures for past priorities and special interests.

Greece and other Southern European countries have suffered a big blow after the financial crisis, due to their resistance to structural change, high debt, low innovation, and lack of practical training. The game changers outlined in this chapter include ensuring that young people and women play a stronger role in societies dominated by old boys' networks. A specific chance for Southern Europe would be to switch to solar and wind energy more quickly than other regions less endowed with sun and wind energy. Greece could also act as a bridge towards Africa and Asia, which are both fast-growing regions in its neighbourhood. Africa needs new technologies and strategies to fight desertification and to promote peace and high growth for its booming population.

Europe has to offer the best social, economic, and ecological model providing more freedom and choices to its citizens than the US or the Chinese model. It can become stronger and larger, not necessarily just through membership, but through partnerships and mutual learning. This may seem like a long way, but it is worthwhile.

References

Aiginger, Karl. 2020. Populism: Root Causes, Power Grabbing and Counter Strategy. *Intereconomics* 55, no.1: 38–42.

Aiginger, Karl. 2018. Harnessing competitiveness for social and ecological goals. In *Competitiveness and Solidarity in the European Union: Interdisciplinary Perspectives*. Edited by Paolo Chiocchetti and Frédéric Allemand. Abingdon: Routledge.

Aiginger, Karl. 2017. "How a strong Europe could create more national scope of action," *Policy Crossover Flash*, Paper No 1, https://static1.squarespace.com/static/5780d6f1579fb375af56974a/t/58b088fc37c581bd4b6c49a8/1487964413615/PCC-Flash+1-2017.pdf (accessed April 29, 2021).

Aiginger, Karl. 2016. "New Dynamics for Europe: Reaping the Benefits of Socio-ecological Transition," Synthesis Report Part I, WWWforEurope, March, https://www.econstor.eu/bitstream/10419/169308/1/849715938.pdf (accessed April 29, 2021).

Aiginger, Karl, and Dani Rodrik. 2020. Rebirth of Industrial Policy and an Agenda for the Twenty-First Century. *Journal of Industry, Competition and Trade* 20, no.2: 189–207.

Aiginger, Karl, and Heinz Handler. 2018. Fostering a Dynamic and Stable Neighborhood for Europe. *Review of Economics & Finance* 14, no.4: 39–54.

Aiginger, Karl, Matthias Firgo, and Peter Huber. 2013. "Südeuropa: Problemzone oder Brücke in die Zukunft [Southern Europe: problem zone or bridge to the future]," *ÖGFE Policy Brief* 7, https://www.oegfe.at/policy-briefs/suedeuropa-problemzone-oder-bruecke-in-die-zukunft/ (accessed April 29, 2021).

European Commission. 2019. The European Green Deal, Communication, 11 December, COM(2019) 640, https://eur-lex.europa.eu/legal-content/EN/TXT/?uri=CELEX%3A52019DC0640 (accessed April 29, 2021).

Gill, Indermit S., and Martin Raiser. 2012. "Golden Growth: Restoring the Lustre of the European Economic Model," The World Bank Report 68168, http://documents1.worldbank.org/curated/en/539371468036253854/pdf/Main-report.pdf (accessed April 29, 2021).

Hermann, Frank. 2020. "Corona-Epidemie: Amerikas Schwarze leiden mehr als die Weißen [Corona epidemic: America's blacks suffer more than whites]," *Der Standard*, 15 April, https://www.derstandard.at/story/2000116848985/corona-epidemie-amerikas-schwarze-leiden-am-meisten (accessed April 29, 2021).

Koundouri, Phoebe. 2020. "Never Waste a Good Crisis: For a Sustainable Recovery from Covid-19," Sustainable Development Solutions Network opinion piece, 1 April, https://www.unsdsn.org/never-waste-a-good-crisis-for-a-sustainable-recovery-from-covid-19 (accessed April 29, 2021).

Richter, Matthias, interview by Robert Pausch, 5 April 2020, transcript, Gesundheit ist eine zutiefst ungleich verteilte Ressource [Health is a deeply unevenly distributed resource], *Zeit online*, 5 April, https://www.zeit.de/gesellschaft/2020-04/risikogruppen-coronavirus-einkommen-gesundheit-vorerkrankungen-gesellschaft?fbclid=IwAR3bdvkZasW3yputDMmKYNKaWsf9iJ4YoLjLHB32G1GdP84-qtuCBCo18nU&page=29&utm_referrer=https%3A%2F%2Fwww.google.com%2F (accessed April 29, 2021).

Rifkin, Jeremy. 2004. *The European Dream: How Europe's Vision of the Future Is Quietly Eclipsing the American Dream*. New York: Tarcher/Penguin.

The Economist. 2020. "Is China winning?" 16 April, https://www.economist.com/leaders/2020/04/16/is-china-winning (accessed April 29, 2021).

PART B:

EU FISCAL AND MONETARY UNION

CHAPTER 3

EXCESSIVE DEFICIT PROCESS AS A BASIS FOR A FISCAL UNION: LESSONS FROM THE EU AUDITORS' POINT OF VIEW

DIMITRIOS V. SKIADAS*

Introduction

There have been extensive and well-founded debates on the need and the foundations of establishing a Fiscal Union within the context of the European Union (hereinafter EU), as the next step in the process of the Economic and Monetary Union (hereinafter EMU). Various proposals have been put forward, which can be categorised according to one or more of the four core arguments each proposal is based on: the enactment of a set of rules for coordination and monitoring of economic policies (including a Banking Union); the establishment of a crisis resolution mechanism; the provision of a joint guarantee scheme for government debt; and the establishment of an insurance and stabilisation fund (Thirion 2017). This chapter will focus on a technical aspect of one of these arguments, namely the "Excessive Deficit Procedure" (hereinafter EDP) provided for by the current fiscal governance scheme of the EMU, as a means of safeguarding and improving the coordination of the national economic policies of the member states.

Main features of the Stability and Growth Pact

In 1992, with the signing of the Maastricht Treaty (Treaty on European Union) and the provision of a three-stage course in order to

* Professor, Department of International and European Studies, University of Macedonia (Thessaloniki, Greece).

establish the EMU, it was decided that, in order for the EMU to operate properly, certain fiscal conditions should be met. These conditions subsequently became known as fiscal rules, and they are supposed to ensure sound public finances in the EU member states, by restricting the political tendency towards a debt-increasing, expansionary fiscal policy. Compliance with them should ensure that deficits and debt are limited, and can be financed on the markets. Thus, they should be simple and consistent, and credible sanctions (in terms of financial as well as political cost) should be provisioned in case of failure to meet the targets (Deutsche Bundesbank 2017). The main fiscal rule focused on setting limitations to the increase of government (or public) deficit, and government (or public) debt ratios to Gross Domestic Product (hereinafter GDP), the corresponding reference values being 3% of GDP on an annual basis and 60% of GDP respectively. These rules were included in Protocol No 12 on the Excessive Deficit Procedure, accompanying the Treaty on European Union. Furthermore, the relevant terms were initially legally defined by Regulation 3605/1993[1] as follows: a) "Government deficit" means the net borrowing of the sector of general government, as defined in the European system of national and regional accounts - ESA 2010 (Eurostat n.d.), i.e., central and state government, local government, and social security funds, excluding commercial operations; b) "Government debt" means the total gross debt at nominal value outstanding at the end of the year of the sector of general government, with the exception of those liabilities the corresponding financial assets of which are held by the sector of general government.

Under pressure to achieve the establishment of the EMU on time, the member states, on Germany's initiative, reached an agreement during the workings of the Intergovernmental Conference that resulted in the signing of the Amsterdam Treaty in 1997. This agreement took the form of a Resolution, and became known as the Stability and Growth Pact (hereinafter SGP) (European Council 1997).

The basic rationale of the SGP is to develop a mechanism for the coordination of economic policy. This coordination is defined as the establishment of, and adherence to, rules commonly accepted by all member states, granting national authorities the main responsibility for national economic planning, setting limits to their discretion, and providing for sanctions in case of their violation. The aim of this coordination is to achieve a mixture of harmonious economic policies that entail a fiscal

[1] Regulation No 3605/1993 has been replaced by Regulation No 479/2009, which has codified its contents.

policy compatible with the monetary policy, which is planned and exercised by the European Central Bank (Begg et al. 2003, 66-67). Thus, the Pact practically contains the following rules: in times of strong growth potential for the member states, they should be careful in their expenditure and create reserves for times of recession, while in times of recession, they should ease the rigidity of their expenditure and tolerate the creation of small deficits (not exceeding 3% of GDP) which, in practice, is an investment to the functioning of the real economy (Barysch 2003, 2). However, this theoretical scheme has not been verified in practice, and this has resulted in severe criticism against the SGP, the most renowned being the Pact's characterisation as "stupid" by the European Commission's former President Romano Prodi (Barysch 2003; Collignon 2003; Begg et al. 2003; De Grauwe 2004; Xenaki 2004). This criticism, as well as the problems identified in the Eurozone fiscal governance model established by the SGP during the 2008-2012 financial crisis, caused the Pact's repeated amendments.[2]

The overall design and operation of the Pact constitute an exemplary scheme of the Open Method of Coordination, which was established as the basic implementing mechanism of policies within the Lisbon Strategy and as the alternative form of action to the so-called "Community Method", which is based on the creation of the acquis communautaire (Closa Montero and Almendral 2005, 8). However, given that the Pact's operation is based on a peculiar scheme of provisions, entailing EU primary and secondary law as well as a Resolution, there is a significant concern about the Pact's legal nature. According to one view, the SGP is a text with exceptional political significance, expressing the commitment of the signatory states, but without legal force (Mparmpas 2006, 89). Another view argues that the significance of the Pact's contents is such that the Pact should be considered as a substantive provision of constitutional level, as the adherence to it is imperative for the achievement and the functioning of the EMU (Closa Montero and Almendral 2005, 6). The Court of Justice of the European Union (hereinafter CJEU) had the opportunity to review the Pact's implementation by the

---

[2] Initially, the main legal tools of EU secondary legislation regarding the Stability and Growth Pact's operation were the following: Regulation 1466/1997 and Regulation 1467/1997. These Regulations were amended for the first time in 2005 by Regulation 1055/2005 and Regulation 1056/2005. They were further amended to incorporate elements in order to tackle the financial crisis by Regulation 1175/2011 and Regulation 1177/2011, Regulation 472/2013 and Regulation 473/2013.

Union's institutions as well as by the EU member states, and thus to provide a judgment on the Pact's legal nature, but unfortunately, it refrained from doing so *expressis verbis*. It merely used the Pact's provisions as a legal basis to review the acts of the Union's institutions and the acts of the EU member states, and finally, it annulled the Council's conclusions on allowing the member states involved in that case (Germany and France) to take further action in order to rectify the excessive deficit recorded by the Commission in their public finances, without, at the same time, obliging the Council and the member states to adopt the Commission's recommendation on this matter (CJEU 2004). It was a politically balanced judgment which, however, with its strange reasoning (Mparmpas 2006, 94), caused several concerns regarding its legal consequences (Skiadas 2004; Dutzler and Hable 2005).

The functioning of the SGP includes the so-called "preventive" and "corrective" arms. The first entails monitoring procedures aiming to identify on time and to take action to avert problematic situations in the public finances of the member states, while the second entails a procedure aiming to correct verified excessive deficits and debts through various means, including sanctions, as follows:

Preventive Arm (Angerer 2014, 1-2)

- With regard to the deficit, each member state has a differentiated medium-term objective (hereinafter MTO) for its budgetary position, entailing a budget close to balance or in surplus, which ensures the sustainability of public finances or a rapid progress towards it, while allowing room for budgetary manoeuvre, in particular for public investment. This objective is to be revised every 3 years, and may be further revised in case of a new structural reform with a major impact on the sustainability of public finances. This MTO is specified, for each member state, within a range between -1% of GDP and balance or surplus. The member states that do not reach their MTO should improve their structural balance by 0.5% of GDP per year as a benchmark, and in case of a "significant deviation" (i.e., 0.5% of GDP in 1 year or cumulatively over 2 years) from the MTO or from its adjustment path, the Commission can express an "early warning". There is a possibility for temporary exceptional deviations from the MTO in the cases of: a) major structural reforms (e.g., pension reforms) that have a verifiable long-term (positive) impact on the public finances; b) an unusual event outside the control of the member state concerned that has a major impact on the financial position of the government; or c) a severe economic downturn for the euro area or the Union as a whole. In any case, all deviations should not endanger fiscal sustainability in the medium term, and must respect the rule of the nominal limit of 3% of GDP.

- With regard to the debt, the Council adopts an annual recommendation regarding the progress towards the MTO, and for countries whose debt is higher than 60% of GDP, on compliance with the debt reduction benchmark (i.e., the agreed rate of reduction which stipulates that the distance to the 60% threshold should be reduced by 5% on average per year —over the past 3 years or in the next 2 years— also taking into account the economic cycle).

The relevant procedure of the preventive arm is as follows:

Figure 3-1: Preventive Arm of the SGP

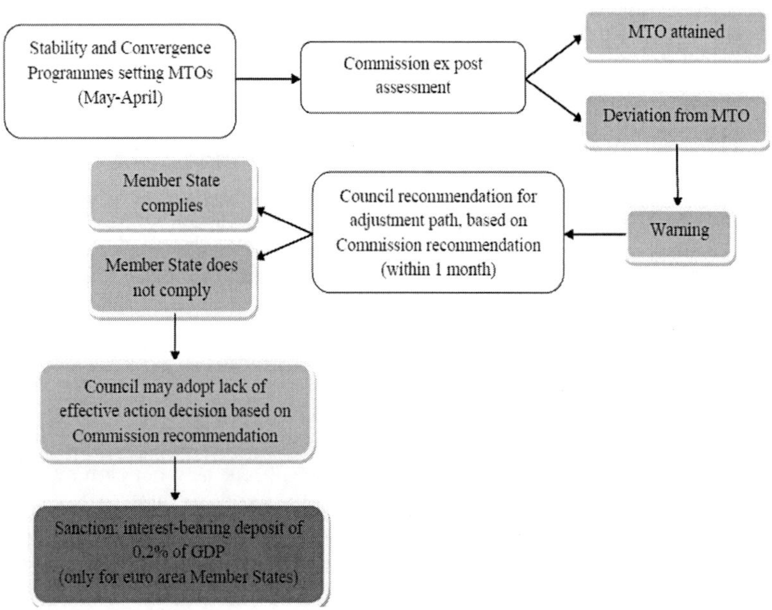

Source: (Angerer 2014, 6)

Corrective arm (Angerer 2014, 3-4)

This entails the EDP. The EDP is triggered if a deficit breaches the 3% of GDP threshold, or if a debt is above 60% of GDP and does not diminish at a sufficiently rapid pace, as defined by the debt reduction benchmark. If the Council decides, on the basis of a Commission recommendation, that a deficit is excessive, the Council issues a recommendation to the member state concerned to correct the excessive deficit and gives it a timeframe for doing so. In its recommendation, the Council shall request that the member state achieve annual budgetary targets which, on the basis of the forecast underpinning the recommendation, are consistent with a minimum annual improvement of the structural balance of at least 0.5% of GDP as a benchmark, in order to ensure the correction of the excessive deficit within the deadline set in the recommendation. The deadline for the correction of the excessive deficit may be extended up to a year if effective action has been taken by the member state concerned and unexpected adverse economic events occur with major unfavourable consequences for government finances, or if there is a severe economic downturn in the euro area or in the EU as a whole, provided that it does not endanger medium-term fiscal sustainability. In the corrective arm, the progress achieved by the member states is measured on the basis of "fiscal effort" in structural terms. If the improvement is in line with the Council recommendation, the Commission and/or Council shall conclude that "effective action" has been taken. The measurement of compliance with the required "fiscal effort" (i.e., of whether "effective action" has been taken or not) is twofold:

First, the Commission and the Council assess whether the annual change in the structural budget balance is in line with the required fiscal effort ("top-down approach"). And second, the Commission carries out a careful analysis that covers the following elements: (a) revisions of potential output growth compared to that assumed at the time of the recommendations; (b) the impact of revisions on the composition of economic growth (tax richness) or of other windfalls/shortfalls on revenue; and (c) quantification of measures taken ("bottom-up approach").

In order to support the member states in their effort to take "effective action", all relevant data used by the Commission, including data on the yields of discretionary fiscal measures, are shared with the member states in a timely manner, enabling them to replicate the calculation underlying the Commission's assessments and recommendations.

The relevant procedure of the corrective arm is as follows:

Figure 3-2: Corrective Arm of the SGP

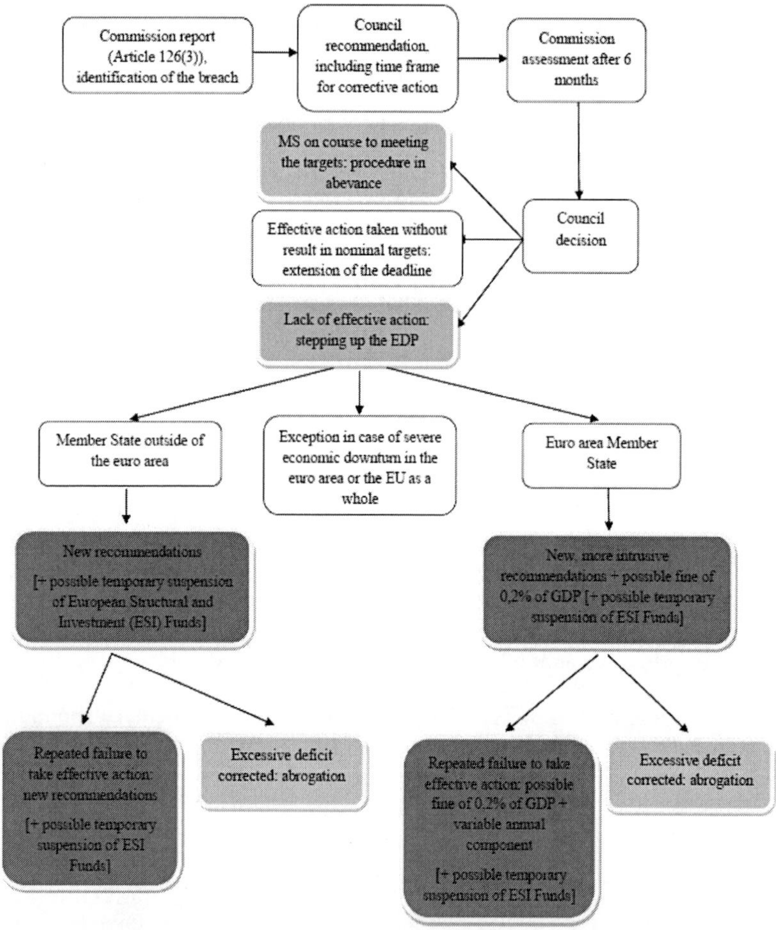

Note: The possible suspensions of up to five ESI funds are in square brackets, since they are formally not belonging to the preventive arm of the Pact but to the so-called regulation on macro-economic conditionality of 5 European Structural and Investment Funds [Regulation (EU) No 1303/2013]

Source: (Angerer 2014, 7)

In both the preventive and the corrective arm proceedings, non-compliance with the recommendations may trigger further steps in the procedures, including the possibility of sanctions for euro area member states, as follows:

Table 3-1: Possible sanctions in the preventive and corrective arms of the SGP

When?	What?
Adjustment towards the MTO/expenditure rule not respected (preventive arm)	Interest-bearing deposit 0.2% of GDP
Opening of the EDP (if the country was already sanctioned under the preventive arm or if the breach of the threshold is particularly serious)	Non-interest-bearing deposit 0.2% of GDP
Failure to take effective action to correct the excessive deficit	Fine 0.2% of GDP
Repeated failure to take effective action to correct the excessive deficit	Fine 0.2% of GDP + variable component

Source: (Angerer 2014, 4)

The first three sanctions in the above Table 3-1 are voted on the basis of a reverse qualified majority in the Council, which means that the sanctions proposed by the Commission will be adopted unless opposed by a qualified majority of countries; this mechanism is also called "semi-automatic". The last sanction (fine for repeated failure to take effective action) is decided on the basis of normal qualified majority voting.

The European Court of Auditors' findings

The entire scheme of the SGP's functioning has been examined by the European Court of Auditors (hereinafter ECA), especially after the amendments introduced to tackle the weaknesses identified during the financial crisis.

With regard to the preventive arm of the Pact, the ECA examined whether the European Commission had used the authority that it was granted by the relevant provisions to ensure both its adequate implementation and its interaction with the corrective arm. The Commission's performance is crucial for the safeguarding of the adherence to the annual MTO set as well as for the correct use of the deviations foreseen. According to the ECA, the implementation rules decided by the Commission and its operational decisions do not ensure that the objectives of the preventive arm are met, i.e., that member states converge toward MTOs in a reasonable period. The Commission's rules include flexibility provisions that are not time-bound to a potential crisis period, and do not distinguish enough between those member states that do have a high level of debt and the others. Thus, these rules result in a very slow pace of convergence to the MTOs and cause concerns as to the member states' capacity to tackle another recession. Furthermore, the assistance provided by the EU for structural reforms is not used to cover the actual budget costs of such reforms, but the Commission uses it as an "incentivising instrument", thus actually increasing public spending for many years.

Another significant finding was that the credibility of the preventive arm has been further eroded by the developments in the corrective arm, as the Commission considers that the requirements of the corrective arm can be fully met just by cyclical recovery (this is also reflected in the Commission's practice of facilitating the extensions for exiting EDPs). As a result, member states in EDP do not have to fulfil the requirements for improving their structural balances, which they would otherwise have to observe if they were under the preventive arm. Finally, the ECA found that fiscal country-specific recommendations (hereinafter CSRs), despite being based on substantive technical assessments, do not explain sufficiently the rationale for the recommended adjustments, nor the risks incurred if member states fail to meet the requirements. The ECA recommended that the Commission address the issue of continuous deviations from the required adjustment path over several years, and ensure that MTOs are reached within a reasonable period, with stricter rules for heavily indebted member states. Also, the ECA stated that the reform assistance should only cover direct costs related to reforms, and the investment financial allowance should not allow increases in non-investment spending in the following years. The adjustments required under the corrective and preventive arms should be harmonised in such a manner that adjustments required under the corrective arm should not be weaker than those required under the preventive arm. The CSRs should provide clearer explanations of their rationale and the risks of not implementing them. According to the ECA's understanding, the existing EU legislation allows the Commission to address these issues and no amendment is necessary, given that the main objective of the relevant rules, which is that member states must make reasonably rapid convergence towards the MTOs, should take precedence over flexibility options (European Court of Auditors 2018b).

Given that the preventive arm of the SGP was reinforced by the 2011 amendments, with the introduction of a scheme called "Macroeconomic Imbalance Procedure" (hereinafter MIP) aiming to prevent and correct macroeconomic imbalances and to provide for enforcement measures to correct excessive macroeconomic imbalances (Regulation 1176/2011, Regulation 1174/2011),[3] the ECA also examined the implementation of this scheme. The MIP operates on an annual cycle, and its starting point is the publication by the Commission of an economic and financial assessment known as the Alert Mechanism Report (AMR), which identifies member states at risk of imbalances that require further analysis in the form of an in-depth review (IDR), focusing on whether these imbalances should be deemed excessive and proposing CSRs to be adopted by the Council and issued to member states. In case of identifying excessive imbalances, an "Excessive Imbalance Procedure" (hereinafter EIP) is initiated, entailing the operation of an enhanced surveillance mechanism that includes the possibility of sanctions for euro area member states.

The overall design of the MIP was found to be beneficial by the ECA. However, its use by the Commission is not considered effective. The CSRs do not provide substantive links between the imbalances identified and the measures proposed, especially with regard to their macroeconomic nature and impact. Also, fiscal policy is not taken into account. The imbalances themselves are correctly identified, yet they have progressively lost their visibility in the Commission's reports. The Commission's assessment usually contains out-of-date data, thus resulting in conclusions that do not refer to recent conditions. The MIP is further weakened by the fact that the Commission does not assess the severity of the imbalances, as it does not employ a relevant classification, thus leading to a lack of transparency on the justification of the Commission's relevant decisions. The most striking finding of the ECA is that the Commission, without providing sufficient justification, has never recommended the activation of the EIP, despite the fact that several member states have been formally identified as having excessive imbalances over a prolonged period. This systematic non-activation of the EIP has reduced the credibility and the effectiveness of the entire MIP. The ECA has suggested to the Commission to establish clear links in its MIP recommendations to specific macroeconomic imbalances, and to provide a clear characterisation

[3] The MIP was introduced by Regulation 1176/2011 on the prevention and correction of macroeconomic imbalances and Regulation 1174/2011 on enforcement measures to correct excessive macroeconomic imbalances in the euro area.

of the severity of the imbalances a member state is facing. The impact of fiscal policy should be examined in analysing imbalances. The activation of an EIP when there is evidence that a member state is facing excessive imbalances is highly recommended, unless there are specific circumstances, in which case the Commission's discretionary action to refrain from activating this procedure should be clearly and publicly explained. Finally, the overall MIP should be more visible by, for instance, allowing the relevant Commissioners to explain it to national Parliaments, especially when excessive imbalances are identified (European Court of Auditors 2018a).

Contrary to what the ECA has found on the frequency of use of the MIP, the EDP, within the corrective arm of the SGP, has been employed repeatedly. 26 out of 28 member states have been involved in such proceedings, Estonia and Sweden being the only member states not to have been found in an excessive deficit situation. The ECA has examined, in its Special Report 10/2016, the use of the EDP, focusing on the Commission's assessment of the quality of member states' statistical data (Eurostat) and on its interpretation of those data (DG Economic and Financial Affairs) leading ultimately to recommendations that the Council initiate or take further action in relation to an EDP, the Commission's monitoring and surveillance tasks within an EDP, and the outcome of the procedure.

With regard to Eurostat, the ECA's findings included the following (European Court of Auditors 2016, 75-78):

The ECA has found that Eurostat, when examining data, has improved its quality-assessment processes since 2011 at the level of both resources and procedures. Standardising and increasing the number of requests for information has allowed EDP data to be more extensively analysed. Yet, it was also found that the process of examining statistical data is not sufficiently documented for the analysis underlying quality assessments to be easily understood. In addition, it is based on data that are not always complete. It could also be made more explicit how the existing rules and guidelines are to be applied. Thus, it is recommended to Eurostat to enhance the transparency of its work in relation to in-house verifications. This would give management and other desk officers a clearer overview of the content of analyses. Eurostat should establish internal written procedures guiding the work of analysis in the quality assessment, and should better assess and document its in-house verification of data in areas such as the delimitation of the general government sector and specific government transactions.

Eurostat does not adequately assess member states' control systems in order to ensure that, despite differences in their statistical systems, there is a consistent approach as to the compilation of data. As there is no documentation on the supervisory and control systems in place for data compilation, it is not possible to implement a systems-based approach for examining the quality of the data received. Therefore, the ECA suggests to Eurostat to examine the supervisory and control systems in place in member states, to clearly document its analyses, and to provide written procedures for consistency.

The "on-the-spot" cooperation between Eurostat and the national statistical authorities of the member states was enhanced by adding to the Eurostat's standard dialogue visits the so-called "upstream" visits that analyse the management and control of upstream data. These new visits have proven to be very useful to the quality assessment tasks of identifying, assessing and monitoring risks and problems. These two types of visits were merged in 2014. However, given the large number of items on their agendas, their duration (2 days) is not sufficient for important data quality issues to be adequately examined. Also, Eurostat has been found to perform limited direct verifications during its on-the-spot visits and, although a well-structured risk analysis has been introduced, it is not used to preselect high-risk issues for visits. The results of the visits are published with considerable delay, thus good practices or identified errors are not disseminated on time. The ECA has recommended to Eurostat to adapt the duration of its dialogue visits to member states in order to ensure more complete coverage, to enhance its direct verifications as part of on-the-spot visits, and to reduce the time taken to publish its visit reports.

Also, given the importance of the national statistical authorities taking action within the recommended deadlines, it has been pointed out to Eurostat by the ECA to make full use of its powers to enforce action in the areas of completeness, methodological responsibility and delivery of documents.

Finally, with regard to Eurostat setting reservations as to data quality and making amendments, it is necessary to state clearly the reasons for such actions. After all, the ECA has suggested that a better documentation of Eurostat's relevant internal procedures and criteria would be beneficial in demonstrating that methodological problems —especially with a potential/actual impact on data affecting net lending/net borrowing of the member states— are addressed in a consistent way.

With regard to the DG Economic and Financial Affairs of the Commission, the ECA's findings included the following (European Court of Auditors 2016, 79-83):

The Commission's proposals for EDP decisions and recommendations are based on analyses which lack transparency and entail vague definitions. The increased complexity of the EDP, caused by its various reforms, has impeded, in several cases, the establishment of a clear link between the analysis made and the conclusions drawn. The ECA suggested to the Commission to further pursue its undeniable efforts to improve transparency and clarity of the EDP in the following areas:

- Assessment process: The key aspects of the Commission's analyses should be more transparent, by devising a methodology to identify and quantify the impact of one-off and temporary measures, by providing sufficiently detailed explanations of assessments and conclusions in country-specific documents (regarding, notably, the concept of "unexpected adverse economic events" when assessing effective action) and by establishing a methodological framework to weigh the impact of the relevant factors taken into account.
- Accessibility of data: The publication of detailed information used to perform the calculations on which the Commission's analyses are based is necessary.
- Bottom-up assessment: The national fiscal councils of the member states should be involved in the assessment process by providing independent scrutiny of the reliability of the figures and information provided by national authorities (i.e., Ministries of Finance).

Another very important issue refers to the debt criterion. The EDP has so far focused more on government deficit than on debt. This was changed by the specific provision in Regulation 1177/2011 on the use of the EDP in assessing compliance also with the debt criterion, in addition to the deficit criterion. This amendment was introduced as a move to "break with the past" and to establish new standards of compliance with the fiscal rules provided for by EU legislation and the SGP, given that the weakness of the enforcement mechanisms of the Pact allowed for failures to abide by the budgetary criteria, and this was allegedly one of the reasons for the outburst of the financial crisis. These considerations are substantively expressed in the Treaty on Stability, Coordination and Governance in the Economic and Monetary Union (also known as the Fiscal Compact), which entered into force on 1 January 2013 (Dehousse 2012; Craig 2012; Fabbrini 2013). A transitional period was enacted until at least 2020 for the implementation of the EDP with regard to the debt criterion. Flexibility add-ons to the EDP have meant that, in unfavourable economic times, compliance may be recognised even if the debt-to-GDP ratio increases. This may undermine the credibility of the process and put at risk the sustainability of public debt, especially during protracted periods of recession (when debt can rise even if the debt criterion is met). Ultimately, whether or not the debt criterion is met, the key thing is to repay or sustainably refinance the actual amount of debt. Taking all these into account, the ECA has recommended to the Commission to focus closely on debt developments, especially in heavily-indebted member states, and to prevent debt-building to unsustainable levels. In case that the 60% debt threshold is exceeded and the concerned member state is placed under the EDP, the ECA has suggested to the Commission to ensure that the required adjustments provide for a realistic and credible convergence path towards compliance with the debt rule, in particular by taking into account the initial level of debt. Also, it has been recommended to the Commission, when setting annual deficit targets in EDP recommendations, to specify the annual debt-to-GDP levels that are consistent with those targets.

Given the importance of structural reforms in tackling excessive deficit conditions, the ECA has suggested to the Commission to make full use of the European Semester and the MIP in monitoring the implementation of structural reforms for member states under an EDP, in particular where fiscal structural reforms are included in an economic partnership program. This monitoring should focus not only on legislative aspects, but also on the actual implementation of the reforms, and should assess their effectiveness.

The reporting requirements for the member states in order to improve the surveillance element of the EDP have been increased, but they are not legally enforceable in the case of a member state failing to meet them. The Commission does not refer to such failures in its assessments, and does not make the best possible use of the information provided. The ECA has suggested to the Commission that it makes clear in its assessments whether the member states have fulfilled their reporting requirements, and also that it examines the possibility of launching infringement procedures (based on the Treaties' provisions) in cases of non-compliance with reporting obligations.

Finally, with regard to financial sanctions, the ECA's understanding has been that the successive EDP reforms have strengthened sanctions against member states that do not comply with recommendations, and have eased the conditions for imposing them. Since the EDP's inception, no sanctions have been applied. Since sanctions are also useful as a deterrent, not applying them when member states fail to fulfil their commitment to budgetary discipline brings the risk that they will be perceived as a tool unlikely to be used. This undermines their credibility and effectiveness, and hence that of the EDP as a whole. The ECA has recommended to the Commission to implement existing legislation and step up the application of sanctions when there is evidence that a member state has not complied with EDP recommendations, and therefore has failed to fulfil its commitment to budgetary discipline under the Treaty.

Final considerations

In conclusion, within the overall EMU framework, as established by the SGP and the relevant legislation, significant steps have been taken towards rationalising and simplifying the use of the EDP as a tool for better economic governance throughout the EU, in a context of increasing complexity. There are now sufficient legal bases to implement the EDP in its entirety. It is up to the EU Institutions' (more importantly the Commission's) commitment to achieve greater clarity and transparency and to maximise the effectiveness of the existing extensive rules and guidelines. If the EDP is to be the instrument for enforcing the fiscal rules decided in the political arena of the EU, in the course of eventually establishing a Fiscal Union, the improvement of its use is imperative. Taking on board the above recommendations made by the ECA would significantly benefit the EDP, in terms of procedural effectiveness as well as of political acceptance and social legitimisation, given that such a scheme may produce results only if those called upon to make the sacrifices needed to meet the goals set within the EDP believe in this scheme's capacity to "bring Ithaca closer".[4]

---

[4] Assimilating the Stability and Growth Pact with Odyssey is not a rarity. The case of Odysseus and his companions trying and managing not to be lured by the Sirens' song (Odysseus by being tied up to his ship's mast and his companions by using wax to cover their ears) has been used to describe the case of the

References

Angerer, Jost. 2014. "Stability and Growth Pact – An Overview," European Parliament Briefing, PE 528.745, 24 July, https://www.europarl.europa.eu/document/activities/cont/201407/20140725ATT87328/20140725ATT87328EN.pdf (accessed March 1, 2021).

Barysch, Katinka. 2003. "A pact for stability and growth," Centre for European Reform Policy Brief, October, https://www.cer.eu/sites/default/files/publications/attachments/pdf/2012/policybrief_stabilityandgrowth_oct03-5403.pdf (accessed March 1, 2021).

Begg, Iain, Dermot Hodson, and Imelda Maher. 2003. Economic Policy Coordination in the European Union. *National Institute Economic Review* 183: 66–77.

Closa Montero, Carlos and Violeta Ruiz Almendral. 2005. The Procedural aspects of the Growth and Stability Pact. Paper presented at the workshop: Which Social and Tax Policy for which European Union?, Stockholm, 10-11 June.

Collignon, Stefan. 2003. Is Europe going far enough? Reflections on the Stability and Growth Pact, the Lisbon Strategy and the EU's economic governance. *European Political Economy Review* 1, no. 2: 222–247.

CJEU. 2004. Judgment of the Court (Full Court) of 13 July 2004, *Commission of the European Communities v. Council of the European Union*, C-27/04, ECLI:EU:C:2004:436.

Craig, Paul P. 2012. The Stability, Coordination and Governance Treaty: Principle, Politics and Pragmatism. *European Law Review* 37: 231–248.

De Grauwe, Paul. 2004. "Towards an Intelligent Stability and Growth Pact," EURO 50 meeting, May, http://www.egmontinstitute.be/content/uploads/2014/01/040526-DeGrauwe.pdf (accessed March 1, 2021).

Dehousse, Renaud. 2012. "The 'Fiscal Compact': legal uncertainty and political ambiguity," Notre Europe Policy Brief, No. 33, February,

---

governments of the member states (as Odysseus) "holding the helm" of the Union, the European Commission and the European Central Bank (as the hero's companions), and the political choices of increasing public expenditure in order to meet existing needs or to achieve popularity (as Sirens). The "companions" remain deaf to the "Sirens' song" despite the reactions of "Odysseus". They thus maintain their course to reach their destination, Ithaca (in the EU's case, the proper functioning of the EMU). See, for instance, Skiadas (2010, 33-34).

https://institutdelors.eu/wp-content/uploads/2020/08/fiscalpact_r.dehousse_ne_feb2012_01-1.pdf (accessed March 2, 2021).

Deutsche Bundesbank. 2017. "Design and implementation of the European fiscal rules," Monthly Report, No. 29, June, https://www.bundesbank.de/resource/blob/667382/cb31f8b7677d2114c89b6f4589ea7507/mL/2017-06-fiscalrules-data.pdf (accessed March 2, 2021).

Dutzler, Barbara, and Angelika Hable. 2005. "The European Court of Justice and the Stability Growth Pact – Just the Beginning?" European Integration online Papers 9, no.5, March, https://eiop.or.at/eiop/texte/2005-005a.htm (accessed March 2, 2021).

European Council. 1997. Resolution on the Stability and Growth Pact Amsterdam, 17 June, OJ C 236: 1–2.

European Court of Auditors. 2018a. "Audit of the Macroeconomic Imbalance Procedure," Special Report, No 03/2018, https://www.eca.europa.eu/Lists/ECADocuments/SR18_03/SR_MIP_EN.pdf (accessed March 3, 2021).

European Court of Auditors. 2018b. "Is the main objective of the preventive arm of the Stability and Growth Pact delivered?" Special Report, No 18/2018, https://www.eca.europa.eu/Lists/ECADocuments/SR18_18/SR_EUROPEAN_SEMESTER_EN.pdf (accessed March 3, 2021).

European Court of Auditors. 2016. "Further improvements needed to ensure effective implementation of the excessive deficit procedure," Special Report, No 10/2016, https://www.eca.europa.eu/Lists/ECADocuments/SR16_10/SR_EDP_EN.pdf (accessed March 3, 2021).

Eurostat. n.d. "ESA 2010: Overview", https://ec.europa.eu/eurostat/web/esa-2010/overview (accessed March 4, 2021).

Fabbrini, Federico. 2013. The Fiscal Compact, the 'Golden Rule,' and the Paradox of European Federalism. *Boston College International & Comparative Law Review* 36, no.1: 1–38.

Mparmpas, Nikolaos. 2006. Η εφαρμογή του Συμφώνου Σταθερότητας και Ανάπτυξης από δημοσιονομικής απόψεως: Η περίπτωση της Ελλάδας [The implementation of the Stability and Growth Pact from a fiscal point of view: The case of Greece], *Δελτίο Φορολογικής Νομοθεσίας* 60, no.1338: 87–98.

Regulation (EU) No 473/2013 of the European Parliament and of the Council of 21 May 2013 on common provisions for monitoring and assessing draft budgetary plans and ensuring the correction of excessive deficit of the Member States in the euro area. 2013. OJ L 140: 11–23.

Regulation (EU) No 472/2013 of the European Parliament and of the Council of 21 May 2013 on the strengthening of economic and budgetary surveillance of Member States in the euro area experiencing or threatened with serious difficulties with respect to their financial stability. 2013. OJ L 140: 1–10.

Regulation (EU) No 1177/2011 of the Council of 8 November 2011 amending Regulation (EC) No 1467/97 on speeding up and clarifying the implementation of the excessive deficit procedure. 2011. OJ L 306: 33–40.

Regulation (EU) No 1176/2011 of the European Parliament and of the Council of 16 November 2011 on the prevention and correction of macroeconomic imbalances. 2011. OJ L 306: 25–32.

Regulation (EU) No 1175/2011 of the European Parliament and of the Council of 16 November 2011 amending Council Regulation (EC) No 1466/97 on the strengthening of the surveillance of budgetary positions and the surveillance and coordination of economic policies. 2011. OJ L 306: 12–24.

Regulation (EU) No 1174/2011 of the European Parliament and of the Council of 16 November 2011 on enforcement measures to correct excessive macroeconomic imbalances in the euro area. 2011. OJ L 306: 8–11.

Regulation (EC) No 479/2009 of the Council of 25 May 2009 on the application of the Protocol on the excessive deficit procedure annexed to the Treaty establishing the European Community (Codified version). 2009. OJ L 145: 291–299.

Regulation (EC) No 1056/2005 of the Council of 27 June 2005 amending Regulation (EC) No 1467/97 on speeding up and clarifying the implementation of the excessive deficit procedure. 2005. OJ L 174: 5–9.

Regulation (EC) No 1055/2005 of the Council of 27 June 2005 amending Regulation (EC) No 1466/97 on the strengthening of the surveillance of budgetary positions and the surveillance and coordination of economic policies. 2005. OJ L 174: 1–4.

Regulation (EC) No 1467/97 of the Council of 7 July 1997 on speeding up and clarifying the implementation of the excessive deficit procedure. 1997. OJ L 209: 6–11.

Regulation (EC) No 1466/97 of the Council of 7 July 1997 on the strengthening of the surveillance of budgetary positions and the surveillance and coordination of economic policies. 1997. OJ L 209: 1–5.

Regulation (EC) No 3605/93 of the Council of 22 November 1993 on the application of the Protocol on the excessive deficit procedure annexed to the Treaty establishing the European Community. 1993. OJ L 332: 7–9.

Skiadas, Dimitrios. 2010. Το Σύμφωνο Σταθερότητας και Ανάπτυξης: Η ευρωπαϊκή επιλογή για την αντιμετώπιση της δημοσιονομικής κρίσης [The Stability and Growth Pact: The European Choice for Tackling the Financial Crisis]. *Διοικητική Ενημέρωση* no.53: 28–45.

Skiadas, Dimitrios. 2004. Υπόθεση Συμφώνου Σταθερότητας: Η θεσμική διάδραση μεταξύ Ευρωπαϊκής Δικαιοσύνης και Ευρωπαϊκής Οικονομικής Πολιτικής [The case of the Stability and Growth Pact: the Interaction between European Justice and European Economic Policy]. *Διοικητική Ενημέρωση* no.31: 29–35.

Thirion, Gille. 2017. "European Fiscal Union: Economic rationale and design challenges," CEPS Working Document, No. 1, January, https://www.ceps.eu/ceps-publications/european-fiscal-union-economic-rationale-and-design-challenges/ (accessed March 4, 2021).

Treaty on European Union (consolidated version). OJ C 326: 13–390.

Xenaki, Athanasia. 2004. Does the EU need the Stability and Growth Pact?, *EPIAScope* 2004, no.2: 29–33.

CHAPTER 4

THE EU RECOVERY INSTRUMENT AS A EUROPEAN SUCCESS STORY

IOANNIS PAPADOPOULOS*

Introduction

The Covid-19 health crisis has undoubtedly shaken the world to its core. On 11 March 2020, Covid-19 was declared a pandemic by the World Health Organization. Since then, the death toll and the pressure on national health systems induced by the new coronavirus have been enormous: as of 22 August 2021, there have been a total of 1.250.224 deaths and 63.296.202 confirmed cases in Europe, and 4.400.284 deaths and 209.876.613 confirmed cases globally (WHO 2021).

The socio-economic impact of the Covid-19 pandemic across the EU was so daunting that it quickly led to a consensus on the need for a common European Recovery Plan complementing the several national stimulus packages that first made their appearance in an uncoordinated way. Indeed, the outbreak of the Covid-19 pandemic in early 2020 changed the economic, social, and budgetary outlook for the years to come in the Union and in the world, calling for an urgent and coordinated response from the European Union (hereinafter EU) in order to cope with the enormous economic and social consequences for all its member states. The spread of the pandemic caused significant disturbances to economic activity throughout Europe: a steep decline in gross domestic product (hereinafter GDP) and a significant impact on employment, social conditions, poverty and inequalities were its almost immediate consequences. Production and supply chains were disrupted. A big part of the workforce

* Associate Professor and Director, Centre for Research on Democracy and Law, Department of International and European Studies, University of Macedonia (Thessaloniki, Greece).

had to stay away from their workplace to prevent further spread of the virus. Many businesses experienced liquidity shortages, which led to a severe deterioration of their financial situation. Key sectors like travel and tourism were particularly hard hit. At the same time, consumer demand dropped precipitously, and the financial markets entered a phase of high volatility.

The pandemic crisis has put the whole world under a state of emergency. It posed significant challenges to the functioning of the Internal Market and to the social and territorial cohesion throughout the EU because of the different fiscal abilities of member states to provide financial support and the ensuing divergence between the national economies. These asymmetrical effects also revealed serious structural weaknesses as well as the need to strengthen the resilience vis-à-vis common risks related to factors beyond human control.

In this context, it quickly became self-evident that a comprehensive set of measures, requiring substantial amounts of public and private investment, was needed, not only to repair the immediate damage brought by the pandemic crisis, but also to set the EU firmly on the path towards a sustainable and resilient recovery by creating high-quality jobs, maintaining an adequate level of social protection, and supporting the EU's green and digital priorities. The EU tried not only to provide direct financial support to member states, but most importantly, to strengthen the framework for support through an innovative approach to underpin long-term reforms and investments, notably in green and digital technologies, that will have a lasting effect on the productivity and resilience of the European economy. An exceptional and coordinated programme of economic and social support was put in place, in a spirit of solidarity between member states, in particular for those member states that experienced the severest impact in their economies and societies.

Hence an innovative EU Recovery Instrument (hereinafter EURI) was established as a dedicated instrument designed to tackle the adverse effects and consequences of the pandemic crisis in the Union, and also to support investment, speed up the recovery, strengthen cohesion among member states, and reinforce the long-term growth potential by stepping up the implementation of sustainable reforms. This very important EU initiative is focused on the green and digital transition of the European economy and on the achievement of fair, inclusive and sustainable growth by restoring labour markets and social protection as well as health care systems and by providing support to businesses affected by the impact of the Covid-19 crisis. The innovative aspect of the EURI is that it strives to ensure a sustainable and resilient recovery throughout the EU by using established mechanisms of spending through Union programmes under the multiannual financial framework (hereinafter MFF), and that support under those programmes is provided in the form of non-repayable support, loans, and provisioning for budgetary guarantees. The ultimate aim of the EU is to reach climate neutrality by 2050. The EURI is instrumental in this effort. Its main goal is to spur public and private investments as well as reforms that will generate European added value and will make the EU more resilient and less dependent by diversifying key supply chains, and thereby strengthening the strategic autonomy of the Union.

This chapter first recounts the path towards a difficult European coordination in front of a crisis that is both symmetrical and asymmetrical. It presents a narrative of the events and the basic points of the discussion that accompanied the endorsement of the EURI, which can be considered as a game changer for Europe. It then goes on to analyse five aspects of the historical agreement at the European Council of July 2020 that stand out, and the reception that they have had. This chapter then proceeds to a thorough critical presentation of the Recovery and Resilience Facility (hereinafter RRF), which surely is the centrepiece of the EU fiscal policy response to the Covid-19 pandemic crisis. The main thesis of the chapter is that the EURI seems to be a European success story, since it has created a European budgetary capacity and new own resources, it has opened the way for direct transfers at unprecedented amounts, and most importantly, it has provided Europe with a strategic sense of orientation for the future. But its posterity will depend on its successful implementation.

The EU Recovery Initiative: A game changer for Europe

The Covid-19 pandemic crisis represents a clearly different approach to the one during the Eurozone sovereign debt crisis of 2011-12 in at least one fundamental aspect: the absence of moral hazard as an ethical device. In the Eurozone crisis, morality played a central role in the management of financial solidarity mechanisms, since the fiscally responsible states accepted to help the needier states in exchange for structural reforms aiming at consolidating the economies of the latter. With the 2020-21 pandemic crisis it became obvious straight away that no EU member state could possibly be held responsible for its economic downfall. Therefore, the exceptional circumstances in the health field compelled the EU decision-makers to pave the way for a new European cohesion and a new solidarity through the mutualisation of efforts to absorb the shock.

With a letter published in the newspapers *Die Zeit* and *Le Monde* on 3 April 2020, twelve high-profile German personalities urged the EU to launch a "Corona fund" with a capacity of long-term borrowing from the international capital markets and of transferring the proceeds to the EU member states so as to alleviate the latter's burden for debts incurred in order to fight against the Covid-19 pandemic (Bofinger et al. 2020). These "Coronabonds" should not be confused with Eurobonds, since the former would collectively guarantee only the extra debt that the states would have to incur since the beginning of the pandemic crisis, and would thus be limited in their duration and scope. It is worth mentioning here that despite the common understanding, the introduction of European "Coronabonds" is not an unprecedented step of debt mutualisation: as Horn, Meyer & Trebesch (2020) have shown, after the first oil crisis in 1973, the European Commission implemented the so-called Community Loan Mechanism (hereinafter CLM) in February 1975 with the goal of issuing European Community bonds on private capital markets to support countries in crisis. The basic design of the CLM was as follows: The European Commission raised community loans on behalf of the European Community, the Council of Ministers made all relevant decisions, while the Commission acted as the executive body. To raise funds, the Commission negotiated with private investors and presented the results to the Council of Ministers. The loans were then transferred to the crisis-hit countries' central banks via the Bank for International Settlements, which acted as an agent. As for the liability structure, the Commission guaranteed the repayment to the private creditors by means of its budget. In addition, the mechanism included a guarantee commitment from the member states, according to fixed quotas.[1] Of course, the "Coronabonds" proposal would go a step further compared to the CLM, which involved country guarantees with maximum quotas. Still, then (as now), the European Community budget played a central role in the European bond guarantee schemes; direct guarantees by member states only served as a second guarantee tier, which would be activated if European funds would not suffice. There is, therefore, a longstanding but not well-known tradition of financial solidarity and cooperation in the European Communities.

---

[1] Through the CLM, more than a dozen community bonds were placed on private markets, and their proceeds were distributed to countries in crisis. These bonds were repaid in full until the 1990s.

The real turning point was the joint announcement by President Macron and Chancellor Merkel on 18 May 2020 of a Franco-German initiative on an EU Recovery Plan of 500 billion euro, to be financed by the issuance of common European debt guaranteed by all EU member states (Présidence de la République 2020). This undoubtedly was an extremely powerful political act and a real novelty, since it demonstrated the need for new instruments to cope with unforeseen challenges. By reactivating the Franco-German axis two months after the decisive initiative by the Commission to suspend the SGP so as to allow EU member states to spend without limits in order to counter the huge economic crisis,[2] the German political elite left aside fiscal orthodoxy and broke the taboo of issuing common EU debt to help redress the European countries that have suffered the severest impact by the pandemic. This timely paradigm shift happened because of the pragmatism of Angela Merkel, who understood that the pandemic crisis was really capable of destroying the EU Internal Market, a development that is definitely not in the German national interest (Requena 2020). In an interview for the French journal *Le Monde* and other European newspapers, Chancellor Merkel made that clear by candidly stating that "it is in the interest of Germany to have a strong internal market, that the EU becomes increasingly united and that it doesn't collapse. What is good for Europe was and remains good for us." She also explained the shift in the German mindset: "In this kind of crisis, we expect from everyone to do what is necessary. What is necessary, in this case, is something extraordinary." Even though she took pains to pinpoint that the EU Recovery Plan does not represent a "federalist leap" leading to the United States of Europe, since it is a one-off initiative for an extraordinary situation, she nevertheless was sanguine about its redistributive effect: "Given that different countries are affected to varying degrees by the pandemic, the distribution key cannot be the same as the ordinary EU budget… For the countries that already have a very high total level of debt, non-repayable assistance makes more sense than supplementary credits." (Wieder 2020)

[2] The SGP was suspended via the activation by the Commission of the "general escape clause" of the SGP on 20 March 2020 (EC 2020b). In parallel, the ordinary EU state aid regime, which imposes limits on financial aid provided by member states to undertakings, was also loosened on 19 March 2020 by the Commission via a temporary state aid framework (EC 2020a) so as to dissolve any apprehension as to the extraordinary right of EU states to keep afloat their businesses during the worst global economic crisis after World War II.

Nine days after this historic initiative, on 27 May 2020, President von der Leyen presented the Commission's draft EURI that was clearly inspired by the Franco-German initiative, confirming thus once again the historic weight of the Franco-German axis as a powerhouse of European integration. In the face of the initial opposition of the so-called "frugal" EU member states (Austria, Denmark, the Netherlands, and Sweden), the Commission surpassed at least three dogmas that had until then obstructed the course of European integration via the issuance of a large European loan by the Commission, an unprecedented increase in intra-Union direct transfers, and the establishment of new EU own resources allowing the Commission to finance the EU independently of member states' contributions. Several analysts (inter alia Kaletsky 2020) welcomed the Commission's plan as a "Europe's Hamiltonian Moment", comparable to the 1790 congressional approval of Alexander Hamilton's plan on public borrowing, which helped to turn the United States, a confederation with a small central government until then, into a genuine political federation. As the first Secretary of the Treasury after the American Independence and a prominent Federalist, Alexander Hamilton had devised a brilliant plan to create a viable American financial system out of nothing. His First Report on Public Credit, presented to the House of Representatives on January 14, 1790, included probably the single most groundbreaking idea in the history of public finance: the "debt assumption plan", i.e., the assumption of state debts incurred to prosecute the War of Independence by the federal government via the issuance of a federal debt instrument, precursor of today's Treasury Bond, and a voluntary swap of old debt for new bonds, backed by the tax base of the federal government (Papadopoulos 2013, 72).

The sums involved, and most importantly, the structure itself of the Commission's EURI (denominated "NextGenerationEU", hereinafter NGEU) were nothing short of revolutionary: 750 billion euro of EU debt, in addition to 1074.3 billion euro of the MFF 2021-27,[3] of which 500 billion in non-repayable support (i.e., grants) and 250 billion in loans.[4] The plan expressed for the first time with such clarity an authentic fiscal solidarity in the EU. The capacity of the Commission to issue common EU bonds up to the amount of 750 billion euro and until the end of 2026 on behalf of the Union in order to subsidise the EU member states that were

[3] These sums are expressed in 2018 prices.

[4] In order to allow the Commission to raise 750 billion euro on the financial markets, the EU own resources ceiling would have to be temporarily lifted to 2% of EU Gross National Income (hereinafter GNI).

economically affected by the Covid-19 pandemic, as well as to establish own resources of the EU budget for the repayment of these bonds, strongly resemble an outline of European Treasury, even though there is no such mention, for political reasons, in the official Commission documents. In any case, this strategic turn towards the constitutive elements of a federal-type Treasury Department clearly represents a big step towards the establishment of a full-blown European Fiscal Union (Papadopoulos 2013, 74). As to the own resources part of the EURI, the Commission had three options: either increase the member states' contributions to the EU budget; or reduce EU spending; or broaden the fiscal basis of the EU via new own resources. The first two options were politically and economically unpalatable in a context of severe crisis; the third option was the one preferred by the Commission. In order to give pledges to the "frugal" member states, who were legitimately worried about the good use of the funds of the EURI, a mechanism of conditionality was provided, whereby the member states who wish to benefit from the Recovery Instrument would have to prepare a plan of investments and reforms compatible both with grand-level priorities and quantified goals of the EU related to the Green Deal and Digital Agenda, and with the country-specific macroeconomic recommendations condensed in the European Semester. The National Recovery and Resilience Plans (hereinafter NRRPs) containing the above would have to be submitted to the Commission and to be approved by the Commission and the Council of the EU, as a prerequisite for the disbursement of funds.

The sheer size of the financial aid[5] available to member states that have suffered economically by the pandemic, and that otherwise would not be able to raise the necessary sums for recovery on their own, but also the structure itself of the budgetary transfers, are the exemplification of European solidarity. Moreover, there is a fairness element in the structure of the EURI, since the own resources under discussion at European level are all associated with fair terms of financing: a digital tax on the digital technology giants (the so-called "GAFA")[6] that have been amassing more profits during the confinement of the populations, and levies that can be used as an incentive to fight against climate change and environmental degradation, such as a carbon border adjustment mechanism or a tax on non-recyclable plastics. And the notion of "conditionality" in this context is not similar, at least in magnitude and invasiveness, to the financial assistance programs during the Eurozone crisis, such as those of

---

[5] Equivalent to almost 75% of the seven-year EU budget.

[6] Google, Amazon, Facebook, and Apple.

Greece during the period 2010-18 (Bini Smaghi 2015), since here there is no reference to spending cuts or tax increases in view of an austerity cure, only to a guarantee that the funds will be disbursed correctly so as to stimulate recovery and to improve long-term resilience vis-à-vis future challenges and risks.[7] On the whole, the NGEU initiative is indicative of a new consciousness in favour of European sovereignty, in the sense of an enhanced capacity of the EU to act autonomously in the international arena in front of the multifaceted challenges and perils of our times, such as health crises, and by extension, potentially in front of risks for the integrity of transnational supply chains and in favour of industrial resilience vis-à-vis foreign economic predators.

The "frugal" member states' viewpoint as to the EURI's philosophy and architecture is interesting and should be analysed in its own right. In an interview for the French journal *Le Monde*, Swedish Minister for Finance Magdalena Andersson explained the reasons for these member states' distrustful, if not downright dismissive, attitude. The minister thought that "we ought to be reasonable and realistic on the size and the time limits and conditions for the granting of this aid"; she emphatically said that the Swedish retired workers, who have paid high taxes and social security contributions for many decades, will not accept grants —and not loans— to Spanish or Italian retired workers because the wide fiscal space that Sweden enjoys is the result of many years of self-disciplined fiscal policies; she also said that the EURI is not that important per se since the EU budget only represents 1% of European GDP, therefore it is just complementary to national fiscal expansionary plans; and she concluded by saying that "the priority should be given to re-establish the normal functioning of the internal market", which is "a much more important motor for the European economy than any recovery fund" (Hivert 2020).

The "frugal" member states are both good Keynesians and good Europeans, since they have been keeping a sound fiscal discipline, and have been saving money during growth periods so as to use them as a countercyclical buffer during recession periods. At the same time, they have built very competitive economies and strong welfare states entitling citizens to a high level of social transfers. In short, they are exemplary as representatives of the European Social Model. Yet this does not legitimise them in their reluctant attitude towards the EURI; on the contrary, such an

---

[7] "Resilience" is defined as "the ability to face economic, social and environmental shocks or persistent structural changes in a fair, sustainable and inclusive way" (art. 2(5) EP and CEU 2021).

attitude is self-destructive in view of the fact that the "frugal" member states are all small-to-medium in size, but have profited enormously from the EU Internal Market, its huge economies of scale, its international commercial negotiating power, as well as its attractiveness for foreign investors. And as Angela Merkel well understood, without a novel and imposing recovery plan at European level, the EU Internal Market —and all the benefits that the "frugal" states obtain from it— would be in mortal danger.

NextGenerationEU: From intergovernmental bargaining to community breakthrough

The European Council of 17-21 July 2020

The European Council that was convened on Friday, 17 July 2020 was destined to be the second longest, and certainly one of the most crucial, in the history of European integration. During this special European Council meeting, numerous concessions were made towards the "frugal" member states so as to reach a unanimous decision: Lump sum rebates on the annual GNI-based contributions were maintained for Austria, Denmark, the Netherlands, Sweden (the four "frugal" states), and Germany; the non-repayable (i.e., grants) part of the EURI funding was reduced and the loans part was raised; and the MFF 2021-27 —that would be completed by the EURI— decreased as a whole (Paulic 2020 and Malingre & Stroobants 2020). Yet, despite these efforts —led by the continuous drafting of agreement texts by President of the European Council Charles Michel—, the Prime Minister of the Netherlands Mark Rutte, followed by the Austrian Prime Minister Sebastian Kurz, persisted in pursuing hard bargaining tactics in favour of more loans and less grants by instrumentalising the "rule of law conditionality", i.e., a mechanism for the respect for EU rule of law values, combined with a right to veto by any member state as a prerequisite to the disbursement of EU funds. The result of the four-day intense backdoor intergovernmental bargaining was the emergence of new rifts in the EU both between North and South (as to the share of grants and loans and as to the total amount of the EURI) and between West and East (as to the mechanism concerning the monitoring and assessment of rule of law violations) (Malingre & Stroobants 2020).

The factor that eventually tipped the balance in favour of a strenuous but conclusive negotiation was not the Commission's prestige or expertise, but the unwavering Franco-German alignment and the political momentum that it produced. The final agreement reached early in the morning of Tuesday, 21 July 2020 was undoubtedly a breakthrough for Europe. It sketched the contours of a more integrated and solidary EU that would open the path for a true Fiscal Union. The aspects of the 21 July 2020 agreement that stand out are five: the massive use of a form of Eurobonds; the onset of a Transfer Union; the substantial redistributive effects of the EURI; the NRRPs as guarantees of good governance; and the necessary expansion of the EU's own resources. On the whole, the EURI truly resembles a "common Marshall Plan", called for in March 2020 by Spanish Prime Minister Pedro Sánchez (Reuters staff 2020).

1) A form of Eurobonds: The European Commission would issue, for the first time on such a scale, EU-Bonds so as to collect the agreed on 750 billion euro at very low interest rates, since the Commission enjoys a AAA credit rating status in the international financial markets.

2) Onset of a Transfer Union: This financial firepower would unequivocally become a solidarity tool, since the 750 billion euro amassed would be transferred towards the EU member states – 390 billion euro in the form of grants to the member states and 360 billion euro in the form of very low-interest rate loans from the EU to those member states who would apply for them.

3) Redistributive effects: The funds collected by the issuance of Eurobonds would have a substantial redistributive effect because the allocation for the grant component of the RRF[8] per member state would take into account both structural elements of the national economies (each member state's population, the inverse of its GDP per capita, and its average unemployment rate between 2015 and 2019, always compared to the EU average), as well as the magnitude of the recession in each member state due to the Covid-19 pandemic (the observed loss in real GDP over 2020 and the observed cumulative loss in real GDP over the period 2020-21). Therefore, the allocation key would mostly benefit those member states that would be economically weaker than the average and most hit by the pandemic crisis.[9] Furthermore, it is obvious that for many member

---

[8] The Recovery and Resilience Facility is discussed *infra* in the subsection "Recovery and Resilience Facility, the centrepiece of the EU Recovery Plan".

[9] Zsolt Darvas, of the European think tank Bruegel, talks about "massive redistribution" in this case because poorer EU countries (like Bulgaria, Croatia, and Greece) and those hardest hit economically by the Covid-19 crisis could obtain up to 15% of their GNI in grants and guarantees from the EU's proposed recovery instruments (Darvas 2020).

states suffering from limited fiscal space due to previous indebtedness, not only the grant, but also the loan component of the RRF was designed to provide them with financing in much more attractive conditions —primarily in terms of interest rates— than they would have obtained in the financial markets by themselves. Hence the indirect redistributive effect of funds borrowed by the Union and redirected towards the most economically and financially vulnerable EU member states.

4) Guarantee of good governance: The design of the reforms and investments necessary for recovery and resilience is made bottom-up via the NRRPs prepared by the member states in order to fit their own economic and social needs, but the NRRPs have to be approved top-down by the Commission and the Council so as to ensure that they reflect to a satisfactory degree the grand European priorities, mainly the green and digital transition of the European economy. The disbursement of the funds by the Commission is made in tranches, following approval of the Commission after consultation with the Council, and if some national government has any objections as to the good use of the funds by another national government, it can bring the issue to the European Council for final decision. Thus, an equilibrated mix between national needs and European priorities and between intergovernmentalism and the Community method was instituted, aiming at an inclusive and consensual recovery in the EU.

5) Expansion of the EU's own resources: Finally, an amendment to the Own Resources decision would become the legal basis for allowing the borrowing of funds on the financial markets to finance NGEU, and in order to increase the credibility and sustainability of the repayment plan, it was decided that the costs related to the Recovery Plan would be fully covered by revenue from genuine new own resources. Consequently, the own resources ceiling would rise permanently from 1.20 % to 1.40 % of the EU GNI, while a temporary increase in the ceiling, worth a further 0.60 % of EU GNI, would be devoted exclusively to borrowing operations for NGEU, and would apply until full repayment of all liabilities and at the latest until December 2058. This temporary increase of the own resources ceiling would thus enable the Commission to borrow on a much larger scale and for lengthier periods than in the past. This mechanism, in turn, would reinforce the economic patriotism of the Europeans by forging a common consciousness of the jointly tackled vulnerabilities and by binding Europeans together for several decades, until full reimbursement of the jointly incurred debt.

The European Parliament's positioning vis-à-vis the EURI was supportive from the outset. Its political priorities were the end of the rebates in some member states' contributions to the EU budget, the establishment of new EU own resources, and the respect of rule of law values. These priorities were reflected in its resolution of 23 July 2020 on the conclusions of the extraordinary European Council meeting of 17-21 July 2020 (EP 2020). There, the Parliament criticised the concessions made to the "frugal" member states in order to reach an agreement, notably the massive cuts to the grant component of the NGEU, which upset the balance between grants and loans and risked undermining the recovery efforts (EP 2020, par. 19), the proposed cuts to the MFF 2021-27,[10] which go against the EU's objectives (EP 2020, par. 4), and the rebates offered to the four "frugal" member states plus Germany, which go against its firm position in favour of ending all rebates and corrective mechanisms altogether, as soon as possible (EP 2020, par. 12). As to the establishment of new EU own resources, the Parliament warned that it would not give its consent for the MFF 2021-27 without an agreement on a broader reform of the EU's own resources system, including the introduction of a basket of new own resources by the end of the MFF 2021-27, which should aim both to cover at least the costs related to the NGEU (principal and interest) in order to ensure the credibility and sustainability of the NGEU repayment plan and to reduce the share of the GNI-based contributions to the EU budget (EP 2020, pars. 10-11). Finally, as to the respect of the rule of law in the framework of the MFF and the NGEU instrument, the Parliament asked to complete the co-legislator's work on the Commission's proposed mechanism to protect the EU budget where there is a systemic threat to the values enshrined in Article 2 of the Treaty on European Union (TEU), and where the financial interests of the Union are at stake, and stressed that, to be effective, this mechanism should be activated by a reverse qualified majority (EP 2020, par. 9).

As to the European Parliament's institutional role in the financing and governance of the NGEU, it was clear that it would not be called to vote on the EURI, even though it is the budgetary authority together with the Council and thus votes (but without the right to amend) on the proposed MFF. Recalling that it is the only directly elected EU institution, and deploring this gap in the NGEU's democratic legitimacy, the Parliament demanded to be fully involved in the financing and the sound

---

[10] Such as the cuts to health, digital transformation and innovation programmes, to programmes supporting the transition of carbon-dependent regions, and to asylum, migration and border management programmes.

management of the recovery instrument, in line with the Community method. More specifically, it called for ex ante democratic and parliamentary scrutiny, and therefore asked to be involved in delegated acts, as well as in the ex post verification that money provided is well spent, in the interest of EU citizens. It also demanded that the Commission present a targeted revision of the Financial Regulation in order to enshrine the role of the budgetary authority in authorising external assigned revenues, such as the NGEU amounts channelled through the budget for expenditure, under the annual budgetary procedure (EP 2020, pars. 21-22). As to the governance of the EURI, the Parliament opposed the position of the European Council, which it considered as moving away from the Community method and endorsing an intergovernmental approach. It stated that such an approach would only complicate the functioning and weaken the legitimacy of the EURI, and was of the firm opinion that the responsible Commissioners should be fully accountable to Parliament (EP 2020, par. 21).

The overall reception of the European Council of 17-21 July 2020 conclusions was positive, both by the main European actors themselves and by scholars. In an interview for the French journal *Le Monde*, European Council President Charles Michel talked about a "Copernican evolution". From the moment that the EU decided to mobilise 750 billion euro through the issuance of common debt for thirty years, to be reimbursed jointly, in order to invest and reform and with the aim of achieving the convergence of national economies, this new mechanism will transform the European project itself by deepening and solidifying the relations between the Union and its member states. To deflect the criticism articulated by the European Parliament, Michel asserted that the combined financing of the whole financial package (composed of the MFF 2021-27 and the NGEU) not only augments the overall EU funds available for spending, but also, from the revenue side, creates a machinery that will impose on the European institutions to make long-awaited decisions on the EU's own resources (Malingre 2020). In a short televised interview on the evening of 21 July 2020, French President Emmanuel Macron talked about the "most important moment in the life of our Europe since the creation of the euro", and pointed out that the 40 billion euro of the EURI that will benefit France will not be financed "neither by our indebtedness nor by our taxes" (Macron 2020).

It is rather striking that the EURI decided by the European Council was met with praise both by the European left and the European right. Then-leader of left-wing Spanish party Podemos and also then-Vice-president of the Spanish Government Pablo Iglesias considered the July

2021 European Council "a turn", and talked about "a historic renouncement of austerity by Europe" and "a manner of tackling the economic crisis diametrically opposed to the one of 2008" (Morel 2020). On the other end of the political spectrum, the high priest of the dogma of German austerity Wolfgang Schäuble, in an article for the German journal *Frankfurter Allgemeine Zeitung* on 6 July 2020, supported the Franco-German proposal of 18 May 2020 for a EU Recovery Plan, and went even further by supporting both the reinforcement of Europe's "strategic autonomy" vis-à-vis "Chinese totalitarianism" and the "correction of the excesses of globalisation", and by using the EURI —that would be agreed on a few days later— as a means to finally move from a Monetary Union to a full-blown Economic Union. With this article, Schäuble surprised the camp of the European fiscal hawks. Not only did he accept the principle of the creation of new own resources for the EU, but he even went so far as to propose a common European investment strategy as the vector of a profound transformation that would lead to a true "European sovereignty" (Schäuble 2020).

The implications of the European Council of 17-21 July 2020 historic decision to issue common European debt urged Professor Sylvain Kahn, a specialist in European history, to talk about the transformation of the EU into a real "state" that has acquired the capacity to finance common needs through fiscal expansion. According to Kahn, this peculiar European state is not a super-state that would replace the twenty-seven EU member states, but a democratic state of mutualised sovereignty that encompasses the latter. Indeed, the NGEU is not the product of pure intergovernmental bargaining; it has derived from democratic mutualisation, since it has to be democratically approved by all national parliaments, networked with the European Parliament, and in some cases also by local or regional parliaments constitutionally required to have their say as well. Moreover, the debate and the fault lines on the EURI have demonstrated the existence of a European deliberative democracy, albeit rudimentary, given that in this respect, there is, on the one hand, a majority (the European stakeholders' alliance wishing for a Fiscal Union) led by a group of leaders (the Franco-German axis), and on the other hand, an opposition (the "frugal" member states), whereas the final decision is a product of compromise after intense debate (Kahn 2020). In any case, the July 2021 agreement on the NGEU instrument came in a timely manner, after the first emergency responses by the national governments and by the European Central Bank (hereinafter ECB), but not too late. And, most importantly, in a world replete with strife and nationalistic antagonisms, the EU member states gained consciousness of their interdependency in front of great hazards and uncertainty, and unequivocally manifested their political will to preserve their Union by transcending their internal —and often paralysing— balance of power.

Recovery and Resilience Facility, the centrepiece of the EURI

The European Council of 17-21 July 2020 decided to establish a novel Recovery and Resilience Facility and gave it the lion's share of the funding under NGEU: 672.5 billion euro, of which 360 billion euro in loans and 312.5 billion euro in grants.[11] The RRF is front-loaded so as to serve also as a countercyclical device: 70% of its grants part is committed in the years 2021 and 2022, and the remaining 30% will be fully committed by the end of 2023 (European Council 2020, paragraph A15).[12] The prefinancing for the RRF amounts to 13% and was paid in 2021.

A very interesting feature of the RRF is that it is fully integrated in the community acquis, and is therefore a purely EU-based facility[13] entirely managed by EU institutions, unlike the ESM, established by an international treaty (the Treaty Establishing the ESM), and its predecessor the European Financial Stability Facility (EFSF), a Luxembourg-based company that had been established as a Special Purpose Vehicle (hereinafter SPV) by the euro area member states in June 2010. This fundamental political decision was made mostly with the aim of integrating the RRF into the European Semester,[14] and thus of assessing

[11] All the rest of the programmes under NGEU were allocated the total amount of 77.5 billion euro, of which: 47.5 billion euro for REACT-EU (Recovery Assistance for Cohesion and the Territories of Europe); 5 billion euro for Horizon Europe; 5.6 billion euro for InvestEU; 7.5 billion euro for Rural Development; 10 billion euro for the Just Transition Fund; and 1.9 billion euro for RescEU. Of all these financial instruments, only REACT-EU was totally new; it was launched as the participation of EU cohesion policy in the EU Recovery Plan following the outbreak of the Covid-19 pandemic.

[12] As for the loans that will be requested under the RRF by the EU member states, their maximum volume will not exceed 6.8% of each member state's GNI.

[13] The legal basis of the RRF is to be found in art. 175 par. 3 TFEU: "If specific actions prove necessary outside the Funds and without prejudice to the measures decided upon within the framework of the other Union policies, such actions may be adopted by the European Parliament and the Council acting in accordance with the ordinary legislative procedure and after consulting the Economic and Social Committee and the Committee of the Regions."

[14] The European Semester of the EU was established in 2010 as a framework for fiscal and macroeconomic policy coordination. It is an annual cycle allowing EU

the NRRPs against the Commission country-specific recommendations included in the European Semester. Indeed, the degree of integration is so strong that given the comprehensive and forward-looking policy nature of the NRRPs, there was no need for the Commission to propose country-specific recommendations in 2021 to the member states that have submitted plans, and member states were encouraged to submit their National Reform Programmes and their NRRPs in a single integrated document that provides an overview of the reforms and investments that each member state will undertake in the coming years, in line with the objectives of the RRF (EC 2020d; art. 18(3) EP and CEU 2021).

The NRRPs prepared by the EU member states and setting out their coherent reform and investment agenda to be implemented up to 2026 are assessed by the Commission, within two months of their submission, as to their consistency with the country-specific recommendations proposed by the Commission (art. 19 EP and CEU 2021), and are approved by an implementing decision of the Council by qualified majority in the context of the European Semester within four weeks of the Commission proposal (art. 20 EP and CEU 2021). They are also assessed as to their capacity for strengthening the growth potential, job creation, and economic and social resilience, as well as their effective contribution to the green and digital transition of the member states (European Council 2020, paragraph A19).

An interesting point of the agreement on the RRF is the commitment of the Commission to cooperate with the member states on the preparation of their NRRPs. The Commission presented guidance and a template to help the member states prepare and present their NRRPs in a clear and coherent way (EC 2020c). Each NRRP must provide that an executive summary should outline the main narrative of the plan, enabling the European Parliament, the other member states, the Commission, and the public at large to have an overview of what the recovery and resilience plan will achieve, and it also gives a detailed explanation of what the member state is expected to provide when submitting the plan (EC 2020d). It is therefore ascertained that the governance process instituted by the RRF is an expression of cooperative European integration; the preparation and implementation of the NRRPs, in the framework and with the financing of the RRF, takes the form of a partnership, not a unilateral decision by any single authority or agency.

---

member states to discuss their budget and economic plans and to monitor progress at specific times throughout the year (EC n.d.a).

The RRF undoubtedly functions as a short-term countercyclical device to offset the recession caused by the pandemic. Yet, its main aim is to serve as a long-term instrument for structural macroeconomic policy reforms that will strengthen the resilience of the European national economies. Therefore, it supports investments and reforms that will have a lasting, positive impact on the economy and society. More specifically, the RRF promotes actions or processes aimed at making lasting improvements to the functioning of markets, institutional structures, public administrations, or relevant policies associated with the green and digital transitions (EC 2020d). It is noteworthy that the structural improvements financed and piloted by the RRF are not purely national; the RRF incentivises the EU member states to create European flagship investment and reform projects that address issues common to all of them, and that need significant investments and create jobs and growth. Therefore, the Commission strongly encourages EU member states to include in their NRRPs investments and reforms in some designated areas of high importance for the twin (green and digital) transition and for the reskill and upskill of human capital in the EU.

The long-term structural reform aspect of the RRF implies a broad conception of "investment" as capital formation in fixed, human, and natural capital, so as to orient the future European economy and society towards lasting and beneficial changes and towards resilience to stress and risk. "Fixed capital" relates to investments in infrastructure, buildings, but also some intangibles like research and development, patents or software. "Human capital" is accumulated by means of spending on health, social protection, education, training and skilling. And "natural capital" is enhanced by actions aiming at increasing the share of renewable natural resources, protecting or restoring the environment, or by mitigating and/or adapting to climate change (EC 2020d).

The quantification of the expenditure targets concerning the green and digital transitions gives a clear sense of priorities in the operation of the RRF. With the ultimate European goal of achieving climate neutrality by 2050 in sight, all NRRPs need to focus strongly on both reforms and investments supporting the climate transition. The means to achieve the aforementioned ultimate goal is that each NRRP will have to include a minimum level of 37% of expenditure related to climate, such as the improvement of energy efficiency of public and private buildings and the acceleration of the development and use of renewable energy sources. Marching in lockstep with the green transition, EU member states need also to ensure in their NRRPs a high level of ambition as to reforms and investments enabling the digital transition. The means to achieve effective implementation in the EU digital agenda is that each NRRP will have to include a minimum level of 20% of expenditure related to it, such as 5G networks, the increase in data cloud capacities, and the digitalisation of public administration and services.

The governance model chosen for the RRF is clearly thought out as a form of "locking in" reforms and investments via the provision of the appropriate incentives, and not as a set of hard law sanctions in case of transgression of commonly accepted rules. The disbursement of financial support by the Commission can be requested by a member state only upon completion of the relevant agreed milestones and targets indicated in its NRRP.[15] Practically, if a member state has not satisfactorily implemented the said milestones and targets, the Commission will suspend all or part of the financial contribution to it. Milestones and targets are the means to measure the progress towards the achievement of a reform or the realisation of an investment. They must be directly determined or otherwise influenced by public policies, and they must be written clearly, realistically and verifiably in order to facilitate the task of the Commission. The Commission will prepare an assessment and ask the opinion of the Economic and Financial Committee on the satisfactory fulfilment of the relevant milestones and targets.

In exceptional circumstances, where a member state considers that there are serious deviations from the satisfactory fulfilment of the relevant milestones and targets of another member state, it may request that the President of the European Council refer the matter to the next European Council, which will exhaustively discuss the matter (European Council 2020). Once operational, a NRRP is monitored through bi-annual reporting on its implementation by the beneficiary (for the grants part) and/or borrower (for the loans part) member state in the context of the European Semester. The Commission established a Recovery and Resilience Task Force (RECOVER) on 16 August 2020 within its Secretariat-General, reporting directly to the Commission President. Its tasks are to support the member states in the elaboration of their NRRPs, steer the implementation of the RRF, and coordinate the process by engaging with the member states to ensure that the notified plans comply with the regulatory requirements set by the legislation and that the proposed reform and investment initiatives deliver on the objectives of the

[15] "Milestones" are qualitative achievements and "targets" are quantitative achievements of a reform or an investment (art. 2(4) EP and CEU 2021).

twin green and digital transition, of recovery and resilience. RECOVER assesses the progress made by the member states in the implementation of their NRRPs, and prepares the necessary implementing acts for the approval of the plans (EC n.d.b).

By mid-February 2021, all the pieces of legislation concerning the NGEU and the RRF were in place. On 14 December 2020, both the EURI Regulation 2020/2094 (CEU 2020a) and the new Own Resources Decision 2020/2053 (CEU 2020b) were enacted. During the same time, the European Parliament and the Council reached an agreement on the specifics of the RRF, which resulted in the enactment of the RRF Regulation on 12 February 2021 (EP and CEU 2021).

The legal basis of the EURI is to be found in art. 122(1) of the Treaty on the Functioning of the European Union (hereinafter TFEU): "Without prejudice to any other procedures provided for in the Treaties, the Council, on a proposal from the Commission, may decide, in a spirit of solidarity between Member States, upon the measures appropriate to the economic situation, in particular if severe difficulties arise in the supply of certain products, notably in the area of energy."[16] In practice, the EURI Regulation is the basic act that creates the external assigned revenue for NGEU (art. 3 CEU 2020a) and allocates the resources from the borrowing operations by type of support (art. 2 CEU 2020a). The EURI Regulation sets up a series of rules for budgetary implementation. It also limits the time within which payments must be made related to legal commitments giving rise to grant support, decisions adopted on the granting of loans, and provisions regarding financial operations, setting 31 December 2026 as the final deadline (art. 3 CEU 2020a). In June 2021, the EURI became operational following the ratification of the new own resources decision by all member states.

The new Own Resources Decision repealed and replaced the earlier Decision of 2014 so as to provide the legal basis for allowing the borrowing of funds on the financial markets to finance the NGEU recovery instrument. The European Parliament had long pushed for the reform of the previous system of own resources, calling for the introduction of new genuine own resources and the elimination of all

[16] It is to be noted that the European Parliament is not involved in this legislative procedure, which requires qualified majority in the Council, and that art. 122 TFEU had already been used for the establishment of SURE, the temporary European instrument to support national safety nets for short time work and unemployment benefits.

correction or rebate mechanisms. The new Decision included an entirely novel article 5 on "extraordinary and temporary additional means to address the consequences of the COVID-19 crisis," which empowered the Commission to borrow funds on capital markets on behalf of the Union up to 750 billion euro in 2018 prices (CEU 2020b).[17] As mentioned before, the new Own Resources Decision increased the own resources ceilings, both permanently from 1.20 % to 1.40 % of the EU GNI (art. 3(1) CEU 2020b) and temporarily to 2% of the EU GNI exclusively for borrowing operations for NGEU (art. 6 CEU 2020b). So as to be perfectly clear on the prohibition of the temporary increase to cover any other liabilities of the Union, it is further specified that "the Union shall not use funds borrowed on capital markets for the financing of operational expenditure" (art. 4 CEU 2020b).

The new Own Resources Decision introduced a new category of own resources, effective as from 1 January 2021, namely a uniform call rate to the weight of plastic packaging waste generated in each member state that is not recycled (art. 2(1)(c) CEU 2020b), whereas the political agreement on the MFF reached on 10 November 2020 between the Parliament and the Council included the incorporation of a roadmap for new own resources in the new interinstitutional agreement on budgetary matters. This roadmap provisions: revenue generated by the allowances to be auctioned under the scheme for greenhouse gas emission allowance trading within the European Union (EU ETS) (from 2023); revenues generated by a border carbon adjustment mechanism (from 2023); revenues from a digital services tax (from 2023); a Financial Transactions Tax-based resource (from 2026); and a uniform call rate to the share of taxable profits attributed to each member state in accordance with the EU rules on the common consolidated corporate tax base (from 2026). On 30 April 2021, the Council adopted the package of implementing legislation accompanying the decision, following the European Parliament's vote in March 2021. In June 2021, all member states had notified the Council of their ratification of the Own Resources Decision, enabling thus the Commission to initiate the borrowing operations for the NGEU recovery instrument. The new own resources system retroactively applies from 1 January 2021.

---

[17] This is reflected in the EURI Regulation, where it is stipulated that the EURI shall be financed up to an amount of 750 billion euro in 2018 prices on the basis of the empowerment provided for in article 5 of the Own Resources Decision (art. 2 par. 1 CEU 2020a).

Yet, on 12 July 2021, the Commission announced that it would postpone the publication of its digital tax proposal for the second semester of 2021, thus temporarily upsetting the political agreement of 10 November 2020, on request of United States of America (hereinafter USA) Treasury Secretary Janet Yellen so as to preserve the work undertaken via the OECD/G20 process on tax base erosion and profit shifting by multinational companies.[18] Prioritising the finalisation of a global tax accord before reassessing one of the new EU own resources applying to the same entities is, of course, perfectly rational; still, it can be perceived as a sign of political weakness vis-à-vis the USA, given that the "GAFA" are American companies. Finally, on 14 July 2021, the Commission presented a legislative proposal to extend the EU ETS system to cover maritime transport and to establish a new separate system of emission trading for emissions from fuels used in road transport and buildings from 2025,[19] as part of the "Fit for 55" legislative package aiming at reducing greenhouse gas emissions at least 55% by 2030 compared to 1990 (EC 2021g). The allowances for the new emissions trading system will be auctioned, as no free allocation is provided, and both national budgets of member states and the EU budget will benefit from the new EU ETS mechanism after the adjustments to the EU budgetary framework that the Commission will present as part of the upcoming Own Resources package (EC 2021h).[20]

---

[18] The OECD/G20 Inclusive Framework on Base Erosion and Profit Shifting has agreed a two-pillar solution to address the tax challenges arising from the digitalisation of the economy. Pillar One aims to ensure a fairer distribution of profits and taxing rights among countries with respect to the largest multinational enterprises, which are the winners of globalisation, while Pillar Two seeks to put a floor on tax competition on corporate income tax through the introduction of a global minimum corporate tax that countries can use to protect their tax bases (OECD 2021).

[19] It is rather significant that this new separate upstream system will regulate fuel suppliers, rather than households and car drivers, so as to incentivise them to decarbonise their product as this will reduce the cost of compliance with the emissions trading system.

[20] It is noteworthy that member states will be required to spend their auction revenues from emissions trading on climate-and energy-related projects, including decarbonisation in the road transport and buildings sectors, and that they should use a part of their revenues from emissions trading in the road transport and building sectors on measures to support vulnerable households and transport users and to match funding under the novel Social Climate Fund, which will be set up to address social impacts of emissions trading on vulnerable households, micro-

Finally, the RRF Regulation is the legal means by which the EU will provide member states with direct financial support to reach their milestones and targets for reforms and investments in order to improve their resilience and adjustment capacity, to mitigate the social and economic consequences of the crisis, and to support the green and digital transitions towards a climate-neutral Europe by 2050. It is interesting that according to the final text adopted by the European Parliament, the Facility will also contribute to the implementation of the European Pillar of Social Rights (art. 4 EP and CEU 2021). The RRF Regulation fixes the basic rules concerning both the non-repayable financial support and the loan support to the member states (arts. 11-16 EP and CEU 2021). As far as grants are concerned, the Regulation determines a maximum amount per member state on the basis of a predefined allocation key taking into account population, GDP per capita, and unemployment.

Member states may also apply for a loan; if they do, the Regulation stipulates that the maximum volume of loans for each member state shall not exceed 6.8% of its GNI (art. 14(5) EP and CEU 2021), and the loan shall be paid in installments subject to the fulfilment of milestones and targets (art. 14(7) and art. 24 EP and CEU 2021). Support under the Facility shall be additional to the support provided under other Union programmes and instruments (art. 9 EP and CEU 2021). To be eligible for funding under the RRF Regulation, NRRPs must focus on key EU policy areas structured in six pillars: a) green transition; b) digital transformation; c) smart, sustainable and inclusive growth; d) social and territorial cohesion; e) health, and economic, social and institutional resilience, with the aim of increasing crisis preparedness and crisis response capacity; and f) policies for the next generation, children and the youth, such as education and skills (art. 3 EP and CEU 2021). Moreover, the Facility will only finance measures that respect the principle of "do no significant harm", i.e., the principle forbidding support to any economic activities that do significant harm to any environmental objective (art. 5(2) EP and CEU 2021).

The Regulation sets the rules concerning the NRRPs (arts. 17-21 EP and CEU 2021). A crucial point for the good management of the facility is that it institutes a mechanism to ensure a conditionality link between the RRF and sound economic governance by allowing the Commission to present a proposal to the Council to suspend all or part of

---

enterprises and transport users, with a view to avoiding social unrest such as the one provoked by the "gilets jaunes" movement in France.

the commitments or payments under the Facility in case of repeated violations of the requirements of either the excessive deficit or the excessive macroeconomic imbalances procedure. The Commission proposal for suspension of commitments or payments will be deemed adopted unless the Council decides, by means of an implementing act, to reject such a proposal by qualified majority within one month of the presentation of the Commission proposal (reverse qualified majority) (art. 10 EP and CEU 2021). Finally, at the insistence of the European Parliament and with the aim of achieving a strong level of democratic legitimacy, specific provisions on dialogue and transparency made their entrance in the RRF Regulation: The Commission must transmit the NRRPs submitted by the member states to the European Parliament and the Council without undue delay, and the competent committee of the European Parliament can, every two months, invite the Commission to address, in a dialogue on recovery and resilience, issues relevant to the implementation of the Facility, notably the state of recovery, resilience and adjustment capacity in the Union, the assessment of the NRRPs, and the status of fulfilment of their milestones and targets (arts. 25-26 EP and CEU 2021). A specific Scoreboard will be set up by December 2021 to display the progress in the implementation of the NRRPs (art. 30 EP and CEU 2021), and an annual report will be provided by the Commission to the European Parliament and the Council (art. 31 EP and CEU 2021).

On 14 April 2021, the Commission adopted a diversified funding strategy so as to operationalise the NGEU borrowing on the most advantageous terms for the EU member states and to raise up to around 800 billion euro in current prices —which represents borrowing volumes of on average roughly 150 billion euro per year— until 2026 (EC 2021a and EC 2021b). The Commission decided to adopt a funding strategy in line with the best practices of sovereign issuers, as a means to raise the needed volumes in a smooth and efficient way and to attract investors to Europe and strengthen the international role of the euro. It is important to note that while the Commission has been borrowing before to support EU member states and third countries on a purely back-to-back basis (whereby the Commission issued bonds and transferred the proceeds directly to the beneficiary country on the same terms that it received in terms of interest rate and maturity), the volumes, frequency and complexity of the NGEU borrowing have called for a fundamental change in the approach to capital markets, adapted to large volumes of debt to be issued on a regular basis over the next years and under changing conditions. The new diversified funding strategy, which combines the use of different funding instruments and techniques with an open and transparent communication to the market participants, will make the EU one of the largest issuers in euro. The new strategy will help the EU to achieve two main objectives: address the large funding needs of NGEU by using a wide range of maturities and instruments,[21] and obtain the desired low cost and low execution risk by allowing flexibility to decide when to execute funding operations and which funding techniques or instruments to use. The introduction of issuance methods employed by large and frequent supranational issuers is yet another step in the direction of the gradual transformation of the EU into a sovereign fiscal entity. The new funding strategy is not only a technical financial issue; it is a clear sign of a breakthrough towards a real Fiscal Union.

On 2 June 2021, the Commission presented the European Semester Spring Package, which focuses on providing fiscal guidance to member states as they continue the process of gradually reopening their economies, and on helping strengthen the economic recovery, making the best possible use of the RRF. With the Spring Package, the Commission prolonged the "general escape clause" of the SGP until the end of 2022, with a view to deactivating it in 2023, so as to encourage the member states to maintain supportive fiscal policies in 2021 and 2022 and to preserve public investment (EC 2021c). As Paolo Gentiloni, Commissioner for Economy, said during the presentation: "The recovery remains uneven and uncertainty is still high, so economic policy must remain supportive in both 2021 and 2022. Thanks also to the Recovery and Resilience Facility, public investment is set to reach its highest level in more than a decade. Our message today is that all countries should also preserve nationally financed investment". The Commission gave thus a very clear message that fiscal policy needs to remain supportive in 2021 and 2022, and that

---

[21] The diversified strategy combines: The setting up of a Primary Dealer Network comprising the banks that will support the issuance programme as financial intermediaries buying, promoting and distributing sovereign debt; the publication of annual borrowing decisions setting a maximum ceiling for the planned borrowing operations over the planning period of one year, and of semi-annually updated NGEU funding plans within the boundaries set by the annual borrowing decisions; the use of multiple funding instruments, namely medium and long-term EU-Bonds —some of which will be issued as green bonds— and short-term EU-Bills issued through auctions, so as to maintain flexibility in terms of market access and to manage liquidity needs and the maturity profile; and a combination of auctions, which offer debt to a group of financial institutions (primary dealers) that can acquire the debt by submitting bids via an electronic platform, and syndications with a group of underwriters (usually banks) whose role is to place the debt with investors.

member states should avoid a premature withdrawal of support and make full use of the RRF funding to implement investments and reforms that will spur the economic recovery, foster higher potential growth and employment, reduce imbalances, and ultimately improve public finances. On the whole, the Commission made clear that the fiscal and macroeconomic environment should continue to stimulate recovery, and avoided the catastrophic error during the Eurozone crisis, when fiscal stimulus programmes were prematurely terminated in the name of fiscal consolidation.

On 15 June 2021, after the ratification of the Own Resources Decision by all EU member states, the European Commission made its first funding operation under NGEU by raising 20 billion euro via a 10-year bond due on 4 July 2031 at a yield of 0.086%. As President Ursula von der Leyen said before embarking on a tour of the European capitals, "Today is a truly historic day for our European Union". In point of fact, this first transaction is at the same time the largest-ever institutional bond issuance in Europe, the largest-ever institutional single tranche transaction, and the largest amount the EU has raised in a single transaction (EC 2021d). The second NGEU transaction, which followed some days later, was oversubscribed more than 11 times and attracted bids exceeding 170 billion euro (EC 2021e), whereas the third 20-year EU-Bond raised further 10 billion euro on very favourable pricing conditions, having been oversubscribed almost 10 times (EC 2021f). Overall, the first three NGEU funding operations have proven beyond any doubt that the novel EU-bonds mechanism has convinced the markets and has attracted strong interest by investors. A deep and internationally appealing EU bond market has become a reality.

Conclusion

Faced with a violent symmetric and asymmetric shock, European political leaders assumed the responsibility of solidarity by adopting an exceptional initiative, the NGEU. Even so, the posterity of Europe's "Hamiltonian Moment" will depend on the effective implementation of this initiative. The NGEU was surcly a brcakthrough. It created a European budgetary capacity and new own resources; it allowed for direct transfers at unprecedented amounts; and it provided Europe with a strategic sense of orientation for the future. The momentum is undoubtedly here. But if the accomplishments of the Plan are not evident to the great majority of European citizens in some years from now, it will ultimately leave the negative impression of another wasted opportunity for the Union, and it will dwindle away. On the contrary, if it contributes to the recovery of the national economies that are now in a difficult situation and if it reinforces political and social cohesion in the Union, it will go down in history as perhaps the most important step in European integration of the 21st century.

References

Bini Smaghi, Lorenzo. 2015. Governance and Conditionality: Toward a Sustainable Framework?. *Journal of European Integration* 37, no.7: 755–768.

Bofinger Peter, Daniel Cohn-Bendit, Joschka Fischer, Rainer Forst, Marcel Fratzscher, Jürgen Habermas, Axel Honneth, Julian Nida-Rümelin, Volker Schlöndorff, Peter Schneider, Simon Strauss, and Margarethe von Trotta. 2020. "Nous appelons Bruxelles à créer un «fonds corona»," *Le Monde*, 3 April, https://www.lemonde.fr/idees/article/2020/04/02/nous-appelons-la-commission-europeenne-a-creer-un-fonds-corona-pour-aider-les-etats-membres_6035262_3232.html (accessed July 14, 2021).

CEU. 2020a. "Council Regulation (EU) 2020/2094 of 14 December 2020 establishing a European Union Recovery Instrument to support the recovery in the aftermath of the COVID-19 crisis," OJ L 433I, 22.12.2020, 23–27.

CEU. 2020b. "Council Decision (EU, Euratom) 2020/2053 of 14 December 2020 on the system of own resources of the European Union and repealing Decision 2014/335/EU, Euratom," OJ L 424, 15.12. 2020, 1–10.

Darvas, Zsolt. 2020. "The EU's recovery fund proposals: crisis relief with massive redistribution," Blog post, Bruegel, 17 June, https://www.bruegel.org/2020/06/the-eus-recovery-fund-proposals-crisis-relief-with-massive-redistribution/ (accessed July 20, 2021).

EC. 2021a. "NextGenerationEU: Commission gets ready to raise up to €800 billion to fund the recovery," Press release, IP/21/1703, 14 April, https://ec.europa.eu/commission/presscorner/detail/en/ip_21_1703 (accessed August 10, 2021).

EC. 2021b. "Funding strategy for NextGenerationEU: Questions and Answers," Questions and answers, QANDA/21/1702, 14 April, https://ec.europa.eu/commission/presscorner/detail/en/ip_21_1703 (accessed August 10, 2021).

EC. 2021c. "European Semester Spring Package: Paving the way for a strong and sustainable recovery," Press release, IP/21/2722, 2 June, https://ec.europa.eu/commission/presscorner/detail/en/IP_21_2722 (accessed August 10, 2021).

EC. 2021d. "NextGenerationEU: European Commission raises €20 billion in first transaction to support Europe's recovery," Press release, IP/21/2982, 15 June, https://ec.europa.eu/commission/presscorner/detail/en/IP_21_2982 (accessed August 10, 2021).

EC. 2021e. "NextGenerationEU: European Commission completes second successful bond issuance to support Europe's recovery," Press release, IP/21/3287, 29 June, https://ec.europa.eu/commission/presscorner/detail/en/IP_21_3287 (accessed August 10, 2021).

EC. 2021f. "NextGenerationEU: European Commission raises further €10 billion in a successful third bond to support Europe's recovery," Press release, IP/21/3682, 13 July, https://ec.europa.eu/commission/presscorner/detail/en/ip_21_3682 (accessed August 10, 2021).

EC. 2021g. "Proposal for a Directive of the European Parliament and of the Council amending Directive 2003/87/EC establishing a system for greenhouse gas emission allowance trading within the Union, Decision (EU) 2015/1814 concerning the establishment and operation of a market stability reserve for the Union greenhouse gas emission trading scheme and Regulation (EU) 2015/757, COM(2021) 551 final, 14 July, https://ec.europa.eu/info/sites/default/files/revision-eu-ets_with-annex_en_0.pdf (accessed August 11, 2021).

EC. 2021h. "Questions and Answers - Emissions Trading – Putting a Price on carbon *", Questions and Answers, 14 July, QANDA/21/3542, https://ec.europa.eu/commission/presscorner/detail/en/qanda_21_3542 (accessed August 11, 2021).

EC. 2020a. "Temporary Framework for State aid measures to support the economy in the current COVID-19 outbreak," Communication, C(2020) 1863 final, 19 March, https://ec.europa.eu/competition/state_aid/what_is_new/sa_covid19_temporary-framework.pdf (accessed July 10, 2021).

EC. 2020b. "Communication on the activation of the general escape clause of the Stability and Growth Pact," COM(2020) 123 final, 20 March, https://ec.europa.eu/info/sites/default/files/economy-finance/2_en_act_part1_v3-adopted_text.pdf (accessed July 10, 2021).

EC. 2020c. "Guidance to Member States. Recovery and Resilience Plans", Staff Working Document, SWD (2020) 205 final, 17 September, https://ec.europa.eu/info/sites/default/files/3_en_document_travail_service_part1_v3_en_0.pdf (accessed July 18, 2021).

EC. 2020d. "Commission presents next steps for €672.5 billion Recovery and Resilience Facility in 2021 Annual Sustainable Growth Strategy," Questions and Answers, 17 September, QANDA/20/1659, https://ec.europa.eu/commission/presscorner/detail/en/QANDA_20_1659 (accessed July 18, 2021).

EC. n.d.a. "The European Semester," https://ec.europa.eu/info/business-economy-euro/economic-and-fiscal-policy-coordination/eu-economic-governance-monitoring-prevention-correction/european-semester_en (accessed July 14, 2021).

EC. n.d.b. "Recovery and Resilience Task Force," https://ec.europa.eu/info/departments/recovery-and-resilience-task-force_en (accessed July 16, 2021).

EP. 2020. "Resolution of 23 July 2020 on the conclusions of the extraordinary European Council meeting of 17-21 July 2020," 2020/2732(RSP), https://www.europarl.europa.eu/doceo/document/TA-9-2020-07-23_EN.html (accessed July 16, 2021).

EP and CEU. 2021. "Regulation (EU) 2021/241 of the European Parliament and of the Council of 12 February 2021 establishing the Recovery and Resilience Facility", OJ L 57, 18.2.2021, 17–75.

European Council. 2020. "Conclusions of the Special meeting of the European Council (17, 18, 19, 20 and 21 July 2020)," https://www.consilium.europa.eu/media/45109/210720-euco-final-conclusions-en.pdf (accessed July 17, 2021).

Hivert, Anne-Françoise. 2020. "'Un fonds de relance européen est nécessaire, pas à n'importe quelles conditions' : entretien Magdalena Andersson," Le Monde, 29 May 2020, https://www.lemonde.fr/international/article/2020/05/27/magdalena-andersson-un-fonds-de-relance-est-necessaire-pas-dans-n-importe-quelles-conditions_6040942_3210.html (accessed July 15, 2021).

Horn, Sebastian, Josefin Meyer, and Christoph Trebesch. 2020. "European Community Bonds since the Oil crisis: Lessons for today?", Kiel Policy Brief No 136, April, https://www.ifw-kiel.de/publications/kiel-policy-briefs/2020/european-community-bonds-since-the-oil-crisis-lessons-for-today-14037/ (accessed July 14, 2021).

Kahn, Sylvain. 2020. "L'Union européenne est maintenant un Etat," Le Monde, 23 July, https://www.lemonde.fr/idees/article/2020/07/22/sylvain-kahn-l-union-europeenne-est-maintenant-un-etat_6046896_3232.html (accessed July 15, 2021).

Kaletsky, Anatole. 2020. "Europe's Hamiltonian Moment," Project Syndicate, 21 May, https://www.project-syndicate.org/commentary/french-german-european-recovery-plan-proposal-by-anatole-kaletsky-2020-05 (accessed July 15, 2021).

Macron, Emmanuel. 2020. Interview au journal télévisé de 20H de TF1, 21 July, https://www.ouest-france.fr/politique/emmanuel-macron/suivez-en-direct-l-interview-d-emmanuel-macron-au-20h-de-tf1-6914081 (accessed July 15, 2020).

Malingre, Virginie. 2020. "Charles Michel: «Une évolution copernicienne»," Le Monde, 26-27 July, https://www.lemonde.fr/international/article/2020/07/25/charles-michel-ce-qui-est-sur-la-table-c-est-une-evolution-copernicienne-pour-l-ue_6047256_3210.html (accessed July 15, 2021).

Malingre, Virginie & Jean-Pierre Stroobants. 2020. "Négociation au forceps à Bruxelles," Le Monde, 21 July, https://www.lemonde.fr/international/article/2020/07/20/plan-de-relance-apres-trois-jours-et-trois-nuits-de-debats-l-ue-toute-proche-d-une-solution_6046724_3210.html (accessed July 15, 2021).

Morel, Sandrine. 2020. "Pablo Iglesias: «Un renoncement historique de l'Europe à l'austérité»," Le Monde, 23 July, https://www.lemonde.fr/international/article/2020/07/22/pablo-iglesias-le-dogmatisme-neoliberal-qui-a-fait-tant-de-mal-a-l-europe-du-sud-a-ete-corrige_6046923_3210.html (accessed July 15, 2021).

OECD. 2021. "Addressing the tax challenges arising from the digitalisation of the economy," July, https://www.oecd.org/tax/beps/brochure-addressing-the-tax-challenges-arising-from-the-digitalisation-of-the-economy-july-2021.pdf (accessed August 11, 2021).

Papadopoulos, Ioannis. 2013. The Efficiency of Debt Crisis Management by EU Mechanisms: Lessons from the Greek Case. In *Reflections on the Greek Sovereign Debt Crisis: The EU Institutional Framework, Economic Adjustment in an Extensive Shadow Economy*. Edited by Aristidis Bitzenis, Ioannis Papadopoulos, and Vasileios A. Vlachos. Cambridge Scholars Publishing.

Paulic, Solenn. 2020. "UE : les détails d'un accord «historique» qui satisfait presque tout le monde," Le Temps, 21 July, https://www.letemps.ch/monde/ue-details-dun-accord-historique-satisfait-presque-monde (accessed July 15, 2021).

Présidence de la République. 2020. “Initiative franco-allemande pour la relance européenne face à la crise du coronavirus,” 18 May, https://www.elysee.fr/emmanuel-macron/2020/05/18/initiative-franco-allemande-pour-la-relance-europeenne-face-a-la-crise-du-coronavirus (accessed July 14, 2021).

Requena, Pilar. 2020. “Angela Merkel and how managing the pandemic crisis can mark her legacy,” Instituto Español de Estudios Estratégicos, Opinion Paper 104/2020, 14 July, http://www.ieee.es/Galerias/fichero/docs_opinion/2020/DIEEEO104_2020PIREQ_Merkel-ENG.pdf (accessed July 14, 2021).

Reuters staff. 2020. “Spain calls for Marshall plan, European debt mutualisation - newspaper,” Reuters, 5 April, https://www.reuters.com/article/health-coronavirus-spain-primeminister-idUSL8N2BT0NM (accessed July 15, 2021).

Schäuble, Wolfgang. 2020. “Aus eigener Stärke [Our own resources],” Frankfurter Allgemeine Zeitung, 6 July, https://www.faz.net/aktuell/politik/inland/gastbeitrag-wolfgang-schaeuble-aus-eigener-staerke-16846887.html (accessed July 15, 2021).

TEU. “Consolidated version of the Treaty on European Union,” OJ C 326, 26.10.2012, 13–390.

TFEU. “Consolidated version of the Treaty on the Functioning of the European Union,” OJ C 326, 26.10.2012, 47–390.

WHO. 2021. “WHO Coronavirus (COVID-19) Dashboard,” Situation by Region, Country, Territory & Area, https://covid19.who.int/table (accessed August 10, 2021).

Wieder, Thomas. 2020. “Angela Merkel : «Il est dans l’intérêt de l’Allemagne que l’UE ne s’effondre pas»,” Le Monde, 28-29 June 2020, https://www.lemonde.fr/international/article/2020/06/26/angela-merkel-il-est-dans-l-interet-de-l-allemagne-que-l-union-europeenne-ne-s-effondre-pas_6044319_3210.html (accessed July 15, 2021).

PART C:

EU BANKING UNION

CHAPTER 5

MONETARY UNION, INTERNAL MARKET, ECONOMIC POLICY COORDINATION, AND THE EUROPEAN BANKING UNION: LEGAL TENSIONS IN TIMES OF ECONOMIC CRISIS

IOSIF KTENIDIS*

Introduction: The position of the Banking Union in the map of EU policies

The establishment of the Banking Union is seen as a major innovation in the constitutional structure of the European Union (hereinafter EU) that emerged without an amendment of the Treaties (Tridimas 2019, 25; Barrett 2019, 10). In a very expedient manner, within less than two years from the introduction of the idea and the basic elements of a Banking Union by the "Four Presidents report" of 26 June 2012 (Rompuy et al. 2012), the basic legal acts establishing the two pillars of the Banking Union, the Single Supervisory Mechanism (hereinafter SSM) and the Single Resolution Mechanism (hereinafter SRM), were adopted by the EU institutions.[1] The European Central Bank (hereinafter ECB) assumed the tasks conferred on it by the SSM Regulation on November 4, 2014 (art. 33(3) Regulation 1024/2013), while the Single Resolution Board (hereinafter SRB) became fully operational by January 1, 2016 (art. 98 (1) Regulation 806/2014). Without doubt, the expedient realisation of the Banking Union project is related to the severity of the Eurozone crisis, which was escalating at the time when the political and

* Associate Professor, Department of International Studies, Faculty of Law, Aristotle University of Thessaloniki (Thessaloniki, Greece).

[1] The SSM Regulation 1024/2013 was issued on October 15, 2013 and the SRM Regulation 806/2014 was issued on July 15, 2014.

legislative debate for the adoption of the Banking Union's legal acts was taking place. To the extent that the Banking Union was mainly conceived as a means of addressing the factors which led to the crisis and of combating the effects of the crisis, its "fast-track" design, institutionalisation and operation are explained and justified.

Crises, regardless of their nature, have always been a driving force for constitutional reform in the EU context. The most important amendment of the Treaty structure from the establishment of the three Communities in the 1950s until today, namely the Maastricht Treaty, has been largely influenced by the fall of the Berlin Wall and the subsequent emergence of a "new Europe". One common feature of the EU's response to crises is that the Union first acts so as to address the new economic and political realities, and it is only later that the legal framework necessary for the action already taken is adopted by the member states in the form of an amendment of the Treaties (Cremona 2011, 226-232). This course of action is not justified from a legal perspective; therefore it raises questions of democratic legitimacy and challenges member states' sovereignty. However, it is politically unavoidable if the EU is to claim and maintain its role as a crucial political and economic actor. More than this, because of the development of the EU as a political and economic project, crises can often only be addressed effectively at the supranational and not at the national level, even if the EU, as a political entity different and independent from the member states, does not possess the legal powers to take the action that is necessary to tackle the crises. This has been particularly evident during the Eurozone crisis, during which measures of financial assistance to member states facing difficulties in financing their public debt had to be introduced by the member states at the EU level, at a time when the relevant Treaty provisions, which were eventually amended, probably prohibited such a course of action. In such instances, the Court of Justice of the EU (hereinafter CJEU) finds itself in the difficult position of having to rule on a measure (EU or national) that appears not to be in conformity with primary EU law from a temporal perspective (because it was adopted before a Treaty amendment), while the measure itself is clearly compatible with the Treaties as applied at the time of the Court's ruling (Pringle v. Ireland, par. 73; Tuori and Tuori 2014, 149-150; Hinarcjos 2015, 123-127).

The establishment of the Banking Union does not follow the "action first – Treaty amendment after" model of the EU's constitutional evolution in response to crises. It appears that EU powers for addressing the crisis from this particular perspective (supervision and resolution of banks) had been granted to the Union by the member states before the crisis. However, some of these powers had not been exercised before the crisis – or, to be more precise, they had been exercised, but not in a manner which efficiently safeguarded the financial stability of the Eurozone, as it became evident by the crisis. In this respect, it might be questionable whether the Banking Union constitutes a novelty from an EU constitutional perspective. One might argue that the Banking Union is a typical example of a condition that is inherent in, and absolutely compatible with, the EU system, in the form it has been designed from the time of its conception in the 1950s: the Communities had been vested with specific powers in limited fields, but there was no Treaty guarantee that they would actually exercise these powers. As a matter of fact, during the first decades of the history of the Communities, the European institutions refrained from exercising most of their competences, mainly for political reasons, which were mirrored in the unanimity requirement that was introduced, as a political compromise, through the Luxembourg Accord (Weiler 1999, 31-39).

The same can be argued for the Banking Union: the empowering provisions (the legal bases) which allowed its realisation were part of EU primary law before the crisis. However, the EU institutions, for reasons related to member state concerns, echoed in the EU legislative process, did not legislate —or did not legislate in the substantive manner they did through the Banking Union legislation—, leaving the field open for regulation at the national level.

This is one way of assessing the Banking Union from an EU constitutional perspective, which stresses its non-innovative character. After all, the Banking Union has been established without a Treaty amendment, and no such amendment is required for its completion through the introduction of the European Deposit Insurance Scheme (EDIS), the third pillar of the Banking Union, which is still pending in the political and legislative process.

However, the novelty of the Banking Union is that its establishment required an extraordinary combination and balancing of various Union competences, in different policy areas, with member states' powers. The outcome of this delicate legal exercise is not the adoption of a single legal instrument, but the introduction of different legal instruments that, when examined together, constitute a single cross-policy legal structure, the Banking Union.

EU competence in the area of prudential supervision

The SSM Regulation legal basis

The first pillar of the Banking Union, the Single Supervisory Mechanism, has been established through the SSM Regulation, the legal basis of which is article 127(6) of the Treaty on the Functioning of the European Union (hereinafter TFEU). According to this provision, "[t]he Council, acting by means of regulations in accordance with a special legislative procedure, may unanimously, and after consulting the European Parliament and the European Central Bank, confer specific tasks upon the European Central Bank concerning policies relating to the prudential supervision of credit institutions and other financial institutions with the exception of insurance undertakings". This legal basis raises many systematic and procedural issues, which have been widely addressed in the legal literature (Gortsos 2019, 24-25; Wolfers and Voland 2014, 1485-1486; Lo Schiavo 2014, 120-122).

Systematically, article 127(6) TFEU is part of Chapter 2, titled "Monetary Policy", of Title VIII of Part Three of the TFEU, as it has been recently pointed out by the CJEU in its "Arkéa" ruling (Crédit Mutuel Arkéa v European Central Bank, par. 54). However, the powers which can be conferred on the ECB on the basis of this provision are not monetary. Monetary powers are attributed to the European System of Central Banks (ESCB) —not directly to the ECB—, and to the Eurosystem in particular,[2] through articles 127(2), 282(1) TFEU and 3.1 of the Statute of the ESCB and the ECB (ESCB Statute), which enumerate the tasks of the ESCB, while the primary objective of EU monetary policy, which is to maintain price stability, is defined in articles 127(1) TFEU and 2 of the ESCB Statute. In this context, although the Treaties do not define monetary policy (Pringle v. Ireland, par. 53; Gauweiler v. Deutscher Bundestag, par. 42; Weiss, par. 50), the CJEU has ruled that "… in order to determine whether a measure falls within the area of monetary policy it is appropriate to refer principally to the objectives of that measure. The instruments which the measure employs in order to attain those objectives are also relevant" (Weiss, par. 53). Prudential supervision of credit institutions does not fall under the monetary policy definition, neither from the scope of the primary monetary policy objective, nor from the perspective of the instruments employed for the maintenance of price stability.

---

[2] The Eurosystem, according to article 282(1) TFEU, consists of the ECB and the national central banks of the member states whose currency is the euro.

ESCB monetary powers constitute an exclusive EU competence (for the member states whose currency is the Euro), as it is specifically stipulated in article 3(1)(c) TFEU. Consequently, in the field of monetary policy, only the Union, and not the member states, can legislate and adopt legally binding acts (art. 2(1) TFEU). Obviously, this exclusive monetary competence does not extend to prudential supervision, which has been a task of national authorities up until the enactment of the SSM Regulation.

Prudential supervision: an internal market EU competence

Since prudential supervision does not fall under the EU monetary policy competence, even though the empowering Treaty provision is found in the monetary policy chapter of the Treaty, the question arises regarding which EU policy covers this particular EU power. Two EU policies appear as candidates for encompassing prudential supervision: internal market and economic policy. In the area of the internal market, the EU shares its competence with the member states (art. 4(2)(a) TFEU), while in the area of economic policy, the powers of the Union are limited to coordination of national economic policies (art. 5(1) TFEU), which, in principle, remain in the hands of the member states (CJEU View of Advocate General J. Kokott in case C-370/12, par. 93).

The function of article 127(6) TFEU rules out the consideration of prudential supervision as an activity falling under the economic policy powers of the Union. When this empowering Treaty provision is activated by an act of secondary law, an EU institution (the ECB) undertakes specific powers, previously exercised by the member states. This conferral of powers from the member states to the Union is limited both by the empowering provision itself, which does not allow the conferral of all but only of specific supervisory tasks, and by the secondary law act, which activates the provision (the SSM Regulation). As a consequence, in this particular area (prudential supervision), powers not conferred upon the Union through the SSM Regulation remain with the member states, in conformity with the principle of preemption, which applies to shared EU and member states competences on the basis of article 2(2) TFEU. However, after the activation of article 127(6) TFEU, the specific banking supervisory powers conferred upon the ECB through the SSM Regulation cannot be exercised anymore by the member states. Such a transfer of powers cannot occur in the area of economic policy, in which the actual power remains with the member states, in spite of the strong coordination of member states' economic policies at the EU level introduced through the Six-Pack and the Two-Pack legislation and the Fiscal Compact (Amtenbrink 2015, 740-748).

The exclusion of economic policy as a competence that can encompass prudential supervision leads to the internal market being the only EU competence which can accommodate the powers attributed to the ECB by the activation of article 127(6) TFEU. This conclusion is in line with the substantial activity that is supervised by the ECB. EU banking legislation, which constitutes the "Single Rulebook"[3] —the compliance with which is supervised by the competent (national or EU) authorities—, has been adopted at the EU level by resorting to internal market legal bases. In the same context, the wording of article 127(6) TFEU confirms the internal market relevance of this provision, because it applies to supervision of "credit institutions and other financial institutions". From this perspective, it could be argued that, in principle, article 127(6) TFEU allows the conferral to the ECB of micro-supervisory powers of individual undertakings that are internal market actors, without covering the transfer of macro-prudential duties that are related to the stability of the financial system in general. Consequently, prudential supervision falls under the internal market EU competence, which is shared with the member states according to article 4(2)(a) of TFEU (Tuominen 2017, 1359).

Prudential supervision: a shared competence

As the CJEU ruled in its "L-Bank" judgment, through the SSM Regulation certain supervisory tasks have been attributed exclusively to the ECB (Landeskreditbank Baden-Württemberg – Förderbank (L-Bank) v. European Central Bank, par. 49). This ruling does not mean that through this act all aspects of prudential supervision fall under the exclusive ECB competence. Other supervisory tasks (for example, supervision of less significant institutions) remain in the sphere of national competence. However, the fact that prudential supervision is a shared competence, which falls under the EU internal market powers, should not rule out, in principle, the full conferral of all supervision of credit institutions to the ECB. In the field of shared competences, the EU institutions decide to which extent they will exercise their Treaty powers through secondary

[3] The basic acts in force today comprising the Single Rulebook are Regulation 575/2013 (CRR) and Directive 2013/36/EU (CRD IV). These acts, together with binding technical standards produced by the European Banking Authority and adopted by the Commission, incorporate the standards laid out in the Basel III accord on capital and liquidity (Joosen and Lehmann 2019, 65).

law, and they can decide to fully cover an area of shared competence without leaving any room for member state action. Nevertheless, in the area of prudential supervision, it is the wording of article 127(6) TFEU that refers to the conferral of "specific tasks" to the ECB, which seems to rule out the exclusive attribution of all banking supervisory powers to the ECB.[4]

The fact that prudential supervision is a shared competence, although it is regulated in the monetary policy chapter of the Treaty, is further illustrated in article 127(5) TFEU, which provides that "[t]he ESCB shall contribute to the smooth conduct of policies pursued by the competent authorities relating to the prudential supervision of credit institutions and the stability of the financial system". This provision confirms that, until the EU legislator activated the legal basis of article 127(6) TFEU, prudential supervision of credit institutions (as well as the stability of the financial system), unlike monetary policy, remained a national duty, in line with the principle of preemption. The EU (in this case acting through the ESCB and not through an EU institution) is mandated only to "contribute" to the smooth conduct of national policies in these areas. After the activation of the legal basis of article 127(6) TFEU, the mandate given to the ESCB under article 127(5) TFEU still applies, but primarily with respect to national policies relating to the stability of the financial system. To the extent that prudential supervision of credit institutions is exercised directly by the ECB (which is a member of the ESCB, and actually, "governs" the ESCB through its decision-making bodies; Ziglioli and Athanasiou 2018, 611), the ESCB's "contribution" to national policies relating to the prudential supervision is limited to those aspects of banking supervision that remain a task of national authorities, according to the SSM Regulation.

Monetary policy and prudential supervision: the role of the ECB

The argument that prudential supervision of credit institutions falls under the internal market EU competence raises the question of the systematic placement of the provision enabling the EU legislator to grant prudential supervisory powers to the ECB in the monetary policy chapter of the Treaties. Should this lead us to the conclusion that powers of prudential supervision of credit institutions can only be granted to the ECB by recourse to article 127(6) TFEU because, although this competence is

---

[4] This is the position endorsed by the German Federal Constitutional Court in the judgment of July 30, 2019, 2 BvR 1685/14, 2 BvR 2631/14.

not monetary, it is closely linked to the exclusive EU monetary policy competence, which is exercised through the ESCB? Alternatively, could it be possible to assign supervisory duties through a different legal basis (with article 114 TFEU being a candidate) to another EU institution (the Commission) or to an EU agency (as it is the case with banking resolution)? After all, the objective of prudential supervision is to safeguard compliance with substantive EU banking legislation (the Single Rulebook), which is adopted in the context of the EU internal market regulatory powers. Also, assigning the task of banking supervision to an EU institution or agency other than the ECB would exclude potential conflicts between the monetary and the prudential supervision functions of the ECB, which is a matter that required complex arrangements in the drafting of the SSM Regulation.[5]

A first remark with respect to this question is generated from economic reality. As it was accurately pointed out in the "Five Presidents" report of 2015 (Juncker et al. 2015, 11), "a single banking system is the mirror image of a single money". In this vein, it is stated in the same report that "[i]n a Monetary Union, the financial system must be truly single or else the impulses from monetary policy decisions (e.g., changes in policy interest rates) will not be transmitted uniformly across its Member States". The uniformity of the financial system is pursued not only through the normative approximation of the regulatory background in all member states, but also through the attribution of prudential supervisory duties of all credit institutions participating in the same system to a single authority, which is the monetary authority.

The aforementioned economic assumption is legally enshrined in article 127(5) TFEU. This provision acknowledges the existence of a linkage between monetary policy and banking supervision. Therefore, it establishes a legal bridge connecting monetary policy to the internal market, which explains why the ESCB —which is entrusted with monetary duties— is asked to "contribute" to the conduct of prudential supervisory policies that form part of the EU internal market policy. It could be argued that this bridge justifies the decision of the drafters of the Maastricht Treaty to entrust banking supervision at the EU level to the supranational central bank (if and when article 127(6) TFEU is activated through secondary legislation) and, at the same time, to rule out the possibility of conferring prudential supervision powers to another EU authority or institution through another legal basis (Pizzolla 2018, 20). The choice to

[5] Especially article 25 of the SSM Regulation.

entrust supranational banking supervision to the ECB, and not to another EU institution or agency, originates in an evaluation of the significance of the interrelation between monetary policy and commercial banking activity.

It should be mentioned that this evaluation was not shared with the same rigour by all member states. Therefore, the formation and function of the legal bridge between monetary policy and banking supervision appear to be the result of a compromise reached among the member states at the time of the drafting of the Maastricht Treaty. In particular, it was not only the prospect of centralisation of prudential supervision at the EU level that was not shared with the same enthusiasm by all member states but, most importantly, it was the attribution of supervisory tasks to the ECB that was not unequivocally supported by all member states. Some member states, including Germany, do not follow the same paradigm domestically, and they assign prudential supervisory duties to national authorities other than the national central banks, in order to safeguard the independence of the central bank in the conduct of its principal task, which is to maintain price stability (Tucker 2017, 325).

The absence of a clear consensus among the member states for the establishment of a direct and undisputable link between monetary policy and prudential supervision, which would result in a constitutional attribution of both competences to the ECB directly through a Treaty provision (without recourse to secondary law), is mirrored in the procedural arrangements of article 127(6) TFEU, especially in the unanimity requirement in Council voting, which does not encourage the actual transfer of prudential supervisory powers to the ECB. This absence of a clear consensus among member states for the consolidation of monetary policy and prudential supervision powers in the ECB is not without significance after the activation of article 127(6) TFEU. It survives in the complex provisions of the SSM Regulation referring to the separation of the monetary and supervisory tasks of the ECB.

Consequently, it could be argued that article 127(6) TFEU is an internal market legal base included in the monetary policy chapter of the Treaties. It functions as lex specialis with respect to the other internal market legal bases, prohibiting the attribution of prudential supervisory powers to the Commission or an EU agency, and allowing the transfer of these powers to the ECB only with the consent of all the member states (Weismann 2018).

Prudential supervision and economic policy coordination

Article 127(5) TFEU does not only establish a bridge between monetary policy and prudential supervision; it also extends this link to the stability of the financial system. However, the stability of the financial system is an economic policy objective, according to the settled case-law of the Court of Justice (Pringle v. Ireland, par. 65), meaning that it falls primarily under the economic policy powers of the member states. The interplay between economic and monetary policy, on the one hand, and the internal market, on the other hand, which is illustrated in article 127(5) TFEU, reflects economic reality that has to be accommodated in the Treaties, and is mirrored in other provisions that form the economic constitution of the Union. Probably the clearest illustration of the inseparability of the three EU policies, in spite of their fundamentally different constitutional design, is article 119 TFEU: the first paragraph brings together economic policy and the internal market, the second refers to monetary policy, and the third stipulates that the activities of the member states and of the Union in all these fields must comply with the same principles (stable prices, sound public finances and monetary conditions, and a sustainable balance of payments).

The significance of this extended legal bridge that brings together monetary policy, the internal market, and the stability of the financial system in general, which is established through article 127(5) TFEU, is highlighted by the macroprudential supervisory tasks assigned to the ECB through the SSM Regulation (Amorello 2018, 265-336). Although article 127(6) TFEU refers only to the supervision of "credit and other financial institutions", implying that the scope of this provision is limited to the microprudential supervision of individual financial institutions, the SSM Regulation explicitly confers on the ECB tasks with a view to contributing to the stability of the financial system "within the Union and each Member State" (art. 1 SSM Regulation). These tasks include the ECB's involvement, not only in the microprudential supervision of credit institutions (which is mainly an exclusive EU competence under the SSM Regulation, as it has been ruled by the Court in the aforementioned L-Bank judgment), but also in the conduct of macroprudential supervision (art. 5 SSM Regulation), which remains, in principle, a competence of the member states, falling within their economic policy powers.

Nevertheless, the extension of ECB supervision to the macroprudential field, which appears not to be supported by the wording of article 127(6) TFEU, does not undermine the rationale of the Treaty construction in this area, and is probably endorsed by the development of EU secondary law. In this context, articles 127(1) and 282(2) TFEU specifically attribute to the ESCB the secondary task of supporting the "general economic policies in the Union". The drafting of these provisions is very careful: it encompasses both the economic policy of each member state and the (coordinating) economic policy of the Union. Also, complementing this task by mentioning that the ESCB's support should contribute to the achievement of the Union's objectives as laid down in article 3 of the Treaty on European Union (hereinafter TEU), the Treaties explicitly mandate the ECB to act for the benefit of the internal market, which is listed among the objectives of article 3 TEU.

Furthermore, the internal market-based EU banking legislation extends to macro-prudential supervision (Tuominen 2017, 1372; art. 458 CRR), although it is not related to individual undertakings, such as market actors. Most importantly, the European Systemic Risk Board Regulation (Regulation 1092/2010), which introduces a system of macro-prudential oversight for the preservation of financial stability, is founded on article 114 TFEU, emphasising, in this respect, the connection of financial stability —which is an economic policy objective— to the establishment of the internal market.

The procedural aspects of article 127(6) TFEU also support the argument that the prudential supervision competence of the ECB is systematically linked to the ESCB's exclusive monetary powers, so that only the ECB, on the basis of article 127(6) TFEU, and no other EU institution or authority, can be the recipient of the attribution of this particular competence under a different legal basis. In this respect, it should be noted that if the EU legislators could assign prudential supervisory tasks to another EU institution or authority through recourse to another legal basis, the unanimous Council decision required by article 127(6) TFEU in order for banking supervisory powers to be exercised at the EU level would be practically circumvented.

The executive nature of prudential supervision: an extraordinary EU competence

A basic condition underlying the division of competences between the EU and the member states is that EU competences are principally legislative in nature, while the implementation of EU legislation, which is mainly an executive function, is not only a national duty (as indicated by article 4(3) TEU), but also a national privilege, which should be respected by the EU (as is evident from articles 291(1) and (2) TFEU). The EU performs executive functions —by applying rules contained in European normative acts in individual situations— only exceptionally. Such exceptions are provisioned in EU primary law, most notably in the area of competition and state aid law. In this context, it is also argued that the EU competence for monetary policy is executive in nature, since monetary policy is not exercised, in principle, through normative acts (Waibel 2017, 90). Other exceptions can be, and have been, introduced through acts of EU secondary law, in principle by recourse to the procedural legal basis of article 291(2) TFEU, in combination with an appropriate substantive legal basis, or even without recourse to article 291 TFEU, when implementing powers are attributed to an EU agency under the Meroni doctrine (Meroni & Co., Industrie Metallurgiche, SpA v. High Authority of the European Coal and Steel Community) in accordance with the ruling of the Court in the ESMA case (United Kingdom of Great Britain and Northern Ireland v. European Parliament and Council of the European Union).

This basic principle, which forms the foundation of a system described as "executive federalism" (Schütze 2015, 304), is reflected — and reinforced, with respect to prudential supervision— in the legal basis of article 127(6) TFEU. This legal basis can be read as introducing an exception to article 291(2) TFEU, because it allows the conferral of implementing powers on an EU institution other than the Commission or the Council, which are the "ordinary" recipients of the conferral of implementing powers under article 291(2) TFEU. For this reason, article 127(6) TFEU can be further considered as introducing an exception to an exception: firstly, article 291(2) TFEU allows the exceptional curtailment of the member states' ordinary implementing powers by allowing the conferral of some of these powers on the EU (on the Commission and, under strict conditions, on the Council) and secondly, article 127(6) TFEU allows the curtailment of the specific member states' implementing powers in the area of prudential supervision by allowing their conferral on the ECB (Pizzolla 2018, 19). As mentioned before, the potential attribution of prudential supervision powers to the ECB is justified due to the link between monetary policy and prudential supervision acknowledged in article 127(5) TFEU. Therefore, especially in the area of banking supervision, implementing powers cannot be conferred on EU institutions by recourse to the procedural legal basis of article 291(2) TFEU, but the only Treaty-compliant method of conferral appears to be article 127(6) TFEU.

The particularly exceptional nature of the legal basis of 127(6) TFEU is not only illustrated by the unanimity voting requirement, but also by the practical exclusion of the European Parliament from the decision-making procedure. Although the regulation transferring banking supervisory powers to the ECB is a legislative act —because, according to article 289(3) TFEU, it is adopted by a procedure labelled as a special legislative procedure—, practically the decision for the attribution of the said powers remains in the hands of the member states, which act in the Council equipped with a veto power, without a decisive involvement of the European Parliament, which is merely consulted for the adoption of the regulation. It is the absence of a rigorous endorsement by the member states of the linkage of prudential supervisory powers to the exclusive monetary policy powers of the central bank that explains why the attribution of these powers to the ECB, although envisaged in the Treaties since 1993, did not take place until the Eurozone crisis. In conclusion, it could be argued that the attribution of banking supervisory powers to an EU institution through EU secondary law is governed exclusively by article 127(6) TFEU. This happens so that member states' executive powers in the area of banking supervision can only be limited in favour of supervision at the supranational level solely by the ECB, with the consent of each member state, due to the unanimous Council decision required in the legal basis.

Additionally, as has already been mentioned, banking supervision is an exceptional EU competence because of its non-regulatory nature (Moloney 2014, 1611). Attributing such an executive power to the EU for the centralised implementation of substantive legislation —regulating banking activity—, which is introduced in an area of shared EU and member states' normative competence, is another particular feature of article 127(6) TFEU. As a result of this particularity, the ECB is required to apply not only EU law when exercising its supervisory duties under the SSM Regulation, but also national law, to the extent that national law governs certain aspects of banking activity which are not regulated by EU legislation (Witte 2014, 89). Notably, national law that is applied by the ECB in the context of the SSM Regulation does not only refer to national acts for the transposition of mandates contained in EU directives, but also national rules that fall outside the scope of EU directives (art. 4(3) SSM Regulation). Such rules are procedurally first appraised by the national competent authorities. However, the binding acts are adopted by the ECB without being bound by the national authorities' assessments of national law.

The ECB would not necessarily have to apply national law if some of the supervisory powers conferred upon it through the SSM Regulation were not of an exclusive scope. However, as is clear from the wording of the SSM Regulation and from the Court's ruling in the L-Bank case (Landeskreditbank Baden-Württemberg – Förderbank (L-Bank) v. European Central Bank, par. 49), the scope of certain ECB prudential supervision powers is exclusive, meaning that when supervision is exercised with regard to these particular areas of the ECB's supervisory competence, all the substantive rules governing the supervised institution's activity must be applied by the supervisor, regardless of whether these rules have been adopted at the EU or at the national level.

The establishment of the SRM and the link between the internal market and member states' fiscal powers

Banking supervision and resolution as interwoven competences

The SRM is closely related to, and supplements, the SSM. The primary objective of prudential regulation is to safeguard the safety and soundness of individual credit institutions, which is essential to ensure the stability of the financial system (recital 16 SRM Regulation). However, regulation of banking activity does not rule out the possibility of failure of individual credit institutions. Accordingly, in order to minimise the impact to the economy and to the financial system caused by the failure of a credit institution, resort to a set of credible resolution tools, prescribed in law, is required, so that the continuity of the failing institution's critical financial and economic functions is guaranteed (recital 5 BRRD).[6]

As argued above, prudential supervision is an executive function, the objective of which is to ensure compliance with substantive banking legislation. In the same manner, banking resolution rules are enforced through an administrative resolution procedure. Through the SSM, prudential banking supervision has been centralised at the EU level, at least for significant credit institutions of Eurozone member states. This centralisation of supervisory tasks necessitated the subsequent centralisation at the EU level of resolution procedures for the institutions subject to the ECB's supervision. This concurrent centralisation at the EU level of supervision and resolution duties serves the objective of coordinating the executive functions of supervision and resolution, which are "interwoven"

---

[6] The Banking Recovery and Resolution Directive (BRRD) 2014/59/EU was issued on May 15, 2014.

(recital 15 SRM Regulation), although they are not exercised, in principle, at the same time: supervision applies during the "normal business life" of a credit institution, while resolution, both in terms of applicable substantive rules, as well as with respect to the administrative process that governs the implementation of the resolution legislation, is initiated at the time it is concluded —because regulation and supervision did not prevent the bank's failure— that the credit institution's "normal business life" is terminated. The strong relation of supervision and resolution is illustrated in the SRM Regulation, which states that "[s]upervision and resolution are two complementary aspects of the establishment of the internal market for financial services whose application at the same level is regarded as mutually dependent" (recital 11 SRM Regulation).

The SRM legal basis

Since transfer of bank resolution executive competence at the EU level is a corollary to the supervisory EU competence envisaged in article 127(6) TFEU, and in light of the fact that the latter provision does not provide a legal basis for the attribution of resolution powers and duties to the ECB, the main questions which arise, from an EU constitutional perspective, are which EU institution should be entrusted with resolution powers and whether an EU agency —either already established at the time of the foundation of the SRM, such as the European Banking Authority, or a new agency to be established specifically for this purpose— can be the recipient of the attribution of resolution competences. In the absence of specific guidance by the Treaties (in contrast to banking supervision, for which article 127(6) TFEU provides a specific legal basis), such a choice should have taken into account not only the various legal bases available, but also the general principles governing the division of competences among the Union and the member states as well as the institutional balance among EU institutions.

The questions of which EU institution can and should be entrusted with resolution powers, and whether an EU agency can or should be the recipient of the attribution of resolution competences, are primarily answered through the choice of the appropriate legal basis for the establishment of the SRM. In the absence of a specific legal basis (as was the case with the SSM), the SRM Regulation is founded on article 114 TFEU. The scope of this provision, with respect to the attribution of powers to EU agencies, was delimited by the CJEU in its ESMA ruling (United Kingdom of Great Britain and Northern Ireland v. European Parliament and Council of the European Union) just before the SRM

Regulation was enacted. Through the SRM Regulation, a special EU agency, the SRB, is established, which is entrusted with powers and duties for the resolution of those banking institutions that are subject to the prudential supervision of the ECB by virtue of the SSM Regulation. Also, a Single Resolution Fund (hereinafter SRF) is established which "supports" the SRM.

Having already argued that prudential supervision, exercised through the SSM, is in essence an internal market EU competence (although the legal basis for the conferral of supervisory powers on the EU is found in the monetary policy chapter of the Treaty), the choice of an undisputedly internal market legal basis (art. 114 TFEU) for the establishment of the mechanism that supplements the SSM, i.e., the SRM, seems to be conceptually justified. As a matter of fact, the establishment of the SRM on the basis of article 114 TFEU signifies the internal market foundations of the whole Banking Union (Van Cleynenbreugel 2014, 64).

Normative differences between the SSM and the SRM Regulation

Although the SRM is a corollary to the SSM, the SRM Regulation is considerably different from the SSM Regulation (Wymersch 2015). Firstly, the SRM Regulation not only transfers from the member states to the EU level certain administrative tasks related to banking resolution, but it also contains substantive provisions that govern the resolution of credit institutions together with the BRRD. In this respect, the scope of the SRM Regulation is considerably broader than that of the SSM, the latter being limited to assigning executive supervisory duties to the ECB for the implementation of substantive rules that are part of other legal acts. This difference reflects the distinct nature of the legal bases on which each regulation is founded. As noted before, article 127(6) TFEU is an exceptional legal basis because it does not provide for the transfer of normative powers to the Union, but only for the assignment of executive supervisory duties to the ECB. For this reason, the SSM Regulation does not contain any rules governing the functioning of credit institutions, while those rules have been adopted under different legal bases, namely article 114 TFEU, which serves as the legal basis for the CRR, and 53(1) TFEU, which is the legal basis of the CRD. Article 114 TFEU, on the other side, is the broader rule-making legal basis for the achievement of the objectives of the internal market. Accordingly, it justifies the adoption of substantive rules for banking resolution, while it can also serve as a substantive legal basis, as was specifically ruled by the Court in the ESMA judgment, for the allocation of implementing powers —meaning powers that do not lead to the adoption of measures of general application, but to measures directed to certain market participants (United Kingdom of Great Britain and Northern Ireland v. European Parliament and Council of the European Union, par. 108)— to an EU institution or an EU agency.

Additionally, while the SRM Regulation appears to have a narrower scope than the SSM, since resolution is only the last act in a credit institution's business cycle, it actually governs —from a substantive perspective— some aspects of the pre-resolution "normal" life of the credit institution as well, which fall, in principle, within the ambit of the SSM. This is because the SRM regulates the substantive content and the drafting process of the resolution plans of credit institutions before they formally enter the resolution stage (after which the SRB assumes its resolution tasks), and it also applies to the early intervention measures that are also adopted before the resolution decision (arts. 8-10, 13 SRM Regulation; Farina and Scipione 2019, 271).

Lastly, the SRM Regulation has an additional aspect that introduces a differentiation from the SSM. Through the foundation of the SRF, a direct link is established between the new EU executive powers in the area of banking resolution and the national powers in the area of economic policy. This is because it has been specifically acknowledged both in the SRM Regulation (recital 20) and in the Agreement on the Transfer and Mutualisation of Contributions to the SRF[7] (recital 7 SRF Agreement) that the EU does not have the competence to levy contributions on credit institutions, but this competence remains with the member states, which undertake, under an international law instrument (the SRF Agreement), the obligation to raise contributions on institutions located in their respective territories and transfer them towards the SRF. Such a direct link between the newly attributed EU executive powers in the area of commercial banking activity and national economic powers is not evident in the SSM Regulation.

The limited role of the ECB in banking resolution

The choice of article 114 TFEU as a legal basis for the foundation of the SRM Regulation justifies the attribution of resolution powers to an EU agency, the SRB. However, it does not rule out the possibility of

[7] The Intergovernmental Agreement on the Transfer and Mutualisation of Contributions to the Single Resolution Fund (hereinafter SRF Agreement) has been ratified by 24 states, including all euro area member states, as of 15 February 2021.

attributing these competences to an EU institution. As a matter of fact, the involvement of EU institutions —the Commission and, exceptionally, the Council— in the resolution process is prescribed in the SRM Regulation itself. The decisive intervention of the Commission and the Council in the SRB's actions ensures that the conditions of the Meroni doctrine —to the extent that they apply after the ESMA ruling— are met.

On the other hand, it is questionable whether the ECB could have been the recipient of banking resolution powers. Attributing both supervision and resolution powers to the ECB would certainly enhance the coherence of the Banking Union architecture, because it would complement the centralisation of banking supervision and resolution executive powers at the EU level with the concentration of both powers to the same EU actor, namely the ECB. Furthermore, the ECB is the only actor that could be the recipient of both supervision and resolution powers, in light of the fact that, as it has been argued above, article 127(6) TFEU prohibits the conferral of prudential supervisory powers on another EU institution or agency.

However, it should be borne in mind that enforcement of EU law remains in principle a member state competence. Implementation of EU law can be conferred on the Union in specific fields, either directly through EU primary law (as in the case of competition law, in which implementing powers are attributed to the Commission directly through the Treaties, or in the case of monetary policy, which is exercised through executive measures of the ECB), or, to the extent that the conferral of executive powers is not prescribed in primary law, through EU secondary law under the conditions of article 291 TFEU. As mentioned above, the latter provision allows the conferral of implementing powers only on the Commission, and exceptionally, to the Council. It is very questionable, in light of article 291(2) TFEU, whether such powers could be attributed to the ECB, which is an EU institution and not an agency —therefore the attribution of implementing powers to the ECB is not directly covered by the ESMA case-law. Also, it is equally questionable whether the exercise of banking resolution duties by the ECB falls within the tasks for which the ECB is empowered to adopt legally binding acts on the basis of article 132 TFEU. For this reason, although the decision not to assign banking resolution tasks to the ECB was a political one and the central bank itself was not willing to undertake the unpopular task of administering banking resolution (Schlosser 2019, 144), it appears that the Treaties themselves did not encourage the attribution of such resolution powers to the ECB. As a result, for a combination of legal and political reasons, the Banking

Union architecture entails an asymmetry from the outset: although the banking supervision and resolution are centralised at the supranational EU level, they are exercised by different EU actors, the ECB, on the one hand, and the SRB together with the Commission and the Council, on the other.

Nevertheless, the ECB does not refrain from any involvement in banking resolution. A careful reading of the SRM Regulation indicates that the ECB retains considerable, although probably indirect, powers in this area, including the power to assess whether a bank is failing or likely to fail (art. 18 SRM Regulation). However, as it has been recently ruled by the General Court of the EU, this assessment of the ECB is a preparatory measure in the procedure, which is designed to allow the SRB to take a decision regarding the resolution of the bank, and cannot, for that reason, form the subject of a direct action for annulment under article 263 TFEU (ABLV Bank AS v. European Central Bank, par. 36).

The limited role of the ECB in banking resolution is not incompatible with the general scheme of the Treaties. The Treaties do not establish an explicit link between banking resolution and monetary policy in the same manner that they establish such a link between monetary policy and prudential supervision through article 127(5) and (6) TFEU. Only such a Treaty-based link could justify an SSM-type involvement of the ECB, which is entrusted with the conduct of the Union's monetary policy, in supranational banking resolution which is an internal market activity. Accordingly, it could be argued that the limited role of the ECB in the SRM is not only politically, but also legally justified.

On the other hand, the lack of a Treaty-based link between monetary policy and banking resolution seems to ignore a basic operation of central banks, which is to act as lenders of last resort (hereinafter LOLR). Central banks are expected to provide credit to individual institutions facing liquidity problems in times of crisis. However, the line between illiquidity and insolvency is not clearly defined, and often insolvency problems of a credit institution are tackled with liquidity injections by the central bank in order to avoid resolution. Accordingly, it could be argued that monetary policy is economically linked to banking resolution, because only the monetary authority can provide unlimited liquidity to individual banks, as a means of dealing with insolvency and avoiding resolution.

The Treaty structure seems to address this pragmatic issue through the peculiar ESCB construction. The ECB itself, being an EU institution, is not in principle assigned with the task of acting as LOLR at the micro level, meaning that the supply of liquidity assistance to illiquid individual banks remains a member state competence. The ECB is mobilised only when liquidity assistance is required at the macro level, if there is a general liquidity crisis affecting the Eurozone banking system. In such a case, lack of liquidity becomes a matter of monetary policy concern, because it does not allow the transmission mechanism of monetary policy to operate. Accordingly, the ECB action of providing liquidity to the whole Eurozone banking system is not related to the potential insolvency of individual credit institutions, but constitutes a monetary policy operation based on article 18 of the ESCB Statute (Steinbach 2016, 361).

On the contrary, LOLR operations addressing individual credit institutions' liquidity problems are potentially related to the solvency of these institutions. In this case, the supply of liquidity at the micro level is an action that serves the preservation of the stability of the financial system, which falls principally under the economic competence of the member states. Therefore, such liquidity is provided by national authorities, i.e., the National Central Banks (hereinafter NCBs), through Emergency Liquidity Assistance (hereinafter ELA) operations. ELA operations are generally considered as functions falling within the national competences of NCBs and that are not related to the monetary mandate of the ESCB. However, even when NCBs exercise national functions, they still remain part of the ESCB. Therefore, NCBs do not operate autonomously when they provide ELA, as they do not operate autonomously when they exercise other national functions unrelated to monetary policy. Accordingly, the ECB has the right to order the suspension of national ELA operations on the basis of article 14.4 of the ESCB Statute, if it considers that the supply of ELA by NCBs compromises the monetary policy objective which is entrusted to the ESCB (Steinbach 2016, 369-373).

Banking resolution and economic policy

As it has been argued, economic policy remains in principle a national competence. According to the CJEU, the role of the Union in this area is restricted to the adoption of coordinating measures (Pringle v. Ireland, par. 60). EU measures have established a "regulatory framework for strengthened economic governance of the Union" based on EU primary law provisions, and supplemented by EU secondary law instruments and intergovernmental agreements (Pringle v. Ireland, par. 58), that admittedly limits substantially member states' discretion in the field of economic policy choices, without transferring the substantial decision-making powers in economic matters from the member states to the Union.

Maintaining financial stability is an economic policy objective (Pringle v. Ireland, par. 64). Therefore, the Court has ruled that the establishment of the European Stability Mechanism (hereinafter ESM) — that serves the objectives of safeguarding the financial stability of the euro area as a whole— by the member states through an international agreement does not encroach on the Union exclusive competences in the field of monetary policy as well as the EU economic policy coordinating powers (Pringle v. Ireland, par. 68).

The SRM is a mechanism that falls in the area of EU internal market competence because it governs an activity of credit institutions, namely their resolution, in their capacity as market participants. However, it also serves the economic policy objective of financial stability both at the national and at the Eurozone level. This is proclaimed in different parts of the SRM Regulation, with recital 61, in particular, mentioning that: "[t]he resolution tools should therefore be applied only to those entities that are failing or likely to fail, and only where necessary to pursue the objective of financial stability in the general interest".

The contribution of the SRM to financial stability establishes a link between banking resolution, which is primarily an internal market function, and the economic policy competence of the member states, as well as the EU coordinating economic powers. This link is justified by the main objective of the SRM and the Banking Union in general, which is "… to break the vicious cycle between banks and sovereigns" (Euro Summit 2012).[8] By establishing an orderly resolution procedure, properly financed by national contributions mutualised at the EU level, taxpayers' money collected at the national level shall not be used for the rescue of insolvent banks. Accordingly, the operation of the SRM should release member states' economic policies and EU coordinating economic powers from the task of addressing the problems of bank failures that have not been prevented by the operation of the SSM.

The link between the SRM, which has an internal market foundation, and national economic policies, is mirrored in the SRF Agreement. In recital 11, the Contracting Parties proclaim that the SRF Agreement "… is rather designed as complementary to the Union legislation on banking resolution and as supportive and intrinsically linked to the achievement of Union policies, in particular the establishment of the internal market in the field of financial services". The conclusion of an international agreement

---

[8] This phrase opened the Euro Area Summit Statement of June 29, 2012.

among the member states as a legal basis for the imposition of contributions to credit institutions for the financing of the SRF, in spite of the fact that these contributions shall eventually be mutualised at the EU level, is underlined by a presumption that the SRM has an economic policy element that falls under the powers of the member states.

The economic policy foundation of the SRF Agreement and the sovereign powers of the member states in this area indirectly affect the functioning of the SRM Regulation. The latter, being an internal market measure based on article 114 TFEU, is adopted by the ordinary legislative procedure, in the course of which the Council decides by qualified majority and no member state has a veto power. However, the SRF Agreement is based on the presumption that the main elements of the SRM Regulation shall not be amended, otherwise any Contracting Party might exercise its rights under public international law regarding a fundamental change of circumstances (art. 9 SRF Agreement). If such an instance occurs, the SRF shall become non-operational and, as a consequence, the SRM shall not be able to exercise its function without the funding provided by the SRF. As a result, through the SRF Agreement, the qualified majority requirement for future amendments of the basic elements of the SRM Regulation is abolished, and only a unanimous Council decision for the amendment of the SRM Regulation shall ensure that no member state shall annul the amendment and the SRM altogether through the exercise of its international law rights as a Contracting Party in the SRF Agreement.

Furthermore, the link between the SRM and economic policy is highlighted by the role of the ESM in the functioning of the SRM. As mentioned before, the CJEU has ruled that the ESM serves an economic policy objective that is not covered by the EU coordinating economic policy competence. This economic policy organisation established by the member states provides a financial backstop for the SRM, as is envisaged in the SRM Regulation (arts. 27(9) and 30(6) SRM Regulation) and the ESM Treaty (article 15), and as it is further elaborated in the SRF Agreement (recital 13). More specifically, the new article 18a of the ESM Treaty, which shall enter into force when the Agreement amending the ESM Treaty is ratified (art. 5 Agreement amending the Treaty establishing the European Stability Mechanism), provides for the grant of a backstop facility to the SRB "covering all possible uses of the SRF as enshrined in European Union law". Most importantly, the ESM operation signalled the establishment not only of the SRM, but of the Banking Union: it was the prospect of mobilising ESM funds for the rescue of Spanish banks in 2012 that led to the establishment of the Banking Union, in order to ensure that member states' funds, mutualised through the ESM, shall be used for the rescue of individual banks that are subject to EU supervision and resolution procedures (Schlosser 2019, 139).

Concluding Remark: The Banking Union as an internal market step towards the completion of the EMU

The establishment of the EU as a new institutional actor coexisting with the European Community, and the introduction of the three-pillar system with the objective of expanding the European integration project to the fields of foreign and security policy and to judicial and home affairs, overshadowed —from a legal and institutional perspective— the foundation of the EMU through the Maastricht Treaty. The international environment and the political and economic developments in the years after the Maastricht Treaty did not encourage a more in-depth analysis of the EMU foundations. The EU had been trying, not always successfully, to establish its position in the international arena as an influential independent actor through the activation of the newly established, but fragile in its conception, Common Foreign and Security Policy, while the right to move and reside freely within the territories of the member states, associated with the new European Citizenship, required recourse to novel third-pillar measures in areas unrelated to the basic economic field of Communities action, the Common Market. At the same time, the Union was pursuing simultaneously the ambitious, but mutually conflicting, objectives of enlargement through the accession of the Central and Eastern European States and of integration through the adoption of a "Constitution of Europe" and an "EU Charter of Fundamental Rights". These developments, combined with the relatively stable economic environment until the financial crisis of 2008, did not draw major attention to the also new in the European architecture EMU. The introduction of the common currency had been seen as a primarily technical exercise, which was left to experts, while the value of economic policy coordination at the EU level had been underestimated because the lack of it —as it was evidenced by the French and German unwillingness to comply with the mandates of the Stability and Growth Pact in the early 2000s (Commission of the European Communities v. Council of the European Union)— did not provoke any significant economic turbulence. At the same time, the internal market had been considered a project that was mainly finalised in 1992 due to the Single European Act. The fundamental progress in the area of the internal market was expected to come not directly, through further integration of the regulatory market framework, but indirectly, due to the influence of the common currency and the abolition of national monetary powers on the functioning of the internal market.

The financial crisis of 2008, which swiftly developed into a Eurozone sovereign debt crisis, brought for the first time the EMU structure at the centre of the institutional debate regarding the evolution of European integration. It also brought attention to the fundamental, albeit politically necessary, asymmetry of the EMU, which is that member states retain, in theory, their economic policy powers, but are deprived of the monetary policy tools that are essential for the conduct of economic policies in times of financial instability. The existence of this asymmetry had been acknowledged from the outset of the EMU, but there was no pressure to address it in times of financial stability (Lastra and Louis 2013, 60-63).

What was probably not equally acknowledged at the time the EMU was conceived was the significance of its interaction with the internal market. There are a number of provisions in the Treaties that link the EMU to the internal market, but they provide limited normative guidance to the EU legislators. The most prominent provision in this respect is article 3(3) TEU, which states that: “The Union shall establish an internal market. It shall work for the sustainable development of Europe based on balanced economic growth and price stability, a highly competitive social market economy, aiming at full employment and social progress, and a high level of protection and improvement of the quality of the environment. It shall promote scientific and technological advance”. Article 3 TEU enumerates the EU objectives, and it lists the establishment of the internal market in paragraph 3 as a different objective from the establishment of the EMU, which is listed autonomously in paragraph 4 of the same article. However, from the wording of article 3(3), it is evident that the establishment of the internal market is not only an autonomous objective having a value of its own, but it also functions as an instrument which serves economic policy objectives (“sustainable development”, “balanced economic growth”, “highly competitive social market economy”, “full employment and social progress”), as well as monetary policy objectives (“price stability”).

Furthermore, it is not only the internal market that is mandated by the Treaties to contribute to the EMU, but the EU and member states’ economic policies are also directed to facilitate the establishment of the internal market. This is stipulated in article 119(1) TFEU, which provides that: “the activities of the Member States and the Union shall include, as provided in the Treaties, the adoption of an economic policy which is based on the close coordination of Member States’ economic policies, on the internal market and on the definition of common objectives, and conducted in accordance with the principle of an open market economy with free competition”. Indirectly, the same applies to the EU monetary policy, which is asked, according to article 119(2) TFEU, without prejudice to its primary objective that is to safeguard price stability, “… to support the general economic policies of the Union, in accordance with the principle of an open market economy with free competition”.

The Treaty mandate for mobilising the EU internal market powers for the attainment of EMU objectives, and the concurrent guidance to the member states and to the EU institutions to take into account internal market concerns in the conduct of economic and monetary policies, were not given specific attention until the outburst of the economic crisis. It was anticipated that the internal market could and would operate independently from economic policy, which was involving political choices and was left to the member states, and from monetary decisions, which would be based on technical assessments to be made by EU institutions. At the end of the day, if member states’ economic, and in particular fiscal, policies failed, also because the EU coordinating powers did not manage to contain unsustainable national choices, a member state’s bankruptcy would not influence the basic functioning of the internal market because the market operates at the European level and market participants are private undertakings and not the member states.

The economic crisis proved that this assumption, although politically convenient under a stable financial environment, was incorrect. The fiscal collapse of certain member states, which was attributed to national economic policy choices that had not been corrected through the EU coordinating powers, led to a fragmentation of the internal market (especially in the banking sector), which did not allow the EU institutions to perform their monetary tasks (Goldmann 2018, 293). Eventually, all the Eurozone member states, which were deprived of national monetary powers, could be left without any monetary policy tools, not only because of the failure of economic policy coordination, but mainly because of the fragmentation of the internal market. This development would compromise price stability for all the Eurozone member states because the internal market, although fragmented, would still remain a common market, meaning that no national obstacles to intra-Community trade could be raised.

It is interesting to note that, as the crisis demonstrated, the fundamental EMU asymmetry (EU monetary competence with no EU economic policy) could be addressed, to a certain extent, through the remobilisation, albeit in an innovative manner, of the most traditional EU powers, the internal market powers. As it has been argued, the Banking Union is mainly an internal market construction. Its infrastructure —the Singe Rulebook, complemented with the BRRD— consists of purely internal market harmonisation measures. The relatively novel addition brought by the Banking Union is the transfer of the power to implement EU regulatory measures in the banking sector from the member states to the EU level through the SSM and the SRM.

As pointed out in the beginning of this chapter, it is often the case that the EU is equipped by the member states through the Treaties with powers it does not exercise. It can be argued that the powers exercised through the Banking Union legislation fall under this category. They constitute internal market powers, which could be exercised by the Union, and they have been exercised to a limited extent even before the Maastricht Treaty. However, the introduction of the EMU necessitated the remobilisation of EU internal market powers in the sensitive area of banking activity in order to avoid fragmentation of the internal market attributable to EMU asymmetries. This is implied by Treaty provisions such as articles 3(3) TEU and 119 TFEU, but was not conceived as a regulatory priority before the crisis. Even after the outbreak of the crisis, the first institutional responses were directed to strengthening the economic coordination framework, without exploring the internal market tools that could contribute to the financial stabilisation of the Eurozone.

The member states and the EU institutions turned to the EU internal market arsenal as a response to the crisis only when it became apparent that member states' budgets would be unlimitedly burdened by the cost of rescuing the most significant, from the EMU perspective, internal market participants, namely the banks. Therefore, the existing EU internal market powers have been activated, through the establishment of the Banking Union, in a manner that bridges the gap between national economic policy choices and EU monetary policy, and consequently, mitigates the destabilising effects of the notorious EMU asymmetry.

References

Agreement amending the Treaty establishing the European Stability Mechanism, 28 January/8 February 2021, European Stability Mechanism, https://www.esm.europa.eu/sites/default/files/esm-treaty-amending-agreement-21_en.pdf (accessed March 5, 2021).

Amorello, Luca. 2018. *Macroprudential Banking Supervision & Monetary Policy: Legal Interaction in the European Union*, Cham: Palgrave Macmillan.

Amtenbrink, Fabian. 2015. The Metamorphosis of the European Economic and Monetary Union. In *The Oxford Handbook of European Union Law*. Edited by Anthony Arnull and Damien Chalmers. Oxford: Oxford University Press.

Barrett, Gavin. 2019. The European Banking Union and the Economic and Monetary Union – A re-telling of Cinderella with an uncertain happy ever after? In *The European Banking Union and the Role of Law*. Edited by Gianni Lo Schiavio. Cheltenham: Edward Elgar Publishing.

BVerfG, Judgment of the Second Senate of 30 July 2019 - 2 BvR 1685/14.

CJEU, Judgment of the Court of 13 June 1958, Meroni & Co., Industrie Metallurgiche SpA v High Authority of the European Coal and Steel Community, C-9/56, ECLI:EU:C:1958:7.

CJEU, Judgment of the Court (Full Court) of 13 July 2004, Commission of the European Communities v Council of the European Union, C-27/04, ECLI:EU:C:2004:436.

CJEU, Judgment of the Court (Full Court) of 27 November 2012, Thomas Pringle v. Government of Ireland, C-370/12, ECLI:EU:C:2012:756.

CJEU, View of Advocate General J. Kokott in case C-370/12 (*Thomas Pringle v. Government of Ireland*), EU:C:2012:675.

CJEU, Judgment of the Court (Grand Chamber) of 22 January 2014, United Kingdom of Great Britain and Northern Ireland v European Parliament and Council of the European Union, C-270/12 (ESMA), ECLI:EU:C:2014:18.

CJEU, Judgment of the Court (Grand Chamber) of 16 June 2015, Peter Gauweiler and Others v Deutscher Bundestag, C-62/14, ECLI:EU:C:2015:400.

CJEU, Judgment of the Court (Grand Chamber) of 11 December 2018, Heinrich Weiss and Others, C-493/17, ECLI:EU:C:2018:1000.

CJEU, Order of the General Court (Eighth Chamber) of 6 May 2019, ABLV Bank AS v European Central Bank, T-281/18, ECLI:EU:T:2019:296.

CJEU, Judgment of the Court (First Chamber) of 8 May 2019, Landeskreditbank Baden-Württemberg – Förderbank (L-Bank) v European Central Bank, C-450/17 P, ECLI:EU:C:2019:372.

CJEU, Judgment of the Court (First Chamber) of 2 October 2019, Crédit Mutuel Arkéa v European Central Bank, C-152/18 P and C-153/18P (Joined Cases), ECLI:EU:C:2019:810.

Cremona, Marise. 2011. External Relations and External Competence of the European Union: The Emergence of an Integrated Policy. In *The Evolution of EU Law*. 2nd ed. Edited by Paul Craig and Gráinne De Búrca. Oxford: Oxford University Press.

Directive 2014/59/EU of the European Parliament and of the Council of 15 May 2014 establishing a framework for the recovery and resolution of credit institutions and investment firms and amending Council Directive 82/891/EEC, and Directives 2001/24/EC, 2002/47/EC, 2004/25/EC, 2005/56/EC, 2007/36/EC, 2011/35/EU, 2012/30/EU and 2013/36/EU, and Regulations (EU) No 1093/2010 and (EU) No 648/2012, of the European Parliament and of the Council. 2014. OJ L 173: 190–348.

Directive 2013/36/EU of the European Parliament and of the Council of 26 June 2013 on access to the activity of credit institutions and the prudential supervision of credit institutions and investment firms, amending Directive 2002/87/EC and repealing Directives 2006/48/EC and 2006/49/EC. 2013. OJ L 176: 338–436.

Euro Summit. 2012. Euro Area Summit Statement, 29 June, https://www.bankingsupervision.europa.eu/about/milestones/shared/pdf/2012-06-29_euro_area_summit_statement_en.pdf (accessed March 6, 2021).

European Council. 2019. Eurogroup Statement on the follow-up of the 29 June Euro Summit, 9 July, https://www.consilium.europa.eu/media/25702/131648.pdf (accessed March 6, 2021).

Farina, Marilena Rispoli, and Luigi Scipione. 2019. Recovery and Resolution Planning. In *The Palgrave Handbook of European Banking Union Law*. Edited by Mario Chiti and Vittorio Santoro. Cham: Palgrave Macmillan.

Goldmann, Matthias. 2018. United in Diversity? The Relationship between Monetary Policy and Prudential Supervision in the Banking Union. *European Constitutional Law Review* 14, no.2: 283–310.

Gortsos, Christos. 2019. European Banking Union Within the System of European Banking and Monetary Law. In *The Palgrave Handbook of*

European Banking Union Law. Edited by Mario Chiti and Vittorio Santoro. Cham: Palgrave Macmillan.

Hinarejos, Alicia. 2015. *The Euro Area Crisis in Constitutional Perspective*. Oxford: Oxford University Press.

Intergovernmental Agreement on the Transfer and Mutualisation of Contributions to the Single Resolution Fund (SRF Agreement), https://data.consilium.europa.eu/doc/document/ST%208457%202014%20INIT/EN/pdf (accessed March 7, 2021).

Joosen, Bart, and Matthias Lehmann. 2019. Proportionality in the Single Rule Book. In *The Palgrave Handbook of European Banking Union Law*. Edited by Mario Chiti and Vittorio Santoro. Cham: Palgrave Macmillan.

Juncker, Jean-Claude, Donald Tusk, Jeroen Dijsselbloem, Mario Draghi, and Martin Schultz. 2015. "The Five Presidents' Report: Completing Europe's Economic and Monetary Union," 22 June, https://ec.europa.eu/commission/sites/beta-political/files/5-presidents-report_en.pdf (accessed March 6, 2021).

Lastra, Rosa, and Jean Victor Louis. 2013. European Economic and Monetary Union: History, Trends, and Prospects. *Yearbook of European Law* 32, no.1: 57–206.

Lo Schiavo, Gianni. 2014. From National Banking Supervision to a Centralized Model of Prudential Supervision in Europe? The Stability Function of the Single Supervisory Mechanism. *Maastricht Journal of European and Comparative Law* 21, no.1: 110–140.

Moloney, Niamh. 2014. European Banking Union: Assessing its Risks and Resilience. *Common Market Law Review* 51, no.6: 1609–1670.

Pizzolla, Agnese. 2018. The role of the European Central Bank in the Single Supervisory Mechanism: a new paradigm of EU governance. *European Law Review* 43, no.1: 3–23.

Regulation (EU) 806/2014 of 15 July 2014 of the European Parliament and the Council establishing uniform rules and a uniform procedure for the resolution of credit institutions and certain investment firms in the framework of a Single Resolution Mechanism and a Single Resolution Fund and amending Regulation (EU) No 1093/2010. 2014. OJ L 225: 1–90.

Regulation (EU) 1024/2013 of the Council of 15 October 2013 conferring specific tasks on the European Central Bank concerning policies relating to the prudential supervision of credit institutions. 2013. OJ L287: 63–89.

Regulation (EU) No 575/2013 of the European Parliament and of the Council of 26 June 2013 on prudential requirements for credit institutions and investment firms and amending Regulation (EU) No 648/2012. 2013. OJ L 176: 1–337.

Regulation (EU) No 1092/2010 of the European Parliament and of the Council of 24 November 2010 on European Union macro-prudential oversight of the financial system and establishing a European Systemic Risk Board. 2010. OJ L 331: 1–11.

Rompuy, Herman V., and the Presidents of the Commission, the Eurogroup and the European Central Bank. 2012. "Towards a genuine Economic and Monetary Union," 26 June, EUCO 120/12 PRESSE 296 PR PCE 102,
https://www.consilium.europa.eu/media/33785/131201.pdf (accessed March 6, 2021).

Schlosser, Pierre. 2019. *Europe's New Fiscal Union.* Cham: Palgrave Macmillan.

Schütze, Robert. 2015. *European Constitutional Law*. 2nd ed. Cambridge: Cambridge University Press.

Steinbach, Armin. 2016. The Lender of Last Resort in the Eurozone. *Common Market Law Review* 53, no.2: 361–383.

Treaty on European Union (consolidated version). OJ C 326: 13–390.

Treaty on the Functioning of the European Union (consolidated version). OJ C 326: 47–390.

Treaty establishing the European Stability Mechanism, Brussels, 11 July 2011, European Stability Mechanism,
https://www.esm.europa.eu/sites/default/files/20150203_-_esm_treaty_-_en.pdf (accessed March 5, 2021).

Tridimas, Takis. 2019. The Constitutional Dimension of Banking Union. In *The European Banking Union and Constitution. Beacon for Advanced Integration or Death-Knell for Democracy?*. Edited by Stefan Grundmann and Hans-W Micklitz. Portland: Hart Publishing.

Tucker, Paul. 2017. Central banks as trustees for monetary system stability: combining banking supervision with monetary policy. In *Shaping a new legal order for Europe: a tale of crises and opportunities: ECB Legal Conference 2017*. Edited by European Central Bank. Frankfurt am Main: European Central Bank.
https://www.ecb.europa.eu/pub/pdf/other/ecblegalconferenceproceedings201712.en.pdf?b452bb9c54dca55f8f5673b21631a4fe (accessed March 8, 2021).

Tuominen, Tomi. 2017. The European Banking Union: A Shift in the Internal Market Paradigm? *Common Market Law Review* 54, no.5: 1359–1380.

Tuori, Kaarlo, and Klaus Tuori. 2014. *The Eurozone Crisis: A Constitutional Analysis*. Cambridge: Cambridge University Press.

Van Cleynenbreugel, P. 2014. Meroni Circumvented? Article 114 TFEU and EU Regulatory Agencies, *Maastricht Journal of European and Comparative Law* 2, no.1: 64–88.

Waibel, Michael. 2017. Monetary Policy: An Exclusive Competence Only in Name?. In *The Division of Competences between the EU and the Member States: Reflections on the Past, the Present and the Feature*. Edited by Sacha Garben, and Inge Govaere. Hart Publishing.

Weiler, Joseph H. H. 1999. *The Constitution of Europe: 'Do the New Clothes Have an Emperor?' and Other Essays on European Integration*. Cambridge: Cambridge University Press.

Weismann, Paul. 2018. The European Central Bank under the Single Supervisory Mechanism: Cooperation, Delegation, and Reverse Majority Voting. *European Journal of Current Legal Issues* 24, no.1.

Witte, Andreas. 2014. The Application of National Banking Supervision Law by the ECB: Three Parallel Modes of Executing EU Law? *Maastricht Journal of European and Comparative Law* 21, no.1: 89–109.

Wolfers, Benedikt, and Thomas Voland. 2014. Level the Playing Field: The New Supervision of Credit Institutions by the European Central Bank. *Common Market Law Review* 51, no.6: 1463–1495.

Wymersch, Eddy. 2015. "Banking Union: Aspects of the Single Supervisory Mechanism and the Single Resolution Mechanism compared," *ECGI Law Working Paper*, No. 290/2015, 28 April, https://papers.ssrn.com/sol3/papers.cfm?abstract_id=2599502 (accessed March 8, 2021).

Ziglioli, Chiara, and Phoebus Athanasiou. 2018. The European Central Bank. In *Oxford Principles of European Union Law, Vol. 1: The European Union Legal Order*. Edited by Robert Schütze and Takis Tridimas. Oxford: Oxford University Press.

CHAPTER 6

THE STRUCTURAL BANKING REFORM PROJECT OF THE EU: TOWARDS A EUROPEAN GLASS-STEAGALL ACT?

IOANNIS PAPADOPOULOS*,
APOSTOLOS KIOHOS**
& NIKOLAOS STOUPOS***

Introduction

During the last decades, the size of the European Union's (hereinafter EU) financial system has increased rapidly, significantly outpacing its Gross Domestic Product (hereinafter GDP) growth. EU financial institutions, and banks in particular, have expanded and become more complex. This has led to the emergence of large financial "one-stop shops" combining within one entity or group the provision of a diverse set of banking services, roughly retail and commercial, on the one hand, and wholesale and investment, on the other. This process allowed banks to provide a broader range of services to their clients by using economies of scale and scope (the "universal banking" model). Notwithstanding these benefits, the unprecedented state aid to banks following the financial crisis ("bail-outs") has clearly illustrated the negative impact on financial

* Associate Professor and Director, Centre for Research on Democracy and Law, Department of International and European Studies, University of Macedonia (Thessaloniki, Greece).

** Associate Professor, Department of International and European Studies, University of Macedonia (Thessaloniki, Greece).

*** Post-Doc Research Fellow, Department of International and European Studies, University of Macedonia (Thessaloniki, Greece).

stability arising from an ever more global and integrated financial system with ever larger financial service providers.

As a response to the financial crisis, the European Commission launched a fundamental overhaul of bank regulation and supervision, in an effort to increase the resilience of banks and to reduce the impact of potential bank failures. Despite this broad-ranging reform agenda, concerns remain that some banks remain too large and complex to manage, supervise in good times, and resolve in bad times (Too-Big-To-Fail – hereinafter TBTF).[1] In this context, then European Commissioner and Vice-President of the European Commission in charge of Internal Market and Services Michel Barnier set up in 2011 a High-level Expert Group (hereinafter HLEG) under the chairmanship of Erkki Liikanen, then Governor of the Bank of Finland, to assess the need for structural reform of the EU banking sector. In October 2012, the HLEG recommended the mandatory separation of proprietary trading and other high-risk trading activities into a separate legal entity within every banking group throughout the EU (HLEG 2012), a proposal largely drawing from the so-called Volcker Rule applicable in the United States of America (hereinafter US).

In July 2013, the European Parliament adopted an own-initiative report titled "Reforming the structure of the EU banking sector" (European Parliament 2013) by a large majority. The Parliament called on the Commission to: (i) provide for a principles-based approach to structural reform of the European banking sector by reducing risk, complexity, and interconnectedness; (ii) ensure the continuity of retail activities; (iii) ensure that trading activities reflect underlying risk and do not benefit from implicit public subsidies; and (iv) ensure that the separated entities have different sources of funding, with no undue or unnecessary shifting of capital and liquidity between these entities and activities. In January 2014, the Commission presented an important proposal for a Regulation on structural measures improving the resilience of EU credit institutions (European Commission 2014a), together with a very extensive Impact Assessment (European Commission 2014b) that will be the focal point of this chapter's discussion on the EU effort to restructure its banking sector.

Following to an important extent the HLEG conclusions, the proposed Regulation concluded that entities within the same banking

---

[1] Too-Big-To-Fail is meant to cover Too-Interconnected-To-Fail (TITF), Too-Complex-To-Fail (TCTF), and Too-Systemically-Important-To-Fail (TSITF) (European Commission 2013, 1-29).

group must be prohibited from engaging in proprietary trading in financial instruments and commodities (art. 6(1) European Commission 2014a), and also that certain other inherently risky trading and investment banking activities —such as market making and sponsorship of risky securitisation products— can be separated from a banking group by the competent authorities if certain metrics are exceeded, so as not to circumvent the above prohibition by engaging in hidden proprietary trading activities (arts. 8-10 and 13 European Commission 2014a). It was also provisioned that trading entities may not carry out the basic banking activities of taking deposits eligible for protection under deposit guarantee schemes and of providing retail payment services (art. 20 European Commission 2014a).

Whereas the Council ultimately reached a common position on this proposal in 2015, the draft report by MEP Gunnar Hökmark stalled in the Committee on Economic and Monetary Affairs (ECON) because of unbridgeable political disagreements between the center-right European People's Party and the center-left Progressive Alliance of Socialists and Democrats. Finally, in July 2018, the European Commission decided to withdraw the proposal because of this continuing political stalemate and because its purpose had in the meantime been achieved to a large extent by other measures adopted at national level (European Commission 2018).

This chapter first makes a comparative assessment of the basic policy scenarios of the European Commission's Impact Assessment concerning the scope and strength of the proposed structural separation between retail and commercial, and wholesale and investment, banking. In particular, we propose a reading of the available materials that is alternative to the Commission's and that, by placing emphasis on the reduction of moral hazard and of capital and resources misallocation, tentatively concludes in favour of a very strong ownership separation (the Glass-Steagall model) instead of either an enhanced functional separation (the Subsidiarisation model) or a light ownership separation (the Volcker Rule), which are the two policy options preferred by the Commission. This tentative conclusion is then closely tested against an analysis of the original purposes of the Glass-Steagall Act in the US and of the problems brought about by a series of legislative interpretations over the years. Our assessment shows that this strict separationist model was proven quite impracticable through the years, since it was riddled with so many problems that it eventually became non-viable. The newest effort to regulate risky trading activity after the demise of the Glass-Steagall Act, i.e., the Volcker Rule, originated once again from the US, but its shortcomings have also become quite obvious, since this American structural banking separation model now in force has presented the same type of definitional and practical conundrums as the previous Glass-Steagall model.

This leads us to shift the perspective by examining a new model of structural banking reform based on the regulation of traders' pecuniary motivation in their specialised labour market, instead of threatening integrated banking groups with sanctions for lack of compliance with a ban on risky investment activities (most notably proprietary trading). We discuss the implications of such a trader pecuniary disincentive model, which is more liberal than the regulatory Glass-Steagall or Volcker Rule-type mechanisms. We conclude that as a matter of public policy, such a model is preferable for a future EU structural banking reform since it does not rely on complicated supervisory and corrective requirements, but rather on rational motivational mechanisms underlying traders' risky behaviour.

The discussion in the European Union

The problem of moral hazard and of resources misallocation

The overall objectives of structural banking reform are to reduce the risk of systemic instability by making it more difficult for banks to become TBTF, and to reduce Single Market fragmentation, since many banks operate across borders and seek to benefit from the opportunities created by divergent national legislations (Basel Committee of Banking Supervisors 2012). Within these overarching objectives, structural reform addresses the following microeconomic aims: (1) to facilitate bank resolution and recovery; (2) to facilitate management, monitoring, and supervision; (3) to reduce moral hazard; (4) to reduce conflicts of interest and to improve bank culture; (5) to reduce capital and resource misallocation; and (6) to improve competition (European Commission 2014b, 10, 25, 39). In this section, we focus on the interconnected issues of moral hazard and of resources misallocation.

Deposit-taking banks are by nature exposed to potentially damaging depositor runs. Therefore, public safety nets in the form of deposit insurance and lender of last resort facilities (as well as bail-outs) have been introduced. Despite these safety nets, deposit-taking banking groups are currently largely unrestricted in the type of banking activities they undertake, and they significantly benefit from the explicit and implicit public safety nets. In their turn, the public safety nets also have the effect of incentivising banks to expand and take excessive risks with the funds available to them because monitoring and market discipline is muted when risk is not appropriately priced (European Commission 2014b, 12). This is the famous "moral hazard" problem, a situation whereby a party A takes on an undue amount of risk because of the presupposition that a counter-party B will be forced to cover the former so as to avoid further damage by negative spillover effects.[2]

The basic problem with moral hazard is the signalling error in risk pricing because of the misalignment between public and private interests, i.e., between the cost of regulation and the risk. This happens in the following way in the universal banking model: The explicit and implicit public safety nets reduce disciplining incentives of depositors and/or bank creditors and lower a bank's funding cost, since there is the reasonable assumption that because of the guarantees and commitments provided to the investment bank by the commercial bank inside a banking group, the group is able to operate on an integrated basis across the two different entities, and thus to ensure competitive financing terms. This allows banks to expand and increase their debt issuance, and hence to leverage up more quickly (Buiter and Rahbari 2012). High leverage, in combination with limited liability, incentivises excessive risk-taking by banks even further, given the asymmetric payoffs to bank managers and shareholders, as upside gains are being privatised, whilst downside losses are being socialised (European Commission 2014b, 12).[3]

Because of moral hazard, much of the bank balance sheet growth that took place, especially after the abolition of the Glass-Steagall Act in 1999, was driven by intra-financial sector borrowing and lending, rather than real economy lending (European Commission 2014b, 13).[4] Of course, market-based and transaction-oriented investment banking activities can be scaled up very quickly and easily because of leveraging, contrary to relationship-oriented commercial banking activities ("boring banking"). This is why it is even more crucial to reduce the scope of the public safety

[2] A moral hazard is an idea that a party protected from risk in some way will act differently than if it didn't have that protection. In the banking context, this applies in the TBTF banks, who often take additional financial risks knowing they will be bailed out by the government (Duca 2013).

[3] Freixas et al. (2007) show that financial conglomerates utilise excessive risk-taking due to their access to the public safety net, and that this effect wipes out any diversification benefits.

[4] In March 2012, loans to households and non-financial corporations only made up 28% of total assets of the EU aggregate bank balance sheet.

net by targeting it as carefully as possible to those core banking activities that deserve subsidisation and protection because they address a market failure. The implicit public safety net also leads to a misallocation of resources, since the expectation of public support artificially increases the size of the financial sector in aggregate, hence diverts resources away from productive sectors of the economy (European Commission 2014b, 15).

The solution to the moral hazard problem must, of course, be systemic. Yet, it cannot be reduced to simply building up banks' capital requirements, either of liquidity buffers (liquid assets that can be sold without loss to meet unexpected cash outflows), or of solvency buffers (sufficient own funds to absorb potential losses). Capital requirements, which depend on the riskiness of the individual entity and/or of the consolidated group, will have to be complemented by structural bank reforms imposing direct constraints on specific activities (European Commission 2014b, 20). The key requirement here is to find and add rational disincentives towards banks that will keep them from excessively expanding their badly priced risky trading activities (Boot and Ratnovski 2012). Marginally increasing the private costs[5] of engaging in excessive trading activities of primarily intra-financial nature can lead to a decline in the number of such activities and hence, all else being equal, to a reduction in bank size. This would, thus, contribute to better deployment and allocation of resources towards the real economy. It would also facilitate the task of resolution authorities, which, in times of stress, would imply lower costs related to bank failures. This would benefit the EU economy overall, as public finances would no longer need to be imperilled to support failed banks (European Commission 2014b, 22).

The counter-problem of losses in economies of scope

At the same time, we cannot say that the widest and strongest possible form of structural separation between commercial and investment banking entities will automatically be the optimal solution since, depending on the scope of activities to be separated and the strength of separation, a degree of efficiency might in principle be lost, notably owing to reduced economies of scope. The Commission's Impact Assessment (European Commission 2014b, 52) makes much of this counter-argument in order to

---

[5] "Private costs" are the costs of a structural separation reform that will have to be incurred by the banking groups themselves, whereas "social costs" are the costs that will have to be incurred by society as a whole when implementing the respective reform (European Commission 2014b, 38).

propose a milder form of structural separation, namely either an enhanced functional separation (the Subsidiarisation model) or a light ownership separation (the Volcker Rule). It is of interest to take a closer look to the economies of scope literature in this context.

In simple, non-technical terms, financial integration has contributed to the convergence of, and decline in, financing costs for corporations and households and to the opening up of investment and diversification opportunities across Europe (European Central Bank 2012, 39-42). This has led to the emergence of large bank groups combining the provision of a diverse set of services. In their quest for economies of scale and scope, banks have also consolidated, first within national borders, then beyond (European Commission 2014b, 26). Alongside the core of the retail banking activity, i.e., insured deposit taking, lending to households and corporations, and management of payment systems, which are critically important for the continuity of a banking group, investment banking activities such as brokerage services, underwriting,[6] securitisation,[7] market making,[8] and proprietary trading[9] have gradually developed.

If we put aside accounting separation (i.e., the simple obligation for integrated financial services to make separate reports for their different business units and make them publicly available), which does not offer much, the two basic degrees of separation are: (a) functional separation, or

---

[6] "Underwriting" of securities is a typical investment banking activity in which banks raise investment capital from investors on behalf of corporations and governments that are issuing securities (both equity and debt securities) in return for a fee (European Commission 2014b, 28, n. 41).

[7] "Securitisation" involves the creation and issuance of tradable securities, such as bonds, that are backed by the income generated by e.g., an asset, a loan or another revenue source (European Commission 2014b, 28, n. 42).

[8] "Market making" involves the purchase and sale of financial instruments (government bonds, corporate bonds, equities, derivatives, etc.) for own account at prices defined by the market maker, on the basis of a commitment to provide market liquidity on a regular and on-going basis (European Commission 2014b, 27).

[9] "Proprietary trading" can be defined as the purchase and sale of financial instruments for own account with the intent to profit from subsequent price changes (European Commission 2014b, 27). It always involves an investment for direct market gain rather than a trade on behalf of clients for a commission. This type of speculative trading activity occurs when a financial firm chooses to profit from market activities rather than thin-margin commissions obtained through client trading activity. Proprietary trading may involve the trading of stocks, bonds, commodities, currencies, or other instruments.

"subsidiarisation", whereby banking groups are obliged to separate the activities of different business units into separate legal entities (European Commission 2014b, 29), and (b) ownership separation, whereby some banking activities will have to be wound down or divested from the banking group so as to reach separate ultimate ownership of assets supporting different activities (European Commission 2014b, 30). Under subsidiarisation, universal banking groups could continue to provide their clients with a diverse set of banking services, but they would have to structure their group differently, with some of the services provided in legal entities separated from the other parts of the group ("structured universal banking" model). This would mean that the moral hazard/resources misallocation problem will still exist to some extent, but that economies of scope will also be preserved to some (varying) extent. Under ownership separation, as was the case with the famous 1933 Glass-Steagall Act in the US, the financial power of depository institutions and, most importantly, the depository institutions' ability to engage in risky securities activities, are reduced; consequently, their managers —focused on prudence— are prevented from entering markets that are focused on risk-taking (Benston 1990). This strong degree of separation seems to put an end to moral hazard issues, but it also seems that some economies of scope, due to financial integration and diversification of risk management inside a consolidated banking group, will be foregone (European Commission 2014b, 51-52, 55-56).

It is very important to understand that in and by itself, the expected increase in private funding costs for the banking group due to structural reform not only is a good thing, but it is also a legitimate and meritorious proposal. The funding costs of the trading entity, that is separated from the deposit entity and hence no longer benefits to the same extent from being implicitly linked to the public safety net, are recurrent private costs. However, they do not necessarily result in any social cost, as the increased funding cost merely reflects the shift of bank risk and contingent liability away from the taxpayer and toward the unsecured debt bank creditors that should, in principle, bear the risk (and be properly remunerated for being exposed to it). The increased private funding cost for the bank reflects, and is being offset by, a decreased (implicit) public subsidy to the benefit of taxpayers (European Commission 2014b, 38-39).

There certainly are genuine scale and scope economies that will be lost by structural reform. Combining different activities within one institution may give rise to genuine economies of scope related to risk diversification, revenue economies of scope, and cost economies of scope

(The Clearing House 2011; European Commission 2014d). For example, integrated banks do have a natural advantage in acting as market makers because of the fact that banks have a variety of other relationships with the clients who want to make trades and the fact that acting as a market maker for a security is often a natural follow-on activity for securities underwritten by the banking group (European Commission 2014b, 40). There may also be genuine economies of scale as an increased scale may allow spreading fixed costs, which can reduce average costs. However, economies of scale are activity-specific and are likely to be relatively small, given that only large, TBTF banks would be subject to structural reform (HLEG 2012; European Commission 2014b, 34). After all, empirical evidence on economies of scale for large banks shows that economies of scale and scope are exhausted at relatively low levels of bank balance sheet size (European Commission 2014d, 176-179). In any case, economies of scale and scope should be evaluated *after* correcting for the implicit funding (and competition) advantage that arises from banks being TBTF (European Commission 2014b, 40-41).

Balancing the reduction of moral hazard and resources misallocation against the losses in economies of scope

Separating proprietary trading, market making, complex securitisation, and complex derivative activities will reduce excessive risk taking. Through subsidiarisation, these activities would not benefit (to the same extent) from the implicit public subsidies, which would also help to re-align private and social interests. This would entail different entities holding separate capital and liquidity buffers, thereby aligning the cost of regulation more closely with the risk, which would promote market discipline, and would also mean that the entities would have separate funding requirements, ending the risky cross-subsidy of trading activities with deposits. If subsidiarisation covers a wide enough range of activities, this would reduce risk-taking incentives by forcing the trading entity to internalise the true cost of its risk-taking and to more strictly separate it from the public safety net associated with insured deposits. The resulting increased funding cost would reflect the inherent riskiness of the activity (although systemic risk may still not be adequately reflected in the institution-specific funding cost). As a result, moral hazard in the trading entity would be reduced (European Commission 2014b, 46-47). Also, to the extent that the additional restrictions reduce the implicit public subsidies and introduce effective market discipline on the trading entity, the latter would no longer be able to artificially and aggressively expand to the detriment of the deposit entity. Hence, this would result in fewer distortions, and would encourage allocation of human and material resources away from trading and towards lending activities (European Commission 2014b, 54; Philippon and Reshef 2009).

Nevertheless, the European Commission itself states, in its Impact Assessment, that "[t]he extent to which funding becomes fully risk sensitive depends on the degree of separation" (European Commission 2014b, 47). Therefore, "[a]n important advantage of ownership separation is that, while intrusive, it is a pure 'structural' reform which after implementation would significantly alleviate the need for continuous enforcement and supervision of the separation. Ownership separation should effectively and significantly reduce the implicit state subsidy (expected bail out) enjoyed by financial institutions that are taking insured deposits and from that perspective remove the moral hazard linked to safety net coverage" (European Commission 2014b, 54). Things seem pretty much clear. The same goes with resources misallocation. Under ownership separation, "[w]ith the most risky trading activities no longer on its balance sheet, a financial institution is able to entirely focus on and allocate more resources to its core and traditional role of lending to the real economy and acting as an intermediary between savers and borrowers" (European Commission 2014b, 54). Ownership separation would eliminate the extension to the prohibited activities of the implicit subsidy resulting from the safety net. Those activities would accordingly become more costly, which would, other things being equal, lead to a reduction in their scale and by extension, to a reduction of systemic risk. Ownership separation clearly wins the day in terms of social benefits, as far as the strength of separation is concerned (European Commission 2014b, 56).

So what about its possible social costs that might offset its social benefits? Of course, ownership separation reform options are no longer compatible with the universal banking model that exists today in the EU. This certainly is the most intrusive form of separation, resulting in the elimination of economies of scale and scope, which argument nevertheless, as we saw, appears rather weak in the relevant literature. Especially for proprietary trading inside a universal banking group, these activities would instead lead to diseconomies, rather than economies, of scope through conflicts of interest, excessive complexity, increased risk taking, increased systemic risk, and even cultural contamination of attitudes towards business practices by risky behaviours typical of the trading floor (European Commission 2014b, 55-56; European Commission 2014d, 182-

183). Thus, at the end of the day, genuine economies of scope related to lost risk diversification opportunities seem to be mainly reduced to market making and securities underwriting, which are of course activities of great importance to the real economy, but —contrary to what the European Commission thinks— do not necessarily deserve to be linked to the public safety net, and thus to enjoy certain subsidies. The empirical proof for the economic rationality of this disconnection is the period stretching between 1933 (enactment) and 1999 (abolition of the Glass-Steagall Act). According to the European Commission itself, "[i]n the era when Glass-Steagall was in place, which went much beyond mere subsidiarisation reform options, the US economy has on average been thriving, compared to the current juncture" (European Commission 2014b, 72), and also securities markets prospered, whereas since its demise, we have been witnessing a steep decline in public equity markets and an explosion of opaque over-the-counter ones (Philippon 2008; Zingales 2012).

The importance of structural banking reform for the EU Banking Union

The framework for the Banking Union that is currently being constructed is meant to reduce the inappropriate links between sovereigns and their banks. Yet, EU member states may be reluctant to mutualise future risks through the Banking Union in the absence of structural reform and credible, orderly resolution mechanisms that would target the public safety net and its implicit subsidies to those core banking activities that deserve subsidisation and protection because they address a market failure. If not, aggressive balance sheet expansion, misallocation of resources to trading instead of lending, and competition distortions will continue to produce moral hazard, thus mitigating the willingness of member states to push ahead with the Banking Union (European Commission 2014b, 21-22). Moreover, uniform rules for the structural reform of the TBTF banks are particularly important for an effective Banking Union, since they will: (1) make supervision easier, by providing for one set of rules contributing to simpler and more transparent group structures; (2) facilitate the task of the Single Resolution Mechanism; and (3) limit the risks to be insured by a future EU Deposit Guarantee Scheme subject to risk mutualisation (and hence increased implicit subsidies) (European Commission 2014b, 24; Haldane 2012).

Some first conclusions

In the consultation of stakeholders made for the purposes of the Impact Assessment, consumer associations and non-bank financials clearly positioned themselves in favour of a "European Glass-Steagall Act". Corporate customers, while acknowledging the need to address the TBTF systemic problem, expressed opposition, mainly because of the fear of the impact of such reform on their financing cost. Banking groups, on the other hand, expressed a resolute opposition to even a mild degree of functional separation (European Commission 2014c).

Yet, as we saw, the issue is ultimately a social one: what is the degree of risk that a society and its components (depositors, consumers, taxpayers, and citizens) are willing to be burdened with so as to subsidise private risk-taking activity for the sake of economic growth? As the European Commission correctly says, "[i]n conclusion, the final balance between the additional benefits in terms of improved *ex ante* financial stability (due to increased resolvability, reduced moral hazard etc.) versus the increased costs in terms of foregone economies of scale and scope and operational costs in this instance is more a matter of political choice than technical ranking" (European Commission 2014b, 64). Regulation by the political sphere via the banks' internalisation of costs from risky trading activities, and the decision-makers' structural ties with civil society, are to be preserved under a rational cost-benefit calculus. It should not be enough to state vaguely, as the European Commission does, that "[g]iven the potential social costs associated with ownership separation, there is a strong imperative to be cautious as regards ownership separation of a broader set of activities at this current juncture. Ownership separation [of more than proprietary trading is] likely to generate social costs, uncertainty and unintended consequences that would be disproportionate to the benefits" (European Commission 2014b, 57). We should err on the side of cautiousness and risk-aversion of the ordinary citizen, as long as a clear political majority has not yet been formed to explicitly promote private risk expansion benefiting from the public subsidy safety net.

The discussion in the United States of America

The Glass-Steagall period of banking regulation: A promised land that ended up riddled with problems

Our analysis up to this point seems to lead us towards a structural banking reform closely resembling the American model of the strict ownership separation between commercial and retail banking, on the one hand, and investment activities, on the other.[10] This model is based on the US Glass-Steagall Act, which lasted sixty-six years from 1933 to its repeal in 1999.[11] But is the Glass-Steagall model ideal, or did it prove itself to rather be a mirage, a promised land that was, in reality, riddled with so many problems that it eventually became non-viable? In order to assess the true value of a Glass-Steagall-type banking structural model today, we need to discern the purposes of the original American legislation, followed by several problematic interpretations of its requirements over the years, which eventually proved the Glass-Steagall separationist model quite impracticable.

The purposes of the Glass-Steagall Act

The inquiry into the structural problems of a banking system must necessarily start with the exploration of the meaning of the term "banking" itself. The classical notion of "banking" is generally considered as synonymous with "commercial" or "retail" banking, and as such, is distinguished from other financial institutions' activities. According to the opinion of a US District Court judge, "[a] commercial bank… is an institution authorized to receive both demand and time deposits, to make loans of various types, to engage in trust services and other fiduciary functions, to issue letters of credit, to accept and pay drafts, to rent safety deposit boxes, and to engage in many similar activities" (United States v. Philadelphia National Bank 1962, 360). In this judicial definition of "commercial banking" we can find the core of classical, well-established banking activities and the essence of the fiduciary and mediating function of the banks vis-à-vis their clients: commercial banks substantially receive deposits subject to repayment, lend money, discount and negotiate promissory

[10] In an important recent book, Arthur Wilmarth concludes as well in favour of the Glass-Steagall model of breaking up TBTF banks (Wilmarth 2020). The author argues that this model would reduce the threat of contagion during a future financial crisis, and would also reduce the political power of the biggest US banks, which he sees as a meritorious goal.

[11] The Act was repealed by the Gramm-Leach-Bliley Act, also known as the Financial Services Modernization Act of 1999, codified in 12 U.S.C. §24a and §1831w. The Gramm-Leach-Bliley Act authorised national banks to control a financial subsidiary, or hold an interest in a financial subsidiary, subject to some conditions and requirements (12 U.S.C. §24a), and also authorised insured state banks to hold financial subsidiaries, subject to some safety and soundness firewalls (12 U.S.C. §1831w).

notes,[12] and manage payment systems. Even if policy considerations of "competition, convenience, or expertise… might otherwise support the entry of commercial banks into the investment banking business" (Investment Co. Inst. v. Camp 1971, 630), the fact remains that the abovementioned functions have always been at the center of classical "banking". It is also a fact that hazards and financial dangers seem to arise when commercial banks engage in the investment banking business, which mainly consists of the underwriting and selling of securities, with an intermediary standing between a corporation issuing securities and the investors who purchase them.

The Glass-Steagall Act was enacted as part of the Banking Act of 1933, which also amended the Federal Reserve Act and established the Federal Deposit Insurance Corporation (hereinafter FDIC), and is considered as a world-wide model of full ownership separation between commercial and investment banking activities. As the US Supreme Court summarised in its renowned decision *Investment Co. Inst. v. Camp* in 1971, "Congress acted to keep commercial banks out of the investment banking business largely because it believed that the promotional incentives of investment banking and the investment banker's pecuniary stake in the success of particular investment opportunities was destructive of prudent and disinterested commercial banking and of public confidence in the commercial banking system" (634). The Glass-Steagall provisions make up only four of the thirty-four sections of the Banking Act: sections 16,[13] 20,[14] 21,[15] and 32.[16] The legislative history of the Act makes it clear

[12] Cf. section 16 US Banking Act of 1933, where the activities "necessary to carry on the business of banking" are described as follows: "discounting and negotiating promissory notes, drafts, bills of exchange, and other evidence of debt; […] receiving deposits; […] buying and selling exchange, coin, and bullion; […] loaning money on personal security; and… obtaining, issuing, and circulating notes […]" (12 U.S.C. §24 (Seventh)).

[13] Section 16 of the Banking Act of 1933 limits commercial banks' purchases and sales of securities to agency executions made solely on a customer's order: "The business of dealing in securities and stock by the [commercial bank] shall be limited to purchasing and selling such securities and stock without recourse, solely upon the order, and for the account of, customers, and in no case for its own account, and the [commercial bank] shall not underwrite any issue of securities or stock", but clearly exempts sovereign bonds that are generally considered as safe ("obligations of the United States, or general obligations of any State or of any political subdivision thereof, or obligations issued under authority of the Federal Farm Loan Act… or issued by the Federal Home Loan Banks or the Home Owners' Loan Corporation;" (12 U.S.C. §24 (Seventh)).

that it was enacted as a strong policy reaction to the excessive security loans and over-investment in securities of all kinds during the pre-1929 Great Depression period, and its central aim was to refocus the banking services to the productive economy, i.e., agriculture, commerce, and industry.[17]

It is crucial to retrace the justifications underlying the prohibition on commercial banks from entering into the business of investment banking, so as to understand the policy determination that outweighed, in the American setting, the possible benefits from economies of scope obtainable by integrated banking groups. To this effect, one of the most vocal proponents of a radical overhaul of the banking sector after the 1929 Great Crash and the failure of the Bank of United States in 1930, Senator Robert J. Bulkley, talked persistently about "hazards" and "financial dangers"[18] that arise when commercial banks engage in the activities later proscribed by the Glass-Steagall Act. The primary one of those hazards was the direct risk that a savings and loans bank might invest its depositors' savings in imprudent stock or security placements in periods of

---

[14] Section 20 of the Banking Act of 1933 prohibits a commercial bank from engaging in the investment activities of underwriting and dealing through affiliation with any organisation "engaged principally in the issue, flotation, underwriting, public sale, or distribution… of stocks, bonds, debentures, notes, or other securities" (12 U.S.C. §377).

[15] Section 21 of the Banking Act of 1933 is the converse of section 16, since it prohibits any organisation engaged in the business of "issuing, underwriting, selling, or distributing… stocks, bonds, debentures, notes, or other securities, to engage at the same time to any extent whatever in the business of receiving deposits" (12 U.S.C. §378).

[16] Section 32 of the Banking Act of 1933 completes the separation of commercial from investment banking by disallowing any "officer or director of any [commercial bank]" from also serving as an "officer, director, or manager of any [organisation] engaged principally in the business of purchasing, selling, or negotiating securities" (12 U.S.C. §78).

[17] See *inter alia* the many remarks to this effect by the sponsors of the bill, Senator Carter Glass and Representative Henry Steagall, in the debate leading to the vote of the Act (US Congressional Record 1933, 3835 and 9884); cf. Preston 1933, 587-590.

The Glass-Steagall isolation of commercial banking from investment banking was eventually extended to multi-banking holding companies in 1956 via the US Bank Holding Company Act (12 U.S.C. §1841-1848).

[18] In the debate during the 1931 Hearings before a Subcommittee of the Senate Committee on Banking and Currency, that paved the way for the Banking Act of 1933 (US Senate 1931).

stock or securities deflation, because "the identity of control and management which prevails between the [commercial] bank and its [investment] affiliate tends to encourage reliance upon the lending facilities of the former" (US Senate 1931, 1058).[19]

But there were also other indirect and "more subtle" hazards stemming from the "promotional and other pressures" on a commercial bank that decides to go beyond its purely fiduciary or managing responsibilities vis-à-vis its clients (Investment Co. Inst. v. Camp 1971, 630). These risks can be codified under two headings: from the public's perspective, the erosion of public confidence in the banking system, and from the banking sector's perspective, the conflicts of interest arising from the mixture of banking and investment activities.[20]

Public confidence in banks is essential to their solvency, and since confidence may be jeopardised because of the potential association on the part of the public between a bank and its investment affiliate, "there might exist a natural temptation to shore up the affiliate through unsound loans or other aid" (Investment Co. Inst. v. Camp 1971, 631; cf. N.a. 1975, 1484; N.a. 1981, 106-107). Public confidence might also be weakened once bank depositors start losing money on investments that they purchased relying on the close relationship between the commercial bank and its investment affiliate. As a general rule, the pressure wrought by the promotional interests in the successful sale of securities might lead otherwise prudent banks to gradually become discredited because of their involvement in risk-taking that is necessarily incident to investment banking.

These same promotional interests might tempt a banking group to "make its credit facilities more freely available to those companies in whose stock or securities the affiliate has invested or become otherwise involved" (Investment Co. Inst. v. Camp 1971, 631), putting thus in danger the banks' ability to function as an impartial source of credit to businesses. Correspondingly, once a banking group has a pecuniary

---

[19] In this regard, Representative Henry Steagall stated: "The purpose of this legislation is to protect the people of the United States in the right to have banks in which their deposits will be safe" (US Congressional Record 1933, 3837).

[20] *Contra* Raab (1988, 615), who thinks that the "primary purpose of the Glass-Steagall Act was to ensure that banks would not divert funds from traditional, productive uses to more speculative endeavors" and consequently, "conflicts of interest and other soundness problems that could arise from bank involvement in securities underwriting or dealing were ancillary to that objective".

interest in promoting, underwriting, trading or distributing specific securities, this most probably will enter into conflict with its obligation to render disinterested and sound investment advice to its corporate customers, who might be pressured to issue a security, and even to use the proceeds from such an issuance to repay bank loans or to pay down bank lines of credit (N.a. 1981, 105). A bank might even go so far as to give out 'bad' loans to its clients, with the expectation that such loans would facilitate the purchase of securities underwritten by it, feeding thus the speculative greed created by the aggressive promotion of financial products to otherwise restrained and risk-averse persons.

All in all, the Glass-Steagall Act was meant to function as a prophylactic measure against the structural tendency towards excessive security loans and over-investment in securities of all kinds, produced by the integration of commercial and investment activities under one single banking group. The prohibition of commercial-bank underwriting of securities that it established was intended to promote banking stability by lowering the overall level of risk in the banking system, as a complement to deposit insurance that the Banking Act of 1933 established in the commercial banking sector. Such was the urge for the reduction of risk inherent in securities dealings, and for the elimination of the potential moral hazard due to the integration of commercial and investment activities, that a fundamental political decision was taken: the aforementioned problems of the banking sector could not possibly be resolved through any form of regulation other than an outright prohibition of the interconnectedness of commercial and investment banking (even though one might, in good faith, imagine some situations where trading in securities would not be detrimental to a banking group's solvency and/or to the overall banking system's stability; Perkins 1971).[21] That is why we must understand Glass-Steagall as a prophylactic model for the protection

[21] *Contra* Langevoort (1987), who thought that the Glass-Steagall objectives could have been accomplished equally well through regulation as by prohibition (690-691). Craft (1983) interprets the Glass-Steagall provisions as not intending to prohibit commercial banks from engaging in investment activities completely, since it allowed banks to continue low-risk related activities such as purchasing investment securities for customer accounts, purchasing limited securities for their own accounts, and underwriting government securities, predicated on a risk analysis of the type of security involved in each type of activity (99-100 and 109-111). Raab (1988) goes even further, arguing that the Glass-Steagall Act should be interpreted to allow banks to underwrite and deal in securities backed by their own assets, since the stated goals of the Act could have been accomplished through regulation as by prohibition (605-607).

of both sound risk management and systemic stability and of the distinctness of the institutional roles played by commercial and investment banks. Moreover, an incidental anti-oligopolistic benefit from this strict separationist model is that it prevents an undue concentration of capital or of authority over capital allocation via investment decisions in a small number of finance power centers that would dominate the economy by tying in, more or less voluntarily, customers that rationally perceive integrated banking groups as providing them with easier access to credit, and thus, as being superior over non-banking investment funds (N.a. 1981, 108-109).

The problematic interpretations of the Glass-Steagall Act requirements over the years

Since the enactment of the Glass-Steagall Act in 1933 and until its abolishment in 1999, capital markets had been evolving in a continuously rapid way. New securities and types of securitisation were created, old securities were changing dramatically in character, and the securities markets themselves were subject to transformations.[22] In the same period, the Glass-Steagall banking structural model seemed to have a growing difficulty in keeping pace with this new banking and finance landscape. The two main legislative aims that we have identified in the relevant literature —the fight against the erosion of public confidence in the banking system and the prevention of conflicts of interest arising from the mixture of banking and investment activities— were being thwarted because the American regulatory agencies and the courts constantly relied on semantic considerations in deciding whether an investment constituted a proscribed "security underwriting" within the terms of Glass-Steagall (Plotkin 1978, 411; Karmel 1980, 632; N.a. 1981, 110-112). The definitional approach of the term "security" proved to be quite fuzzy, since in some cases it was overinclusive (when the debt instrument in question was considered a "security", even though it clearly fell into some legitimate commercial banking activity; for example, loan participations, i.e., negotiations of large loans by a lead bank with the accompanying sale of participations to other commercial banks and financial institutions) and in other cases it was underinclusive (when the debt instrument in question was not considered a "security", even though it clearly permitted activity that the Act was intended to preclude; for example, commercial paper, i.e.,

[22] One of the first to have reflected on these changes and to have concluded that the Glass-Steagall Act was no longer working well as a regulatory scheme was Karmel (1980).

short-term promissory notes that financial and industrial corporations issue to raise capital). The definitional approach of whether a debt instrument is a "security", and if so, whether a bank is "underwriting, trading, or dealing" in such a security, gradually became outdated, since financial markets became more sophisticated and viewed both loans and securities merely as financing vehicles. Consequently, semantic distinctions came to be seen as matters of pure form, oblivious to the real function of financial markets. The formalistic administrative and judicial interpretation of "securities" actually served for some time as a barrier to entry in favour of incumbent market participants, and therefore as protection from competition.

This formalistic conundrum in the actual working of the Glass-Steagall regulatory scheme could not logically be resolved in any other way than resorting to a teleological interpretation or a functionalist approach (e.g., N.a. 1981, 112-114). Since the universally recognised purpose of the Glass-Steagall Act is to separate commercial from investment banking, in order to achieve the legislative purposes, we need to determine whether a commercial bank is engaging in a pattern of conduct that cannot be construed as permissible, traditional commercial banking, but presents instead the fundamental qualities of investment banking. At the core of the investment function of banking institutions lies the establishment of a network for sales and distribution of bonds and securities, and the solicitation of corporate issuers to support said network. The fundamental characteristic of such a network for the sales and distribution of debt and equity instruments is its promotional character, since a bank acts with the expectation of earning fees in the form of commissions from the sale of securities of non-financial corporations. Even if one accepts that a functionalist approach allows better implementation of Glass-Steagall, since it may be more consistent with the legislative intentions or the underlying philosophy of the Act, the fact remains that such an approach is a first breach in the wall of conceptual separation between commercial and investment banking.

A further problem in the interpretations of the Glass-Steagall Act requirements occurred due to the regulatory loophole in several provisions of the Act, since sections 16, 20, and 32 only covered national and state member banks, i.e., all banks that are members of the Federal Reserve System and thus are automatically covered by the FDIC. This regulatory gap allowed state nonmember banks, i.e., banks chartered under state law that may either obtain or forego federal deposit insurance, to expand their product offerings and therefore their balance sheets, as well as their geographic coverage, by circumventing the Glass-Steagall regulatory scheme. Even section 21, that applies also to state nonmember banks, was held not to refer to bank affiliates, i.e., companies effectively controlled by said banks (Board of Governors of the Federal Reserve Board v. Investment Co. Inst. 1981, 58 n. 24, 60). This regulatory scheme of incomplete separation between retail and investment activities was interpreted as reflecting the legislative intention of allowing some interaction between these two sectors, to the extent that it involved only low-risk activities not endangering bank deposits.[23] This assessment nonetheless produced problems of its own, since it was necessarily predicated on a risk analysis of the security involved in each type of activity, i.e., on a more or less imprecise functional evaluation, distorting thus the supposedly clean-cut distinction between authorised commercial and unauthorised investment banking activities. Once we accept a risk analysis as the distinguishing criterion of permissible bank activity, whereby an act involving some sort of "security" underwriting can be accepted as legitimate with regard to the Glass-Steagall Act if it does not pose the risks that said Act was designed to prevent, then we must necessarily allow the regulators, and eventually also judges, to assess the comparative risks involved in any new financial product vis-à-vis standard commercial loans. Yet, such an assessment is not really rule-based anymore; it must rely on the combined interpretation of several risk indicators and on the underlying policy considerations of the Act, i.e., ultimately on subjective interpretative criteria.

As the years went by, competition between strictly regulated commercial banks and wholly unregulated firms offering financial services started to increase, and this gradually led to a significant decline in the profitability of American banks (J.P. Morgan & Co. 1984, 20). This led to a growing chorus of criticism during the deregulation era of the 1980s that emphasised the need for a healthy banking system to operate smoothly, and therefore to engage in trading activities that would improve the banks' financial position, for the benefit of the general public and of the economy at large.[24] Since, as we saw, previous developments in the field of the Glass-Steagall separation between commercial and investment activities gradually eroded the strict definitional approach of "prohibited securities underwriting" in favour of a more indefinite functional and policy test, the

---

[23] On this interpretation, see Craft 1983, 95-101, 109-111; cf. supra footnote 21.

[24] The first comprehensive study to examine the separation of American commercial and investment banking and to call for a far-reaching deregulation of corporate finance in favour of increased competition for corporate securities business was Walter (1985); see also N.a. 1984; Litan 1987, 60-72.

pressure towards relaxing the prophylactic measures themselves started to give way to a new deregulating approach: the Glass-Steagall Act should either be entirely repealed, or should at least allow for more securitisation by commercial banks backed by their own assets, so as to augment their liquidity and to allow them to remain competitive in increasingly volatile financial markets.

In the 1980s, the Office of the Comptroller of the Currency (hereinafter OCC)[25] started to accept the purchase and sale of securities backed by pools of federally insured mortgage loans and issued by national banks, acting as principals and not as agents of their clients (Raab 1988, 607-615). According to the "transparency theory" of the OCC, these securities were considered as "legally transparent", since their holders have essentially the same rights, liabilities, and risks as if they were directly in possession of the underlying low-risk, federally guaranteed mortgage loans. This interpretation of securities' "underwriting" and "dealing" was held to cover only the process of purchase (underwriting) or purchase and sale (dealing) of another company's securities, either newly issued (underwriting) or traded in the secondary market (dealing). Such an expanded scope of the exceptions to the Glass-Steagall prohibition would actually allow the commercial banks to securitise any of their assets, regardless of their underlying risk, based on an inherently fuzzy definition of bank assets "held for investment, rather than trading, purposes" (Raab 1988, 614). Therefore, regulators would be entrusted with the task of ensuring that banks are securitising only assets that they either originated or purchased solely for investment purposes, and such an assessment would mean that "bank examiners would perform the following procedures: (1) review internal bank memoranda and minutes of Board of Directors' meetings; (2) conduct interviews with key bank personnel; (3) review the elapsed time between asset acquisition and securitisation and sale; and (4) review the bank's current and historical activity in transactions similar to those at issue" (Raab 1988, 614). Everyone can understand that this kind of banking supervision is very intrusive, and thus may produce serious administrative costs, without ruling out possible conflicts of interest otherwise than by regulating the securitisation process, and without excluding systemic risk otherwise than counting on the banks' capacity to avoid unwise loans and imprudent management in general. Such a regulatory landscape would effectively sound the death knell of the

[25] The regulator of American national banks, i.e., those chartered by the federal government.

Glass-Steagall clear-cut and strict separationist model regarding the structure of the banking system.

The Volcker Rule: The newest effort to regulate risky trading activity

Description and goals of the Volcker Rule

In 1933, the Securities Act of 1933 and the Glass-Steagall Act were enacted within the first three months of President Franklin D. Roosevelt's New Deal. The Glass-Steagall Act provided for the regulatory separation of commercial banking from investment banking (including securities underwriting, market making, and other capital market activities) and insurance. This created a US banking model that was quite distinct from the "universal banking" model in many other countries of the world, most notably those in Europe (Neal and White 2012).

One of the principal goals of the Glass-Steagall Act, as we saw, was to ensure that the US banking industry, which had just been provided with federal deposit insurance, would be safe and sound and protected from "non-banking" capital market risks. The idea was that federal deposit insurance created a contingent liability for US taxpayers, thus mechanisms had to be put in place to contain the size of this liability. One such mechanism was the adoption of restrictions on the permissible activities of insured banks, and the exclusion of investment banking and insurance from the permissible set was such a restriction. In addition to other factors, the Glass-Steagall restrictions were remarkably successful in ensuring the safety and soundness of American commercial banking (Calomiris 2000).

One of the cornerstones of the Glass-Steagall Act was the distinction between a loan and a security. Commercial banks were allowed to provide loans, but not to underwrite securities, whereas investment banks were allowed to underwrite securities. For numerous decades after the Glass-Steagall Act, this distinction was both conceptually and operationally useful. However, in the 1980s and 1990s, securitisation emerged as a major force in banking. Securitisation is a process whereby illiquid assets, like mortgages or credit card loans (receivables), are pooled together in a portfolio and placed in a trust, following which, claims are issued against this portfolio that are sold to capital market investors. These claims are given ratings by the credit rating agencies, are traded in the capital market, and have market-determined yields (Bernanke 2000).

One of the consequences of the rise of securitisation was that it blurred the boundary between loans and securities. Because securitisation is a process of converting loans into securities, banks were effectively involved in the process of securities underwriting when they were participating in securitisation. Carpenter et al. (2016) criticised the process of securitisation between banking entities as an economically impractical effort, which could hardly stick to the "letter of the law" of the Glass-Steagall Act. Additionally, according to the same researchers, during the 1980s (especially after 1985, when US commercial banking truly embraced securitisation) and the 1990s, the economics of the financial services industry gradually but inexorably eroded the *de facto*, although not *de jure*, separation between loan origination and securities underwriting that was at the heart of Glass-Steagall. Banks continued to play a pivotal and ever-increasing role in not only originating the various loans that were securitised, but also in making a market in the claims against bank pool loans[26] that were sold to investors. To a large extent, this relentless weakening of the separation provisions of Glass-Steagall was a direct consequence of market forces and the underlying shift in the economics of the financial services industry, rather than lobbying efforts or political forces (Neal and White 2012). Eventually, the Glass-Steagall Act was formally dismantled in 1999 with the passage of the Gramm-Leach-Bliley Act, also called the Financial Services Modernization Act. This act repealed Sections 20 and 32 of the Glass-Steagall Act and authorised bank holding companies and foreign banks that meet eligibility criteria to become financial holding companies, thus allowing them to engage in a broad range of financially related activities (Krainer 2012).

The Volcker Rule, contained in the Dodd-Frank Act, attempts to bring the situation around, in a manner of speaking. The Dodd-Frank Act does not re-enact the Glass-Steagall Act, but it does revive some of its features through limitations imposed on the ability of commercial banks and affiliated companies to engage in trading "unrelated to customer needs" and investing in, and sponsoring of, hedge funds or private equity funds. The Volcker Rule refers to section 619 of the Dodd-Frank Wall Street Reform and Consumer Protection Act. The Rule restricts US banks from conducting certain kinds of speculative investments that do not benefit their clients. The Volcker Rule prohibits financial institutions from

[26] A bank pool loan is a fairly new form of loan, used by US-based firms trading on public markets that need funding of under $10,000,000 (University of California 2020).

using their own accounts for short-term proprietary trading[27] of securities, derivatives, and commodity futures, as well as options on any of these instruments. The Rule also bars banks, or insured depository institutions, from acquiring or retaining ownership interests in hedge funds or private equity funds, subject to certain exemptions. Alternatively, the Rule aims to discourage banks from taking too much risk by barring them from using their own funds to make these types of investments to increase profits (Acharya et al. 2010).

The benefits from the implementation of the Volcker Rule

There have been multiple claims that the Volcker Rule is an effective method to eliminate risk and regulate the banking environment. There are five argued major benefits of the Volcker Rule for banks and the overall economy, according to its supporters (Elliot and Rauch 2014; Lehmann 2016; Krahnen et al. 2017):

- First and foremost, prohibiting proprietary trading activities from banks is believed to make single institutions and the banking system safer as a whole. It shields banks from market risks and high earnings volatility, and reduces the risk of systemic failure from common shocks or contagion.
- Second, banks will also be smaller, which, all else being equal, further reduces systemic risk. Research on the interconnectedness of different banking activities suggests that lower trading risk exposure also has a beneficial risk-mitigating effect on classic bank activities, such as lending.
- Third, prohibiting banks from private equity and hedge fund activities directly addresses one source of bank default risk. By studying the causes of bank failures during the recent financial crisis, one can conclude that private equity and venture capital activities contributed significantly to the banks' probability of default.
- Fourth, another factor contributing indirectly to future bank stability is an increased transparency and lower risk of fraud through the heightened compliance standards of the Volcker Rule. The Rule calls for a very detailed compliance plan, in which a bank has to list its securities positions and the reasons for holding them. It

[27] The Volcker Rule defines prohibited proprietary trading as "engaging as principal for the trading account of the banking entity in any purchase or sale of one or more financial instruments" (12 C.F.R. §44.3 (a)).

also has to be documented that compensation schemes of traders are not linked to revenues or income from proprietary positions. The fact alone that a bank has to actively demonstrate transparency in its securities-related business is assumed to deter fraud. Recent illegal trading-related activities, such as the cases of Jérôme Kerviel of Société Générale and Kweku Adoboli of UBS, might therefore be prevented in the future. Also, clients are no longer potential counterparties in banks' proprietary trades. Cases in which clients are defrauded as part of proprietary securities deals, like the recent scandal involving Goldman Sachs trader Fabrice Tourre, may therefore be avoided as well. Of course, most sizeable frauds involve the perpetrators' lying to their own management, so it is unlikely that these documentation requirements will completely eliminate frauds of this nature.

- On a more general note, many supporters of the Rule also cite a "cultural change" argument. Although rather intangible in nature, the argument states that in the absence of proprietary trading, banks may drift towards a more risk-averse business culture. "High octane" prop-traders are laid off or relocated to other departments, hence losing their —perhaps negative— influence on other employees' risk-taking behaviour. The overall approach of the bank to do business is therefore likely to become more conservative.

The concerns with the implementation of the Volcker Rule

While the intent of the Volcker Rule is to foster economic stability at the global financial markets and to minimise risk-oriented practices, the actual effects of the Rule are open to question. In specific, government agencies and official banking regulation institutions have reported that the Rule may prove difficult to enforce. Moreover, even if financial regulators manage to detect ways to effectively enforce the Rule, the economic impacts might not be what defenders of this law had in mind. The law could, in practice, end up having the opposite of its intended impact. A number of researchers (Carpenter and Murphy 2010; Whitehead 2011; Thakor 2012; Viñals et al. 2013; Elayan et al. 2018; Ando and Matsumura 2020) have discussed the disadvantages of the Volcker Rule's implementation to the financial institutions.

1) Increased volatility

Critics of the Volcker Rule argue that it will restrict the activity of market-making —which serves as a ready buyer and seller of securities— even though the law explicitly permits commercial banks to practice market making. Companies that engage in market making must possess a large inventory of securities in order to readily purchase and sell them. Their decisions as to which securities to hold are influenced by the expected changes in the prices of those securities. Since enterprises will be more likely to keep securities that they expect to appreciate in value, some have argued that market making is effectively proprietary trading by another name. Hence, it is entirely possible that constraints against trading in securities for banks' own accounts will decrease market-making activity among commercial banks (Elayan et al. 2018). A distinct consequence of banking institutions ceasing to conduct market making may be reduced liquidity due to the diminished ability of institutions issuing securities to find buyers for those instruments. Less liquidity will limit firms' ability to raise capital, which will make them more susceptible to negative economic shocks (both asymmetric and symmetric).

The Volcker Rule may also increase economic volatility for other reasons. Hedge funds and private-equity companies generally experience more difficulty in attracting investors as a result of limitations placed on commercial banks' affiliations with them. Actually, they will have fewer funds to invest in constrained businesses that experience trouble meeting temporary liquidity restrictions, which will lead to more business failures. Hedge funds and private-equity firms typically assume a far greater risk than most conventional financial institutions, in the hope of securing high returns (Jackson 2015). Businesses that face severe liquidity constraints in conventional markets typically have the choice to secure investments from such firms, but only by paying a substantial premium greater than market rates. The Volcker Rule necessarily limits the funding available to hedge funds and private-equity firms, thereby forcing them to be more discriminating in deciding where to invest their funds. Also, the likelihood of bankruptcies due to temporary liquidity constraints will significantly increase (Jackson 2015). The frequency and intensity of disruptions in the financial system, and consequently in the economy overall, may increase as a result.

In addition, proprietary trading is a lucrative source of profit for commercial banks. If the Volcker Rule succeeds in eliminating proprietary trading as a source of profits, financial institutions will have the option to pass the higher remaining costs of business onto their customers. In fact, the clients absorb the losses themselves, or replace proprietary trading with other profitable activities. Restrictions against proprietary trading could thus incentivise banks to become more dependent on real-estate lending, which is historically a volatile and risky market, for a greater portion of their earnings. This effect is exacerbated by the fact that the Volcker Rule restricts proprietary trading even at the level of bank-holding firms, which traditionally remained exempt from such regulation because they are not covered by deposit insurance (Carpenter and Murphy 2010).

Furthermore, speculative trading necessarily requires institutions to assume a certain level of risk. The trades that brought about the collapse of the subprime mortgage market and led to the 2008 crisis resulted from banks holding very highly rated mortgage-backed securities (hereinafter MBS) that were widely considered to carry little to no risk (Morgan and Sheehan 2015). As a consequence, had the Volcker Rule been in place before the crisis, it is likely that regulators would not have considered large holdings of MBS to constitute proprietary trading (Whitehead 2011). To the extent that regulators allow activity that appears safe but only turns out to be risky after a crisis, as tends to be the case in major market disruptions, the frequency of disruptions may not change at all or may even rise, depending on how effectively regulators identify speculative trading.

2) Difficulty of enforcement

A main concern with the Volcker Rule is that it will prove difficult and costly in its enforcement. One of the reasons for this difficulty of enforcement is that the Volcker Rule focuses on the intent behind trades rather than the trades themselves, and the specific restrictions in the law against proprietary trading and affiliations with hedge funds and private-equity firms require interpretation on the part of the regulatory agencies that are responsible for enforcing them. This might be the Rule's fundamental vulnerability. The confusion over the definitions of restrictions and exemptions made by the Volcker Rule could lead to greater volatility. Peter Wallison (2013) notes that "since banks will not know at what point permitted risk-mitigating hedging crosses the line into becoming proprietary trading in the view of regulators, banks may hedge less and will therefore exhibit more procyclicality and volatility in their returns". In fact, the Rule seeks to eliminate situations in which banks hold securities for the exclusive purpose of benefiting from short-term price movements, and regulators will essentially have to second-guess as to whether or not banks are holding securities for that purpose.

Some scholars have pointed out that the many exceptions to the Volcker Rule make properties inseparable from proprietary trading, and that firms will therefore be able to use legally permitted activities to trade for their own accounts (Ando and Matsumura 2020). Although banks have been shutting down their segments that were specifically devoted to proprietary trading, and will continue to do so as regulators implement the Volcker Rule, they might still be continuing to engage in proprietary trading, but secretly rather than openly. Depositors, other creditors, and investors will then face more difficulty in comparing options as to where to put their money, because risky activity may be deliberately hidden in response to the law's restrictions. Even if the law did not make exceptions for certain types of activities and simply banned proprietary activity altogether, distinguishing proprietary trading from trading on behalf of a company's customers could still prove difficult for regulators. This may occur because the same traders typically undertake trades that are made both on behalf of customers and on behalf of the enterprise (Viñals et al. 2013).

Elliot and Rauch (2014) predicted that the Volcker Rule in its current form will prove ineffective and counterproductive. Part of their reasoning is that the ability of the Rule to effectively deter proprietary trading depends on the ability of regulators to distinguish between allowed and prohibited activities in situations where the difference between the two is based on an arbitrary distinction at best. They argue that regulators, whose responsibility is to enforce the Rule, would recognise that market making can become proprietary trading if banks hold securities for the purpose of benefiting from short-term price movements rather than simply holding securities in order to facilitate purchasing and selling securities. In fact, the point at which market making becomes speculative trading depends on the size of the inventory and the types of securities in the inventory, and such distinctions are sometimes difficult to make. Also, the point in which a permitted activity becomes a prohibited activity will depend on an ex-post judgment by regulators. According to Elliot and Rauch (2014), the correct judgment will likely only be clear in retrospect, so the Volcker Rule will not be able to achieve an effective limitation of the overall amount of risk in the financial system.

Due to the expense and complexity of limiting the scope of banking activity through a regulation such as the Volcker Rule, some experts in the field have argued that a far simpler, cheaper, and more enforceable method of achieving financial stability would be to simply limit the size of banks, rather than their scope. Arnold Kling (2012) argues that systemic risk in the financial system can be addressed by simply breaking up the banks that would create systemic risk if they failed. A related concern is that uncertainty over how regulators will enforce the law could reduce activity in financial markets. Moreover, the Rule offers regulators the authority to subject banks to a "prudential backstop", through which they may restrict activity that the Rule explicitly allows (Elayan et al. 2018). Uncertainty over how agencies will enforce the Rule could lower the availability of financial services, because financial institutions may be deterred to offer products that they fear could potentially be perceived by regulators as violating the Volcker Rule.

3) Reduced economic growth

If the Volcker Rule restricts the ability of banks to trade securities for their own account or to invest in private-equity firms and hedge funds (which also profit by identifying price discrepancies), overall economic efficiency may decline. Concerns over proprietary trading focus on the fact that speculative trading could cause financial institutions to incur substantial losses that may ultimately be borne by other institutions or by taxpayers. It is important to note also that banning proprietary trading will prevent institutions from earning potentially high returns from such activity, which creates costs not only for banks but also for the overall economy (Morgan and Sheehan 2015). If financial institutions earn returns on investments that exceed the return of the overall market, then the high returns signal will generate economic value by allocating savings more effectively than their rivals. Companies that engage in speculative trading serve that purpose by profiting from situations in which the market has priced financial instruments incorrectly. When many different institutions engage in this activity, the prices of financial instruments are more likely to reflect their true economic value (Viñals et al. 2013).

4) Undue influence by private interests

Thakor (2012) and Krahnen et al. (2017) argue that, while the Volcker Rule is considered by its proponents as being necessary to protect the public interest, private interests have also attempted to leverage the Rule in order to seek rents to profit at the expense of others through obtaining favours from the government. Financial institutions outside of the commercial-banking sector may stand to profit from the Volcker Rule. The Rule explicitly seeks to move speculation in securities outside of commercial banking, which will reduce the competition that investment banks, hedge funds, and similar financial institutions face from traders at commercial banks (Thakor 2012).

Large financial institutions also have an interest in seeking rents by pushing for complex regulatory structures in order to limit competition. The Volcker Rule will necessitate that commercial banks create complicated infrastructures in order to monitor their activities and comply with the Rule, which may create an expensive barrier for new rivals to entry in commercial banking. The number of new rivals entering the market would consequently decrease, thereby making the profitability of larger banks more secure (Krahnen et al. 2017). One consequence of this outcome is that large incumbent financial institutions will gain greater earnings than it is justified by their value to society. Yet another consequence is that large institutions will expend resources on lobbying rather than on creating products that consumers value, which represents a loss to society. Most importantly, the reduced competition increases the prices of financial products and provides consumers with fewer options. This happens because of the fact that large firms do not need to innovate in order to maintain their market niche (Nabilou 2013). Smaller firms generally gain a niche market by offering new products. If regulation impedes such innovation, new products will not displace old products and as a result, consumers will have fewer choices than they would have if the financial industry were more competitive.

According to the above scholarship, the Volcker Rule faces plenty of problems, especially regarding the sustainable operation of the banking sector. In summary, these problems are presented as follows:

- Impact on Risk Management in Financial Institutions: A rigid implementation of the Volcker Rule may interfere with efficient risk management in banks.
- Loan Quality Signaling in Securitisation: Banks that securitise the loans they originate can signal the quality of the loans they securitise by the amount of the securitised tranches they hold on their balance sheets. If the Volcker Rule impedes their ability to do this, it will interfere with the signalling that banks can engage in, potentially causing a decline in the prices at which the securitisation tranches can be sold.
- Reduction in the Value of Financial Services Sold by Banks: A diminished role for banks as market makers is capable of reducing the amount of information about market conditions that

banks gather, and hence of diminishing the value of advisory and other services that banks provide to their customers.

- Effect on the Coevolution of Banks and Markets: Banks and capital markets coevolve. Advances in one sector propel advances in the other. A rigid implementation of the Volcker Rule may impede this coevolution.

Conclusion: The shortcomings of the Volcker Rule and a new policy proposal

Paul Volcker (2012) himself expounded the basic aim of the rule named after him: "The basic public policy set out by the Dodd-Frank legislation is clear: the continuing explicit and implicit support by the Federal government of commercial banking organisations can be justified only to the extent those institutions provide essential financial services. A stable and efficient payments mechanism, a safe depository for liquid assets, and the provision of credit… clearly fall within that range of necessary services. Proprietary trading of financial instruments —essentially speculative in nature— engaged in primarily for the benefit of limited groups of highly paid employees and of stockholders does not justify… tax payer subsidy implicit in routine Federal Reserve credit, deposit insurance or emergency support." After the demise of the Glass-Steagall strict separationist model because of the insuperable problems in its implementation that we identified, the problems of excessive bank risk-taking resurfaced during the deregulation parenthesis between 1999 and 2010. These systemic problems were exacerbated by the moral hazard resulting from the government safety net on insured depository institutions with which large banking groups are affiliated, so that TBTF banking groups would informally develop an expectation that they are actually enjoying an informal guarantee in their speculative trading activities, since they would not be left to go bankrupt, but would be bailed out instead in case of trouble.

This era of deregulation resulted in the Lehman Brothers collapse and in the global financial meltdown of 2008. In such a setting, the Volcker Rule was enacted so as to reduce once again systemic risk and to increase financial stability, only this time the separation of commercial banks from speculative financial activity was limited to proprietary trading, while market making, underwriting, and hedging were maintained as valuable services provided by the banking system.[28] Therefore, the degree of separation is the same as it was in Glass-Steagall, but the scope of separation now is (theoretically, at least) narrower than the previous model.

However, this prima facie targeted regulatory scheme did not prevent the reappearance of numerous implementation problems, not only of those that existed under the Glass-Steagall Act, but also of new ones. Once again, the root of the problem seems to be the fundamental definitional challenge of what actually constitutes banned "proprietary trading", as opposed to permitted market-making, underwriting, and hedging. This new semantic sting once again produced over- and under-inclusiveness, since sometimes rules also capture and deter desirable banking activities, and sometimes they leave room for speculative proprietary trading in the grey area between permissible and impermissible trading movements. It also came with a myriad of practical problems: When is a "trading account" considered as used for the purpose of reselling financial instruments in the short term or of profiting from arbitrage or short-term price movements? When is an inventory of securities held to provide a client with a buyer or seller or to meet anticipated needs of the banks' clients, and when is it held purely for profiting from price movements? When is hedging a counterbalance to some risky position, and when is its purpose a straight profit, especially when it is done on a portfolio basis? Can the use by the regulators of cutoff rules and presumptions provide clear guidance to the market players, or can it lead instead to market distortions in the banks' trading activities? To sum up, the new Volcker Rule structural banking model presented the same type of conundrums as the Glass-Steagall model. Therefore, we are of the opinion that it cannot be relied upon by the EU to define and ban overly risky trading by banks, if one day the European Commission decides to reformulate a legislative proposal to that effect.

So is the whole effort a dead end? We think not. The EU has only to gain from the American regulatory shortfalls that we have been retracing in this chapter, since it can shift directly to another paradigm

---

[28] The Volcker Rule's exceptions permit the "purchase, sale, acquisition, or disposition of securities and other… instruments… in connection with underwriting or market-making-related activities", in quantities "designed not to exceed the reasonably expected near term demands of clients, customers, or counterparties" (12 U.S.C. §1851 (d)(1)(B)), and also the "risk-mitigating hedging activities… designed to reduce the specific risks to the banking entity" (12 U.S.C. §1851 (d)(1)(C); see also 12 C.F.R. §44.4(a), §44.4(b)).

instead of dilapidating scarce resources by trying once again to make such regulatory efforts worthwhile. An interesting alternative approach that is actually implied in the American implementing regulations of the Volcker Rule, and that has been recently formulated in the literature, is one that is based on an obligatory remodelling of the trader compensation schemes that apply in investment banking, in lieu of the current "define-and-ban" approach. The idea that seems to us worth exploring is the following: Instead of defining and banning "proprietary trading" as such, regulators should rather make sure that proprietary risk-taking in trading activities is no longer financially rewarding to the traders, or in other words, that even if a trader were to engage in any kind of proprietary trading activities, he would not be allowed to participate in any profits made from this trade.[29] As Bubb and Kahan (2018) summarise this approach, rather than seek to identify the motivation behind a trade, it seeks to disincentivise banks' proprietary trading by handicapping banking groups relative to their unregulated competitors, since a common incentive for the attraction and motivation of highly skilled traders in the labour market is the compensation contract that pays the individual trader a fraction of his trading profits— and this possibility will vanish under this new policy proposal (1033). This approach can become a checkmate for the solution of the insurmountable problems encountered with both the Glass-Steagall and the Volcker Rule models of structural banking separation.

This new policy proposal is already implied in the existing American framework. In the Final Rule "Prohibitions and Restrictions on Proprietary Trading and Certain Interests In, and Relationships With, Hedge Funds and Private Equity Funds" adopted by the four main US regulatory agencies for the banking sector (Office of the Comptroller of the Currency, Board of Governors of the Federal Reserve System, Federal Deposit Insurance Corporation, and Securities and Exchange Commission) in 2014 so as to implement section 619 of the Dodd-Frank Act, there are three requirements concerning traders' compensation arrangements that need to apply before a bank benefits from an exemption to the prohibition of proprietary trading, and the language used in all three of them is common. First, the underwriting exemption is allowed provided that inter alia "the compensation arrangements of persons performing underwriting activities are designed not to reward or incentivize prohibited proprietary trading" (Department of the Treasury et al. 2014, 967, iv). Second, the market-making exemption to the prohibition of proprietary trading is

[29] This "simple compensation-based approach" has been forcefully expounded and argued for recently in Bubb and Kahan (2018).

allowed provided that "the compensation arrangements of persons performing market making-related activities are designed not to reward or incentivize prohibited proprietary trading" (Department of the Treasury et al. 2014, 971, v). And third, the hedging exemption to the prohibition of proprietary trading is allowed provided that "the compensation arrangements of persons performing risk-mitigating hedging activities are designed not to reward or incentivize prohibited proprietary trading" (Department of the Treasury et al. 2014, 975, (3)).

The justification behind these requirements for any possible exemption is analytically explained in the text. If we take market making, "the Agencies continue to hold the view that activities for which a banking entity has established a compensation incentive structure that rewards speculation in, and appreciation of, the market value of a position held in inventory, rather than use of that inventory to successfully provide effective and timely intermediation and liquidity services to customers, are inconsistent with permitted market making-related activities" (Department of the Treasury et al. 2014, 311). Even though compensation incentives are not disallowed per se, since revenues resulting from movements in the price of principal positions can serve as a good guide for the effectiveness with which personnel has managed the risk involved, still "a banking entity relying on the market-making exemption should provide compensation incentives that primarily reward customer revenues and effective customer service, not prohibited proprietary trading" (Department of the Treasury et al. 2014, 311-312). Consequently, the implementation of the Volcker Rule implies that a compensation plan based purely on net profit and loss is not consistent with the market-making exemption (Department of the Treasury et al. 2014, 312). An analogous reasoning applies also to the underwriting and the hedging exemptions. As a general matter, Appendix B "Enhanced Minimum Standards for Compliance Programs" of the Final Rule requires "written procedures for determining compensation arrangements for traders engaged in underwriting or market making-related activities… or risk-mitigating hedging activities… so that such compensation arrangements are designed not to reward or incentivize prohibited proprietary trading and appropriately balance risk and financial results in a manner that does not encourage employees to expose the banking entity to excessive or imprudent risk" (Department of the Treasury et al. 2014, 1064).

Apart from the abovementioned Volcker Rule implementing regulations, a general authorisation derives from section 956 of the Dodd-Frank Act, which requires US financial regulators to issue rules prohibiting incentive compensation arrangements that encourage inappropriate risk-taking at Covered Financial Institutions, either by providing excessive compensation, fees, or benefits, or that could lead to material financial loss (12 U.S.C. §564(b)). In 2016, the relevant agencies issued a Joint Agency Proposed Rule (Department of the Treasury et al. 2016), which provides that an incentive-based compensation arrangement is considered to encourage inappropriate risks, and thus is proscribed, unless some enumerated exceptions apply. This statutory basis can be used in the future for the issuance of a rule purely and simply banning compensation on the basis of trading profits (Bubb and Kahan 2018, 1046). And even though, as they stand, the Volcker Rule implementing regulations that we pointed out regulate the exceptions to prohibited proprietary trading rather than traders' compensation as such, and can prove quite complex to manage, they could be reformulated on the basis of section 956 of Dodd-Frank so as to draw a clear-cut line prohibiting payment of traders via a percentage of their trading profits.

The relevant literature has recently formulated in a persuasive manner this alternative approach in the American context. Bubb and Kahan (2018) correctly argue that speculative proprietary trading is basically a zero-sum game, since one of the parties that make opposing bets will make money while the other(s) will lose money (1046). Short-term bets based on the identification and exploitation of mispriced securities only affect who gets what share of the total return. Of course, returns to the activity depend on the relative skills of competing traders. Now, under the new policy proposal, banks who hire traders with lower skills in proprietary trading because of their profound disadvantage vis-à-vis unregulated hedge funds in the competition for trading talents in the labour market, take risks of actually making *losses* in these trades because of the zero-sum nature of trading. In other terms, once the most talented traders are incentivised to flock at hedge funds so as to continue to earn a percentage of the returns on their trades, banks will not just lower their chances of making money in proprietary trading; they will actually hire traders that risk *losing* money.

This new element is a real game-changer, since it fundamentally alters the incentive scheme for banks. Banks will now no longer have, as before, an incentive to still want to engage in speculative proprietary trading despite the Glass-Steagall or the Volcker Rule's "define-and-ban" framework, by exploiting possible regulatory loopholes or ambiguities; they will actually have a rational incentive to keep away altogether from the proprietary trading market, even though such activity will not be formally proscribed by law. It goes without saying that in such case, regulators will no longer have the tedious task of trying to identify possible frauds in the grey area between permissible and impermissible types of bank trading, and therefore administrative costs will be drastically reduced. In sum, the new policy proposal is likely to be both simpler and more effective than the current define-and-ban approach of the Volcker Rule, since it does not even require any rules distinguishing between various types of trading, nor any kind of relevant regulatory supervision (Bubb and Kahan 2018, 1035-1037). It just needs to take notice of the banks' trading profits, in the sense of the change in value of their securities portfolios over the supervision period. Even better: the new prohibition of increasing traders' compensation for trading gains can be combined with a voluntary bank scheme that reduces compensation for trading losses, which will actually motivate banks to be more prudent and to enable traders to incentivise hedging.

This new structural banking model, based on the regulation of traders' pecuniary motivation in their specialised labour market, appears to us simpler and sounder than the current Volcker Rule, as applied in the US. A future EU structural banking reform can be inspired by such a model, which does not anymore threaten banks with sanctions for lack of compliance with a ban on proprietary trading, but instead targets the banks' abilities to engage in profitable proprietary trading directly. As a public policy choice, such a model is preferable, since it does not rely on a complicated supervisory and corrective machinery for the compliance of institutional actors, which necessarily comes with an administrative cost; it relies instead on the motivational mechanism underlying traders' risky behaviour and on the capacity of banking management to be incentivised by policy signals. All in all, such a model is more liberal than the regulatory Glass-Steagall or Volcker Rule-type mechanisms, which is important for it to gain political traction also by the center and right-wing part of the political spectrum in the EU. And in any case, this model can also be fruitfully combined with additional heavier regulations, if such a political decision is made, for example with the imposition of caps on the amount of the overall compensation paid to the bank executives and to those bank employees who take risks, which is something closer to the European regulatory tradition than to the American one.[30]

[30] In this respect, see the discussion of bankers' compensation schemes incorporating market discipline so as to constrain excessive risk-taking in Tung (2011).

References

Acharya, Viral V., Thomas F. Cooley, Matthew P. Richardson, and Ingo Walter eds. 2010. *Regulating Wall Street: The Dodd–Frank Act and the New Architecture of Global Finance*. Hoboken, New Jersey: John Wiley & Sons, Inc.

Ando, Sakai, and Misaki Matsumura. 2020. Intensive margin of the Volcker rule: Price quality and welfare. *Journal of Financial Intermediation* 43, 100814.

Basel Committee of Banking Supervisors. 2012. "Report on intra-group support measures," Bank for International Settlements, February, https://www.bis.org/publ/joint28.pdf (accessed May 5, 2021).

Benston, George J. 1990. *The Separation of Commercial and Investment Banking: The Glass-Steagall Act Revisited and Reconsidered*, Basingstoke and London: Palgrave Macmillan.

Bernanke, Ben S. 2000. *Essays on the great depression*. Princeton, New Jersey: Princeton University Press.

Boot, Arnoud W. A., and Lev Ratnovski. 2012. "Banking and Trading," IMF Working Papers, No. 12/238, 2 October, https://www.imf.org/en/Publications/WP/Issues/2016/12/31/Banking-and-Trading-40031 (accessed May 10, 2021).

Bubb, Ryan, and Marcel Kahan. 2018. Regulating Motivation: A New Perspective on the Volcker Rule. *Texas Law Review* 96, no.5: 1019–1052.

Buiter, Willem, and Ebrahim Rahbari. 2012. "Debt of Nations: Mr. Micawber's Vindication: Causes and Consequences of Excessive Debt," Citi GPS: Global Perspectives & Solutions, November, https://willembuiter.com/DoN2.pdf (accessed May 8, 2021).

Calomiris, Charles W. 2000. *US bank deregulation in historical perspective*. Cambridge: Cambridge University Press.

Carpenter, David H., Edward V. Murphy, and M. Maureen Murphy. 2016. "The Glass-Steagall Act: A Legal and Policy Analysis," Congressional Research Service Report for Congress 7–5700, 19 January, https://fas.org/sgp/crs/misc/R44349.pdf (accessed May 9, 2021).

Carpenter, David H., and M. Maureen Murphy. 2010. "The 'Volcker Rule': Proposals to Limit 'Speculative' Proprietary Trading by Banks," Congressional Research Service Report for Congress 7–5700, 22 June, https://fas.org/sgp/crs/misc/R41298.pdf (accessed May 9, 2021).

Craft, Rebecca A. 1983. Avoiding the Glass-Steagall and Bank Holding Company Acts: An Option for Bank Product Expansion, *Indiana Law Journal* 59, no.1: 89–111.

Department of the Treasury, Federal Reserve System, Federal Deposit Insurance Corporation, Federal Housing Finance Agency, National Credit Union Administration, and Securities and Exchange Commission. 2016. "Joint Agency Proposed Rule Incentive-based Compensation Arrangements," https://www.sec.gov/rules/proposed/2016/34-77776.pdf (accessed May 9, 2021).

Department of the Treasury, Board of Governors of the Federal Reserve System, Federal Deposit Insurance Corporation, and Securities and Exchange Commission. 2014. "Prohibitions and Restrictions on Proprietary Trading and Certain Interests In, and Relationships With, Hedge Funds and Private Equity Funds," https://www.sec.gov/rules/final/2013/bhca-1.pdf (accessed May 9, 2021).

Duca, John V. 2013. "Subprime Mortgage Crisis: 2007-2010," Federal Reserve History, 22 November, https://www.federalreservehistory.org/essays/subprime-mortgage-crisis (accessed May 6, 2021).

Elayan, Fayez A., Rafet Aktas, Kareen Brown, and Parunchana Pacharn. 2018. The impact of the Volcker rule on targeted banks, systemic risk, liquidity, and financial reporting quality. *Journal of Economics and Business* 96, C: 69–89.

Elliot, Douglas J., and Christian Rauch. 2014. "Lessons from the Implementation of the Volcker Rule for Banking Structural Reform in the European Union," SAFE White Paper, No. 13, https://www.econstor.eu/bitstream/10419/96515/1/783722435.pdf (accessed May 9, 2021).

European Central Bank. 2012. "Financial Integration in Europe," Report, April, https://www.ecb.europa.eu/pub/pdf/fie/financialintegrationineurope201204en.pdf (accessed May 5, 2021).

European Commission. 2018. "Commission implements 2018 Work Programme commitment to withdraw 15 pending legislative proposals," 3 July, https://ec.europa.eu/luxembourg/news/commission-implements-2018-work-programme-commitment-withdraw-15-pending-legislative-proposals_fr (accessed May 9, 2021).

European Commission. 2014a. "Proposal for a Regulation of the European Parliament and of the Council on structural measures improving the resilience of EU credit institutions," COM(2014) 43 final, 29 January (withdrawn), https://eur-lex.europa.eu/legal-content/EN/ALL/?uri=CELEX%3A52014PC0043 (accessed May 9, 2021).

European Commission. 2014b. "Commission Staff Working Document, Impact Assessment accompanying the document Proposal for a Regulation of the European Parliament and of the Council on structural measures improving the resilience of EU credit institutions and the Proposal for a Regulation of the European Parliament and of the Council on reporting and transparency of securities financing transactions," SWD (2014) 30 final, Part 1/3, 29 January (withdrawn), https://eur-lex.europa.eu/resource.html?uri=cellar:e186dd0b-89b3-11e3-87da-01aa75ed71a1.0001.05/DOC_1&format=PDF (accessed May 9, 2021).

European Commission. 2014c. "Annex A2 to Commission Staff Working Document, Impact Assessment accompanying the document Proposal for a Regulation of the European Parliament and of the Council on structural measures improving the resilience of EU credit institutions and the Proposal for a Regulation of the European Parliament and of the Council on reporting and transparency of securities financing transactions. Summary of replies to the stakeholder consultation," SWD (2014) 30 final, Part 2/3, 29 January (withdrawn), https://eur-lex.europa.eu/resource.html?uri=cellar:e186dd0b-89b3-11e3-87da-01aa75ed71a1.0001.05/DOC_1&format=PDF (accessed May 9, 2021).

European Commission. 2014d. "Annex A9 to Commission Staff Working Document, Impact Assessment accompanying the document Proposal for a Regulation of the European Parliament and of the Council on structural measures improving the resilience of EU credit institutions and the Proposal for a Regulation of the European Parliament and of the Council on reporting and transparency of securities financing transactions. Summary of the main findings in literature on economies of scale and scope in the banking sector," SWD (2014) 30 final, Part 3/3, 29 January (withdrawn), https://eur-lex.europa.eu/resource.html?uri=cellar:e186dd0b-89b3-11e3-87da-01aa75ed71a1.0001.05/DOC_1&format=PDF (accessed May 9, 2021).

European Commission. 2013. "European Financial Stability and Integration Report 2012", SWD(2013) 156 final, Part 2, 24 April, https://ec.europa.eu/transparency/regdoc/rep/10102/2013/EN/10102-2013-156-EN-F1-2.Pdf (accessed May 7, 2021).

European Parliament. 2013. "European Parliament resolution of 3 July 2013 on reforming the structure of the EU banking sector," 2013/2021(INI), https://www.europarl.europa.eu/doceo/document/TA-7-2013-0317_EN.html (accessed May 9, 2021).

Freixas, Xavier, Gyongyi Loranth, and Alan D. Morrison. 2007. Regulating Financial Conglomerates, *Journal of Financial Intermediation* 16, no.4: 479–514.

Haldane, Andrew G. 2012. "On being the right size," 2012 Beesley Lecture, Institute of Directors, London, 25 October, https://www.bis.org/review/r121030d.pdf (accessed May 11, 2021).

HLEG. 2012. "Final Report of the High-Level Expert Group on reforming the structure of the EU banking sector," 2 October, https://ec.europa.eu/info/sites/info/files/liikanen-report-02102012_en.pdf (accessed May 12, 2021).

Hökmark, Gunnar MEP. Draft report on the proposal for a regulation of the European Parliament and of the Council on structural measures improving the resilience of EU credit institutions, 22 December 2014, 2014/0020(COD) (withdrawn), https://www.europarl.europa.eu/doceo/document/ECON-PR-546551_EN.pdf (accessed May 13, 2021).

J.P. Morgan & Co. 1984. "Rethinking Glass-Steagall: The Case for Allowing Bank Holding Company Subsidiaries to Underwrite and Deal in Corporate Securities," December, http://3197d6d14b5f19f2f440-5e13d29c4c016cf96cbbfd197c579b45.r81.cf1.rackcdn.com/collection/papers/1980/1984_1231_RethinkingGlass.pdf (accessed May 9, 2021).

Jackson, Howell E. 2015. Substituted Compliance: The Emergence, Challenges, and Evolution of a New Regulatory Paradigm. *Journal of Financial Regulation* 1, no.2: 169–205.

Karmel, Roberta S. 1980. Glass-Steagall: Some Critical Reflections, *Banking Law Journal* 97, no.7: 631–641.

Kling, Arnold. 2012. "Once Again, Break up the Banks," Commentary, May 15, https://www.cato.org/commentary/once-again-break-banks (accessed May 9, 2021).

Krahnen, Jan-Pieter, Felix Noth, and Ulrich Schüwer. 2017. Structural Reforms in Banking: The Role of Trading. *Journal of Financial Regulation* 3, no.1: 66–88.

Krainer, Robert E. 2012. Regulating Wall Street: The Dodd-Frank Act and the New Architecture of Global Finance, a review. *Journal of Financial Stability* 8, no.2: 121–133.

Langevoort, Donald C. 1987. Statutory Obsolescence and the Judicial Process: The Revisionist Role of the Courts in Federal Banking Regulation, *Michigan Law Review* 85, no.4: 672–733.

Lehmann, Matthias. 2016. Volcker rule, ring-fencing or separation of bank activities – Comparison of structural reform acts around the world. *Journal of Banking Regulation* 17, no.3: 176–187.

Litan, Robert E. 1987. *What Should Banks Do?*. Brookings Institution Press.

Morgan, Jamie, and Brendan Sheehan. 2015. Has Reform of Global Finance been Misconceived? Policy Documents and the Volcker Rule. *Globalizations* 12, no.5: 695–709.

N.a. 1984. Restrictions on Bank Underwriting of Corporate Securities: A Proposal for More Permissive Regulation. *Harvard Law Review* 97, no.3: 720–738.

N.a. 1981. A Conduct-Oriented Approach to the Glass-Steagall Act. *Yale Law Journal* 91, no.1: 102–120.

N.a. 1975. The Legality of Bank Sponsored Investment Services. *Yale Law Journal* 84, no.7: 1477–1504.

Nabilou, Hossein. 2013. Bank Proprietary Trading and Investment in Private Funds: Is the Volcker Rule a Panacea or Yet Another Maginot Line?. *Banking and Finance Law Review* 32, no.3: 297–341.

Neal, Larry, and Eugene N. White. 2012. The Glass-Steagall Act in historical perspective. *The Quarterly Review of Economics and Finance* 52, no.2: 104–113.

Perkins, Edwin J. 1971. The Divorce of Commercial and Investment Banking: A History. *Banking Law Journal* 88, no.6: 483–528.

Philippon, Thomas, and Ariell Reshef. 2009. "Wages and Human Capital in the US Financial Industry: 1909-2006," National Bureau of Economic Research, Working paper No. 14644, January, https://www.nber.org/system/files/working_papers/w14644/w14644.pdf (accessed May 6, 2021).

Philippon, Thomas. 2008. "The Evolution of the US Financial Industry from 1860 to 2007: Theory and Evidence," New York University, NBER, CEPR, Working paper, November, http://diyhpl.us/~bryan/papers2/financial/The%20evolution%20of%20the%20US%20financial%20industry%20from%201860%20to%202007.pdf (accessed May 7, 2021).

Plotkin, Robert S. 1978. What Meaning Does Glass-Steagall Have for Today's Financial World?. *Banking Law Journal* 95, no.5: 404–411.

Preston, Howard H. 1933. The Banking Act of 1933. *American Economic Review* 23, no.4: 585–607.

Raab, Michael S. 1988. The Transparency Theory: An Alternative Approach to Glass-Steagall Issues, *Yale Law Journal* 97, no.4: 603–622.

Thakor, Anjan V. 2012. "The economic consequences of the Volcker Rule," Center for Capital Markets Competitiveness, Summer, https://www.centerforcapitalmarkets.com/wp-content/uploads/2010/04/17612_CCMC-Volcker-RuleFINAL.pdf (accessed May 9, 2021).

The Clearing House. 2011. "Understanding the Economics of Large Banks," 7 November, https://bpi.com/wp-content/uploads/2018/07/20111107-tch-study-understanding-the-economics-of-large-banks.pdf (accessed May 14, 2021).

Tung, Frederick. 2011. Pay for Banker Performance: Structuring Executive Compensation for Risk Regulation, *Northwestern University Law Review* 105, no.3: 1205–1252.

University of California. 2020. "Loan Terminology Dictionary," https://www.ucop.edu/loan-programs/resources/loan-terminology-glossary.html (accessed May 9, 2021).

US Dodd-Frank Wall Street Reform and Consumer Protection Act. 2010. Public Law 111–203, 124 Statutes 1376, 21 July, https://www.congress.gov/111/plaws/publ203/PLAW-111publ203.pdf (accessed May 7, 2021).

US Gramm-Leach-Bliley Act. 1999. Public Law 106–102, 113 Statutes 1338, 12 November (US Financial Services Modernization Act of 1999), https://www.govinfo.gov/content/pkg/PLAW-106publ102/pdf/PLAW-106publ102.pdf (accessed May 7, 2021).

US Bank Holding Company Act. 1956. Public Law 84–511, 84th Congress, H.R. 6227, 9 May, https://www.govinfo.gov/content/pkg/STATUTE-70/pdf/STATUTE-70-Pg133.pdf (accessed May 7, 2021).

US Banking Act. 1933. Public Law 73–66, 73d Congress, H.R. 5661, 16 June (Glass-Steagall Act), https://fraser.stlouisfed.org/title/banking-act-1933-glass-steagall-act-991 (accessed May 7, 2021).

US Securities Act. 1933. Public Law 73–22, 48 Statutes 74, 27 May, https://www.govinfo.gov/content/pkg/COMPS-1884/pdf/COMPS-1884.pdf (accessed May 7, 2021).

US Congressional Record. 1933. Volume 77, 73rd Congress, 1st Session.

US Senate. 1931. "Operation of the National and Federal Reserve Banking Systems," Hearings on Senate Resolution 71 before a Subcommittee of the Senate Committee on Banking and Currency, 71st Congress, 3rd session, Part 7: Appendix, https://fraser.stlouisfed.org/title/operation-national-federal-reserve-banking-systems-675/part-7-appendix-22460 (accessed May 15, 2021).

US District Court for the Eastern District of Pennsylvania. 1962. United States v. Philadelphia National Bank, 201 F. Supp. 348 (E.D. Pa. 1962).

US Supreme Court. 1971. Investment Co. Inst. v. Camp, 401 U.S. 617 (1971).

US Supreme Court. 1981. Board of Governors of the Federal Reserve Board v. Investment Co. Inst., 450 U.S. 46 (1981).

Viñals, José, Ceyla Pazarbasioglu, Jay Surti, Aditya Narain, Michaela Erbenova, and Julian Chow. 2013. "Creating a Safer Financial System: Will the Volcker, Vickers, and Liikanen Structural Measures Help?," IMF Staff Discussion Note, SDN/13/4, https://www.imf.org/external/pubs/ft/sdn/2013/sdn1304.pdf (accessed May 9, 2021).

Volcker, Paul A. 2012. "Commentary on the Restrictions on Proprietary Trading by Insured Depository Institutions," *Wall Street Journal*, 13 February, https://online.wsj.com/public/resources/documents/Volcker_Rule_Essay_2-13-12.pdf (accessed May 9, 2021).

Wallison, Peter J. 2013. "Why the Volcker Rule Will Harm the U.S. Economy," 13 December, https://www.aei.org/articles/why-the-volcker-rule-will-harm-the-u-s-economy/ (accessed May 9, 2021).

Walter, Ingo ed. 1985. *Deregulating Wall Street: Commercial Bank Penetration of the Corporate Securities Market.* New York: Wiley.

Whitehead, Charles K. 2011. The Volcker Rule and Evolving Financial Markets, *Harvard Business Law Review* 1, no.1: 39–73.

Wilmarth, Arthur E. Jr. 2020. *Taming the Megabanks: Why We Need a New Glass-Steagall Act*. New York: Oxford University Press.

Zingales, Luigi. 2012. "Why I was won over by Glass-Steagall," *Financial Times*, 10 June, https://www.ft.com/content/cb3e52be-b08d-11e1-8b36-00144feabdc0 (accessed May 12, 2021).

CHAPTER 7

TOWARDS AN EFFECTIVE BANKING UNION: THE CASE OF THE MONTE DEI PASCHI DI SIENA BANK

KORNILIA VIKELIDOU*

Introduction

The financial crisis originated in 2008 in the USA after the failure in the Mortgage-Backed Securities (MBS) market and the crash of Lehman Brothers. The subsequent sovereign debt crisis in the European Union (hereinafter EU) revealed that the main factors leading to the crisis include macroeconomic imbalances[1] with debt sustainability issues, repercussions of the vicious circle between the banking sector and state finances, pervasive banking nationalism,[2] the lack of appropriate financial regulation, as well as EU mechanisms able to identify, prevent and tackle upcoming financial crises of such magnitude. These conditions greatly amplified negative spillover effects observed after the near-collapse of the economies of several member states, and exposed shortcomings of the

* PhD, Department of International and European Studies, University of Macedonia (Thessaloniki, Greece).

[1] The subsequently enacted Regulation 1176/2011 defines "imbalance" as "any trend giving rise to macroeconomic developments, which are adversely affecting or have the potential adversely to affect the proper functioning of the economy of a Member State or of the economic and monetary union, or of the Union as a whole" (art. 2(1)).

[2] According to Véron (2013), "banking nationalism", by analogy with "economic nationalism", is an expression which has become commonly used to refer to a government supporting or protecting domestic corporate actors perceived as "national champions", or undermining foreign such actors seen as champions of competing national interests, usually in contexts which involve an element of cross-border economic competition.

existing economic policy coordination framework. Indicative examples include makeshift decision-making in relation to financial support and failure to act at European level, even in cases of existing EU rules. This, in turn, triggered a loss of credibility for the euro area and a decrease in the political influence of the EU, which turned the financial crisis into an existential crisis of the latter.

Taking into account the developments and the existing research concerning the Italian Bank Monte dei Paschi di Siena (hereinafter BMPS), this chapter critically examines the extent to which the ongoing situation of this bank interacts with the implementation and the progress concerning the still incomplete Banking Union framework. The aim of the chapter is to provide an insight into the extent to which the Banking Union framework has been implemented so far, to shed light on the missing elements, and to draw some tentative conclusions. Given that the case of BMPS is considered to be the first big test of how the Banking Union functions in practice, this chapter attempts to advance some suggested thought-provoking proposals that could make a positive contribution to EU policies towards an effective Banking Union.

Recent Developments in the Bank Monte dei Paschi di Siena

The Italian Bank Monte dei Paschi di Siena was founded in 1472. It is considered the oldest bank in the world still operating and the third-largest bank in Italy (Treanor 2016). However, the stress tests conducted by the European Banking Authority (hereinafter EBA) reveal that BMPS has almost failed the EU-wide stress tests carried out since 2010. This is mainly due to the fact that one third of BMPS's total loan book is not performing, compared to about one fifth as an average for the Italian banking system (De Groen and Gros 2016). However, in October 2016, BMPS had 5 billion euro of subordinated debt, of which 65% was sold to retail clients. This represents the complexity of implementing resolution under the Bank Recovery and Resolution Directive (hereinafter BRRD)[3] regime (Merler 2016b), also taking into consideration the definition of Non-Performing Loans (hereinafter NPLs), which delineates that a loan is

[3] The EU Bank Recovery and Resolution Directive (Directive 2014/59/EU) was enacted on 15 May 2014. On 1 January 2016, the Single Resolution Board acquired its resolution authority and the key bail-in provision of the BRRD entered theoretically into force, entailing the ability of resolution authorities to impose losses on shareholders, creditors and uninsured depositors of non-viable banks.

qualified as NPL when it is 90 days past-due or unlikely to be paid without collateral realisation. Moreover, all exposures to a debtor should be considered non-performing when 20% of said exposures are 90 days past-due (De Groen 2016).

Italian banks had low exposure to US sub-prime products —the collapse of which was the primary reason for the financial crisis— and there was no pre-crisis housing bubble in Italy. Although in 2009 BMPS seemed to be financially sound, when it participated in the Italian bank recapitalisation scheme and received state guarantees as a form of liquidity support, it incurred huge losses in 2011 and 2012, mainly due to the previous acquisition of Banca Antonveneta in 2008 for the unreasonable price of 9 billion euro and to the convoluted and questionable accounting practices on two structured transactions with Nomura and Deutsche Bank in 2011 and 2012 for a total amount of 1.2 billion euro (Ewing and Pianigiani 2013). This resulted in a second state recapitalisation in 2013 for a total amount of 4.1 billion euro. The European Commission approved this recapitalisation as restructuring aid (EBA 2016; Mesnard et al. 2017), and even the International Monetary Fund (IMF) acknowledged, until 2013, the proven ability of the Italian banking system to mitigate the effects of the crisis and to ensure capitalisation by resorting to the market. However, low economic activity, along with company failures and job losses, triggered a further rise in NPLs. The situation was negatively affected by fruitless managerial decisions and precarious allocation of credit, in combination with the specific conditions of each bank and the fact that the real value of the NPLs cannot be determined, since every NPL is a special case (De Groen and Gros 2016). The comprehensive assessment carried out by the European Central Bank (hereinafter ECB) and the EBA in 2014 implicitly revealed that the ECB, as the Single Supervisor of the Eurozone banks, should timely focus on the Italian banking sector in order to avoid any systemic effect.

When BMPS started being supervised by the ECB in November 2014, it decided to raise 5 billion euro of capital due to the Comprehensive Assessment conducted in the context of the Single Supervisory Mechanism (hereinafter SSM) and the losses it had incurred in 2013. However, BMPS reported the highest capital shortfall, amounting to 2.1 billion euro, which was more than 20% of the total shortfall of all participating banks. Consequently, BMPS was penalised and had to write down 4.2 billion euro following the Asset Quality Review, thus incurring significant losses again. In 2015, BMPS managed to raise 3 billion euro of capital, following the capital plan decided in cooperation with the ECB. Overall, from 2011 to 2015, BMPS experienced net losses amounting to 14.3 billion euro, raised equity from private investors amounting to 8 billion euro, and repaid 2 billion euro of state aid (Mesnard et al. 2017).

In November 2015, the Italian Parliament transposed the BRRD into national legislation. Thus, the Italian authorities were left with rather little time to implement the new rules on crisis management before the full implementation of bail-in (Gehrig et al. 2016). However, the main issue for Italy was not the time available to implement the new crisis regime for BMPS, but the unwillingness to impose a bail-in, since this would provoke political implications. In support of this, there has been a letter that was sent in November 2016 to Ms Elke Koenig, Chair of the Single Resolution Board (hereinafter SRB), by Mr. Marco Zanni and Mr. Marco Valli, Members of the European Parliament (MEPs), asking for other suggested solutions to be implemented rather than bail-in, taking into consideration the possible social impact of the latter (Zanni and Valli 2016). Moreover, on 12 May 2017, Mr. Zanni posed a question to the Chair of the Single Supervisory Mechanism Board regarding the precautionary recapitalisation with state aid of two Venetian banks, Banca Popolare di Vicenza and Veneto Banca. This question focused on the ineffectiveness and the dangers involved in case of a bail-in, as stipulated by the BRRD (Zanni 2017).

In this context, earlier attempts for "creative" solutions that would avert a potential implementation of bail-in took place in early 2016. Specifically, a guarantee scheme on NPLs and Atlante, a bank-financed backstop fund, were established. The guarantee scheme for Italian NPLs entailed that Italy would offer a state guarantee on them in order to help limit the balance sheet impact. The banks needed to pay a fee for the guarantee so that it would not be considered state aid. This fee would be increasing over time. It would be calculated based on the guaranteed amount, and the price of the guarantee would be computed taking as reference the prices of credit default swaps for issuers with a comparable level of risk to the guaranteed bonds. Before the establishment of the guarantee scheme on NPLs, 50% of the less senior tranches needed to be placed with private investors. However, taking into account the low market appeal of riskier tranches and the difference between the market price of NPLs and their value as accounted for on banks' balance sheets, this guarantee scheme might have turned out to be ineffective, unless Italian banks pool their funds together and buy a significant part of the junior products themselves (Merler 2016b). In support of this, the example of Banca Popolare di Bari is noteworthy, since the relevant deal proved that the Italian guarantee scheme has floundered (Hale and McCrum 2017).

The Atlante fund, endowed with an initial capital of 4.25 billion euro by a large majority of Italian financial institutions, was launched in April 2016 acting as a shareholder of last resort with the view to ensuring the success of capital raising of banks that could not raise capital on the market. Specifically, Atlante was designed to underwrite new recapitalisations by Italian banks up to 70% of its capital. Moreover, Atlante was created as a purchaser for the junior tranches of securitised Italian NPLs for up to 30% of its capital. Atlante may have prevented bank resolution in the short run, but one year later, the problematic nature of this fund came up to the surface. First, it accumulated risk on the balance sheets of an already interdependent banking system, thus increasing the possibility of systemic risk in the long run. Besides, Atlante's endowment was inadequate to reach its aim, since two recapitalisations of Banca Popolare di Vicenza and Veneto Banca could consume the biggest part of its initial capital (Gehrig et al. 2016). However, Atlante did not manage to boost confidence in the Italian banking system since, on the one hand, it could trigger conflicts of interest based on the fact that its main shareholders, i.e., the Italian banking groups, were also its contracting parties, and on the other hand, it resulted in subscribing almost completely the capital raises it participated in (Merler 2017). In support of these arguments, there is also the fact that Giuseppe Guzzetti, one of the persons participating in the Atlante venture, explicitly regretted his participation. Moreover, lack of trust in the success of Atlante was revealed by the fact that participating banks made a significant write-down to the values of their investment (Merler 2017).

In light of this negative legacy, the poor performance of BMPS in the EU-wide stress tests carried out by the EBA and the ECB and published on 29 July 2016 was not a surprise (EBA 2016). As a response to this, and induced by an earlier demand by the ECB to take drastic action to reduce NPLs (Monte dei Paschi di Siena 2016), BMPS announced that it would seek to raise capital amounting to 5 billion euro from private investors. However, attracting foreign capital in politically uncertain circumstances was rather doomed to fail due to the size of the amount to be gathered, as well as the existing uncertainty stemming from the forthcoming, at the time, Italian referendum in December 2016. Thus, additional losses were noticed in BMPS since September 2016, which led to new guidelines from the ECB.

Indeed, after the negative outcome of the Italian referendum on 4 December 2016, BMPS managed to raise only 1 billion euro. The ECB refused to grant more time to BMPS, and that triggered the approval of a precautionary recapitalisation (ECB 2016) from the Italian government on 23 December 2016, which allowed BMPS to benefit from a 20 million euro bail-out package (The Economist Intelligence Unit 2016). The ECB subsequently raised the capital requirements of BMPS from 5 billion to 8.8 billion euro. This provoked serious criticism, as well as further doubts concerning the credibility of the common supervisory framework (Merler 2016c). Besides, this considerable raise for capital requirement reflected the divergent philosophies on state aid between the ECB and the European Commission. It highlighted that the ECB aims at securing financial stability by securing the health of the lender regardless of the cost to the taxpayer, whereas for the European Commission, the size of taxpayer support matters, as any special treatment for BMPS can trigger protests from other lenders (Barker et al. 2017). The most convincing argument, however, seems to be that this raise of capital requirements for BMPS reflects the risk profile of the Italian banks.

According to the Canadian rating agency DBRS, the overall stock of bad loans for 15 Italian banks fell in 2016 for the first time in the past eight years. However, the worst class of bad loans, where banks are exposed to insolvent borrowers, has slightly risen. DBRS, when analysing this data, found out that only 9 billion euro came from NPLs turning into performing, with the rest coming from write-offs, recoveries and sales. By contrast, 32 billion euro of performing loans turned into NPLs (Hale and McCrum 2017).

The impact on the still incomplete Banking Union

The case of BMPS exposed Italy's opposition to the implementation of the bail-in rule by the establishment of the Atlante fund and by the use of "precautionary recapitalisation" in order to avoid national political turmoil. Consequently, it cannot be ignored that a transition period may be required in order to avoid a creative or, in other words, flexible enforcement of the BRRD/Single Resolution Mechanism Regulation (hereinafter SRMR) rules, which would undermine their safe and consistent application. This transition period should take into consideration that there are different banking products and legal systems within the Eurozone's 19 countries.

Given that the national solutions have not brought until today the expected results and the fact that two other Italian banks, Banco Popolare di Vicenza and Veneto Banca, asked in March 2017 for access to precautionary recapitalisation, like the one discussed for BMPS, it has been clear that: a) a bail-out of BMPS is not enough, since more rescues might be needed, and b) although measures that should have been taken earlier may have now become unavoidable (Merler 2017), the fear of a potential panic makes taxpayers' help seem safer than the implementation of a bail-in, even though this cannot be a long-term solution and raises serious issues of moral hazard.

The case of BMPS has been, for the time being, the most important reputational test for the two already established pillars of the Banking Union, i.e., the Single Supervisory Mechanism and the Single Resolution Mechanism. These two pillars must resolve issues that developed long before the emergence of the Banking Union architecture. Nevertheless, they have still not been effective enough to build the necessary confidence that would make participating countries more receptive regarding the implementation of the new banking resolution tools. Following the publication of the stress tests in July 2016, the ECB, as the prudential supervisor, demanded that Italy raise new capital and move towards a drastic reduction of NPLs. When Italy failed to come up to the expected standards, the ECB refused to give more time to BMPS. Critics say that this had a positive impact on the ECB's credibility, but the subsequent lack of action raised fresh doubts over the ECB's reputation. In support of this, there has also been Germany's view, which explicitly expressed that "soft treatment of BMPS would set a legal precedent that undermines post-crisis EU rules designed to end taxpayer bail-outs" (Barker et al. 2017). Such a situation is particularly worrying, when at the same time the SSM has faced charges that it has been too soft on Deutsche Bank since, in the context of the stress tests conducted in 2016, the SSM allowed Deutsche Bank to count the sale of a unit to a Chinese company though the sale was not completed at the time (Jones and Brunsden 2017).

It is also remarkable that the desperate attempts of BMPS to close big capital shortfalls made Germany less willing to cooperate regarding further risk sharing, thus slowing progress in the completion of the Banking Union. Germany explicitly claimed that "first Italian banks must get rid of their bad loans and only later would richer countries agree to put their money in common funds to shield depositors and lenders from future failures" (EurActiv.com with Reuters 2016). This means that progress on the third pillar of the Banking Union concerning a European Deposit Insurance Scheme (hereinafter EDIS) has been postponed for much later, until there has been significant progress on the issue of NPLs.

Due to the complex and evolving nature of the latest situation concerning BMPS, and given the European multilevel bank regulatory structure, there is much confusion about which set of regulations and institutional arrangements applies to the Banking Union that currently consists of 19 euro area members. Although much responsibility for the mishandling of the BMPS case is mistakenly attributed to the still unfinished Banking Union, the handling of the BMPS problem indicates the political character of the situation, which consists in the non-implementation of the bail-in rule, and more generally, in the resolution framework stipulated in BRRD. The latter applies across the entire EU and is not Banking Union legislation.[4] Moreover, the Italian banking fragility, particularly noticed in the case of BMPS, has been revealed since October 2014, and that was when the results of the Comprehensive Assessment were published (ECB 2014). That was two years before the crisis management regime entered into force and that, in any case, applies to all member states of the EU and not just to countries participating in the Banking Union. Consequently, for the time being, the Banking Union is not to blame for the incompetent management of the failing or likely to fail (hereinafter FOLF) Italian bank, but rather the politically driven impediments posed by the competent authorities that refuse to face the political cost of past mis-selling of loans that are currently non-performing, as well as the perilous allocation or investment of bank assets.

According to article 18(1) Regulation 806/2014 (SRMR Regulation) (or article 32(1) BRRD), a resolution is triggered when the following conditions are all met. Firstly, when the competent or resolution authority determines that the institution is FOLF. The criteria for this are determined by objective tests, including breach of the Capital Requirements Directive (CRD) capital requirements, having more liabilities than assets, being unable to pay obligations as they fall due, or requiring extraordinary public finance. Secondly, when there is no reasonable prospect, in regard to the circumstances and taking other relevant factors into account, for any alternative action preventing the failure of the institution within a reasonable timeframe. Thirdly, when a resolution action is necessary for the public interest. The action must achieve, and be proportionate to, one

[4] As far as countries outside the Banking Union are concerned, the rules of the BRRD are implemented by national authorities, whereas for countries in the Banking Union, according to the Single Resolution Mechanism and as provisioned in Regulation 806/2014, the Single Resolution Board decides on resolution schemes, but the execution of such resolution is done by the National Competent authorities (hereinafter NCAs).

of the resolution objectives, and must only be taken if a winding up or insolvency of the institution or parent undertaking would not meet those objectives to the same extent.

From the outset, the case of BMPS mirrored obscurity and uncertainty as to the applicable rule of law against a background in the context of which calling upon taxpayers to bail out failing banks is still falsely deemed as a first best recourse. However, as already mentioned, the most remarkable issue is that the results of the previous stress tests in October 2014, which had been carried out among others by the ECB as the Single Supervisor of the most significant Eurozone banks,[5] had revealed that the Italian banking system, and particularly BMPS, was in distress (EBA 2016; Véron 2014). Specifically, nine out of the fifteen participating Italian banks were among the twenty-five banks that failed the stress test. Four of them (BMPS, Banca Popolare di Vicenza, Veneto Banca and Carige) were still undercapitalised when the results were announced in October 2014, and happened to be the same ones that needed fresh capital at least until December 2016. Notwithstanding, the ECB has been rather slow in taking any corrective action that would avert BMPS from being on the edge of resolution. It was only in March 2017 that the ECB published guidance to banks on tackling NPLs (ECB 2017). Before that, and after the Italian constitutional referendum on 4 December 2016, we only witnessed the ECB's initiative to force BMPS to find new capital before the end of 2016, implying that similar initiatives would be expected from the other three significant problematic banks as well as from Italy's smaller banks that remain supervised by the Bank of Italy (Véron 2017). According to Véron's view, who is a senior fellow at Bruegel think tank in Brussels, there are two good excuses for the belated action of the ECB: First, the lack of consensus on behalf of the Bank of Italy concerning any suggestion by the ECB, and second, the constitutional referendum in Italy on 4 December 2016, which deterred the ECB from interceding in order to avoid being accused of any political interference (Véron et al. 2017).

[5] The 2014 EU-wide stress test was coordinated by the EBA and was carried out in cooperation with the ECB, the European Systemic Risk Board, the European Commission and the competent authorities from all relevant national jurisdictions. In this process, the EBA has developed a common methodology and plays an important role in ensuring a comprehensive, consistent and comparable disclosure of the results. The European Systemic Risk Board and the European Commission have developed the adverse and the baseline scenarios respectively. Competent authorities, including the ECB for the euro area, are responsible for the quality assurance of banks' data, as well as for supervisory actions banks will have to take in response to the outcome of the exercise.

The case of BMPS, and generally the NPL situation in the euro area, has shed light on the inadequate harmonisation of certain key supervisory tools at the EU level as well as their inefficiency to prevent the development of new NPLs. It has become conspicuous that it is a key priority to tackle this issue in a coordinated way at the European level since the respective national strategies only in exceptional cases brought fruitful results. This was the case for both Spain and Ireland (Darvas et al. 2016), which used state-backed "bad banks" to cleanse their banking systems of toxic loans after the financial crisis. The case of BMPS has also stressed the need to set up a European Asset Management Company (hereinafter AMC), or alternatively develop a European blueprint for national AMCs, so as to overcome market failures and ensure a speedy resolution to the NPL problem, along with the Single Resolution Mechanism for the Banking Union member states, in order to bring some Single Market consistency to the application of resolution and to activate a resolution tool in the context of the crisis management regime. This is under the condition that a suitable price is agreed at which the banks will be able to offload their bad loans to the vehicle. If this price is too low, it will not reassure the markets because of the impact of the write-down on banks' balance sheets. On the other hand, if the government guarantees were such that the selling price resulted too high compared to the market value of the loans, then the involvement of the AMC would be considered state aid (Merler 2016a). It was also made clear that the early intervention measures available to the SSM under the SRMR and BRRD, as well as any other related issue that needs to be implemented under the resolution framework, must be clarified in a directly applicable regulation in order to be effective and fully usable in practice (Bassot and Hiller 2017).

It is noteworthy that in the context of tackling the NPL problem, the case of BMPS highlighted the role of the SSM in requiring realistic and ambitious strategies to be adopted by national banks. Such strategies have to include revamped governance and risk management, along with quantitative objectives concerning the reduction of the NPL portfolio, taking also into consideration the potential conflict of interests. This was highly the case for BMPS, since the Bank of Italy is both the national supervisory and the national resolution authority (Gehrig et al. 2016).

During the latest developments of BMPS, it was often implied that many of the Italian bad loans were sold to retail clients without rendering them aware of the risks involved in these transactions (Bernabei and Za 2015). Regarding this vast issue of banking policy, neither the Bank of Italy nor the ECB have taken any measure (Véron 2017). Moreover, the case of BMPS depicted the tendency of the Italian authorities to minimise their own costs by keeping the bank alive through support from the ECB, as well as their attempt to avoid resolution. This type of potential conflicts would have been mitigated if a EDIS and a fiscal backstop were already in place, ensuring the stability of the new integrated banking system, and eventually the needed alignment of responsibilities. Thus, it is clear that the case of BMPS proved in practice that a European underpinning of deposit insurance and resolution is an indispensable complement to moving supervision to the ECB.

However, it was also made evident that a fiscal backstop for the euro area banks would ensure, for instance, that the ECB would have no incentive to offload the fiscal cost of any problem to the national authorities. Overall, the BMPS case showed that European supervision and resolution, on the one hand, and deposit insurance and a lender of last resort at the national level, on the other hand, are not incentive-compatible. Consequently, the missing elements of deposit insurance, as well as the lack of fiscal backstop at European level, "might actually backfire" as long as they are not established under the Banking Union framework (Schoenmaker 2012). This becomes even more urgent given that the limited amount of the existing Single Resolution Fund will hardly be enough for a systemic banking crisis, since it is designed to reach at its final stage, in 2024, the amount of 55 billion euro (SRB n.d.).

Equally important was the lack of provision of a transition stage that would give member states the time to adjust to the new regime introduced by the BRRD, which entered into force in January 2016 putting an end to state-funded solutions to banks. This lack of a transition stage favoured the use of the Atlante fund as "a shareholder of last resort", mitigating the possibility of activating the resolution procedure, even for banks that would fail to find new capital (The Corner 2016).

Steps towards an Effective Banking Union

Taking into consideration the BMPS case, the toxic mix of excessive NPL levels, stagnant growth, and persistent excess debt in other euro area countries,[6] it is clear that further harmonisation is needed. This should not result in a "race to the bottom", but in putting together common

---

[6] Notably in Italy, with almost 30% of the total euro area NPL stock, Greece and Cyprus regarding households and companies, and Portugal regarding large enterprises (Demertzis and Lehmann 2017).

elements in terms of scope and identification criteria, and in shaping the respective rules for resolution.[7] This must be done in a form that will provide a harmonised understanding of these substantial concepts, strengthen the function of resolution tools,[8] and prevent diverging national requirements from annihilating the enforcement of rules at European level, such as those demanded for the effectiveness and completion of the Banking Union. To this end, the strengthening of the Banking Union should comprise the introduction of sovereign exposure limits, the establishment of a EDIS, and additional harmonisation of relevant features of bank insolvency regimes, such as the hierarchy of liabilities.[9]

At this point, Ronny Mazzocchi's view,[10] who was the parliamentary assistant to Roberto Gualtieri, then Chair of the Committee on Economic and Monetary Affairs (ECON) of the European Parliament, is noteworthy. He alleges that due to the vague but strict legal framework of BRRD, the latter favoured a large public uproar and the conditions for a potential financial crisis in Italy when the Bank of Italy and the Italian government

---

[7] "Resolution" means the restructuring of a bank by a resolution authority, through the use of resolution tools, to ensure the continuity of its critical functions, to preserve financial stability, and to restore the viability of all or part of that institution, while the remaining parts are put into normal insolvency proceedings (European Commission 2014).

[8] According to article 37(3) BRRD, when an institution is failing, a resolution authority should have a harmonised minimum set of resolution tools, including: a) a sale of business tool: this enables the authorities to sell part of the business without shareholder consent, b) a bridge institution tool: this allows authorities to transfer all or part of the business to an entity owned by the authorities, which continues to provide essential financial services pending onward sale or entity wind-down, c) an asset separation tool: this enables the transfer of bad assets to a separate vehicle of bad bank, and d) a bail-in tool: this allows equity and debt to be written down and is intended to ensure that most unsecured creditors of an institution bear appropriate losses.

[9] "The legal requirement in BRRD that no creditor should be worse off in a resolution than if the bank had gone through a court-ordered insolvency, prevents the resolution process from being consistent across countries as long as bank insolvency frameworks remain different or even increasingly divergent from one another following several recent national law changes" (Véron 2016a, 5).

[10] Ronny Mazzocchi, parliamentary assistant to Roberto Gualtieri, then Chair of the Committee on Economic and Monetary Affairs (ECON) of the European Parliament, was interviewed by the author on 5 September 2016 at Mr. Gualtieri's office in the European Parliament in Brussels. The interview forms an annex to the PhD dissertation of the author "The European Banking Union as a contributing factor to financial stability".

announced plans to resolve four small Italian banks in November 2015,[11] and invoked the bail-in of holders of equity and subordinated debt that amounted to EUR 798 million losses imposed on junior bondholders, around half of which were held by retail investors. This caused irreparable harm on Italy's banking system, since it had further undermined trust and no one wanted to be involved in investment in bonds. This view entails that a bail-in cannot be automatically implemented. On the contrary, it must be applied after a transition period, according to a flexible interpretation, and in a coordinated way that will respect the particularity of the banking sector and avoid a fire-sale environment and negative spillover effects.

To make countries more receptive concerning bail-ins, Nicolas Véron is of the view that, assuming minimally competent public communication, a reasonable compromise would involve bailing-in junior creditors, presumably in the form of a debt-equity swap; compensating the retail victims of mis-selling; and sparing all senior creditors and depositors under the BRRD's exemption for precautionary recapitalisations (Véron 2016b). The above arguments are strengthened by the view that a joint act by European governments is crucial to convince investors that bank liabilities are safe, which did happen in 2008. Likewise, the European governments must offer a public guarantee for bank liabilities, temporarily suspending European regulations governing state aid and the bail-in provisions. Banks should be allowed to obtain a public backstop to cover the potential losses from securitising and restructuring their NPLs. This could be based on article 107 of the Treaty on the Functioning of the EU (TFEU),[12] which explicitly allows the Commission to declare state aid compatible with the Treaty in the face of especially turbulent economic conditions (Micossi 2016).

Unless the NPL problem is tackled, debt overhang will be a systemic obstacle to recovery, since high debt levels act as a disincentive to new investment (Myers 1977 in Demertzis and Lehman 2017, 4). This will have a negative impact on banks' profitability, rendering thus European banks unable to meet the increased capital needs and regulatory

[11] Banca delle Marche, Banca dell' Eturia e del Lazio, Cassa di Risparmio di Chieti and Cassa di Risparmio di Ferrara (Garrido et al. 2016).

[12] According to the Treaty, "aid to make good the damage caused by natural disasters or exceptional occurrences" (art. 107(2)(b) TFEU), and "aid to promote the execution of an important project of common European interest or to remedy a serious disturbance in the economy of a Member State" (art. 107(3)(b) TFEU), shall be compatible with the internal market.

standards of the Banking Union and other EU financial regulations. Besides, debt is the outcome of a contract. Debt in excess of sustainable levels has a negative impact on the supply as well as on the demand side of debt that is related to the borrower, who becomes considerably unable to be involved in profitable investments without potentially endangering financial stability. Under these conditions, bad debts prevent growth, and in turn, lack of growth generates bad debt (Demertzis 2017 in Demertzis et al. 2017). This creates a vicious circle with potential repercussions on financial stability and the completion of the Banking Union.

Taking into account the abovementioned parameters, the ECB published its final guidance on NPLs in March 2017 (ECB 2017) with the view to advancing measures, processes and best practices that banks should incorporate when tackling NPLs. Although its guidance is a non-binding instrument, the ECB expects banks to fully adhere to it in line with the severity and scale of NPLs in their portfolios or, in any case, give adequate explanations regarding any deviation. This guidance comprises incentives to carry out NPL reduction strategies backed by credible operational plans, sale, write-off, foreclosure, and other appropriate options for each portfolio. The ECB's guidance is expected to increase supervisory reporting requirements of the SSM for banks with a high level of NPLs in order to make the latter disclose more information that will render solutions easier to be adopted and NPL reduction strategies more effective. If this guidance leads to credible measures, investors will recognise the shift in policy and, in turn, will price higher expected future returns into loan valuations. Consequently, the SSM can favour a coordinated effort of several European and national authorities towards resolving the NPL problem by taking into consideration not only the supply, but also the demand side of this issue (Constancio 2017).

There is also the view that legacy assets,[13] such as the NPLs, should have been dealt with by the Asset Quality Review in 2014, prior to the ECB assuming its role as the SSM of the largest euro area banks in the Banking Union (Gros and Belke 2015). However, even in retrospect, it cannot be ignored that the SSM, having taken steps at European level, can timely spot and address the issues inherent in cases of debt distress, such as information asymmetry, conflict of divergent interests and coordination problems. Due to political reasons of the member states, it is the delay in

[13] According to the Commission's Implementing Regulation 680/2014, "legacy assets" comprise the stock of NPLs as determined in line with the EBA's asset quality methodology (European Commission 2014).

the enforcement of the Banking Union rules that makes negotiations notoriously lengthy, and sometimes ineffective.

In January 2017, the proposed solution by the EBA to NPLs involving the establishment of a European AMC, the so-called "bad bank", could significantly contribute to overcoming the various failures by removing distressed assets from banks' balance sheets. The European bad bank is proposed to have to sell its toxic loans into the market after a fixed time period, with the power to recoup any losses from the lenders themselves. It is to be noted that typically, these institutions require some form of government support (Constancio 2017). This could revive the loop between banks and sovereigns, which the Banking Union has initially targeted to weaken. However, within the existing framework of the Banking Union providing for supervision and resolution at European level, a broader use of AMCs could be accommodated within the existing rules on bank resolution and state aid, with minimum mutualisation of legacy assets. The argument for the establishment of an AMC is also supported by Marco Zanni MEP, who has been dealing with BMPS (Zanni and Valli 2016). However, Mr. Zanni is of the view that this bad bank must be established, for the time being, only at national level and be state-funded. Otherwise, there will be no investment interest in the private sector. In his opinion, this is mainly due to the lack of clarity regarding the bail-in rule introduced by BRRD, which should be applied in cases from 2016 onwards so that in the meantime the way can be paved for a level-playing field that will render the bail-in rule of BRRD fairer and easier to be politically accepted (Zanni 2017).[14]

There is also the view that, taking into consideration the US banking model, widespread securitisation and large banks operating throughout the euro area are significant shock absorbers, besides banking integration introduced by the Banking Union. These two characteristics of the US financial system proved to have lessened the need for fiscal backstops for the federal institutions in the US and have mitigated the dominance of banks and debt instead of markets and equity respectively, thus increasing risk sharing. However, for such a regime, it should be taken into account that big banks are not only too big to fail, but also too big to be saved (Gros and Belke 2015). This also sheds light on the fact

[14] Marco Zanni MEP was interviewed by the author on 8 February 2017 at his office in the European Parliament in Brussels. The interview forms an annex to the PhD thesis of the author "The European Banking Union as a contributing factor to financial stability".

that the ECB's one-size-fits-all monetary policy can never be perfectly tailored for any individual member state, since neither all situations can be foreseen in legislation nor all risks can be measured. Regulation at EU level can often signal warnings or provide solutions, but banking nationalism, the lack of devotion to EU interests, overconfidence, and herd behaviour weaken the signals and, in the long run, prove that it is often the case that "one size fits none" (The Economist 2009).

An effective Banking Union requires, among other factors, an effective resolution that creates a level-playing field and addresses moral hazard, as one of its key functions is to enhance discipline within the markets. The SSM can take a more objective look at borrowers' financial health provided that the national supervisory authorities of the Banking Union member states have a fruitful cooperation with the ECB in a way that can at least mitigate information asymmetries. This can reveal cases of NPLs before they reach a threatening level to financial stability. Should there be cases of irredeemable insolvent borrowers, the timely intervention of the SRB, which is an independent EU agency stipulated in the SRMR, could cut them off from credit and promote efficient liquidation of assets and collateral, a solution that may not be favoured under national insolvency laws. This entails that the Banking Union, designed to have enhanced authority over most aspects of bank supervision and resolution, can de-link overlapping tasks between the prudential and executive authorities, typically resulting in a failure to protect savers, as was strongly the case of BMPS. Provided that the Banking Union legislation is politically accepted and timely implemented, it can: firstly, promote prudential supervision that ensures the protection of investors' and savers' interests considerably, while protecting the reputation of banks and NCAs; secondly, scrutinise banks' strategies, while constraining credit risk by requiring respective measures from national authorities; and thirdly, provide the necessary consistency in the regulatory architecture in order to promote banks' profitability as well as financial stability. Without the full consent of the respective national banks and authorities, the Banking Union will provide a meaningful framework that, however, lacks teeth in terms of implementation should an upcoming systemic crisis strike.

Conclusion

The developments in BMPS shed light on the vast impact of NPLs on financial stability, rendering imperative the need for a collective policy response at EU level. This policy response should tackle debt distress, avert a potential new stock of NPLs, and restore market sentiment under conditions that promote trust and operational capacity, leading thus to profitable investments and consumption. These conditions can be achieved only with mechanisms at European level, since banking crises are the result of a combination of negative and persisting factors not encountered in just one country. Against this background, the BMPS case provided an indication of the strengths and weaknesses of the current form of the Banking Union. It also highlighted the fact that the home bias towards domestic sovereign debt in Italian banks' portfolio has not yet been put to an end.

EU strategy should not constrain national solutions. However, in the context of the still incomplete Banking Union, a clear EU institutional framework that averts and addresses market failures could move banking systems more broadly to a stronger equilibrium that advances collective solutions, which do not undermine the credibility of the existing framework for bank resolution and do not distract from rigorous supervision by the SSM.

As long as legal reforms are politically accepted in time, a fully-fledged Banking Union with supervision, resolution and, in the long run, the still missing elements of a European Deposit Insurance Scheme and a fiscal backstop, could provide the legal framework, along with the necessary mechanisms and certainty, so that viable debt remains serviced, while non-viable debt gets timely resolved, which is a guiding principle for resolving NPLs. This could gradually generate the right incentives, and pave the way for a coordinated approach to correcting current imbalances in the euro area and to resolving the post-crisis legacy issues in the banking sector. In turn, this could lessen the influence of national counterproductive measures that may be unduly lengthy, costly, or just resulting in perpetuating unsustainable debt or non-viable banks.

Without common orientation, it is hardly possible to reach at national level solutions to tackling Europe's bad loans or to prevent an upcoming economic crisis, taking into account the cross-border nature of the current European banking sector. Due to imbalances existing long before the introduction of the euro, but widely revealed due to the increasing requirements of a fully-fledged currency union, financial integration exacerbated political fragmentation, resulting in a division of core and periphery countries and thus creating a multispeed Union. This gradually disorientated member states from serving the common interest to protecting their national interest in an effort to reach the demanded standards of the new regulations related to cross-border banking. Indicative highlights of relevant impediments include information asymmetry, inefficient debt enforcement mechanisms, regulatory barriers for loan servicing and loan transfers, supervisory forbearance, delayed loss recognition, and lack of existing mechanisms with the necessary loss-absorbing capacity. This situation brought the necessary political convergence to a stalemate, hardening thus the prospects of a potential leeway towards common steps that promote financial stability.

The Banking Union framework could provide the cross-border banking sector with a broader sense of transparency, fairness and accountability. Whether this regime is effective will be shaped by the ongoing progress on delivering the promised outcomes related to expected opportunities, risks and costs. It will also be determined by the extent of the regained trust in common European targets and the commitment of the member states to achieve them. It is ultimately all about striking the right balance between sovereignty and integration in a voluntary European Union that will map out the optimal path towards financial stability.

References

Barker, Alex, Claire Jones, and Rachel Sanderson. 2017. "Brussels and ECB split on Monte dei Paschi's capital proposals," *Financial Times*, 23 February, www.ft.com/content/9635b04c-f923-11e6-bd4e-68d53499ed71 (accessed May 31, 2021).

Bassot, Étienne, and Wolfgang Hiller. 2017. "The Juncker Commission's ten priorities: State of play at the start of 2017," European Parliamentary Research Service, In-Depth Analysis, PE 595.876, January, https://www.europarl.europa.eu/RegData/etudes/IDAN/2017/595876/EPRS_IDA(2017)595876_EN.pdf (accessed May 29, 2021).

Bernabei, Stefano, and Valentina Za. 2015. "Italian bank rescue leaves bitter families marooned," *Reuters*, 21 December, http://www.reuters.com/article/italy-banks-bonds-idUSL8N1490SJ20151221 (accessed May 28, 2021).

Commission Implementing Regulation (EU) No 680/2014 of 16 April 2014 laying down implementing technical standards with regard to supervisory reporting of institutions according to Regulation (EU) No 575/2013 of the European Parliament and of the Council. 2014. OJ L 191: 1–1861.

Constancio, Vitor. 2017. "Resolving Europe's NPL burden: challenges and benefits," 3 February, https://www.ecb.europa.eu/press/key/date/2017/html/sp170203.en.html (accessed May 30, 2021).

Darvas, Zsolt, Dirk Schoenmaker, and Nicolas Véron. 2016. "Reform of the European Union financial supervisory and regulatory architecture and its implications for Asia," Bruegel Working Paper, No. 9, https://www.bruegel.org/wp-content/uploads/2016/11/WP_09_16.pdf (accessed May 28, 2021).

De Groen, Willem Pieter. 2016. "A closer look at Banca Monte dei Paschi: Living on the edge," CEPS Policy Brief, No. 345, July, https://www.ceps.eu/download/publication/?id=9550&pdf=MPSLivingontheEdge.pdf (accessed May 26, 2021).

De Groen, Willem Pieter, and Daniel Gros. 2016. "The continuing saga of Banca Monte dei Paschi di Siena," Centre for European Policy Studies Commentary, 28 July, https://www.ceps.eu/ceps-publications/continuing-saga-banca-monte-dei-paschi-di-siena/ (accessed May 26, 2021).

Demertzis, Maria, Sharon Donnery, Piers Haben, and Alexander Lehmann. 2017. "Banks and borrowers in distress – Europe's NPL crisis," Bruegel Podcast, 10 March, https://www.bruegel.org/2017/03/banks-and-borrowers-in-distress-europes-npl-crisis/ (accessed May 25, 2021).

Demertzis, Maria, and Alexander Lehmann. 2017. "Tackling Europe's crisis legacy: a comprehensive strategy for bad loans and debt restructuring," Bruegel Policy Contribution, Issue No. 11, https://www.bruegel.org/wp-content/uploads/2017/04/PC-11-2017-2004.pdf (accessed May 25, 2021).

Directive 2014/59/EU of the European Parliament and of the Council of 15 May 2014 establishing a framework for the recovery and resolution of credit institutions and investment firms and amending Council Directive 82/891/EEC, and Directives 2001/24/EC, 2002/47/EC, 2004/25/EC, 2005/56/EC, 2007/36/EC, 2011/35/EU, 2012/30/EU and 2013/36/EU, and Regulations (EU) No 1093/2010 and (EU) No 648/2012, of the European Parliament and of the Council. 2014. OJ L 173: 190–348.

EurActiv.com with Reuters. 2016. "Germany blocks small progress on banking union at EU summit," 16 December, https://www.euractiv.com/section/euro-finance/news/germany-blocks-small-progress-on-banking-union-at-eu-summit/ (accessed May 28, 2021).

EBA. 2016. "EBA publishes 2016 EU-wide stress test results," Press release, 29 July, https://www.eba.europa.eu/eba-publishes-2016-eu-wide-stress-test-results (accessed May 26, 2021).

ECB. 2017. "ECB publishes guidance to banks on tackling non-performing loans," Press release, 20 March, https://www.bankingsupervision.europa.eu/press/pr/date/2017/html/sr170320.en.html (accessed May 25, 2021).

ECB. 2016. "What is precautionary recapitalisation and how does it work?," 27 December, https://www.bankingsupervision.europa.eu/about/ssmexplained/html/precautionary_recapitalisation.en.html (accessed May 29, 2021).

ECB. 2014. "Results of the 2014 Comprehensive Assessment," 26 October, https://www.bankingsupervision.europa.eu/banking/tasks/comprehensive_assessment/2014/html/index.en.html (accessed May 27, 2021).

European Commission. 2014. "EU Bank Recovery and Resolution Directive (BRRD): Frequently Asked Questions," Memo, 15 April, https://ec.europa.eu/commission/presscorner/detail/en/MEMO_14_297 (accessed May 27, 2021).

Ewing, Jack, and Gaia Pianigiani. 2013. "Patron of Siena Stumbles," *The New York Times*, 23 February, https://www.nytimes.com/2013/02/23/business/global/the-patron-of-siena-monte-dei-paschi-stumbles.html (accessed May 29, 2021).

Garrido, José, Emanuel Kopp, and Anke Weber. 2016. "Cleaning-up Bank Balance Sheets: Economic, Legal and Supervisory Measures for Italy," International Monetary Fund Working Papers, No. 16/135, July, https://www.imf.org/en/Publications/WP/Issues/2016/12/31/Cleaning-up-Bank-Balance-Sheets-Economic-Legal-and-Supervisory-Measures-for-Italy-44075 (accessed May 30, 2021).

Gehrig, Thomas, Marcello Messori, Antonio Nogueira Leite, André Sapir, Sascha Steffen, Philippe Tibi, David Vegara, Casper G. de Vries, and Miranda Xafa. 2016. "European Banking Supervision: The first eighteen months," Edited by Dirk Schoenmaker and Nicolas Véron, Bruegel, Blueprint series 25, https://www.bruegel.org/wp-content/uploads/2016/06/Blueprint-XXV-web.pdf (accessed May 26, 2021).

Gros, Daniel, and Ansgar Belke eds. 2015. *Banking Union as a Shock Absorber: Lessons for the Eurozone from the US*, Centre for European Policy Studies, Lanham: Rowman & Littlefield.

Hale, Thomas, and Dan McCrum. 2017. "Italy's bad debt problem refuses to go away," *Financial Times*, 8 May, https://www.ft.com/content/5be3608c-3182-11e7-9555-23ef563ecf9a (accessed May 28, 2021).

Jones, Claire, and Jim Brunsden. 2017. "Doubts grow over performance of Eurozone banking watchdog," *Financial Times*, 22 March, https://www.ft.com/content/19f809b4-0b1e-11e7-97d1-5e720a26771b (accessed May 26, 2021).

Merler, Silvia. 2017. "Italian banks: not quiet on the eastern front," Bruegel Blog Post, 31 March, https://www.bruegel.org/2017/03/italian-banks-not-quiet-on-the-eastern-front/ (accessed May 25, 2021).

Merler, Silvia. 2016a. "Bad banks and rude awakenings: Italian banks at a crossroads," Bruegel Blog Post, 26 January, https://www.bruegel.org/2016/01/bad-banks-and-rude-awakenings-italian-banks-at-a-crossroads/ (accessed May 31, 2021).

Merler, Silvia. 2016b. "An Italian take on banking crisis," Bruegel Opinion, 27 October, https://www.bruegel.org/2016/10/an-italian-take-on-banking-crisis/ (accessed May 27, 2021).

Merler, Silvia. 2016c. "The strange case of the MPS capital shortfall," Bruegel Blog Post, 27 December, https://www.bruegel.org/2016/12/the-strange-case-of-the-mps-capital-shortfall/ (accessed May 27, 2021).

Mesnard, B., M. Magnus, and A. Margerit. 2017. "The precautionary recapitalisation of Monte dei Paschi di Siena," European Parliament, Briefing, PE 587.392, 6 July, https://www.europarl.europa.eu/RegData/etudes/BRIE/2017/587392/IPOL_BRI(2017)587392_EN.pdf (accessed May 31, 2021).

Micossi, Stefano. 2016. "Banking crisis yet again and how to fix it," CEPS Commentary, 15 February, https://www.ceps.eu/publications/ banking-crisis-yet-again-and-how-fix-it (accessed May 29, 2021).

Monte dei Paschi di Siena. 2016. Press release, 26 December, https://www.gruppomps.it/static/upload/archivio/16911/CS_2016_12_26_ENG.pdf (accessed May 29, 2021).

Myers, Stewart C. 1977. Determinants of corporate borrowing. *Journal of Financial Economics* 5, no.2: 147–175.

Regulation (EU) No 806/2014 of the European Parliament and of the Council of 15 July 2014 establishing uniform rules and a uniform procedure for the resolution of credit institutions and certain investment firms in the framework of a Single Resolution Mechanism and a Single Resolution Fund and amending Regulation (EU) No 1093/2010 (SRMR). 2014. OJ L 225: 1–90.

Regulation (EU) No 1176/2011 of the European Parliament and of the Council of 16 November 2011 on the prevention and correction of macroeconomic imbalances. 2011. OJ L 306: 25–32.

Schoenmaker, Dirk. 2012. "Banking union: Where we're going wrong," VoxEU & CEPR Policy Portal, 16 October, http://voxeu.org/article/banking-union-where-we-re-going-wrong (accessed May 27, 2021).

SRB. n.d. "What is the Single Resolution Fund?," https://srb.europa.eu/en/content/single-resolution-fund (accessed May 27, 2021).

The Corner. 2016. "Italy's Rescue Fund Atlante: No Sector Solution, But An Effective Tool For Pressing Issues," 13 April, https://thecorner.eu/news-europe/italys-rescue-fund-atlante-no-sector-solution-but-an-effective-tool-for-pressing-issues/53454/ (accessed May 29, 2021).

The Economist. 2009. "One size fits none," Special report, 13 June, https://www.economist.com/special-report/2009/06/13/one-size-fits-none (accessed May 25, 2021).

The Economist Intelligence Unit. 2016. "Italy approves precautionary recapitalisation for MPS," 23 December, http://country.eiu.com/article.aspx?articleid=1494952133&Country=Italy&topic=Economy&subtopic=For_9 (accessed May 29, 2021).

Treanor, Jill. 2016. "Monte dei Paschi di Siena: a brief guide to the world's oldest bank", *The Guardian*, 22 December, https://www.theguardian.com/business/2016/dec/22/monte-dei-paschi-the-history-of-the-worlds-oldest-bank (accessed May 29, 2021).

Véron, Nicolas. 2017. "ECB finally addressing Italian bank woes," Bruegel Opinion, 4 January, https://www.bruegel.org/2017/01/ecb-finally-addressing-italian-bank-woes/?utm_content=buffer76686&utm_medium=social&utm_source=twitter.com&utm_campaign=buffer+(bruegel) (accessed May 29, 2021).

Véron, Nicolas, Dirk Shoenmaker, and Silvia Merler. 2017. "How will Europe's banking system respond to future challenges?," Bruegel Podcast, 5 May, https://www.bruegel.org/2017/05/how-will-europes-banking-system-respond-to-future-challenges/ (accessed May 25, 2021).

Véron, Nicolas. 2016a. "Market turbulence highlights bumpy transition to Europe's new bank policy regime," Bruegel Blog Post, 8 March, https://www.bruegel.org/2016/03/market-turbulence-highlights-bumpy-transition-to-europes-new-bank-policy-regime/ (accessed May 26, 2021).

Véron, Nicolas. 2016b. "Italy's banking problem is serious but can be fixed," Bruegel Blog Post, 14 July, https://www.bruegel.org/2016/07/italys-banking-problem-is-serious-but-can-be-fixed/ (accessed May 26, 2021).

Véron, Nicolas. 2016c. "Breaking the vicious circle," Bruegel Opinion, 21 October, https://www.bruegel.org/2016/10/breaking-the-vicious-circle/ (accessed May 28, 2021).

Véron, Nicolas. 2014. "Testimony: European Banking Union: Current Outlook and Short-Term Choices," Statement presented at the conference: "Banking Union and the Financing of the Portuguese Economy," 26 February, https://www.piie.com/sites/default/files/publications/testimony/veron20140226.pdf (accessed May 26, 2021).

Véron, Nicolas. 2013. "Banking Nationalism and the European Crisis," Peterson Institute for International Economics and Bruegel, 27 June, https://www.piie.com/sites/default/files/publications/papers/veron20130627.pdf (accessed May 30, 2021).

Zanni, Marco. 2017. "Solvency characteristics of the two Venetian banks," Question for a written answer Z-029/2017 to the Chair of the Single Supervisory Mechanism Board (Rule 131a), https://www.europarl.europa.eu/doceo/document/ECON-QZ-603023_EN.pdf?redirect (accessed May 29, 2021).

Zanni, Marco, and Marco Valli. 2016. "Letter from MEP to Elke Koenig, Chair of the Single Resolution Board," 24 November, https://www.europarl.europa.eu/cmsdata/112323/D52587%20-%20Koenig%20-%20Letter%20by%20MEP%20Zanni%20Valli%20-%20BS.pdf (accessed May 29, 2021).

CHAPTER 8

POWERS OF THE BANK OF GREECE UNDER THE BANKING UNION: INTERPLAY WITH THE ECB

MARTHA KAVVATHA*

Introduction

In 2012, under the pressure of the evolving financial crisis, the Banking Union was proclaimed by the European Commission (European Commission 2012) in order to break the link between private and public debt and to restore confidence in banking supervision by ensuring the impartial and uniform implementation of a stringent regulatory and supervisory framework for all euro area banks. The first pillar of the Banking Union was put in place with the creation of the Single Supervisory Mechanism (hereinafter SSM), which introduces an integrated approach, where supervision is being exercised by the European Central Bank (hereinafter ECB) either directly or via national supervisors, under the oversight of the ECB.

The SSM is governed by two regulations: Regulation 1024/2013 (SSMR) that establishes the SSM, which is composed of the ECB and the National Competent Authorities (hereinafter NCAs), and Regulation 468/2014, called the 'framework regulation' (SSMFR), that puts in place and organises the technical arrangements for their cooperation.

---

* PhD, Attorney at law, Bank of Greece. The author is working on banking supervisory issues.
This chapter should not be reported as representing the views of the Bank of Greece. The views are those of the author and do not necessarily reflect those of the Bank of Greece.

The delineation of competences between the European and the national level of supervision is reflected in principle in two articles of the SSMR. According to art. 4(1) SSMR, headed "Tasks conferred on the ECB", the ECB has exclusive competence to carry out the tasks stated in that provision, within an SSM composed of the ECB and the NCAs, in relation to all credit institutions established in the Eurozone. Furthermore, according to art. 6(6) SSMR, "national competent authorities shall carry out and be responsible for the tasks referred to in points (b), (d) to (g) and (i) of art. 4(1) and adopting all relevant supervisory decisions with regard to credit institutions classified as less significant".[1]

Art. 4(1) in combination with art. 6(6) SSMR have for a long time been interpreted as introducing a distribution of competences between the ECB and the NCAs, according to which the former is competent for the direct supervision of Significant credit Institutions (hereinafter SIs), while the latter institutions remain competent for the direct supervision of Less Significant credit Institutions (hereinafter LSIs) under the oversight of the ECB (Wymeersch 2014). However, the General Court, in its first ruling relating to the SSM (Landeskreditbank Baden-Württemberg - Förderbank v European Central Bank 2017),[2] rejected the idea of a distribution of competences between the ECB and the NCAs and accepted the exclusive competence of the ECB to pursue and achieve the tasks listed in art. 4 SSMR for all credit institutions, while the direct prudential supervision by the NCAs under the SSM was envisaged "as a mechanism of assistance to the ECB rather than the exercise of autonomous

[1] Whether the status of a supervised entity is significant or less significant is determined on the basis of criteria set out in the SSMFR (arts. 39-42 and 50-66 SSMFR), which include the size of the credit institution, the importance of the credit institution for the economy of the Union or any participating member state, the significance of the credit institution with regard to cross-border activities, a request for or the receipt of direct public financial assistance from the European Stability Mechanism, and the fact that the supervised entity is one of the three most significant credit institutions in a participating member state. Nevertheless, the ECB may, upon its decision, assume direct supervision of credit institutions that do not fulfil any of the significance criteria if the NCA requests so or on the ECB's own initiative in order to ensure a high quality of supervisory standards.

[2] In March 2015, L-Bank went before the General Court to challenge the ECB's final decision that defined L-Bank as a significant credit institution. It essentially claimed that the ECB had incorrectly applied article 6(4) SSMR and article 70 SSMFR because it had based its assessment of the bank's significance solely upon size and did not take into account the existence of particular circumstances which make it inappropriate to classify a supervised entity as significant under article 70 SSMFR.

competence" (Landeskreditbank Baden-Württemberg - Förderbank v European Central Bank 2017, par. 58). Under the interpretation of the General Court, which has thereafter been confirmed by the Court of Justice of the European Union (hereinafter CJEU) (Landeskreditbank Baden-Württemberg - Förderbank v European Central Bank 2019), it is within a decentralised framework of cooperation (as defined by both art. 6 SSMR and the SSMFR) that an allocation of tasks, powers, and responsibilities is operated between the European and national levels of supervision, depending on whether the supervised entity is classified as SI or LSI.

Nevertheless, a few months following the ruling of the CJEU, the German Federal Constitutional Court (hereinafter GFCC) ruled that the adoption of the SSMR and the transfer of supervisory powers to the ECB does not exceed the competences conferred on the European Union (hereinafter EU) by the Treaties, and in particular by art. 127(6) of the Treaty on the Functioning of European Union (hereinafter TFEU),[3] in a sufficiently qualified manner, provided that this article is interpreted strictly (2 BvR 1685/14). In the view of the GFCC, a restrictive interpretation of art. 127(6) TFEU would mean that the SSMR does not confer full banking supervision on the ECB, but provides for a division of supervisory competences between the ECB and the NCAs. Essentially, only specific supervisory powers, which are crucial in order to ensure the coherent and effective implementation of the EU's policy in this domain, are conferred to the ECB. Meanwhile, national authorities retain their competences, as attributed to them by national law, and not on the basis of a re-delegation of powers conferred to the ECB.[4] Conversely, in the view of the GFCC, any interpretation pursuant to which the SSMR confers the entire prudential supervision of credit institutions to the ECB amounts to an *ultra vires* act.

---

[3] According to this provision, specific tasks relating to the prudential supervision of credit institutions and other financial institutions, with the exception of insurance undertakings, may be conferred on the ECB.

[4] In the view of the GFCC, such a re-delegation of powers by the ECB would entail that all supervisory tasks had fully been conferred on the ECB, which is specifically not what art. 127(6) TFEU allows and what the SSM Regulation provides. A full conferral of all tasks would exceed the limits of the European integration agenda in an evident and structurally significant manner, and would deprive member states of a central part of their economic governance. Such an interpretation of the SSMR is neither compatible with the wording of art. 127(6) TFEU, nor tenable in light of a systematic analysis.

Although the CJEU's interpretation of the SSMR differs from the interpretation of the GFCC in regard to both the methodology[5] and final outcome,[6] the GFCC finds that its ruling is in line with the decision of the CJEU, as the CJEU's interpretation in respect to the general division of supervisory competences between the ECB and the NCAs does not belong to the crucial elements of the case and is, therefore, not binding.[7] Despite their differences, both courts suggest that, in practice, the NCAs carry out the direct supervision of the LSIs subject to the ECB's specific powers laid down in the SSMR.[8] In this sense, the current organisation of banking supervision with respect to the LSIs, as presented therein, seems to fit both views, even though the interpretation of the CJEU could justify a more active and decisive role of the ECB.[9]

The functioning of the SSM relies on the obligation of cooperation in good faith and of exchange of information between the ECB and the NCAs (art. 6(2) SSMR), which are enshrined in the SSMR and underpin all aspects of the interaction between the European and the national level of supervision. These principles are further specified throughout the SSMR and SSMFR, and define the tasks and powers of national authorities, not only in regard to the supervision of LSIs, but also to the Eurozone's most important banks. Both levels of supervision are coordinated in the SSM, but the ECB remains ultimately responsible for the effective and consistent functioning of the entire mechanism, and to this end, it holds important coordinating powers. In the subsequent analysis, the tasks and powers that remain with the Bank of Greece (BoG)

---

[5] The CJEU interpreted the SSMR but did not assess its conformity with art. 127(6) TFEU.

[6] According to the interpretation of the CJEU, the ECB is the sole competent supervisor in a system of decentralised prudential supervision, while in the view of the GFCC, the SSM is a system of cooperation between the European and national prudential supervisors, where each of them has its own competences.

[7] The CJEU has held that exclusive competence is conferred on the ECB for determining the content of the definition of "particular circumstances" within the meaning of art. 6(4)(2) SSMR, which grants the ECB exclusive supervisory powers in relation to institutions that are considered significant according to the criteria laid down in the same art. 6(4)(2) SSMR.

[8] In particular, the power of the ECB to issue regulations, guidelines, or general instructions to NCAs, or to take over the direct supervision of LSIs (article 6(5) SSMR).

[9] Further, the interpretation of the SSMR that will be upheld may lead to different solutions in cases where the ECB and the NCA(s) have a different approach with regard to LSI supervision, or if questions of the supervisor's liability arise.

within the SSM, in its quality of NCA,[10] are identified in correlation to those conferred on the ECB.

The SSM scope and relevant powers

The scope of the ECB's competence for direct prudential supervision is limited by the Treaty to credit institutions, in the sense used in the Capital Requirements Regulation 575/2013/EU (CRR), meaning "an undertaking the business of which is to receive deposits or other repayable funds from the public and to grant credits for its own account".[11] Institutions that qualify as "credit institutions" under national law, but do not fulfil the criteria of the European definition, lay beyond the ECB's competence and are under the remit of national authorities. The ECB also conducts supervision on a consolidated basis, as provided for by art. 111 of Directive 2013/36/EU (CRD IV) in respect to credit institutions, financial holding companies, or mixed financial holding companies that are significant on a consolidated basis (art. 4(1)(g) SSMR and art. 8(1) SSMFR). Furthermore, the ECB is responsible for the direct supervision of branches established within a participating member state by a credit institution established in a non-participating member state insofar as the branches are classified as significant (art. 14 SSMFR).

The BoG retains its competence for the supervision of insurance companies,[12] as well as financial institutions that qualify as leasing or factoring companies and non-performing loans (NPL) servicers. Furthermore, pursuant to the wording of the SSMR (recital 28 SSMR), the BoG still performs those supervisory tasks not conferred to the ECB by the SSMR, including the power to receive notifications from credit institutions in relation to the right of establishment and the free provision of services, the supervision of credit institutions from third countries establishing a branch or providing cross-border services in the Union, the supervision of payments services, the day-to-day verifications of credit institutions, and

[10] According to art. 4(40) Regulation (EU) 575/2013 (CRR), "competent authority" means a public authority or body officially recognised by national law, which is empowered by national law to supervise institutions as part of the supervisory system in operation in the member state concerned.

[11] Art. 2(3) SSMR, which refers to article 4(1) point 1 CRR. Nevertheless, the TFEU, in its article 127(6), would allow other financial institutions to be included in the SSM's remit.

[12] Supervisory tasks concerning insurance undertakings are expressly excluded from the scope of art. 127(6) TFEU, which serves as the legal basis for the creation of the SSM.

finally, the application and enforcement of legislation regarding the prevention of the use of the financial system for the purpose of money laundering and terrorist financing (Directives 2015/849 and 2018/843) (AML/CTF). The BoG also shares competences with the Hellenic Capital Markets Commission (HCMC) in relation to markets in financial instruments and with the competent Ministry of Development in regard to certain aspects of consumer protection.

The powers conferred on the ECB are meant to enable it to pursue the micro- and macro-prudential tasks it has been vested with, pursuant to arts. 4(1)(2) and 5 SSMR (Lackhoff 2017). In order to carry out those tasks, the ECB is regarded as the competent authority[13] in terms of European law,[14] and has therefore been given supervisory, investigatory, and sanctioning powers. According to art. 9 SSMR, for the performance of the tasks listed in arts. 4(1), 4(2) and 5 of said Regulation, the ECB shall have the powers set out in the SSMR, as well as the powers attributed to NCAs under Union law (where "Union" shall be construed as including EU Regulations, as well as national law implementing EU Directives or exercising a legislative option granted by a Regulation to member states).[15] The ECB may also require, by way of instructions, that the national authorities make use of their own powers, under and in accordance with the conditions set out in national law, in cases where the SSMR does not confer such powers to the ECB, but these powers are necessary in order for the ECB to carry out its tasks (art. 9(1) third subpar. SSMR). The most debated issue concerning the ECB's powers is whether prudential tasks and powers provided by national law but not stemming from Union law[16] can be exercised directly by the ECB, which is known as "the national power issue" (Lackhoff 2017). Currently, the ECB consistently opts to exercise these powers directly, insofar as it can be argued that the relevant power falls within a task conferred on the ECB

---

[13] Or the designated authority as the case may be.

[14] According to art. 4(40) CRR, "competent authority" means a public authority or body officially recognised by national law, which is empowered by national law to supervise institutions as part of the supervisory system in operation in the member state concerned.

[15] On the contrary, the ECB is not bound by the exercise of the options granted by a Regulation to competent or designated authorities, and has the power, in its quality of competent authority, to exercise itself such options and/or discretion for significant institutions (see, for instance, Regulation 2016/445, 60).

[16] Meaning that they do not stem from the implementation of EU Directives or from the use of an option under EU Regulations.

and underpins its supervisory function.[17] Supervisory powers provided by national law that do not fulfil the above two criteria are still exercised by the BoG.[18]

In this context, the ECB and the NCAs exercise their supervisory, investigatory, and sanctioning powers within the SSM in accordance with the allocation introduced by the SSMR and the SSMFR.

Micro-prudential powers

Pursuant to the delineation of powers set out in the SSMR, micro-prudential supervision of SIs falls within the remit of the ECB. The main aspects of such supervision are reflected in art. 4(1) SSMR and include, inter alia, compliance of the supervised entities with prudential requirements in the area of own funds requirements, liquidity, leverage and reporting (art. 4(1)(d) SSMR); compliance with requirements regarding robust governance arrangements, including the fit and proper requirements for the persons responsible for the management of credit institution, risk management processes, internal control mechanisms, and remuneration policies (art. 4(1)(e) SSMR); conduct of supervisory reviews and stress tests and imposition on credit institutions, on the basis of such supervisory reviews, of specific additional own funds, publication or liquidity requirements, and other measures (art. 4(1)(f) SSMR); supervision on a consolidated basis (art. 4(1)(g) SSMR); participation in supplementary supervision of a financial conglomerate in relation to the credit institutions included in it (art. 4(1)(h) SSMR); and finally, exercise of supervisory tasks in relation to recovery plans, and early intervention measures, excluding any resolution powers (art. 4(1)(i) SSMR).

In relation to the supervision of SIs, the ECB has, along with the powers granted to competent authorities under national law, the power to adopt the supervisory measures provided for in art. 16 SSMR, if at least

---

[17] Such powers include the approval of acquisitions by SIs of holdings in non-banks or banks outside the EU, of mergers/demergers involving a significant institution, of asset transfers/divestments by significant institutions, of a significant institution's statutes, and of the appointment of key function holders in significant institutions.

[18] Or by other national authorities as the case may be (e.g., the Hellenic Competition Commission is competent for the approval of mergers from a competition law perspective).

one of the conditions of art. 16(1) is met.[19] Supervisory powers under art. 16(2) SSMR include the power to impose capital add-ons to credit institutions (art. 16(2)(a) SSMR); to require the reinforcement of the arrangements, processes, mechanisms and strategies (art. 16(2)(b) SSMR); to require institutions to present a plan to restore compliance with supervisory requirements and set a deadline for its implementation (art. 16(2)(c) SSMR); to require institutions to apply a specific provisioning policy or treatment of assets in terms of own funds requirements (art. 16(2)(d) SSMR); to restrict or limit the business, operations or network of institutions, or to request the divestment of activities that pose excessive risks to the soundness of an institution (art. 16(2)(e) SSMR); to require the reduction of the risk inherent in the activities, products and systems of institutions (art. 16(2)(f) SSMR); to require institutions to limit variable remuneration as a percentage of net revenues (art. 16(2)(g) SSMR); to require institutions to use net profits to strengthen own funds (art. 16(2)(h) SSMR); to restrict or prohibit distributions by the institution to shareholders, members or holders of Additional Tier 1 instruments where the prohibition does not constitute an event of default of the institution (art. 16(2)(i) SSMR); to impose additional or more frequent reporting requirements (art. 16(2)(j) SSMR); to impose specific liquidity requirements (art. 16(2)(k) SSMR); to require additional disclosures (art. 16(2)(l) SSMR); and, finally, to remove at any time members from the management body of credit institutions who do not fulfil the requirements set out in prudential Union law (art. 16(2)(m) SSMR).

In exercising its tasks in relation to SIs established in Greece, the ECB cooperates closely with the BoG. Acknowledging the important and long-established expertise of national supervisors in the supervision of

---

[19] Pursuant to article 16(1) SSMR, the ECB may exercise the supervisory powers of par. 2 of said article to take the necessary measures at an early stage to address relevant problems in any of the following circumstances: (a) the credit institution does not meet the requirements of the prudential Union law, (b) the ECB has evidence that the credit institution is likely to breach the requirements of prudential EU law within the next 12 months, (c) based on a determination, in the framework of a supervisory review in accordance with point (f) of article 4(1), that the arrangements, strategies, processes and mechanisms implemented by the credit institution, and the own funds and liquidity held by it, do not ensure a sound management and coverage of its risks. It is noted that for the purpose of assessing if conditions under (a) or (b) are met, prudential Union law should be understood as including the CRR, the national provisions transposing EU Directives, as well as any other prudential provision that may be found, for example, in regulatory technical standards.

credit institutions within their territory, and their economic, organisational and cultural specificities, as well as the existence of a large body of dedicated and highly qualified staff for those purposes, the SSMR entrusts the national authorities with the task of assisting the ECB in the preparation and implementation of any acts relating to the exercise of the ECB's supervisory tasks (recital 37 SSMR). In this context, the BoG is involved in the supervision of SIs by appointing at least one of its staff as members of the Joint Supervisory Teams (hereinafter JSTs) responsible for the day-to-day supervision of significant Greek institutions, while also designating a sub-coordinator of those JSTs. The sub-coordinator shall assist the coordinator of the team, who is assigned by the ECB, in regard to the organisation and coordination of the tasks in the JST (art. 6 SSMFR). Furthermore, the national supervisor will assist the ECB in the performance of its tasks, by submitting draft decisions to the ECB on his own initiative or upon request (arts. 90(1)a and 91 SSMFR), by assisting the ECB in the preparation and implementation of any supervisory acts, by assisting in verification activities and day-to-day assessment of the Greek SIs (art. 90(1)(b) SSMFR), by participating in on-site inspection teams (art. 144(1) SSMFR), by enforcing the ECB's decisions, using when necessary the powers he has under national law and may not be exercised directly by the ECB, or by facilitating the access by the ECB to the business premises of the persons in relation to whom the ECB exercises its general investigatory powers (art. 90(1)(c) SSMFR). Investigatory powers of the BoG remain intact and may be exercised vis-à-vis SIs, although their exercise is subject to the obligation of the BoG to inform, report, and closely coordinate with the ECB (art. 6(6) 2nd and 3rd subpar. SSMR).

A special aspect of the assistance provided by the BoG to the ECB concerns the assessment of the suitability of members of the management bodies of significant supervised entities.[20] Although the competence for conducting the "fit and proper" assessment lies with the ECB, appointments are declared by the credit institutions (or exceptionally by the appointee) to the BoG, which then informs the ECB. Together they collect the necessary information, carry out the assessment, and present a detailed proposal for a decision, following which the ECB prepares a decision with the assistance of the NCA. In 2018, and in order to streamline the supervisory decision-making process, the ECB implemented a system of intensified NCA assistance called "alternative fit and proper

[20] It is noted though that the "fit and proper" assessments that are part of a licensing or qualifying holding procedure are conducted by the ECB for SIs and LSIs alike.

process", which allows, under certain conditions, ECB decisions addressed to SIs to be taken based solely on NCAs' assessments (Hernández Saseta 2018).

The role of the BoG is more important in relation to the micro-prudential supervision of LSIs, which fall under its direct supervision. The BoG carries out and is responsible for the tasks referred to in art. 4(1)(b), (d) to (g), and (i) SSMR, and is authorised to adopt all relevant supervisory decisions in relation to LSIs. Acknowledging, however, the fact that even smaller institutions may pose a threat to financial stability (recital 16 SSMR), the SSMR reserves an overseeing and coordinating role for the ECB, which is declared responsible for the effective and consistent functioning of the SSM as a whole and for the establishment of an overarching framework for the supervision of LSIs. In this context, the BoG, in exercising its supervisory powers, shall follow the recommendations (art. 4(3) 2nd subpar. SSMR), regulations, guidelines and general instructions (art. 6(5)(a) SSMR)[21] issued by the ECB for the exercise of specific supervisory tasks and the adoption of specific supervisory decisions, while the ECB can take over the direct supervision of an LSI in order to ensure consistent application of high supervisory standards (art. 6(5)(b) SSMR). Furthermore, the SSMFR introduces a twofold obligation of notification and reporting for the NCAs in order to enable the ECB to exercise its overseeing role in relation to LSI supervision effectively. On the one hand, the BoG shall notify ex ante[22] the ECB of any material supervisory procedures regarding the LSIs under its direct supervision. Procedures that are considered material and are subject to prior notification include those that concern the removal of members of the management boards and the appointment of special managers to take over the management of an LSI (art. 97(2)(a) SSMFR), those that have a significant impact on the LSI (art. 97(2)(b) SSMFR), those that may negatively affect the reputation of the SSM (art. 97(4)(b) SSMFR), and any other procedure that is considered material by the BoG (art. 97(4)(a) SSMFR). Furthermore, supervisory decisions for high-priority LSIs[23] that

[21] Such instructions, being of a general nature, may not concern an individual LSI, but rather "groups or categories of credit institutions".

[22] The information shall be provided by the NCAs ex ante or in duly justified cases of urgency simultaneously to opening a procedure (art. 97(1) SSMFR).

[23] High-priority LSIs are less significant supervised entities which the ECB considers that, based on the general criteria defined by the ECB regarding their risk situation and potential impact on the domestic financial system, should be the object of a closer monitoring by the ECB.

are considered material[24] shall be notified to the ECB before their adoption,[25] and the ECB shall express its views on the draft decision within a reasonable time before their planned adoption. In addition, the BoG shall report ex post to the ECB annually on the measures it has taken and on the performance of the tasks it carries out in accordance with art. 6(6) of the SSM Regulation (arts. 99-100 SSMFR).

Common procedures

Apart from the tasks carried out in respect only to significant institutions, art. 4(1) SSMR confers to the ECB certain tasks to be carried out in relation to all credit institutions of the Eurozone in order to ensure that only operators with a sound economic basis, an organisation capable of dealing with the specific risks inherent to deposit taking and credit provision, and suitable directors, carry out these activities (recital 20 SSMR). In this vein, the ECB is vested with the power to grant prior authorisation for taking up the business in a participating member state (art. 4(1)(a) SSMR), to assess notifications of the acquisition and disposal of qualifying holdings in credit institutions (art. 4(1)(c) SSMR), and to withdraw authorisations (art. 4(1)(a) SSMR) in relation to all credit institutions ("common procedures"). The contribution of the BoG is also important in the context of the aforementioned common procedures. The BoG remains the point of entry for applications for prior authorisation for taking up the business of credit institution, and shall assess such requests and verify whether conditions set out in national law are met.[26] If, following the assessment, the BoG considers that the requirements of national law are met, it submits a draft proposal to the ECB to be taken

[24] Decisions that relate to the removal of members of the management boards of the less significant supervised entities and the appointment of special managers, that have a significant impact on the less significant supervised entity, that may negatively affect the reputation of the SSM, or decisions for which the ECB's views are sought (art. 98(2) and (3) SSMR).

[25] Pursuant to art. 98(4) SSMFR, the draft decision shall be notified to the ECB ten days in advance of the planned date of adoption, while in cases of urgency, a reasonable time period for sending a draft decision that meets the criteria laid down in paragraphs 1, 2 and 3 to the ECB shall be defined by the relevant NCA.

[26] This includes national law that implements the CRD IV Directive (Greek Law 4261/2014).

into consideration for the adoption of the final decision.[27] If not, the BoG may reject the application by issuing the final (negative) decision.

The national supervisor is also the point of entry for notifications of the intention to acquire a qualifying holding in a credit institution established in Greece. The BoG shall assess whether the proposed acquisition complies with the requirements set out in national law, and shall submit a draft proposal to the ECB for the objection or not to the acquisition. In these cases, contrary to what happens in the authorisation procedure, the BoG cannot adopt a final decision rejecting the request, and the final decision always lies with the ECB.

Finally, the BoG actively assists the ECB in regards to the withdrawal of an authorisation. A proposal for the withdrawal of an authorisation may be submitted to the ECB by the BoG in cases set out either in the relevant Union or the national law. In the latter case, the decision adopted by the ECB takes into account the justification behind the withdrawal put forward by the BoG, whose role is thus crucial. In all cases, the BoG consults closely with the ECB in order to examine necessary remedial measures, including resolution measures.

An important aspect of the role reserved for NCAs —which are also competent authorities in the sense of the AML/CTF Directive— such as the BoG, has come to light in view of the recent cases of withdrawal of authorisation due to breaches of anti-money laundering legislation (European Parliament 2018).[28] Infringements of AML legislation justify the withdrawal of authorisation under EU law,[29] and are thus among the cases in which the ECB may proceed with the withdrawal on its own initiative without any relevant proposal by the NCA (art. 14(5) SSMR). Nevertheless, supervisory tasks related to the AML are expressly excluded from the tasks conferred to the ECB by the SSMR and are exercised by national authorities. Since the ECB's tasks do not include AML/CTF, it cannot conduct its own investigations (for example, on-site inspections) into AML/CTF compliance. To decide whether a license should be

[27] Whether such proposal may be accompanied by recommendations, conditions or restrictions depends largely on the national administrative law of each member state. If the NCA does attach such recommendations, conditions or restrictions, it shall be responsible for assessing compliance with these.
[28] ABLV Bank in Latvia and Versobank in Estonia.
[29] Art. 18(f) in combination with art. 67(1)(o) CRD IV. Alternatively, withdrawal due to AML/CTF breaches could be initiated on the basis of deficiencies of the governance [art. 18(f) in combination with art. 67(1)(d) CRD IV].

withdrawn as a result of breaches of national AML-related provisions, the BoG would need to inform the ECB of the circumstances and facts justifying the withdrawal, and the ECB has to rely on the facts as investigated by the BoG in its quality of competent authority for AML/CTF. Drawing conclusions from these facts, in particular whether they justify for a license withdrawal, would, however, be a competence of the ECB, who will need to assess inter alia whether the withdrawal of authorisation respects the principle of proportionality (Nouy 2018).

Macro-prudential powers

Furthermore, the ECB's tasks include measures aimed at macro-prudential stability for all credit institutions of the Eurozone. Nevertheless, in the domain of macro-prudential supervision, the ECB shares powers with the NCAs, which remain primarily responsible for the application of macro-prudential tools aimed at addressing systemic or macro-prudential risks in their jurisdictions, including the imposition of additional capital buffers.[30] Pursuant to art. 5(2) SSMR, the ECB shall be duly notified by the NCAs prior to the adoption of such measures,[31] and shall have the power to apply higher requirements and more stringent measures, if deemed necessary.[32]

Investigatory powers

Within the SSM, the ECB is also vested with important investigatory powers (arts. 10-13 SSMR) that may be exercised in relation to all credit institutions, regardless of whether they are classified as SI or LSI, and also in relation to legal and natural persons listed in art. 10(1) SSMR.[33] Pursuant to the relevant Section of the SSMR, the ECB has

---

30 The buffer requirements mentioned in art. 5(1) SSMR mean the buffers provided for in arts.129 to 142 CRD IV, i.e., the capital conservation buffer, the institution-specific countercyclical buffer, risk buffers for systemically relevant institutions, and the systematic risk buffers.

31 The obligation of notification also exists in relation to the intention of national authorities to designate a credit institution as an Other Systemically Important Institution (hereinafter O-SII) also when there is no simultaneous imposition of an O-SII buffer.

32 This includes the power of the ECB to impose a buffer requirement in cases where the NCA does not impose any such requirement (art. 102 SSMFR).

33 Art. 10(1) SSMR concerning the request of information refers to "(a) credit institutions established in the participating Member States; (b) financial holding

information-gathering powers that may be exercised either through ad-hoc information requests and/or obligatory reporting at recurring intervals. The ECB may also conduct all necessary investigations as well as on-site inspections. At the same time, however, the BoG retains its investigatory powers that may be exercised in relation to all institutions established in Greece, in close cooperation and coordination with the ECB.

Sanctioning and enforcement powers

Finally, following a rather convoluted delineation of powers, the SSMR confers to the ECB certain enforcement and sanctioning powers only regarding SIs, while the BoG remains competent for sanctions vis-à-vis LSIs. In this context, the ECB may impose administrative pecuniary penalties to legal persons[34] for the breach of requirements under directly applicable EU law, provided that such penalties are made available to competent authorities under the relevant EU law (art. 18(1) SSMR). It may also impose fines and periodic penalty payments for breaches of an ECB decision or Regulation in accordance with the provisions of Regulation 2532/98/EC (art. 18(7) SSMR).

Important sanctioning powers in regard to SIs remain, however, in the remit of the BoG (art. 18(5) SSMR). The BoG still has the power to impose non-pecuniary administrative penalties for breaches of directly applicable EU law,[35] pecuniary and non-pecuniary penalties for breaches

---

companies established in the participating Member States; (c) mixed financial holding companies established in the participating Member States; (d) mixed-activity holding companies established in the participating Member States; (e) persons belonging to the entities referred to in points (a) to (d); (f) third parties to whom the entities referred to in points (a) to (d) have outsourced functions or activities". Art. 11 concerning the conduct of general investigations refers to "any person referred to in Article 10(1) established or located in a participating Member State," while art. 12 concerning on-site inspections applies to "legal persons referred to in Article 10(1) and any other undertaking included in supervision on a consolidated basis where the ECB is the consolidating supervisor in accordance with point (g) of Article 4(1)".

[34] Such legal persons include significant credit institutions and financial holding companies or mixed financial holding companies that fall into the perimeter of ECB consolidated supervision.

[35] For example, a cease and desist order to the credit institution (art. 67(2)(b) CRD IV) for breach of its reporting obligations (art. 67(1)(e) CRD IV) shall be issued by the BoG.

of non-directly applicable Union law[36] or national law, as well as all kinds of administrative penalties or measures imposed on members of the management board of credit institutions or any other individuals who, under national law, are responsible for a breach by a credit institution, financial holding company or mixed financial holding company.[37] Nevertheless, the sanctioning powers of the BoG regarding SIs within the SSM may not be exercised autonomously, but only following a request of the ECB. In such cases, the ECB shares with the BoG the facts establishing the alleged breach and requires the BoG to open proceedings. The latter shall notify the ECB of the completion of any penalty procedure initiated at the request of the ECB, and in particular of any penalties imposed (art. 134(3) SSMFR). The BoG retains the power to open proceedings on its own initiative regarding LSIs or the application of national law for tasks not conferred on the ECB (art. 134(1) last subpar.).

The distribution of powers between the European and the national levels of supervision in the area of enforcement and sanctions is a vivid example of the unique institutional set-up of the SSM, in which the NCAs formally retain certain powers, but these can no longer be autonomously exercised for the purpose of carrying out tasks that have been attributed to the ECB (Pizzolla 2018, 3-23).

Conclusion

The SSM, established in the aftermath of the financial crisis, results in a transfer of powers from national competent authorities to an EU institution (namely the ECB) in relation to banking supervision. The language of the SSM Regulation, being the outcome of a political compromise between those pushing for a full Europeanisation of prudential supervision affecting any bank, on the one hand, and those wanting to preserve an autonomous field of competence for NCAs regarding LSIs, on the other hand, may give rise to diverging interpretations, which mirror this original divide. However, regardless of the interpretation that is

[36] This includes national law transposing relevant Directives. For example, for breaches listed in art. 66(1) CRD IV (as transposed in Greek Law 4261/2014), all administrative penalties and measures provided for in par. 2 of the same article shall be imposed by the BoG, given the fact that the provisions that have been breached are those of an EU Directive (i.e. of non-directly applicable Union law).

[37] For example, pecuniary penalties to natural persons under art. 67(2)(f) CRD IV (as transposed in Greek Law 4261/2014) will be imposed by the BoG, regardless of the origin of the provision that has been breached.

adopted, it is indisputable that despite the centralisation of decision-making at the European level, national authorities, including the Bank of Greece, retain a substantial role, while cooperation and coordination between the national and the European levels is deemed crucial for the fulfilment of the objectives of this undertaking.

References

CJEU, Judgment of the Court (First Chamber) of 8 May 2019, Landeskreditbank Baden-Württemberg - Förderbank v European Central Bank, C-450/17 P, ECLI:EU:C:2019:372.

CJEU, Judgment of the General Court (Fourth Chamber, Extended Composition) of 16 May 2017, Landeskreditbank Baden-Württemberg - Förderbank v European Central Bank, T-122/15, ECLI:EU:T: 2017:337.

Directive (EU) 2018/843 of the European Parliament and of the Council of 30 May 2018 amending Directive (EU) 2015/849 on the prevention of the use of the financial system for the purposes of money laundering or terrorist financing, and amending Directives 2009/138/EC and 2013/36/EU (AML/CTF). 2018. OJ L 156: 43–74.

Directive (EU) 2015/849 of the European Parliament and of the Council of 20 May 2015 on the prevention of the use of the financial system for the purposes of money laundering or terrorist financing, amending Regulation (EU) No 648/2012 of the European Parliament and of the Council, and repealing Directive 2005/60/EC of the European Parliament and of the Council and Commission Directive 2006/70/EC (AML/CTF). 2015. OJ L 141: 73–117.

Directive 2013/36/EU of the European Parliament and of the Council of 26 June 2013 on access to the activity of credit institutions and the prudential supervision of credit institutions and investment firms, amending Directive 2002/87/EC and repealing Directives 2006/48/EC and 2006/49/EC (CRD IV). 2013. OJ L 176: 338–436.

European Commission. 2012. "Communication A Roadmap towards a Banking Union," COM(2012) 510 final, 12 September, https://eur-lex.europa.eu/legal-content/EN/TXT/?uri=CELEX%3A52012DC0510 (accessed June 1, 2021).

European Parliament. 2018. "Money laundering – Recent cases from an EU banking supervisory perspective", European Parliament, In-depth analysis, April, PE 614.496, https://www.europarl.europa.eu/cmsdata/142725/EGOV%20Briefing%20on%20EU%20Banking%20supervisory%20perspective.pdf (accessed June 1, 2021).

GFCC, Judgment of the Second Senate of 30 July 2019, 2 BvR 1685/14.

Greek Law 4261/2014. 2014. Access to the activity of credit institutions and prudential supervision of credit institutions and investment firms (transposition of Directive 2013/36/EU), repeal of Law 3601/2007, and other provisions. OJ Hellenic Republic A 107: 3673–3780.

Hernández Saseta, Carmen. 2018. Assignments to the national competent authorities in the preparation of the ECB's decisions: legal challenges, European Central Bank ed., ESCB Legal Conference 2018, December, https://www.ecb.europa.eu/pub/pdf/other/ecb.escblegalconfeenceproceedings201812.en.pdf (accessed June 1, 2021).

Lackhoff, Klaus. 2017. *The Single Supervisory Mechanism: A Practitioner's Guide*. München, Oxford and Baden-Baden: C.H. Beck-Hart-Nomos.

Nouy, Danièle. 2018. "Re: Your letters (QZ026-28)," Letter of the Chair of the Supervisory Board to Mr. Giegold MEP on money laundering risks, 3 May, https://www.bankingsupervision.europa.eu/ecb/pub/pdf/ssm.mepletter180503_giegold.en.pdf (accessed June 1, 2021).

Pizzolla, Agnese. 2018. The Role of the European Central Bank in the Single Supervisory Mechanism: A New Paradigm for EU Governance. *European Law Review* 43, no.1: 3–23.

Regulation (EU) 2016/445 of the European Central Bank of 14 March 2016 on the exercise of options and discretions available in Union law. 2016. OJ L 78: 60–73.

Regulation (EU) No 468/2014 of the European Central Bank of 16 April 2014 establishing the framework for cooperation within the Single Supervisory Mechanism between the European Central Bank and national competent authorities and with national designated authorities (SSMFR). OJ L 141: 1–50.

Regulation (EU) No 1024/2013 of the Council conferring specific tasks on the European Central Bank concerning policies relating to the prudential supervision of credit Institutions (SSMR). 2013. OJ L 287: 63–89.

Regulation (EU) 575/2013 of the European Parliament and of the Council of 26 June 2013 on prudential requirements for credit institutions and investment firms and amending Regulation (EU) No 648/2012 (CRR). 2013. OJ L 176: 1–337.

Regulation (EC) No 2532/98 of the Council of 23 November 1998 concerning the powers of the European Central Bank to impose sanctions. 1998. OJ L 318: 4–7.

Treaty on the Functioning of the European Union (consolidated version). OJ C 326: 47–390.

Wymeersch, Eddy. 2014. "The Single Supervisory Mechanism or 'SSM', Part One of the Banking Union," European Corporate Governance Institute, Law Working Paper No. 240, February, https://papers.ssrn.com/sol3/papers.cfm?abstract_id=2397800 (accessed June 1, 2021).

PART D:

THE LEGAL AND ECONOMIC DIMENSION OF CREDIT RATING AGENCIES

CHAPTER 9

CREDIT RATING AGENCIES: EVOLUTION OR EXTINCTION? THE CASE FOR THE INDEPENDENT CREDIT RATING AGENCIES

PERIKLIS GOGAS,*
THEOPHILOS PAPADIMITRIOU,**
ATHANASIA DIMITRIADOU***
AND ANNA AGRAPETIDOU****

Introduction

Credit Rating Agencies (hereinafter CRAs) have been around for more than 150 years (White 2009). Their role has evolved from mere information collectors and providers to quasi-official arbitrators of credit risk throughout the global financial system. They were originally paid by potential investors who subscribed to their services. They also compiled information that —at the time— was too difficult and costly for their clients to gather on their own. After the market crash in 1929, they started to play a more formal role. The stricter rules that were imposed by New Deal regulators with the Glass-Steagall Act in the mid-1930s (US Banking Act 1933) limited banking, insurance, and other financial institutions to

* Professor, Department of Economics, Democritus University of Thrace (Komotini, Greece). Corresponding author, pgkogkas@econ.duth.gr.
** Professor, Department of Economics, Democritus University of Thrace (Komotini, Greece).
*** PhD Candidate, Department of Business, Law and Social Sciences, University of Derby (Derby, United Kingdom).
**** PhD, Department of Economics, Democritus University of Thrace (Komotini, Greece).

only investing in "investment grade" securities that were assessed by the CRAs. Since then, we have been seeing a growing reliance of investors and other market participants on CRAs' ratings, as they were increasingly incorporated in private contracts, investment guidelines for pension funds, endowment funds, and other private entities that also came to rely on them. After the "dust" of the global financial crisis of 2007 settled, which itself led to abrupt events of default for many large financial corporations and also international governments, CRAs became the focal point of criticism by economists, politicians, the media, market participants, and official regulatory agencies (Mullard 2012). The reason was obvious: CRAs failed to perform the job they were supposed to do in financial markets, i.e., efficient, effective, and prompt measuring and signalling of financial (default) risk (for more, see Shiller 2008).

The main criticism has focused on the inherent conflict of interest in the CRAs' operation due to the "issuer-pays system"; CRAs are being paid by the issuers of the debt instruments they are rating. This is a situation classically prone to generating sub-optimal results. Being private for-profit corporations, their main operating goal is to maximise profits by retaining and increasing their market share, instead of the economy-wide optimal goal of producing the most accurate credit ratings. This results in a situation that can be described as "rating-shopping". Parties interested in issuing new debt have a strong incentive to employ a CRA that will assign the highest possible rating to their debt instrument. Thus, in this market, CRAs effectively rate-compete.

But the issuer-pays system is not the only problem identified in the relevant debate. Other issues relate to the relatively loose regulatory oversight from government agencies. The importance of credit ratings has skyrocketed, and the related complexity of both the methodologies used in this process and the modern hybrid financial instruments that are subject to these ratings has increased dramatically in the modern financial world. Nonetheless, regulators have only marginally increased their oversight over CRAs. Critics point to various objectives, and even questionable reasoning, for this lagging behaviour on the part of regulators. Additionally, the overreliance on credit ratings in various private contracts amplifies any problems already existent in the rating process. Another serious disadvantage of the current system is that ratings often change ex post, especially when important events of default come into play, i.e., significant downgrades of credit ratings. Experience shows that ratings produced by CRAs change long after significant price changes in the markets. Finally, there is the important issue of the limited liability of CRAs that may be playing an important role in all or most of the above problems; there is limited civil liability of CRAs, as well as low penalties and limited level of enforcement by financial markets' regulatory authorities.

The regulatory authorities in the United States of America (hereinafter US), after the financial crisis of 2007 and in light of the abovementioned criticisms, decided to take action in 2008. They tried to address the areas of conflict of interest between rating agencies and issuers of structured securities. They also prohibited CRAs from issuing a rating on a structured product, unless information on the underlying assets was available, and from structuring the same products that they rate. They also required the public disclosure of the information CRAs use to determine a rating on a structured product. The last requirement is designed to facilitate "unsolicited" ratings of structured securities by rating agencies that are not paid by the issuers.

Moreover, in recent years, these new regulations, the abundance of economic and financial data, and the availability of powerful new methodologies and inexpensive computing power, have brought us to a new era of independent ratings. These can be produced by non-market, not-for-profit Independent Credit Rating Agencies (hereinafter ICRAs), which can either compete with CRAs or be used as an auxiliary risk-gauging mechanism by market participants. These independent ratings — as we will show— are free from the problems inherent in traditional CRAs. Due, especially, to the requirement for public disclosure of the information CRAs use to produce a rating on a structured product, CRAs will be unable to play an oligopolistic role in information gathering and processing. They can now be benchmarked against the ICRAs, which can be set by either public or governmental regulatory authorities, such as the Securities and Exchange Commission (hereinafter SEC), the Federal Deposit Insurance Corporation (hereinafter FDIC), the European Central Bank (ECB), national or international specialised entities, or universities, research institutions, etc. New forecasting techniques from the area of Machine Learning and Artificial Intelligence systems are proving to be even more efficient than traditional ones.

In the last part of this chapter, we present two relevant methodologies that can be used by an ICRA to produce probabilities of default and/or assign credit risk ratings to banking institutions. In the first case, we create a model that is able to forecast bank credit ratings in the US. We use 46 individual variables and financial ratios from four continuous years to our target rating year, producing a total of 184 variables for each bank. All these data come from their publicly reported financial statements as they were obtained from the FDIC. Our model reaches an overall 83.70% accuracy in bank credit ratings.

Next, we also employ a machine learning classification approach, namely the Support Vector Machines, to classify a set of 1443 US banks as solvent or insolvent. Our sample comes from the period 2003-13 and includes all 468 banks that failed in that period. We use 36 variables for each bank over a four-year window, resulting in 144 variables for each bank. From this set of possible regressors, we use a technique called "local-learning for high-dimensional data" to refine the variables. Finally, a shrinking procedure is used to further refine the input set. The final selected variables are only two: the tier 1 risk-based capital over total assets that is a measure of leveraging, and the total interest expense over total interest income that represents a measure of operational efficiency, both set one year before the forecast. This model achieves a 99.21% overall accuracy in forecasting the failure or not of a banking institution, one year ahead.

History and evolution of the CRAs

The history of Credit Rating Agencies dates back to the 1850s, when Henry Poor, editor of the American Railroad Journal, decided to publish statistical information on the property of railroads. This decision proved to be very useful for the investors around the world, as they were seeking credit information in order to make investment decisions. At the time, it was too difficult and costly for investors to gather information on their own. Adding to that, the traditional way of obtaining information (via business or banking relationships) was insufficient. In response to this market need, in 1909, John Moody started providing credit information by publishing an opinion on the creditworthiness of various bonds. This opinion was based on industry information and statistical analysis. He was the first to have assigned a rating on a bond instead of just providing statistical information. Two companies, Poor and Standard Statistics merged to form a ratings company, the Standard and Poor's. In 1913, the Fitch Publishing Company was founded by John Knowles Fitch, a 33-year-old entrepreneur. The sole purpose of the company was to publish financial statistics on equity and bonds. In 1913, Fitch developed a debt rating system based on a company's ability to pay its liabilities —the now familiar "AAA" to "D" rating scale that is widely used. The Fitch Publishing Company issued the first rating in 1924. These three credit rating agencies (Standard and Poor's, Moody's and Fitch) were making money by merely collecting and compiling data, and by providing financial information to interested individuals that invested in various financial instruments, such as bonds, stocks, etc. For these information and rating services they were charging subscription fees. This payment method was known as the "subscriber-pays" or "investor-pays" model. By the end of 1920, a vast majority of bonds were rated by these ratings agencies.

The increased importance of CRAs after the 1929 crash

After the US stock market crash in 1929, the need for credit ratings increased sharply. The vast number of bond defaults motivated the investors and regulators to rely more on independent third-party credit information. As a response to the financial crisis, regulators imposed stricter rules with the Glass-Steagall Act of 1933. The Act limited banking, insurance and other financial institutions to only investing in "investment grade" securities. This assessment was made by the CRAs. This was the first regulatory rule that incorporated credit ratings and granted CRAs a more formal role in the financial markets. In 1970, another recession led the SEC to officially designate Moody's, Fitch and Standard and Poor's as Nationally Recognised Statistical Rating Organisations (hereinafter NRSROs). Over the years, regulators increased their reliance on these SEC-identified NRSROs for the evaluation of bond portfolios. We witness a growing reliance on the CRAs' ratings, as they were increasingly incorporated in private contracts as well, investment guidelines for pension funds, endowment funds, and other private entities. The demand for an independent opinion on the creditworthiness of investments had increased both by investors and bond issuers, as the asymmetric information in the form of adverse selection increased risk for the investors and financing cost for the borrowers. As a result, CRAs became the quasi-official arbitrators of credit risk throughout the global financial system (Partnoy 2002). At that point, we observe a significant change: a transition from the "investor-pays system" to the "issuer-pays system". Since then, the investor is not anymore the customer of the CRAs. Rather, debt issuers are, as they seek to rate their new bond issues in order to reduce the investor's risk and become more attractive, especially in the primary (first issue of debt instruments) financial markets.

To summarise, the business model by which CRAs operate was significantly modified over the years. The changes that they adopted were either dictated by their voluntary response to the growing importance of financial markets and the way they could best serve the changing information needs of their potential customers, or imposed by the legal regulatory framework under which they were required to operate.

The 2007 financial crisis

In the US

After every financial crisis, and the subsequent defaults of large companies or governments of significant national economies, CRAs become the focal point of criticism by economists, politicians, the media, etc. The main reason is the inability of CRAs to do the job they were supposed to do in the financial markets, which of course is measuring and signalling risk. For example, Enron and Lehman Brothers had been assigned with high ratings just a few days before their collapse. Also, many worthless subprime-related securities maintained a high rating during the recent financial crisis. More specifically, in January 2007, nearly 10% of all subprime loans were delinquent, an increase of 68% over the prior year. Nonetheless, during the first half of 2007, both Moody's and S&P continued to issue AAA ratings for mortgage-backed securities (hereinafter MBS) and collateralised debt obligation (hereinafter CDO) securities. It was only after July 10, 2007 that downgrades began. Thus, it took almost 6 months for the CRAs to respond and downgrade assets, long after the markets had done it already on their own. In 2012, Senator Levin stated at the US Congress that "rating agencies are incentivised to offer the highest ratings, as opposed to offering the most accurate ratings, in order to attract business" (Levin 2011, 273). Thus, the issuers and the investment banks are engaged in "rating shopping", i.e., choosing the rating agency that offers the highest ratings. In other words, "rating shopping" is a situation in which the publisher of debt comes into contact with various CRAs and selects the one that guarantees to issue a high credit rating. This problem is related to an inherent conflict of interest in CRAs' operation: the so-called "issuer-pays system" that incorporates incentives to assign high ratings in order to maximise profits, instead of producing the most accurate credit ratings.

Furthermore, CRAs played an important role during 2007-08 in the MBS crisis, which led to the great recession of 2008-09. It is a fact that not all major market players, including CRAs, had foreseen the depth of the financial crisis in September 2008 (Shiller 2008). This is acknowledged by policymakers, market participants, and by CRAs themselves. Because of the depth of the crisis, CRAs were unable to sufficiently eliminate the flaws in their evaluation methods. The main purpose of CRAs' management teams was to maintain their market share and issue bond ratings, even when their analysts were concerned about the creditworthiness of the securities following the financial collapse. Essentially, the agencies underestimated the credit risk associated with structured credit products, and failed to adjust their ratings quickly enough to the deteriorating market conditions.

CRAs were supposed to fit in a system in which every investor would be able to invest in international securities (government and corporate bonds). Their role was to enable investors from all over the world to diversify portfolios internationally. Nevertheless, their contribution to the outbreak of the 2007-08 MBS crisis brought about distrust as to their overall creditworthiness.

In the EU

In October 2008, then President of the European Commission, José Manuel Barroso, commissioned Jacques de Larosière to chair a committee that would provide advice on the future of European financial regulation and supervision. In February 2009, the Committee published a report identifying the following gaps (de Larosière 2009):

- CRAs were able to reduce credit risk perception by providing AAA ratings on the largest installments of structured financial products, and
- The disadvantages of evaluation methodologies were the main reason for the depreciation of credit.

In March 2009, the UK Financial Services Authority published the Turner Review, which held the CRAs responsible for the financial crisis (UK Financial Services Authority 2009). There were three possible mechanisms through which the CRAs influenced the financial crisis of 2007. First, rating agencies were considered to be facilitators of the process due to the AAA rating of securities backed by assets, including residential mortgage-backed securities (RMBS) and the collation of CDOs made up of different MBSs and synthetic credit default swaps (CDS). Secondly, the original mortgage lenders could now lend their mortgages to investment banks, allowing the original lender new funds to create new home loans. Finally, AAA credit ratings reduce banks' capital requirements, creating a climate for higher leverage and increased exposure to mortgage loans. After all, AAA ratings meant reduced risk on assets that, in turn, lowered minimum capital requirements.

Criticism and identified issues

Despite the significant role which CRAs play in the financial markets, their credibility has been under scrutiny, as we have seen, especially during the recent financial crisis. CRAs evolved from the market's demand for independent third-party information for investment decisions. One main criticism is that CRAs do not meet the criterion for independence anymore. The "issuer-pays system" has raised a real and apparent conflict of interest, as it creates the incentive to issue higher ratings to the issuer who pays fees to the agencies in order to attain a rating. This model is criticised because it may lead to "rating shopping", as we have seen. Moreover, they have been accused of loose regulatory oversight and limited supervision, especially when taking into account the overreliance of banks, investors, organisations, and many contracts on them. Additionally, there is limited civil liability of CRAs, as well as low penalties and level of enforcement. Another issue is the lack of competition in the industry. By the end of 2000 there were only three designated NRSROs (US House of Representatives 2003, 145).

New regulations

In the past 15 years, regulators enacted a series of rules to foster transparency and accountability in the CRA industry. In 2006, the US Congress passed the Credit Rating Agency Reform Act (US Credit Rating Agency Reform Act 2006) aiming to open the barrier to new NRSROs. To that point, it was not clear how the designation process worked, so that some agencies did become NRSROs, while others did not. As a result, there are currently nine designated NRSROs (US SEC 2021):

- S&P Global Ratings
- Moody's Investors Service, Inc.
- Fitch Ratings, Inc.
- A.M. Best Rating Services, Inc.
- Kroll Bond Rating Agency, Inc.
- DBRS, Inc. (Dominion Bond Rating Service)
- Japan Credit Rating Agency, Ltd.
- Egan-Jones Rating Co.
- HR Ratings de México, S.A. de C.V.

Nonetheless, even after these reforms, the rating industry is still a characteristic example of an oligopoly. A larger competition would force CRAs to provide more accurate and up-to-date ratings, as they have been criticised for not providing ratings on a timely basis. This is also referred to as "the problem of ex post ratings". Another serious concern of CRAs was the conflict of interest between the CRAs and the issuer. In June 2008, the SEC took some regulatory action implementing new rules to address this issue. These rules prohibit a CRA from issuing a rating on structured products, unless information on the underlying assets is available (US SEC 2008). Moreover, they prohibit them from structuring the same products that they rate. Also, the new regulations require the public disclosure of the information a CRA uses to determine a rating on a structured product. The last requirement is designed to facilitate "unsolicited" ratings of structured securities by rating agencies that are not paid by the issuers. Thus, the regulators seem to find an important step towards the reliability, transparency and efficiency of the CRAs' system, as well as towards the inclusion of other independent players that may issue competitive credit ratings that do not suffer from the "issuer-pays system" inherent problems.

The era of Independent Credit Rating Agencies (ICRA)

From the very beginning of the CRAs, their main purpose was to provide independent third-party information to investors. Since then, their expanding role has highlighted issues related to conflict of interest and transparency in their rating process. These identified issues bring us to the new era of ICRAs. ICRAs can be formed in the international market and can directly compete with the already established CRAs in terms of rating accuracy and timeliness, the two main issues with the role and performance of the CRAs. The role of ICRAs can be assumed by dedicated subsidiaries of national or international institutions, such as Central Banks, specialised governmental entities, or independent ratings providers operating within universities, research institutions, etc. Currently, there are several factors facilitating the transition to ICRAs: a) the abundance of relevant data, as we live in the era of "big data", b) the cheaper and faster computer processing, c) the significant progress in traditional forecasting techniques, and d) the wide use of new forecasting techniques, i.e., Machine Learning and Artificial Intelligence systems. These methodologies (Machine Learning, Deep Learning, Complex Networks, etc.) treat large datasets, both under a theory-based and an a-theoretical setting, producing very accurate results.

The advantages of such independent ratings are many. They come with full transparency in the ratings procedure, since they employ publicly available data that are easy for anyone to access, and also the methodologies employed are readily available to be used by anyone with little to moderate technical training and experience. More importantly, they will increase competition, as there can be alternative sources of ratings of financial instruments in the markets, thus minimising the oligopolistic power of the existing CRAs in information gathering and processing. Moreover, the ICRAs will be subjected to "market discipline" or "market rewards", depending on the accuracy and fairness of the ratings they provide to market participants. These disciplinary actions can be performed either unofficially by the markets or in a structured and regulated framework under the supervision of a relevant authority. The investors will learn to trust the sources that are more accurate and, most importantly, fairer in assigning ratings. Inevitably, any forecaster is faced with forecasting error and thus, the size of the forecasting error determines the quality of the forecasts. Nonetheless, it is important to note here that even sub-optimal forecasts —in terms of standard deviation of errors—are superior and preferred to biased ones, as the former would be, at least on average, accurate.

In the following sections, we present two such methodologies that can be used by market participants, either as competing with CRAs or as an auxiliary risk-gauging mechanism to the traditional CRAs' ratings. The proposed models use only publicly available information that enhances the transparency of the rating process and minimises the possibility to exploit instances of conflict of interest. First, we present a forecasting model for bank credit ratings and then a forecasting model for bank failures.

Forecasting Bank Credit Ratings

Many methodological approaches have been used in the relevant literature in the effort to forecast bank, bond and other credit ratings. We find traditional methodologies from econometrics and statistics, as in Pinches and Mingo (1973), but we also find plenty of machine learning approaches. Such examples are: Kwon et al. (1997), Huang et al (2004), and Chen and Shih (2006).

In this section, we present an empirical model designed to forecast bank credit ratings using only quantitative and publicly available information from banks' financial statements (Gogas et al. 2014). The authors identify the most important variables that contribute to the long-term ratings of the US banks, as they are assigned by Fitch, using only quantitative, non-proprietary information. Their proposed model achieved 83.70% forecasting accuracy.

The methodology is as follows:

1. The regressors are selected from various economic variables and financial ratios, and by applying the step-wise backward method for variable selection, different sets are selected as alternative explanatory variables.
2. These sets are then used in an ordered probit regression model, and are then used to predict the credit rating of each bank.

The Data

The dataset consists of 92 US banks that had freely available long-term ratings from Fitch in 2012. For each bank, 46 individual variables and financial ratios are collected from their financial statements from 2008 to 2011. All financial information is publicly available from the FDIC. Overall, there are 184 variables for each and every one of the banks that Fitch reported freely accessible ratings for in 2012. The dependent variable is the rating and the independent variables are the 184 variables from the financial statements of banks. In the sample, initially, there are six reported ratings categories, which are then grouped into three course categories as follows: ratings of AA and A are classified as “2”, ratings of BBB are classified as “1”, and ratings of BB, B and CCC are classified as “0”. Table 9-1 lists the 46 independent variables. All variables from the balance sheets are expressed as ratios of total assets except for total employees (TOEM) and total assets (TASSET). All the variables from the income and expense statements are expressed in terms of total interest income.

Table 9-1: List of independent variables (Gogas et al. 2014)

Assets and Liabilities	Income and Expenses	Performance Ratio	Condition Ratio
Total employees (TOEM)	Total interest expense (TIE)	Yield on earning assets (YOEA)	Loss allowance to loans (LATL)
Total assets (TASSET)	Provision for loan and lease losses (PLLL)	Net interest margin (NIM)	Net loans and leases to deposits (NLLTD)

Cash and due from depository institutions (CASH)	Total noninterest income (TNI)	Net operating income to assets (NOIA)	Net loans and leases to core deposits (NLLCD)
Net loans & leases (NLL)	Service charges on deposit accounts (CHARGE)	Return on assets (ROA)	Equity capital to assets (EQCTA)
Loan loss allowance (LLA)	Trading account gains & fees (TRACC)	Return on equity (ROE)	Core capital (leverage) ratio (LEV)
Goodwill and other intangibles (GOI)	Additional noninterest income (ANI)	Assets per employee (ASSPE)	Tier 1 risk-based capital ratio (T1RBC)
Total deposits (TD)	Total noninterest expense (TNE)		Total risk-based capital ratio (TRBCR)
Interest-bearing deposits (IBD)	Salaries and employee benefits (SAL)		
Trading liabilities (TL)	Pre-tax net operating income (PTNOI)		
Subordinated debt (SD)	Securities gains (SEC)		
Total bank equity capital (TBEC)	Net income attributable to bank (NIA)		
Long term assets (LTA)	Cash dividends (DIVDS)		
Average Assets (AA)	Net operating income (NOI)		
Volatile liabilities (VL)			

Loans and leases held for sale (LLHFS)
Unused loan commitments (ULC)
Tier 1 (core) risk-based capital (T1CRC)
Tier 2 risk-based capital (T2RBC)
Total unused commitments (TUC)
Derivatives (DER)

Methodology

We first follow a thorough variable selection procedure to identify the most important variables for the forecasting of credit ratings. The primary step is to calculate the correlations $r_{i,R}$, where *i* refers to each individual variable and R to the ratings' dependent variable. Next, as a pre-filtering step, six different groups of regressors are created based on the correlation between the dependent variable (ratings) and the 184 independent variables. The groups are created as follows:

Group 1: All variables with $|r_{i,R}| \geq 0.5$ along with their lags. E.g., if the variable Net Operating Income of the year 2010 has a correlation higher than 0.5, then the Net Operating Income for all the years 2011, 2009 and 2008 are included in Group 1. There are 5 variables that meet the correlation restriction ($|r_{i,R}| \geq 0.5$). By adding their lags Group 1 includes 20 variables.

Group 2: All variables with $|r_{i,R}| \geq 0.4$ along with their lags. By doing this, Group 2 includes 44 variables.

Group 3: All variables with $|r_{i,R}| \geq 0.4$ without their corresponding lags. This group includes 15 variables.

Group 4: This group includes the 5 variables with the highest positive correlation and the 5 variables with the highest negative correlation, resulting in a total of 10 variables.

Group 5: This group includes the 30 variables with the highest correlation.

Group 6: This group includes all 184 explanatory variables of the sample.

Table 9-2 summarises the number of variables in each group, as mentioned above.

Table 9-2: The number of variables selected in each of the 6 groups (Gogas et al. 2014)

Group	1	2	3	4	5	6
Number of variables	20	44	15	10	30	184

After that, the following step is to identify the most significant variables in terms of the bank ratings for each one of the six groups. This is done with the following alternative techniques:

a) A combinatorial exhaustive search methodology of all possible sets of 4 variables. Then the one set that produces the highest R^2 is selected.
b) A combinatorial exhaustive search (as above) that selects the 8 most informative variables in terms of credit ratings.
c) A stepwise forward method of least squares that selects all variables from each one of the above 6 groups of possible regressors that have a p-value less than 0.1.

According to the above, a total of 18 alternative sets of regressors have been created to be used and compared on their forecasting accuracy with respect to bank credit ratings.

Table 9-3 summarises the above results for the six groups of variables. The first line reports the highest R^2 for the 4 regressors of each group, using an exhaustive research for all possible combinations within the group. The next line reports the same for 8 regressors. The third line reports those variables which have p-value < 0.1, according to the stepwise-forward method of least squares. The numbers in parenthesis refer to the number of variables that the stepwise-forward method selects for each one of the six groups of regressors.

Table 9-3: R^2 values for the optimum set of regressors for the six groups of variables (Gogas et al. 2014)

Regressors selection	Group 1	Group 2	Group 3	Group 4	Group 5	Group 6
Combinatorial 4	0.49	0.54	0.54	0.53	0.53	0.59
Combinatorial 8	0.53	0.61	0.57	0.49	0.60	0.70
Stepwise-forward (Selected Variables)	0.40 (4)	0.55 (5)	0.55 (5)	0.46 (3)	0.53 (4)	0.71 (11)

Table 9-4 shows all the variables selected as best regressors, according to the three different variable selection methodologies, and for each one of the six groups. Panels A and B report the selected variables with the highest R^2 for a set of 4 best regressors and for a set of 8 best regressors accordingly. Panel C reports the selected variables using the stepwise-forward method. This selects four variables from group 1 and group 5, five variables from group 2 and group 3, three variables from group 4, and eleven variables from group 6 that includes all 184 variables.

Table 9-4: Variable selection from each method (Gogas et al. 2014)

Group 1	Group 2	Group 3	Group 4	Group 5	Group 6
Panel A. Methodology: combinatorial 4 (set of four best regressors)					
NOIA10	NOI10	NOI10	L_TASSET 11	L_TAS SET11	L_TAS SET11
PTNOI1 0	L_TASSET 11	L_TASSET 11	L_TASSET 10	L_TAS SET10	TIE11
NOIA8	IND11	IND11	NOIA10	NOIA10	SEC8
NOA08	AA10	AA10	TNE11	TNE11	PTNOI1 0
Panel B. Methodology: combinatorial 8 (set of eight best regressors)					
NIA10	L_TASSET 11	L_TASSET 11	NOI10	L_ TASSE T11	L_TAS SET11
ROA10	IND11	ABD11	AA10	L_TAS SET10	L_TAS SET10
PTNOI1 0	NIA10	NIA10	IBD11	TNE11	SEC8

ROA09	PTNOI10	L_TASSET10	NIA10	TNI10	LTA7
NOIA8	TNI11	NOIA10	PTNOI10	DIVDS11	YOEA11
ROA08	TNI9	L_TASSET9	ROA10	ROE09	NIM10
NIA11	ROE08	L_TASSET8	NOIA10	PTNOI9	NOIA10
ROA11	NOIA8	TNI11	PLLL10	PTNOI10	TBEV9
Panel C. Methodology stepwise forward (set of regressors with p> 0.1)					
NOI10	NOI10	NOI10	NOI10	TNE11	NOI10
NIA10	L_TASSET11	L_TASSET11	IND11	L_TASSET11	L_TASSET11
ROA10	IBD11	IBD11	AA10	L_TASSET10	TIE11
NOIA10	AA10	AA10		NOIA10	L_TASSET10
	L_TASSET10	L_TASSET10			SEC8
					GOI8
					ASSPE10
					LTA8
					TRL11
					SD11
					T2RBC8

Results

As described above, a total of 18 alternative sets of regressors have been created to be used and compared on their forecasting accuracy with respect to bank credit ratings. The selected variables of each group are used in an ordered probit framework to forecast Fitch's long-term ratings for 2012. Table 9-5 shows the forecasting accuracy of each one of the 18 models tested.

Table 9-5: Rating Forecasting Accuracy (Gogas et al. 2014)

Regressor Selection	Group 1 (%)	Group 2 (%)	Group 3 (%)	Group 4 (%)	Group 5 (%)	Group 6 (%)
Combinatorial 4	69.57	70.65	70.65	68.48	68.48	71.74
Combinatorial 8	68.48	75.00	76.09	71.74	71.74	81.52
Stepwise-forward	65.22	71.74	71.74	71.74	68.48	81.52

The best forecasting accuracy is achieved with the combinatorial 8 and the stepwise-forward selection criterion with the regressors from group 6. The forecasting accuracy in both cases is 81.52%. In the next table (Table 9-6) we list the regressors of the two best forecasting models. A description of each variable is provided as well as their source. The regressor source is classified as A/L when they come from Assets and Liabilities, I/E when they come from Income and Expense accounts, and P/R stands for a Performance Ratio.

Table 9-6: List of regressors in the optimal forecasting models (Gogas et al. 2014)

Variable	Source	Description
Panel A. Group 6 using the combinatorial 8 criterion		
L_TASSET11	A/L	Log of total assets in 2011
L_TASSET10	A/L	Log of total assets in 2010
SEC8	I/E	Securities gains (losses) over total interest income in 2008
LTA8	A/L	Long-term assets (5+ years) over total assets in 2008
YOEA11	P/R	Yield on earning assets in 2011
NIM10	P/R	Net interest margin in 2010
NOIA10	P/R	Net operating income to assets in 2010
TBEC9	A/L	Total bank equity capital over total assets in 2009

Panel B. Group 6 using the stepwise-forward criterion

NOI10	I/E	Net operating income over total interest income in 2010
L_TASSET11	A/L	Log of total assets in 2011
TIE11	I/E	Total interest expense over total interest income in 2011
L_TASSET10	A/L	Log of total assets in 2010
SEC8	I/E	Securities gains (losses) over total interest income in 2008
GOI8	A/L	Goodwill and other intangibles over total assets in 2008
ASSPE10	P/R	Assets per employee ($ millions) in 2010
LTA8	A/L	Long-term assets (5+ years) over total assets in 2008
TRL11	A/L	Trading liabilities over total assets in 2011
SD11	A/L	Subordinated debt over total assets in 2011
T2RBC8	A/L	Tier 2 risk-based capital over total assets in 2008

Finally, these models are augmented with additional regressors from the list of 184 variables. The optimum model, in that case, is when the long-term assets over total assets from the year 2009 (LTA9) is added to the model from group 6 and the combinatorial 8 criterion. The forecasting accuracy for this model reaches 83.70% with nine explanatory variables. It is interesting that two of the variables of the optimum model pertain to the year 2008 and two to the year 2009, three variables pertain to the year 2010, and only one pertains to the year 2011. The target rating pertains to the year 2012.

According to the above empirical analysis, we can see that we can produce a model that can replicate or anticipate the CRAs' ratings within reasonable margins of accuracy based on publicly available data. As a result, such empirical forecasting models can be used as an alternative to the CRAs' ratings. These can help to enhance the transparency of the rating process and minimise the possibility to exploit instances of conflict of interest between the CRAs and the rated banks, as they will result in significant deviations in the assigned ratings by the two methodologies.

Forecasting bank failures

The issue of bank failures is of great importance to the economy as a whole and not only to the banking sector. Bank failures may create cascading effects that can significantly increase systemic risk in an economy. There are plenty of studies in the literature that deal with the issue of the accurate and timely forecasting of bank failures. These approaches include traditional econometric techniques such as Meyer and Pifer (1970), Canbas et al. (2005), Arena (2008), Li et al. (2011) and many others, or advances in forecasting methodologies beyond traditional econometrics and statistics. Some relevant examples are: Tam and Kiang (1990) that dates three decades in the past and uses the emergent —at that time— neural networks technique. Other examples are Bell (1997), Olmeda and Fernández (1997), Swicegood and Clark (2001), Ravi et al. (2008), Ravi and Pramodh (2008), Ioannidis et al. (2010), Ekinci and Erdal (2011), Ekinci and Erdal (2013), Ekinci and Halil İbrahim (2017), Boyacıoğlu et al. (2009), etc.

In this section, we present a machine learning-based model to forecast bank failures using only publicly available information. The proposed methodology defines a linear decision boundary that separates the forecasted solvent from the failed banks using only two explanatory variables. This setup generates a novel and alternative stress testing tool that is easy to be replicated by anyone with moderate or little technical training.

Methodology – Support Vector Machines

In recent years, support vector machines have gained popularity due to some attractive characteristics, such as great generalisation ability and unique global solutions. In 2018, we proposed a forecasting model for bank failures based on Support Vector Machines (SVMs), with 99.21% forecasting accuracy (Gogas et al. 2018). To the best of our knowledge, this is the state-of-the-art in forecasting default risk and bank failures.

The basic idea of support vector classification is to separate the data in two classes (for binary classification) by finding the hyperplane that maximises the distance between the two classes. The hyperplane is defined by only a small number of data points that are called "support vectors" and are derived through a minimisation procedure. In case a perfect separation of data is not possible, an error-tolerant parameter can be introduced that allows misclassification; then, the goal of the SVM is to maximise the margin between the two classes and to minimise classification errors (Figure 9-1).

Figure 9-1*:* Support vectors lie on the margin lines, which are represented with the dotted lines and define the hyperplane (Gogas et al. 2014)

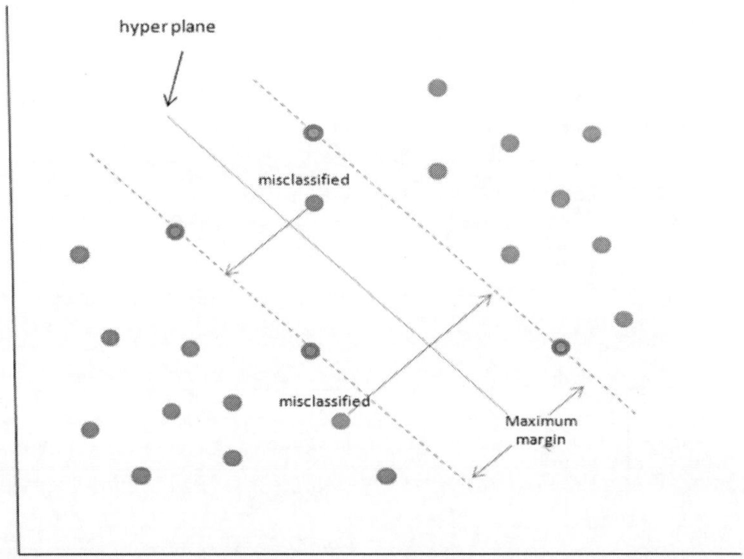

One main advantage of the SVM is that it can efficiently deal with non-linear data by using the kernel trick (non-linear projection function). Kernels allow the projection of data points to a higher dimensional feature space, where the data are linearly separable (Figure 9-2). The projection can be done in a very computationally efficient way (using just dot multiplication).

Figure 9-2: The data cannot be separated by a hyperplane in the two-linearly separable in a higher dimensional feature space (down) (Gogas et al. 2014).

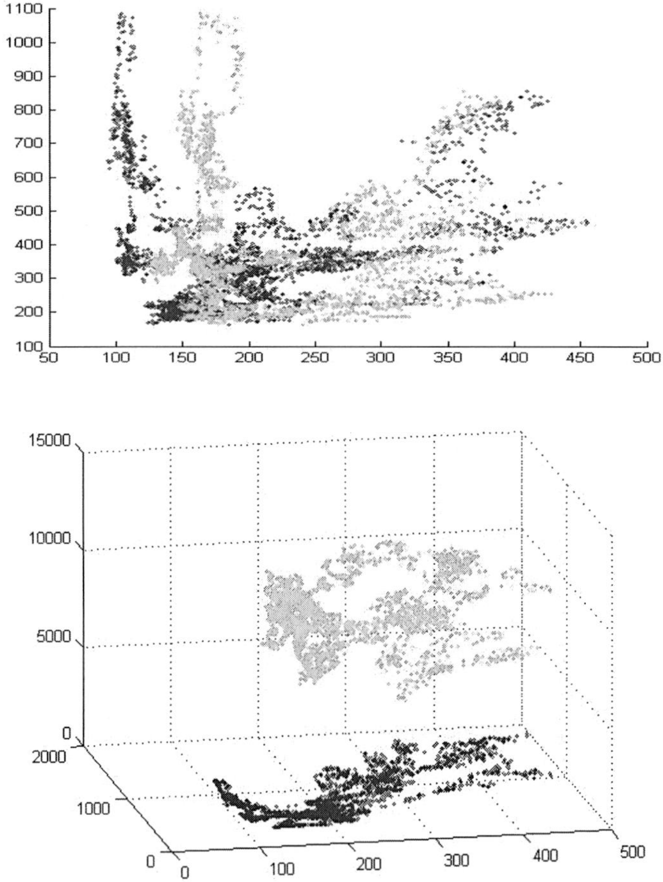

The SVM implements the structural risk minimisation rule for the selection of the hyper parameters and as a result, it yields an optimal global solution and avoids selecting local ones, a property that leads to great generalisation ability. The model has two basic steps: the first one is the training and the second one is the testing. The largest part of the dataset is used in the training process for the estimation of the separating hyperplane, while in the out-of-sample testing step, the generalisation ability of the model is evaluated by investigating the model's performance in a small subset that was left aside in the first step.

The Data

The dataset consists of 1443 US banks that include the complete set of the 481 failed banks during the 2007-2013 period and 962 banks that were solvent. For each bank, 36 variables and financial ratios were collected from their financial statements over a four-year window, resulting in 144 variables for each bank. Table 9-7 shows the 36 variables collected for each bank. All data come from the FDIC.

Table 9-7: The list of the 36 initial variables collected for each bank (Gogas et al. 2014)

Source	Variable	Description
A/L	TASSET	Total assets
A/L	CASH	Cash and due from depository institutions/total assets
A/L	NLL	Net loans and leases/total assets
A/L	LLA	Loan loss allowance/total assets
A/L	GOI	Goodwill and other intangibles/total assets
A/L	TD	Total deposits/total assets
A/L	IBD	Interest-bearing deposits/total assets
A/L	SD	Subordinated debt/total assets
A/L	AA	Average assets year-to-date/total assets
A/L	VL	Volatile liabilities/total assets
A/L	ULC	Unused loan commitments/total assets
A/L	T1CRC	Tier 1 (core) risk-based capital/total assets
A/L	T2RBC	Tier 2 risk-based capital/total assets
A/L	TUC	Total unused commitments/total assets
I/E	TIE	Total interest expense/total interest income
I/E	PLLL	Provision for loan and lease losses/total interest income
I/E	TNI	Total noninterest income/total interest income

I/E	TRACC	Trading account gains & fees/total interest income
I/E	ANI	Additional noninterest income/total interest income
I/E	TNE	Total noninterest expense/total interest income
I/E	SAL	Salaries and employee benefits/total interest income
I/E	PTNOI	Pre-tax net operating income/total interest income
I/E	SEC	Securities gains (losses)/total interest income
I/E	NIA	Net income attributable to bank/total interest income
I/E	DIVDS	Cash dividends/total interest income
I/E	NOI	Net operating income/total interest income
P/R	YOEA	Yield on earning assets
P/R	NIM	Net-interest margin
P/R	ROA	Return on assets
P/R	ROE	Return on equity
P/R	ASSPE	Assets per employee ($ millions)
C/R	NLLTD	Net loans and leases to deposits
C/R	EQCTA	Equity capital to assets
C/R	LEV	Core capital (leverage) ratio
C/R	T1RBC	Tier 1 risk-based capital ratio
C/R	TRBCR	Total risk-based capital ratio

Since the initial input set of possible explanatory variables is large, a technique called "local-learning for high-dimensional data" is used to identify the most informative of these variables in terms of bank failures. This selects 6 out of the initial set of 144 variables as the most important ones. Next, the input set is scrupulously refined by following an iteratively shrinking procedure. First, we calculate the forecasting accuracy for the six-variable input set, and then we measure the forecasting accuracy for every possible quintet of variables taken from our initial set of six and keep the quintet that outperforms the rest of the tested sets as our base input set. We continue in a similar way by checking sequentially the quartets, the triads, and couples of variables. Thus, in every round, the variable set is pruned by one. Under this scheme, the final selected variables are only two: the tier 1 risk-based capital over total assets that is a measure of leveraging, and the total interest expense over total interest income that represents a measure of operational efficiency, both one year before the forecast.

Results

From the total number of 1443 banks, the 1100 are used to train the model (≈76%), and the remaining 343 banks were set aside and used to test the generalisation ability of the model to unknown data (out-of-sample forecasting). The results are presented in Table 9-8.

Table 9-8: Out-of-sample forecasting accuracy (Gogas et al. 2014)

Optimum model Year t-1	Real Solvent 1164	Real Failed 115
Predicted Solvent	1157	3
Predicted Failed	7	112
Accuracy	99.40%	97.39%

For the 1164 real solvent banks, the forecasting accuracy is 99.40%, while for the 115 failed banks, the forecasting accuracy is 97.39%. Thus, the overall accuracy of the model is 99.21%. The model produced a total of ten errors: seven solvent banks were misclassified as insolvent (false alarms) and three insolvent banks were misclassified as solvent. After close examination of these banks, we found that all misclassified as insolvent banks had received enforcement action from the FDIC, and one had received financial help from the US Treasury as part of the Troubled Asset Relief Program. These findings mean that without this intervention by the regulators, these banks would probably have failed, as it was predicted. As for the misclassified as solvent banks, one was discovered with unreported losses and was closed for fraud. So, it was impossible to predict its failure from the fraudulent financial statements. Finally, the other two failed banks were both very small banks with total assets of \$43.5 and \$24.8 million respectively. Figure 9-3 provides a graphic representation of the results. The dashed line is the classification boundary that separates the solvent banks that are marked with dark grey, on the right, from the failed banks marked with light grey, on the left. With black dots we mark the banks that were misclassified. These are the 7 solvent banks depicted as insolvent and the 3 insolvent banks that were classified as solvent. The horizontal axis represents the variable Tier 1 (core) risk-based capital/total assets for year t-1, while the vertical axis is the Total interest expense/total interest income for year t-1.

Figure 9-3: Graphic representation of the results[1] (Gogas et al. 2014)

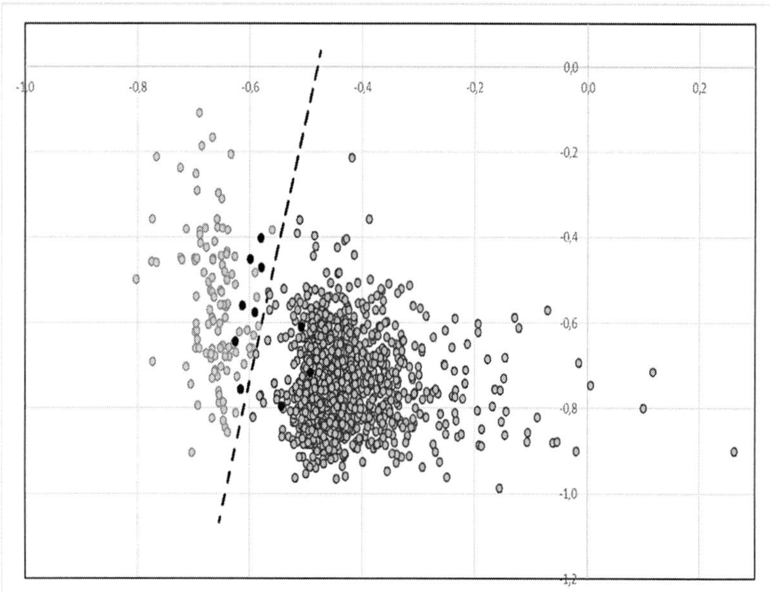

A Machine Learning Credit Ratings Scheme

Combining the two methodologies presented in "Forecasting Bank Credit Ratings" and "Forecasting bank failures" above, we can create classification bands, as marked in Figure 9-4, with colours that correspond to different credit ratings. This produces a fully transparent, replicable and independent credit ratings system that can be used by the ICRAs.

[1] Dashed line separates the two-dimensional data space in two sub-spaces; the solvent (right) and the insolvent (left). Black points represent misclassified banks in each class.

Figure 9-4: Combination of the two methodologies "Forecasting Bank Credit Ratings" and "Forecasting bank failures" (Gogas et al. 2014)

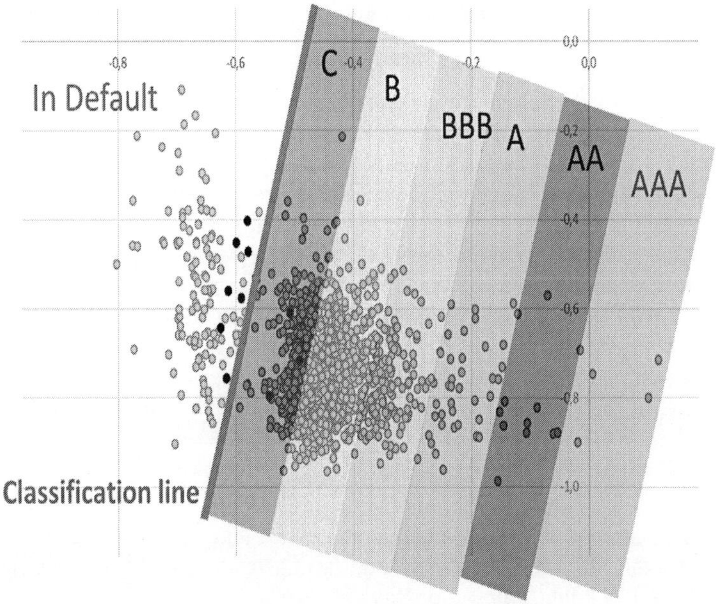

Conclusion

CRAs play an important, albeit many times controversial, role in financial markets. The assessment of credit risk is of the outmost importance for all participants in these markets: debt issuers, investors, arbitrages, governments, financial institutions, and regulators. Nonetheless, CRAs have faced a lot of criticism over the last two decades, and especially in periods following major financial crises or economic distress. Most of this criticism seems to be justified. CRAs seem to respond sluggishly and mostly ex post in downgrading securities and their debt issuers. Moreover, despite the regulatory changes effected after the 2007 financial crisis, their procedures still seem not to be fully transparent. The major disadvantage of the current CRAs' system of assigning ratings is the apparent conflict of interest inherent to the issuer-payer system that is in effect. ICRAs, on the other hand, do not suffer from this disadvantage. Historically, the major comparative advantage of CRAs has always been their ability and specialisation in obtaining and processing data to produce their ratings. This advantage is now limited due to significant developments in computer technology and progress in scientific research techniques. More specifically, we are now in the "big data" era, where there are plenty of available and high-quality data, either free or at low cost. The computer processing power, on the other hand, is vastly better, and the associated computing costs are minimal. Finally, and most significantly, we now have new methodologies that can produce very accurate results. Since public disclosure is now mandatory for transparency reasons, ICRAs must come into play in this market. ICRAs do not suffer from the issuer-payer conflict of interest. They will be subject to "market discipline" or "market rewards" depending on the accuracy and fairness of the ratings they provide. Even sub-optimal forecasts are preferred to biased forecasts, as the former are on average accurate. Finally, investors are more likely to trust the ICRAs, since they can be highly specialised and independent, and they are not subject to any conflict of interest. In this chapter, we provided two examples of such innovative machine learning methodologies that can be used in forecasting credit ratings and economic failure or distress.

References

Arena, Marco. 2008. Bank failures and bank fundamentals: a comparative analysis of Latin America and East Asia during the nineties using bank-level data. *Journal of Banking & Finance* 32, no.2: 299–310.

Bell, Timothy B. 1997. Neural nets or the logit model: A comparison of each model's ability to predict commercial bank failures. *International Journal of Intelligent Systems in Accounting, Finance and Management* 6, no.3: 249–264.

Boyacıoğlu, Melek Acar, Yakup Kara, and Ömer Kaan Baykan. 2009. Predicting bank financial failures using neural networks, support vector machines and multivariate statistical methods: A comparative analysis in the sample of savings deposit insurance fund (SDIF) transferred banks in Turkey. *Expert Systems with Applications* 36, no.2: 3355–3366.

Canbas, Serpil, Altan Cabuk, and Suleyman Bilgin Kilic. 2005. Prediction of commercial bank failure via multivariate statistical analysis of financial structure: The Turkish case. *European Journal of Operational Research* 166, no.2: 528–546.

Chen, Wun-Hwa, and Jen-Ying Shih. 2006. A study of Taiwan's issuer credit rating systems using support vector machines. *Expert Systems with Applications* 30, no.3: 427–435.

de Larosière, Jacques. 2009. "The high-level group on financial supervision in the EU report," 25 February, https://ec.europa.eu/economy_finance/publications/pages/publication14527_en.pdf (accessed June 2, 2021).

Ekinci, Aykut, and Halil İbrahim Erdal. 2017. Forecasting Bank Failure: Base Learners, Ensembles and Hybrid Ensembles. *Computational Economics* 49, no.4: 677–686.

Ekinci, Aykut, and Halil Ibrahim Erdal. 2013. A Comparison of Various Artificial Intelligence Methods in the Prediction of Bank Failures. *Computational Economics* 42, no.2: 199–215.

Ekinci, Aykut, and Halil Ibrahim Erdal. 2011. An application on prediction of bank failure in Turkey. *Iktisat Işletmeve Finans* 26, no.298: 21–44.

Gogas, Periklis, Theophilos Papadimitriou, and Anna Agrapetidou. 2018. Forecasting bank failures and stress testing: A machine learning approach. *International Journal of Forecasting* 34, no.3: 440–455.

Gogas, Periklis, Theophilos Papadimitriou, and Anna Agrapetidou. 2014. Forecasting Bank Credit Ratings. *Journal of Risk Finance* 15, no.2: 195–209.

Huang, Zan, Hsinchun Chen, Chia-Jung Hsu, Wun-Hwa Chen, and Soushan Wu. 2004. Credit rating analysis with support vector machines and neural networks: a market comparative study. *Decision Support Systems* 37, no.4: 543–558.

Ioannidis, Christos, Fotios Pasiouras, and Constantin Zopounidis. 2010. Assessing bank soundness with classification techniques. *Omega* 38, no.5: 345–357.

Kwon, Young, Ingoo Han, and Kun Chang Lee. 1997. Ordinal Pairwise Partitioning (OPP) Approach to Neural Networks Training in Bond Rating. *International Journal of Intelligent Systems in Accounting Finance and Management* 6, no.1: 23–40.

Levin, C. 2011. "Wall Street and the financial crisis: Anatomy of a financial collapse," United States Senate, Permanent Subcommittee on Investigations, Majority and minority staff report, April 13, https://www.hsgac.senate.gov/imo/media/doc/PSI%20REPORT%20-%20Wall%20Street%20&%20the%20Financial%20Crisis-Anatomy%20of%20a%20Financial%20Collapse%20(FINAL%205-10-11).pdf (accessed June 3, 2021).

Li, Guo, Lee W. Sanning, and Sherril Shaffer. 2011. Forecasting bank failures: timeliness versus number of failures. *Applied Economics Letters* 18, no.16: 1549–1552.

Meyer, Paul A. and Howard W. Pifer. 1970. Prediction of Bank Failures. *Journal of Finance* 25, no.4: 853–868.

Mullard, Maurice. 2012. The Credit Rating Agencies and Their Contribution to the Financial Crisis. *The Political Quarterly* 83, no.1: 1–199.

Olmeda, Ignacio, and Eugenio Fernández. 1997. Hybrid Classifiers for Financial Multicriteria Decision Making: The Case of Bankruptcy Prediction. *Computational Economics* 10, no.4: 317–335.

Partnoy, Frank. 2002. The Paradox of Credit Ratings. In *Ratings, Rating Agencies and the Global Financial System*. Edited by Richard M. Levich, Giovanni Majnoni, and Carmen Reinhart. New York City: Springer.

Pinches, George E., and Kent A. Mingo. 1973. A Multivariate Analysis of Industrial Bond Ratings. *The Journal of Finance* 28, no.1: 7–18.

Ravi, Vadlamani, H. Kurniawan, Peter Nwee Kok Thai, and P. Ravi Kumar. 2008. Soft computing system for bank performance prediction. *Applied Soft Computing* 8, no.1: 305–315.

Ravi, Vadlamani, and Chelimala Pramodh. 2008. Threshold accepting trained principal component neural network and feature subset selection: Application to bankruptcy prediction in banks. *Applied Soft Computing* 8, no.4: 1539–1548.

Shiller, Robert. 2008. *The subprime solution: How today's global financial crisis happened and what to do about it.* Princeton: Princeton University Press.

Swicegood, Philip, and Jeffrey A. Clark. 2001. Off-site monitoring for predicting bank under performance: A comparison of neural networks, discriminant analysis, and professional human judgment. *International Journal of Intelligent Systems in Accounting, Finance and Management* 10, no.3: 169–186.

Tam, Kar Yan, and Melody Kiang. 1990. Predicting bank failures: A neural network approach. *Applied Artificial Intelligence* 4, no.4: 265–282.

UK Financial Services Authority. 2009. "The Turner Review. A regulatory response to the global banking crisis," March, http://www.actuaries.org/CTTEES_TFRISKCRISIS/Documents/turner_review.pdf (accessed June 2, 2021).

US Banking Act (Glass-Steagall Act). 1933. Public Law No. 73-66, 73d Congress, H.R. 5661.

US Credit Rating Agency Reform Act. 2006. Public Law No. 109-291, 109th Congress.

US House of Representatives. 2003. "Rating the Rating Agencies: The State of Transparency and Competition," Committee on Financial Services, Hearing before the Subcommittee on Capital Markets,

Insurance, and Government Sponsored Enterprises, 180th Congress, 1st session, 2 April, https://books.google.gr/books?id=VVznyhQ9eVgC&printsec=frontcover&hl=el&source=gbs_ge_summary_r&cad=0#v=onepage&q&f=false (accessed June 3, 2021).

US SEC. 2021. "Current NRSROs," 25 January, https://www.sec.gov/ocr/ocr-current-nrsros.html (accessed June 3, 2021).

US SEC. 2008. "SEC Proposes Comprehensive Reforms to Bring Increased Transparency to Credit Rating Process," Press release, No. 2008-110, 11 June, https://www.sec.gov/news/press/2008/2008-110.htm (accessed June 3, 2021).

White, Lawrence J. 2009. "A Brief History of Credit Rating Agencies: How Financial Regulation Entrenched this Industry's Role in the Subprime Mortgage Debacle of 2007-2008," *Mercatus on Policy*, No. 59, October, https://www.mercatus.org/system/files/59_CRA_history_%28web%29.pdf (accessed June 2, 2021).

CHAPTER 10

ASSESSING THE EU REGULATORY FRAMEWORK ON CREDIT RATING AGENCIES AS AN ANCHOR OF FINANCIAL STABILITY

DESPOINA ANAGNOSTOPOULOU*
AND KORNILIA VIKELIDOU**

Introduction

Credit ratings provide an opinion on the relative ability (and willingness) of an obligor to meet financial commitments (OECD 2010, 5). Credit Rating Agencies (hereinafter CRAs) play an important role in global securities and banking markets because their credit ratings are used by investors, borrowers, issuers, and governments as part of making informed investment and financing decisions, since they cover information asymmetries between investors and debt issuers (Miller 2016, 605; Petit 2011, 588). Their credit ratings are also used by credit institutions, investment firms, or insurance undertakings as a reference for the calculation of their capital requirements for solvency purposes or for calculating risks in their investment activity (Directive 2013/36/EU). CRAs provide an opinion on the relative ability and willingness of parties with debt obligations to meet financial commitments. They have three functions: to measure the credit risk of the issuer, to provide a means of comparison, and to provide a common standard (OECD 2010, 1).

CRAs were gradually given a "gatekeeper" role that permitted access of issuers to capital markets and reduced or increased their cost of

* Associate Professor, Department of International and European Studies, University of Macedonia (Thessaloniki, Greece).
** PhD, Department of International and European Studies, University of Macedonia (Thessaloniki, Greece).

capital, according to their rating (Veil 2017, 552; Coffee 2006, 2). In addition, they obtained a regulatory role accorded first by the United States of America (hereinafter US) and then by the European Union (hereinafter EU) and other third countries (Veil 2017, 552-553). As the Economist states in May 2020:

> The accuracy of ratings matters, because the licensed firms that issue them [the CRAs] wield great power over capital markets. A downgrade can cause a company's funding costs to rocket, or a run on a bank. It can also force a corporate or sovereign borrower out of an index, draining the pool of investors willing or permitted to lend to it (Economist 2020).

Despite their importance and their effects, CRAs were not subject to binding regulation. Their behaviour was self-regulated by following the non-binding International Organisation for Securities Commissions (hereinafter IOSCO) Code, and was influenced by their need to keep their reputation for diligence (Veil 2017, 555; European Commission 2006).

CRAs were created in the US in 1909, when Moody's was established (Miller 2016, 605), and have flourished after the Great Depression of 1929. In 1936, the US Federal Reserve Bank mandated that commercial banks invest only in "investment grade bonds", with reference to "recognised rating manuals" (i.e., CRA ratings). It thus prohibited their investment in speculative bonds that could undermine their solvency. The same prohibition applied for insurance companies and broker-dealers (Cantor and Packer 1995, 16-17). In 1975, the US Securities and Exchange Commission (hereinafter SEC) established guidelines for designating "National Recognized Statistical Rating Organizations" (hereinafter NRSROs) (Levich et al. 2002).[1] At the same time, the SEC endorsed Moody's and Standard & Poor's (hereinafter S&P) that were the large rating firms, and later Fitch as well, as well as seven more CRAs in 2010 (Petit 2011, 592). In 1991, the SEC mandated that bonds and other debt instruments that were held as assets by money market mutual funds (MMMFs) had to have a CRA rating of AAA/Aaa or AA+/Aa1. That meant regulatory reliance on the CRAs' ratings for prudential regulatory purposes (European Commission 2015b, 67). The "Big Three"[2] expanded their rating business globally and provided investors and financial

---

[1] The term was used solely for determining capital charges on different grades of debt securities under 17 CFR §240.15c3-1, the SEC's "Net capital requirements for brokers or dealers" rule.

[2] The "Big Three CRAs" are S&P, Moody's, and Fitch.

institutions with guidance regarding creditworthiness and default risk of corporate and sovereign issuers of debt securities.

In 2003, the IOSCO published a Statement of Principles Regarding the Activities of Credit Rating Agencies as high-level objectives, describing the terms and conditions of their operation and the manner in which their opinions should be used (IOSCO 2015, A-2; European Commission 2006). In 2004, the Basel II Accord[3] included the Market Risk Pillar, with a standardised approach to Credit Risk (Petit 2011, 592, n. 31), while increasing the reliance on ratings. In September 2006, the US Credit Rating Agency Reform Act, among other things, added Section 15E to the Securities Exchange Act of 1934 in order to establish self-executing requirements on NRSROs and to provide the SEC with authority to implement a registration and oversight programme for NRSROs.

The unfolding of the financial crisis in 2007-08, revealing cases such as Lehman Brothers assessed by the CRAs with high ratings just a few days before their collapse, without adapting them fast enough to changes in the markets, exposed the insufficiency of the regulatory framework of CRAs regarding their capacity to evaluate the associated risks as well as avert or mitigate such downward spirals that threaten financial stability. In addition, a lot of criticism was voiced against the lack of transparency in their criteria (Veil 2017, 555).

In the US, the Financial Crisis Inquiry Commission,[4] nicknamed the "Angelides Commission" after its chairman, Phil Angelides, concluded (with four committee members dissenting) that:

> …the failures of credit rating agencies were essential cogs in the wheel of financial destruction. The three credit rating agencies were key enablers of the financial meltdown. The mortgage-related securities at the heart of the crisis could not have been marketed and sold without their seal of approval.

---

[3] The Revised Framework for Capital Measurement and Capital Standards (Basel II Accord) was endorsed by the central bank governors and the heads of banking supervisory authorities of the G10 countries in June 2004, and was revised in June 2006 (Basel Committee on Banking Supervision 2006). For the European comprehensive approach of Basel II, see ECB 2004.

[4] The Financial Crisis Inquiry Commission (FCIC) was a ten-member commission appointed by Democrats and Republicans (ratio of 6-4) of the US Congress with the goal of investigating the causes of the financial crisis of 2007-10. It was created by section 5 of the Fraud Enforcement and Recovery Act of 2009 (Public Law 111-21), which was signed into law by US President Barack Obama on May 20, 2009 (US Financial Crisis Inquiry Commission 2011, xi).

> Investors relied on them, often blindly. In some cases, they were obligated to use them, or regulatory capital standards were hinged on them.... [T]he forces at work behind the breakdowns at Moody's... includ[ed] the flawed computer models, the pressure from financial firms that paid for the ratings, the relentless drive for market share, the lack of resources to do the job despite record profits, and the absence of meaningful public oversight (US Financial Crisis Inquiry Commission 2011, xxv).

The response of the US was the Dodd-Frank Wall Street Reform and Consumer Protection Act of July 21, 2010, which made changes to the federal financial regulatory framework and institutions. It mandated the SEC to establish the Office of Credit Ratings (OCR) in order to supervise NRSROs, e.g., the CRAs registered with the SEC (US SEC 2017). The Dodd-Frank Act includes enhanced regulation of the NRSROs and, in particular, an effective internal control structure, implementation of the SEC's rules to prevent sales and marketing considerations from influencing the ratings issued by a NRSRO, as well as guidelines, avoidance of conflicts of interest, processing of complaints regarding non-compliance by the NRSRO, reward policy, duty to report credible allegations of unlawful conduct by issuers, public disclosure of initial and revised credit ratings, methodology and data used, annual public inspection report for each of the NRSROs, and more powers to the SEC to suspend or revoke registration in case of non-integrity (US Dodd-Frank Act, Title IX—Investor Protections and Improvements to the Regulation of Securities, Subtitle C). In addition, Section 939A of the Dodd-Frank Act requires federal agencies to review their regulations that require the use of a creditworthiness assessment of a security or money market instrument, to remove any reference to or reliance on credit ratings, to substitute an appropriate standard of creditworthiness, and to develop uniform standards of creditworthiness (US Commodity Futures Trading Commission 2010).

In the EU, the massive amount of power of the CRAs was evident even before the crisis. Thus, in 2002, the Italian food industry Parmalat S.p.A. was rated "investment grade" for its newly-issued bonds until a few days before it declared bankruptcy (De Pascalis 2017, 65). Thyssenkrupp AG, one of the world's largest steel producers, with a revenue of 37.303 million in 2003 (Thyssenkrupp 2005, 5) and 34.77 billion in 2018, saw its stocks downgraded to junk (BBB+), with its director finding this incomprehensible (Langohr and Langohr 2009, 191, 198). When the euro area financial crisis began, subsequent downgrades to junk status occurred in Portugal, Ireland, Italy, Greece, and Spain,[5] followed by abrupt bond sell-offs and higher borrowing costs.

In October 2010, the Financial Stability Board (hereinafter FSB)[6] published the "Principles for Reducing Reliance on CRA Ratings" in order to "end mechanistic reliance on CRA ratings by banks, institutional investors and other market participants by reducing the 'hard wiring' of CRA ratings in standards, laws, and regulations and by providing incentives for firms to develop their own capacity for credit risk assessment and due diligence" (Financial Stability Board 2010). The FSB Principles recognise that CRAs play an important role and that their ratings can appropriately be used as an input to a firm's internal credit assessment processes. However, any use of CRA ratings by a firm should not be mechanistic nor lessen a firm's responsibility to ensure that its credit exposures are based on sound risk assessments. The Principles are based on the assumption that financial institutions should not invest in credits without conducting their own due diligence. At the same time, this does not imply that market participants should avoid all use of credit ratings, as long as they combine the use with exercise of their own judgment (Financial Stability Board 2010).

In 2014, the SEC imposed new rules on the rating industry, but it did not ban the issuer-pays model under which the rating agencies operate (Cavallaro and Trotta 2019). In 2015, the IOSCO published the Code for

---

[5] "In the aftermath of the global financial crisis, the unflattering acronym "PIGS" or "PIIGS" entered the popular lexicon to describe EU Member States – Portugal, Ireland, Italy, Greece and Spain – that were unable to refinance government debt or bail out stricken banks without the help of third parties. Almost a decade on, Italy and Greece remain at risk of default, but Portugal has undergone a remarkable turnaround in fortunes. Portugal left a stringent EU and IMF-led austerity program four years ago and its economy has expanded for 15 consecutive quarters. GDP grew 2.7% last year – its strongest rate of expansion since the millennium" (Robinson 2018).

[6] The FSB was established by the G20 in April 2009 as the successor to the Financial Stability Forum (FSF), established in 1999 by the G7 Finance Ministers and Central Bank Governors. In September 2009, the G20 endorsed the FSB's original Charter, with which the FSB aims to promote the reform of international financial regulation and supervision. In June 2012, the G20 endorsed the FSB's restated and amended Charter, which reinforces its role in standard-setting and in promoting members' implementation of international standards and agreed G20 and FSB commitments and policy recommendations. On 28 January 2013, the FSB established itself as a not-for-profit association under Swiss law, with its seat in Basel, Switzerland (Financial Stability Board 2018).

fundamentals, including quality and integrity, independence and conflicts of interest, transparency and timeliness of ratings disclosure, as well as keeping confidential information (IOSCO 2015). The EU reacted by enacting the first Credit Rating Regulation 1060/2009 in September 2009 (CRA I), amended by the second Credit Rating Regulation 513/2011 in 2011 (CRA II), and enhanced by the third Credit Rating Regulation 462/2013 in 2013 (CRA III).

Shedding light on the EU regulatory framework on CRAs, it is the aim of this chapter to assess its role in restoring market confidence and increasing investor protection in terms of safeguarding financial stability.

The development of the EU regulatory framework on Credit Rating Agencies

CRA I was adopted in September 2009. It established a regulatory framework for CRAs with the view to enhancing the integrity, transparency, responsibility, good governance and independence of credit rating activities.[7] According to the CRA Regulation (as has been amended and applies in its consolidated version), its aim is to promote the smooth function of the internal market and a high level of consumer and investor protection in the EU (art. 1 CRA Regulation).

The CRA Regulation introduced a registration procedure with a national supervisor and the Committee of European Securities Regulators (hereinafter CESR)[8] when a CRA operates in the EU, by providing in its application the complete information mentioned in Annex II of the CRA Regulation (arts. 14-20 CRA Regulation). This procedure allowed the certification of non-EU established CRAs based on equivalence of supervision (art. 5 CRA Regulation; European Commission 2019a). The CRA Regulation provided for supervision by national competent authorities and their eventual obligatory cooperation in colleges of national supervisors, in

---

[7] Art. 3(1)(a)(b) Regulation 1060/2009: "'Credit rating' means an opinion regarding the credit-worthiness of an entity, a debt or financial obligation, debt security, preferred share or other financial instrument or of an issuer of such a debt or financial obligation, debt security, preferred share or other financial instrument, issued using an established and defined ranking system of rating categories. 'Credit rating agency' means a legal person whose occupation includes the issuing of credit ratings on a professional basis".

[8] The CESR was the supervising EU authority of capital markets and was succeeded by the European Securities and Markets Authority (hereinafter ESMA) (Regulation 1095/2010).

case that different EU member states were involved in investigations or on-site inspections or delegation of tasks. It also provided for cooperation with third countries and exchange of information (arts. 34-35 CRA Regulation). In addition, it established specific rules under penalties (art. 36 CRA I) on: a) issuing ratings (art. 5 CRA Regulation), b) avoiding the existing and potential conflicts of interest between the CRAs, their governors and rate analysts, on the one hand, and the organisations they rate, on the other hand, including outsourcing (art. 6 CRA Regulation), and c) respecting transparency as regards models, methodologies and key assumptions related to ratings in order to enhance their quality (art. 8 CRA Regulation).

The CRA Regulation established ESMA at the center of the EU regulatory framework, with many supervisory powers. ESMA was established by Regulation 1095/2010 (ESMA Regulation) and succeeded national competent authorities, which were no longer responsible for the supervision and sanctions of CRAs (Veil 2017, 556). In addition, the CRA Regulation includes rating outlooks for the first time, i.e., the CRAs' opinion on the possible prospects of a rating (recital 4 CRA III; Veil 2017, 558).

CRA III regulated the issuance of "sovereign rating" of a state, or a regional or local authority of a state (art. 3(1)(v) CRA III).[9] Hereinafter, sovereign ratings shall be issued in a manner which ensures that the individual specificity of a particular member state has been analysed and at a specific calendar at the ESMA Rating Platform (art. 8a(1) CRA Regulation), accompanied by individual country reports made publicly available. Other public communications about potential changes in sovereign ratings shall not be based on information within the sphere of the rated entity that has been disclosed without the consent of the rated entity, unless it is available from generally accessible sources, or unless there are no legitimate reasons for the rated entity not to give its consent to the disclosure of the information (art. 8a(2) CRA Regulation).

CRA III aimed at applying its strict rules to all CRAs, even if they are established outside the EU. "Credit institutions, investment firms,

---

[9] The concept includes the case where the issuer of the debt or financial obligation, debt security or other financial instrument or debt vehicle is a state or a regional or local authority of a state, or where the issuer is an international financial institution established by two or more states, which has the purpose of mobilising funding and providing financial assistance for the benefit of its members experiencing, or threatened by, severe financing problems.

insurance undertakings, reinsurance undertakings, institutions for occupational retirement provision, management companies, investment companies, alternative investment fund managers and central counterparties may use credit ratings for regulatory purposes only if they are issued by CRAs established" in the EU and registered in accordance with CRA III (art. 4(1) CRA III), or that the conduct of the credit rating activities by CRAs established in a third-country resulting in the issuing of the credit rating to be endorsed fulfils requirements, which are at least as stringent as the requirements of CRA III and subject to legally binding rules that are equivalent to those of CRA III (arts. 4(3)(b) and 5(6)(b) CRA III). CRA III attempts to limit the regulatory role of CRAs by reviewing over-reliance on credit ratings by financial institutions, obliging them to make their own credit risk assessment and to stop relying solely or mechanistically on credit ratings for assessing the creditworthiness of an entity or financial instrument (art. 5a CRA III). This is done in accordance with the G20 conclusions and the FSB principles for Reducing Reliance on External Credit Ratings, while emphasising the need for control of structured finance instruments (recital 71 Directive 2013/36/EU; Veil 2017, 559).

Over-reliance on credit ratings by the European Supervisory Authorities (hereinafter ESAs) and the European Systemic Risk Board (Regulations 1092/2010; 1093/2010; 1094/2010; 1095/2010; Directive 2010/78/EU) had to stop by 31 December 2013, after review of all such references and their removal in existing guidelines and recommendations (art. 5b CRA Regulation). In addition, the European Commission had to review whether references to credit ratings in EU law trigger sole or mechanistic reliance on credit ratings by supervisors and market participants deleting all references for regulatory purposes by 1 January 2020, if appropriate alternatives to credit risk assessment have been implemented (art. 5c CRA Regulation). The CRA Regulation also provides for safeguards, such as double rating for securitisation instruments (art. 8c CRA Regulation), and a limited contractual relationship for re-securitisations up to four years (art. 6b CRA Regulation). At the same time, it established a legal basis for the CRAs' civil liability (art. 35(a) CRA III).[10]

The EU credit rating regulatory framework was complemented by many other acts. The most important relevant acts are:

---

[10] See below ("Liability issues").

a) Directive 2011/61/EU (art. 64), which amends art. 4(1) CRA Regulation so as to provide that "credit institutions, investment firms, insurance undertakings, assurance undertakings, reinsurance undertakings, UCITS, institutions for occupational retirement provision and Alternative Investment Funds may use credit ratings for regulatory purposes only if they are issued by credit rating agencies established in the Union and registered in accordance with this Regulation";
b) Directive 2013/14/EU, which amends the CRA Regulation to require financial institutions and investors to carry out their own evaluation of credit risks and not to rely solely or automatically on external ratings in order to evaluate the creditworthiness of an organisation or financial instrument;
c) Directive 2013/36/EU, which provides that institutions should have internal methodologies that enable them to assess the credit risk of exposures to individual obligors, securities or securitisation positions, and credit risk at the portfolio level without relying solely or mechanistically on external credit ratings. "Where own funds requirements are based on a rating by an External Credit Assessment Institution (hereinafter ECAI) or based on the fact that an exposure is unrated, this shall not exempt institutions from additionally considering other relevant information for assessing their allocation of internal capital" (art. 79 Directive 2013/36/EU). In addition, starting from 2014, the ESAs shall "publish a biannual report analysing the extent to which Member States' law refers to external credit ratings for regulatory purposes and the steps taken by Member States to reduce such references" (art. 161 Directive 2013/36/EU);
d) Directive 2014/51/EU, which aligned the recognition of CRAs and ensured the consistency with macro-prudential supervision on credit institutions;[11] thus, "external credit assessment institution" (ECAI) means a CRA that is registered or certified in accordance with the CRA Regulation (art. 13 Directive 2009/138/EC, as amended by art. 2 Directive 2014/51/EU);
e) Regulation 2017/2402, which establishes a specific more risk-sensitive prudential framework for simple, transparent and standardised securitisation (hereinafter STS) (recital 5 and arts. 19-26 Regulation 2017/2402),[12] in order to prevent a new subprime

---

[11] See, for example, Regulation 575/2013 and Directive 2013/36/EU.

[12] "Securitisation" is the process where a financial instrument is created, typically by a lender such as a bank, by pooling assets (for example, car-loans or SME-

mortgage crisis as the one that took place in 2007 in the US. It aims to establish the framework for securitisation as a major building block of the EU Capital Markets Union (European Commission 2017; European Commission 2015a). The Regulation provides that the originator, sponsor or securitisation special purpose entity (SSPE) may use the service of a "third party" authorised by the competent authority to check and assess whether a securitisation complies with its provisions and the STS criteria, without affecting their liability (art. 27(2) Regulation 2017/2402). The Regulation expressly prohibits a competent authority to grant the authorisation to a CRA (art. 28(1)(b) Regulation 2017/2402); and

f) Regulation 2017/1131, which states that Money Market Funds (hereinafter MMFs) should invest in high-quality eligible assets after a prudent internal credit quality assessment procedure, under certain criteria, without over-reliance on ratings issued by rating agencies. "Taking note of the work done on reducing investor over-reliance on credit ratings by international bodies, such as IOSCO and the FSB [and EU law]… it is not appropriate to prohibit any product, including MMFs, from soliciting or financing an external credit rating", if the selection is made for the most suited to the specific investment portfolio of the CRA after an internal procedure in a consistent manner (rec. 31-34 and arts. 19-21 Regulation 2017/1131).

Assessment

Registration process and perimeter activities

All CRAs established in the EU must apply for registration with ESMA (art. 15 CRA Regulation), whereas CRAs established in non-EU countries and whose credit ratings are used in the EU should be certified by ESMA. According to the data published by ESMA, there are 27 CRAs authorised by ESMA to issue credit ratings within the EU (ESMA 2018a). The registration is a two-phase process that comprises: a) the completeness of the application (art. 15(1) CRA Regulation; Annex II CRA Regulation), and b) the compliance of the applicant CRA with the conditions with the CRA Regulation (art. 16(1) CRA Regulation). ESMA should verify that

---

loans) for investors to purchase. This facilitates access to a greater range of investors, thereby increasing liquidity and freeing up capital from the banks for new lending (European Commission 2017; Regulation 2017/2402).

there are no non-registered or non-certified CRAs issuing credit ratings in the EU. In order to facilitate the application of the CRA Regulation and ensure a level playing field, ESMA is entitled to establish harmonised regulatory technical standards concerning the information to be provided by CRAs in their application for registration of certification (recitals 10-12 CRA II; art. 21(4) CRA Regulation). Although ESMA shortened the registration process, the latter remains cumbersome due to the regulatory requirements (European Court of Auditors 2015). In the case of ESMA rejecting the application for registration, the ESA Board of Appeal will rule on the appeal, as it has already done in 2014 and 2017 (Moloney 2018, 270).

The scope of the CRA Regulation covers only credit ratings issued by the CRAs registered in the EU. Thus, "this Regulation does not apply to credit ratings that a credit rating produces pursuant to an individual order and provides exclusively to the person who ordered it and which are not intended for public disclosure or distribution by subscription" (art. 2(2)(a) CRA I). In the same context, investment research, investment recommendations, and other opinions about a value or a price for a financial instrument or a financial obligation are not considered as credit ratings (recital 20 CRA I). This provision has led the Big Three to register since 31 October 2011: Moody's registered in 5 member states (UK, Cyprus, Germany, France, Italy, and Spain), S&P Global Ratings Europe Limited registered in Ireland, and Fitch registered in 6 member states (UK, Poland, Germany, France, Italy, and Spain). There are 4 more certified CRAs with seat outside the EU: two US CRAs (Kroll Bond Rating Agency and Egan-Jones Ratings Co.), one Japanese (Japan Credit Rating Agency Ltd), and one Mexican (HR Ratings de México, S.A. de C.V.).[13]

Credit institutions may only use "for regulatory purposes"[14] ratings that have been issued by a CRA that is registered within the EU or that satisfies the equivalence criteria in the CRA Regulation. Registered CRAs can endorse credit ratings issued in third countries under specified conditions (art. 4(3) CRA Regulation). The most important conditions to be met entail that: a) the registered CRA can verify on an ongoing basis that the conduct of the third-country CRA operates under a no-less

[13] The list of CRAs registered or certified by ESMA can be found at ESMA (2021).

[14] "'Regulatory purposes' means the use of credit ratings for the specific purpose of complying with Union law, or with Union law as implemented by the national legislation of the Member States" (art. 3(1)(g) CRA Regulation).

stringent supervisory regime (art. 4(3)(b) CRA Regulation), b) there is an objective reason for the rating to be elaborated in the third country (art. 4(3)(e) CRA Regulation), and c) there is an appropriate cooperation arrangement between ESMA and the relevant supervisory authority of the credit rating agency established in the third country (art. 4(3)(h) CRA Regulation).

According to the CRA Regulation (art. 5(1) CRA Regulation), the credit ratings "that are related to entities established or financial instruments issued in third countries and that are issued by a CRA established in a third country" may be used by credit institutions for regulatory purposes under conditions, such as: a) an equivalence decision by the European Commission confirming that the standards of regulation in the specific third country are equivalent to EU standards (art. 5(1)(b) CRA Regulation); b) a cooperation agreement in effect between the European Commission and the regulator of that third country (art. 5(1)(c) CRA Regulation); and c) the certification of the third country CRA by ESMA (art. 5(1)(e) CRA Regulation).

Regarding securitisation instruments,[15] the CRAs are required to have an additional symbol, as well as to disclose information on the credit quality and the performance of the underlying assets, the structure of the securitisation transaction, the cash flows, and any necessary information in order to conduct comprehensive and well-informed stress tests (art. 8b CRA III). However, after obtaining technical advice from ESMA, the Commission shall review the situation in the credit rating market for securitisation instruments, and shall submit a report to the European Parliament and to the Council accompanied by a legislative proposal in order to ensure transparency (art. 39(4) CRA Regulation).

According to the CRA Regulation, ESMA is entitled to impose fines in case of infringements (art. 36a CRA Regulation) or to delegate specific supervisory tasks to competent national authorities. National supervisors are responsible for the supervision of the use of credit ratings by financial institutions, and they have the power to demand ESMA to withdraw a license. In order to ensure a level playing field and identify cases of credit ratings that have not been registered with ESMA, perimeter

---

15 "'Securitisation instrument' means a financial instrument or other assets resulting from a securitisation transaction or scheme referred to in Art. 1(1) of Regulation (EU) 2017/2402 (Securitisation Regulation)" (art. 3(1)(l) CRA Regulation).

assessments are conducted by ESMA using a variety of information sources (ESMA 2018b).

ESMA has recently found five banks infringing on the provisions of the CRA Regulation by issuing credit ratings without being authorised to do so. On 23 July 2018, ESMA fined Danske Bank, Nordea Bank, SEB, Svenska Handelsbanken and Swedbank €495.000 each, and issued five public notices for negligently breaching the CRA Regulation (ESMA 2018a). Between June 2011 and May 2016, these five banks issued credit research to their clients, which included the issuance of what the banks describe as shadow ratings. ESMA considered these reports to include opinions that meet the criteria of a credit rating as stipulated in the CRA Regulation. Consequently, these reports were considered to be infringements of the CRA Regulation, since none of these banks had obtained prior authorisation, and neither of them was or is registered as a CRA, nor had they applied for registration prior to issuing these ratings. The calculation of the amount of the five fines levied took into consideration the fact that the infringement had been committed for more than 6 months, and also the mitigating factor that each bank has voluntarily taken measures to ensure that similar infringements could not be committed in the future.

Quality of the rating process, conflicts of interest, transparency

One of the main objectives of the CRA Regulation is to improve the quality of the rating process and to ensure that credit ratings are independent and objective. To this end, ESMA works on numerous areas to enhance the quality of ratings related to portfolio risk, validation of methodologies, the methodology development, the rating process, validation practices, and analyst rotation. With the view to improving the quality of the CRAs' work, the CRA Regulation addresses measures to increase competition, such as the measures on conflict of interests and transparency intended to reduce barriers to entry. However, provisions for competition alone can do little towards boosting the quality of the credit ratings in a market, which is dominated from the outset by the same Big Three. Additionally, according to the European Court of Auditors, "the current approach of the Eurosystem does not guarantee that all ESMA-registered CRAs are on an equal footing" (European Court of Auditors 2015).

Another important issue in the regulatory framework of the CRAs concerns the conflict of interest arising mainly from the issuer-pays model dominating the CRAs market; an apt analogy would be making teachers being paid by their students to give good grades for fear of losing business

(Petit 2011, 590). In order to limit conflicts of interest, the CRA Regulation requires CRAs to meet certain organisational requirements (annex I CRA Regulation). Specifically, CRAs must have an administrative or supervisory board from which at least one third are not involved in credit rating activities. These independent members are responsible for monitoring the development of the credit rating policy and the effectiveness of the measures introduced to prevent conflicts of interest. Additionally, the CRAs are required to adopt and disclose policies and procedures intended to ensure the independence of their rating activity. "A credit rating shall ensure that the provision of ancillary services does not present conflicts of interest with its credit rating activities and shall disclose in the final rating reports any ancillary services provided for the rated entity or any related third party".[16] Besides, the CRA Regulation sets operational requirements to ensure the independence of the CRAs' employees. To this end, it provides for a mandatory rotation of analysts, the prohibition of an analyst's involvement regarding the negotiation of fees, and the decoupling of the analysts' remuneration from the revenues stemming from the entities they rate. It is also worth noting, concerning re-securitisation products with underlying assets from the same originator, that the CRA Regulation sets a rotation mechanism by defining a maximum four-year duration of any contractual relationship between issuers and CRAs and a minimum period during which the CRA is prohibited from entering into a new contract (art. 6(b) CRA Regulation).

The EU regulatory framework on CRAs focuses significantly on transparency rules. According to the CRA Regulation, an annual transparency report is required to be published and remain available on ESMA's website (ESMA 2020b) for at least five years (art. 12 & annex I, section E, part III, CRA Regulation). This annual report shall comprise detailed information on the legal structure and ownership of the CRA, a description of internal control mechanisms, statistics on the allocation of the staff to new CRAs, and the different asset classes, credit rating reviews, methodology or model appraisal, senior management, a description of the CRA's record-keeping policy, the outcome of the CRA's annual internal review of its independent compliance function, a description of the CRA's management and rating analyst rotation policy, as well as financial information on the revenue of the CRA (annex I, section D CRA

[16] Annex I, Section B, point 4 CRA Regulation: "Ancillary services are not part of the credit rating activities; they comprise market forecasts, estimates of economic trends, pricing analysis and other general data analysis as well as related distribution services".

Regulation). The CRA III Regulation introduced the European rating platform, which comprises the credit ratings of registered or certified CRAs that are published by ESMA on a website (art. 11a CRA Regulation).

The sovereign ratings have to be issued in a manner which ensures that the individual specificity of a particular member state has been analysed and accompanied by individual country reports (art. 8a(1) CRA Regulation). Besides, sovereign ratings shall be reviewed every six months (art. 8(5) CRA Regulation), and policy recommendations shall not be included (annex I, section D, part III, point 4 CRA Regulation). Against this background, sovereign ratings are expected on a constant basis, and this contributes to a more informed and less vulnerable market.

The quality of the rating process and the prevention of conflicts of interest are safeguarded through the enactment of deterrence rules in the CRA Regulation. This is achieved notably through the mitigation of over-reliance on credit ratings for regulatory purposes by requiring supervised by ESMA entities to make their own credit risk assessments (art. 5a CRA Regulation) and by stipulating that the ESAs do not refer to credit ratings in their guidelines and draft technical standards where such references have the potential to trigger sole reliance on credit ratings by the competent authorities (art. 5b CRA Regulation), as well as through the introduction of civil liability rules for CRAs in case of specific infringements having a reasonable impact on a credit rating (Art. 35a CRA Regulation).

Supervision of Credit Rating Agencies

In May 2011, the CRA II Regulation gave general competence to ESMA regarding the ongoing supervision of registered CRAs.[17] Accordingly, ESMA is entitled to assess the periodic information provided by the supervised entities, draw remedy-oriented action plans, and monitor their application. The ongoing supervision of ESMA comprises: a) analysis of information sent periodically by the CRAs, which is used for

[17] On the other hand, certified CRAs follow the certification process. "Certification" is a specific regime introduced by art. 5 CRA Regulation that can be used by small CRAs from third countries with no presence or affiliation in the EU, to provide for the use of credit ratings issued in third countries in the EU, in case that these CRAs are not systemically important for the financial stability or integrity of the financial markets of one or more member states. Certification is possible after determination by the Commission of the equivalence of the legal and supervisory framework of a third country to the requirements of the CRA Regulation.

the individual risk assessment of the respective CRA along with the general risk analysis function within ESMA, b) regular engagements such as on-site inspections to CRAs, organised after receiving the periodical information, c) other tasks such as follow-up remedial action plans from investigations, providing feedback to queries from CRAs on an ad hoc basis and handling complaints from third parties, which might entail the involvement of national competent authorities (arts. 21-23d CRA Regulation).

The supervisory authority of ESMA is based on the risks posed by market participants. This entails that when the ongoing supervision identifies cases of non-compliance with the applicable requirements, then ESMA takes further investigatory actions, which comprise: a) requests for information (art. 23b CRA Regulation), b) general investigations (art. 23c CRA Regulation), and c) on-site inspection (art. 23d CRA Regulation).

Following a public consultation in July 2018,[18] ESMA published on 5 February 2019 guidelines on supervisory reporting for CRAs (ESMA 2019b), which mainly aim at streamlining the information that is reported on a periodic basis by CRAs to ESMA, as well as increasing the predictability of ESMA's supervisory interactions with CRAs with respect to the requests for information that ESMA submits to CRAs (ESMA 2019b). These guidelines constitute a revision to ESMA's existing guidelines that were published in 2015 (ESMA 2015b) and apply to the CRAs registered in the EU. They provide for the information that should be submitted by the CRAs both to enable ESMA's ongoing supervision of the CRAs on a consistent basis and to clarify expectations of the information that should be submitted to ESMA for the calculation of supervisory fees and the CRAs' market share. According to the ESMA Regulation (art. 16(3) Regulation 1095/2010), "financial market participants shall make every effort to comply with those guidelines and recommendations". The main features of these revised guidelines comprise: i) differentiated reporting calendars for entities, depending on the required level of supervisory engagement, ii) individual reporting instructions for each reporting item, which have been elaborated and expanded in areas where ESMA has identified a supervisory need, and iii) standardising reporting templates for specific reporting items (ESMA 2019b, 4). These main features aim at shedding light on when and where

[18] The nineteen responses to the consultation paper derived from a mixture of fifteen CRAs, industry associations, and other market participants (ESMA 2019b, 4). These guidelines do not apply to certified CRAs (ESMA 2019b, 40).

thematic investigations may be necessary, or where remedial actions may need to be taken by the CRAs to ensure that the required information by ESMA is timely and relevant in order to favour a consistent application of the CRA Regulation. To this end, these guidelines propose the following changes: a) clarification of key aspects and concepts in the existing requirements and standardised templates for a number of reporting areas, b) refined reporting frequencies, c) a new basis for determining a CRA's reporting requirements, and d) additional requirements where ESMA has identified information gaps (ESMA 2019b, 81). Specifically, ESMA expects that the suggested clarifications and templates will gradually lessen the compliance cost for CRAs by reducing the time they spend on responding to requests for information from ESMA. Besides, the proposed revised guidelines are tailored to align the reporting requirements of the CRAs with ESMA's risk-based approach to supervision. Accordingly, ESMA will be able to adjust the reporting categorisation of an individual CRA in response to changes in ESMA's assessment of that CRA. It may thus be the case that small and medium-sized CRAs are assessed by the new approach as representing high risk, and thus as being required to report more often to ESMA. This might entail additional costs to higher-risk small CRAs, which, however, could be justified as a safeguard to investors and orderly markets. Against this background, the standardised format and reporting frequency suggested by these new guidelines are less burdensome than ad hoc requests at different intervals. In the same way, the introduced new items, such as the annual review of credit ratings and methodologies and the attestation on internal controls, are considered as written confirmation that the CRA is meeting specific requirements in the CRA Regulation and consequently, they are not expected to aggravate the cost for CRAs (ESMA 2019b, 81-82).

ESMA is also responsible for: i) submitting draft Regulatory Technical Standards (hereinafter RTS) for endorsement by the European Commission (art. 21(4) CRA Regulation). In December 2011, ESMA submitted its RTS on: a) information to be provided by CRAs for applications for registration and certification, b) information provided by CRAs to ESMA through the CEREP platform,[19] c) the assessment of the compliance of the rating methodologies, and d) the content and format of ratings data periodic reporting to be requested from CRAs for the purpose of ongoing supervision by ESMA, and ii) the assessment of third country regimes under the endorsement and certification provisions in the CRA

[19] CEREP is a central repository for publishing the rating activity statistics and rating performance statistics of credit rating agencies.

Regulation (art. 5 CRA Regulation). Additionally, ESMA actively participates in global supervisory colleges (art. 5(7) CRA Regulation), which consist of ESMA and of the main CRA Regulators outside the EU for the three largest and internationally operating CRAs. It is noteworthy that during 2017, ESMA also had bilateral interactions with regulators from third countries on smaller CRAs operating globally, as well as on specific topics, such as methodology disclosures and conflicts of interest in shareholdings (ESMA 2021).

The first recommendations of ESMA, published in 2012, concerned the results of the first examination on the three groups of registered CRAs. Specifically, these recommendations concerned the CRAs' internal policies and procedures, such as the recording of internal meetings, the timing of the distribution of documents ahead of Rating Committees, the adequacy of resources devoted to the analytical business, the internal control functions, the Independent Directors, the disclosure of rating methodologies, the process for the disclosure of rating actions, and the IT environment.

The CRA Regulation stipulates that in case of specific infringements concerning: a) conflicts of interest, organisational or operational requirements, b) obstacles to the supervisory activities, and c) disclosure provisions (annex III CRA Regulation), the supervisory measures entitle ESMA to: a) withdraw the registration of the CRA, b) temporarily prohibit the CRA from issuing credit ratings in the EU, c) suspend the use of credit ratings of a specific CRA for regulatory purposes, d) require the CRA to bring the infringement to an end, and e) issue public notice depending on the seriousness of the breach (art. 24(1) CRA Regulation). ESMA has taken four enforcement actions against CRAs, three of which concern infringements of sovereign debt disclosures: on Moody's (no disclosure on methodology: fine of 1.24 million euros imposed in May 2017); on Fitch (no notification of downgrading: 1.38 million euros in July 2016); on S&P (erroneous email alert, issuance of public notice by ESMA), and on DBRS Ratings (organisational requirements, fine of 30.000 euros; Moloney 2018, 268).

Competition issues: The significant market power of the Big Three and new entrants

Market share

The global credit ratings market is highly concentrated. This is a fact that has been observed throughout several successive decades. In 2010, the OECD Competition Committee confirmed that "the credit rating market is a natural oligopoly, with three CRAs accounting for more than 90% of the market" (OECD 2010). In 2016, the European Commission, based on 2014 turnover from credit rating activities and ancillary services in the EU, confirmed that the rating industry was "dominated by three US-based firms (S&P, Moody's and Fitch), with a global geographic coverage of all asset classes (corporate bonds, sovereign bonds, SFIs and covered bonds)… and a cumulative market share in revenues of approximately 92% percent in the EU". It concluded that the EU CRA Regulation did not prevent a slight increase in concentration in the overall CRA market, based on revenues from rating activity only.[20] In 2020, Moody's, S&P and Fitch still seem to have a combined global market share of almost 95% (Economist 2020).

Table 10-1 by ESMA demonstrates the market shares in 2014 and the absence of significant relevance by EU rating agencies (European Commission 2016), while table 10-2 demonstrates the market share in 2018.

[20] However, the concentration is lower for total revenues (i.e., revenues from rating activity and ancillary services). Ancillary services seem to constitute an important activity for smaller CRAs, while larger CRAs rely more on rating revenues. The most concentrated market is the market of corporate bonds, while concentration has decreased in the sovereign ratings and in SFIs (European Commission 2016, 12).

Table 10-1 Market share calculation based on 2014 turnover from credit rating activities and ancillary services at group level in the EU (ESMA 2015a; European Commission 2016, 8)

Registered Credit Rating Agency	Market Share
AM Best Europe-Rating Services Ltd. (AMBERS)	0.79%
ARC Ratings, S.A.	0.02%
ASSEKURATA Assekuranz Ratings-Agentur GmbH	0.21%
Axesor S.A.	0.61%
BCRA-Credit Rating Agency AD	0.02%
Capital Intelligence (Cyprus) Ltd.	0.12%
CERVED Group S.p.A.	1.20%
Creditreform Rating AG	0.50%
CRIF S.p.A.	0.33%
Dagong Europe Credit Rating Srl	0.02%
DBRS Ratings Limited	1.47%
Euler Hermes Rating GmbH	0.20%
European Rating Agency, a.s.	0.00%
EuroRating Sp. Zo.o.	0.00%
FeriEuroRating Services AG	0.64%
Fitch Group[21]	16.80%
GBB-Rating Gesellschaft für Bonitätsbeurteilung mbH	0.32%
ICAP Group SA	0.55%
INC Rating Sp. Zo.o.	0.00%
ModeFinance S.A.	0.00%
Moody's Group[22]	34.67%
Rating-Agentur Expert RA GmbH	0.00%
Scope Credit Rating GmbH	0.14%
Spread Research SAS	0.11%
Standard & Poor's Group[23]	40.42%
The Economist Intelligence Unit Ltd.	0.87%
Total	100%

[21] Fitch France S.A.S; Fitch Deutschland GmbH; Fitch Italia S.p.A.; Fitch Polska S.A.; Fitch Ratings España S.A.U.; Fitch Ratings Limited and Fitch Ratings CIS Limited.

[22] Moody's Investors Service Cyprus Ltd; Moody's France S.A.S.; Moody's Deutschland GmbH; Moody's Italia S.r.l.; Moody's Investors Service España S.A.; Moody's Investors Service Ltd; and Moody's Investors Services EMEA Ltd.

[23] Standard & Poor's Credit Market Services France S.A.S.; Standard & Poor's Credit Market Services Italy S.r.l.; and Standard & Poor's Credit Market Services Europe Limited.

Table 10-2 Market share calculation based on 2018 turnover from credit rating activities and ancillary services at group level in the EU (ESMA 2019a, 8)

Name of CRA	Market Share %	Less than 10%	Previous Year	YoY Change
S&P Global Ratings	42.09%	-	42.26%	↓
Moody's Investor Service	33.39%	-	32.04%	↑
Fitch Ratings	16.62%	-	15.10%	↑
DBRS Ratings	2.46%	Yes	1.88%	↑
The Economist Intelligence Unit	0.87%	Yes	0.86%	↑
AM Best Europe-Rating Services	0.82%	Yes	0.77%	↑
Cerved Rating Agency	0.81%	Yes	0.82%	↓
Creditreform Rating	0.55%	Yes	0.51%	↑
Scope Ratings	0.49%	Yes	0.28%	↑
GBB-Rating	0.32%	Yes	0.28%	↑
Axesor Risk Management	0.21%	Yes	0.14%	↑
CRIF Ratings	0.21%	Yes	0.17%	↑
Assekurata	0.20%	Yes	0.19%	↑
ICAP	0.19%	Yes	0.12%	↑
Euler Hermes Rating	0.18%	Yes	0.20%	↓
ARC Ratings	0.15%	Yes	0.06%	↑
ModeFinance	0.13%	Yes	0.10%	↑
Capital Intelligence Ratings	0.12%	Yes	0.11%	↑
QIVAUO SAS	0.08%	Yes	0.04%	↑
Kroll Bond Rating Agency Europe	0.03%	Yes	-	↑
DG International Rating	0.02%	Yes	0.03%	↓
BCRA Credit Rating Agency	0.02%	Yes	0.01%	↑
INC Rating	0.01%	Yes	0.01%	-
EuroRating	0.01%	Yes	<0.01%	↑
Nordic Credit Rating AS	0.01%	Yes	-	↑
Rating-Agentur Expert RA GmbH	<0.01%	Yes	<0.01%	-
ACRA Europe	<0.01%	Yes	<0.01%	-
Inbonis	-	-	-	-
TOTAL	100			

As ESMA explains, "the purpose of the market share calculation is to facilitate issuers and related third parties in their evaluation of a CRA with no more than 10% total market share in the EU, as the CRA Regulation, under Article 8(d), states that issuers or related third parties are required to consider appointing a CRA with no more than 10% total market share whenever they intend to appoint one or more CRAs to rate an issuance or entity" (ESMA 2020c). Based on tables 10-1 and 10-2, one can ascertain the proliferation of very small CRAs (28 registered in the EU), with a market share below 1%, and only one being the fourth CRA, DBRS, which is supported by the Deutsche Bank.

The same surveillance for competition control takes place in the US, where the SEC reported the market shares of the NRSROs: S&P holds 49.5%, Moody's 32.3%, and Fitch 13.5%. Therefore, the SEC reported that the 3 larger NRSROs "account for 95.4% of all the ratings outstanding as of December 31, 2018—slightly lower than their 95.8% share as of December 31, 2017". DBRS holds 2.4% and takes the fourth place. The remaining 2.2% of the ratings market is held by 6 CRAs: A.M. Best (0.4%), EJR (0.9%), HR Ratings (0.1%), JCR (0.2%), KBRA (0.6%), and Morningstar (0.2%) (US SEC 2020, 11). Therefore, S&P holds the first place in the EU and the US, with a market share between 42 and 49.5%. Moody's holds the second place, with around 32% on both sides of the Atlantic, and Fitch is between 13.5 to 16.6%, respectively. And as if by a coincidence, at the fourth place there is again the EU-established DBRS, with a share of 2.4% on both sides of the Atlantic. One cannot but observe how balanced the market shares are.

The question of competition infringement and parallel conduct

As early as 1996, US authorities investigated Moody's for restraints upon, or monopolisation of, interstate or foreign trade or commerce, and in 2001, the oldest CRA was condemned by a US District Court because of intentionally obstructing compliance, since it unlawfully withheld, concealed, and/or destroyed documentary material that was the subject of such demand (U.S. v. Moody's Investors Service Inc. 2001).[24]

No concerns were expressed, however, in the EU. In 2006, the European Commission stated that it "does not share the European Parliament's concerns about the degree of concentration in the ratings industry, since there is no indication of any anti-competitive practices in this industry [while] excessive market fragmentation could have adverse consequences (i.e., credit rating agencies may face undue pressure to issue favourable ratings in order to attract clients)" (European Commission 2006, 5).

From the point of view of competition law, it is evident that the credit rating industry exhibits structural oligopoly and behavioural parallelism of ratings. But does this infringe on competition rules?

[24] Moody's was convicted on April 10, 2001 for violation of 18 U.S.C. §1505 for obstruction of justice.

Oligopolistic markets are characterised by a small number of competitors with "roughly equal shares and a mutual dependence that invites parallel conduct" (Dashwood et al. 2011, 738). Oligopolistic markets are also characterised by high barriers to entry, little product differentiation, and price transparency, where prices are almost the same because of natural interdependence leading to similar responses and rational actions (Craig and de Burca 2015, 1007-8). However, the theory of interdependence may be criticised as over-simplistic due to "supra competitive profits" CRAs earn (Whish and Bailey 2012, 565).

In the EU framework, eventual application of art. 101(1) TFEU requires proof of a collusive agreement or "firm, concise and consistent body of evidence" by the European Commission that they have gone beyond independent parallel conduct to a "concerted practice", e.g., simultaneous and identical price announcements not caused by the features of the market, transparency of prices, or other coincidence (Dashwood et al. 2011, 738; CJEC 1988, par. 127). What is important is that at the time of the first announcement, the "pilot competitor" did not know the approach of the other competitors, since no previous contacts to coordinate their conduct, and thus no concerted practice, was proven to avoid competition risks. Parallel conduct does not constitute *ipso facto* concerted practice, but a strong indication that there is one (Pliakos 2018, 600-602; CJEC 1972, par. 118).

In addition, CRAs have a very significant market power in the relevant market of ratings (information and experience goods), which is not reduced even if their ratings are not accurate (Petit 2011, 594-597). This could lead the European Commission to initiate an inquiry to investigate for abuse of dominant position in the market according to art. 102 TFEU, on the grounds of either individual dominant position or of collective dominance. In such case, the market definition and the determination of dominance through significant market shares, e.g., for S&P, seem easy to confirm. However, the criterion of abuse of dominant position is not easily confirmed, since there does not seem to exist refusal to supply, price discrimination, or selective or predatory pricing (Craig and de Burca 2015, 1072-1085). The CRA III Regulation introduced a provision requiring fees charged to the CRAs' clients for the provision of credit ratings and ancillary services not to be discriminatory and to be based on actual costs, which may be reviewed by ESMA (European Commission 2016, 14).

Many times, the Big Three have demonstrated parallel conduct by downgrading the same financial instruments (Petit 2011, 615), but if the European Commission cannot prove that this constitutes a "concerted practice", unexplainable by objective data, the CRAs may be exonerated (compare Craig and de Burca 2015, 1010). A highly concentrated market constitutes a risk for financial stability if the CRAs observe each other's behaviour and respond by posting similar opinions about creditworthiness of issuers, as demonstrated during the latest financial and sovereign debt crisis (European Commission 2016, 12). Their conduct should have been reviewed *ex officio* and should lead to the adoption of remedies, e.g., standard regulatory obligations (Neyrinck and Petit 2011).

Entry barriers —Registration of new entrants

After the sovereign debt ratings in 2010, Wolfgang Schäuble, the German Federal Finance Minister (2009-2017), stated in 2011: "We need to break the ratings agencies' oligopoly" (Deutsche Welle 2019). The CRA Regulation aimed to encourage new entrants to register in the EU. However, it established the same rigorous standards for reporting, quality, and transparency of their assessments for all CRAs, thus creating many regulatory barriers to market entry for new CRAs, which confronted the same standards as the Big Three, albeit equipped with lesser means to cope. The European Commission suggested that the standards should be more proportional to the size of the CRAs and their capabilities, by "simplifying reporting requirements in order to reduce compliance costs or clarifying certain existing exemptions for companies up to a certain threshold in terms of turnover or number of employees" (European Commission 2016).

In its report, the European Commission confirmed that the majority of issuers still tend to use one or two of the CRAs that are most acceptable among investors, regulators, and central banks and have a global coverage, as well as "a highly reputational nature" and "name recognition" (European Commission 2016, 12). The European Commission also found that the role of the Big Three is still important, as they are CRAs of systemic importance to the financial system, recognised as ECAIs by the European Central Bank (ECB), and therefore, it advised that reliance on ratings within the ECB's European Credit Assessment Framework (ECAF) should be reduced (European Commission 2016, 12).

The CRA III Regulation attempted to stop the CRAs' permanent client relations and to open the market to new entrants by establishing a maximum duration of four years for every contractual relationship with a CRA for the issuing of credit ratings on re-securitisations (art. 6b CRA Regulation). It also increased competition in the CRAs market by obliging a double credit rating of securitisation instruments, i.e., the issuer must appoint two CRAs to provide a credit rating of a securitisation instrument, independently of each other (art. 8c CRA Regulation). A recommendation is made that at least one CRA of the two should have no more than 10% of the total market share (art. 8d CRA Regulation). This provision is very important since the usual practice was to ask ratings from two of the Big Threes, thus leading to "partner monopoly" (Petit 2011, 597). Though not a binding obligation, it is an attempt to increase competition by promoting the appointment of a smaller CRA to provide the second rating. However, this recommendation is in practice blocked by the traditional and reputable Big Three that produce higher quality ratings compared to other smaller CRAs, and have already established business relationships with issuers.

It is evident that forecast accuracy and reputation, and not price, are quite important in the credit rating market (Petit 2011, 596), and these could be gradually recognised to the small CRAs entering the market by clients like the ECB and other institutions, which have their own internal ratings. However, the result continues to be disappointing since in 2020, the Big Three "exploit the reluctance of many bond issuers to stray from them", which allowed them to raise prices by 3-4% per year, while their profits are very high even during the coronavirus era, since companies need liquidity (Economist 2020). One cannot but wonder whether this alleged conduct of raising prices each year demonstrates an infringement of competition rules or is just "parallel conduct".

Liability issues

To hold liable or not?

Before the financial crisis, it was considered that "the value of a rating business derives from the agency's reputation in issuing high-quality ratings and therefore no liability was needed since the market would punish those CRAs that issued inaccurate ratings" (Cavallaro and Trota 2019, 219). However, after 2008, voices increased that the CRAs should not be immune to liability, instead they should be treated "like other gatekeepers", e.g., banks, accountants, and lawyers (Partnoy 2006). "If one accepts the fact that reputational capital does not provide sufficient incentives for accurate ratings, the question then becomes whether increased civil liability is the answer" (Cavallaro and Trotta 2019, 216).

In the US

Since 1933, Rule 436(g)(1) of the US Securities Act of 1933 has held the CRAs explicitly immune from certain violations of securities law, except fraud, even when they were granted regulatory advantages (Partnoy 2006, 30). When lawsuits for their civil liability were filed in courts, the CRAs argued that their opinion is protected by the First Amendment of the US Constitution and that they should have the same protection as journalists enjoy, being financial gatherers for financial publishing, and making thus their statements a matter of public concern. As Partnoy (2006) explains, in disputes concerning securities, the US courts held different approaches, according to the context and the active or passive "role of the CRAs in structuring the transaction it rated", e.g., in case of unsolicited ratings, or whether they considered ratings as commercial speech (investment advice) and then, whether their protection is absolute or qualified (Partnoy 2006, 31-36, 45). It was therefore advised that a threat of strict liability should be established for rating malfeasance, and should limit the extent to which the First Amendment protects the CRAs' opinions (Partnoy 2006, 45).

In 2010, Section 933 of the US Dodd-Frank Act established a new regime for the liability of the NRSROs to counter the immunity that CRAs obtained under the protection of the First Amendment in the US. After the Act and the 2009 Congress inquiry by the Angelides Committee, several lawsuits were filed before the US Courts by the US Department of Justice, several states and investors, because of an overly positive assessment of structured financial products, i.e., Residential Mortgage-Backed Securities (hereinafter RMBSs)[25] and Collateralised Debt Obligations (hereinafter CDOs).[26] The lawsuits were settled, with the CRAs admitting facts against them and complying with obligations imposed. Below are some notable cases:

1) Investors filed lawsuits against Morgan Stanley, Moody's Investors Service and S&P for "negligent misrepresentation over their activities regarding the Cheyne and Rhinebridge structured investment vehicles (SIVs)… [so that the SIVs] received ratings as high as triple-A, … even though much of the underlying collateral was low-quality or

---

[25] A RMBS is a debt-based security (similar to a bond), backed by the interest paid on loans for residences (Australia Reserve Bank 2015, 43).

[26] A CDO is a complex structured finance product that is backed by a pool of loans and other assets and sold to institutional investors (Longstaff and Rajan 2008, 529).

subprime mortgage debt". The accused CRAs and the collaborating bank agreed to pay about $225 million for settlement (Reuters 2013).[27]

2) The US Department of Justice and several US states filed a lawsuit against S&P based on the allegation that in 2007-08 its positive ratings caused damage of US $5 billion (US Department of Justice 2017; Veil 2017, 571). In its complaint, the Justice Department stated that S&P delayed updates to its ratings criteria and analytical models between September 2004 and October 2007, weakening its criteria in a desire to gain more business from the investment banks that issued the securities (Reuters 2015) and it falsely represented that its ratings were objective, independent and uninfluenced by S&P's business relationships with the investment banks that issued the securities (US Department of Justice 2017). S&P argued that its ratings were protected under the First Amendment right to free speech, and described the lawsuit as retaliation for the firm downgrading the credit rating of the United States (Reuters 2015).

In 2013, a settlement was reached, according to which S&P acknowledged it had not uncovered evidence to support its allegations of retaliation despite the fact that 290 million documents have been examined (Reuters 2015). S&P did not admit to any violations of law, but it did sign a statement of facts acknowledging that its executives in 2005 delayed implementing new models that produced more negative ratings. S&P agreed to pay $687.5 million to the US Department of Justice as penalty and $687.5 million to 19 states and the District of Columbia. This sum exceeds the company's profits earned for rating mortgage-backed securities from 2002-07 (Reuters 2015). In its agreed statement of facts, S&P admitted that its decisions on its rating models were affected by business concerns and that it maintained and continued to issue positive ratings on securities despite a growing awareness of quality problems with those securities.[28]

[27] US District Court, Southern District of New York, Abu Dhabi Commercial Bank et al v. Morgan Stanley & Co et al; US District Court, Southern District of New York, King County, Washington et al v. IKB Deutsche Industriebank AG et al. (cases cited in Reuters 2013).

[28] S&P acknowledged that it promised investors at all relevant times that its ratings must be independent and objective and must not be affected by any existing or potential business relationship; its executives admitted, despite its representations, that decisions about S&P's model for rating CDOs were made, at least in part, based on the effect that any update would have on S&P's business relationship

3) The public pension fund California Public Employees' Retirement System filed a lawsuit against S&P in 2009, claiming its inaccurate ratings caused considerable loss. The case was closed with a $125 million settlement (Reuters 2015).

4) On January 13, 2017, the US Department of Justice ratified a nearly $864 million settlement agreement with Moody's group over allegations arising from Moody's role in providing credit ratings for RMBSs and CDOs.[29] The settlement included the Statement of Facts, where Moody's acknowledged key aspects of its conduct, and a Compliance Agreement to prevent future violations of law. The Statement of Facts addressed Moody's representations to investors and the general public about: (1) its objectivity and independence, (2) its management of conflicts of interest, (3) its compliance with its own stated RMBS and CDO rating methodologies and standards, and (4) the analytic integrity of certain rating methodologies. In the Compliance Agreement, Moody's undertook to improve its business practices, including: separation of Moody's commercial and credit rating functions, independent review and approval of changes to rating methodologies, changes to ensure that key personnel is not compensated on the basis of the company's financial performance, enhancing Moody's oversight over its press releases and methodology development, and certifications of compliance for at least five years (US Department of Justice 2017). The settlement did not have any negative impact on the stock market. On the contrary, the Moody's share price even climbed four percent (Rodemann 2017).

The CRA III Regulation

Before 2009, the EU had not attached any importance to a specific legal basis for CRAs' liability towards issuers and investors. In

---

with issuers; relevant people within S&P knew in 2007 many loans in RMBS transactions S&P was rating were delinquent and that losses were probable; and its representatives continued to issue and confirm positive ratings without adjustments to reflect the negative rating actions that it expected would come (US Department of Justice 2015).

[29] The agreement resolved pending state court lawsuits in Connecticut, Mississippi, and South Carolina, as well as potential claims by the Justice Department, 18 states, and the District of Columbia. The settlement followed an investigation by the Consumer Protection Branch and the US Attorney's Office for the District of New Jersey into potential claims pursuant to the Financial Institutions Reform, Recovery and Enforcement Act (FIRREA) and to investigations conducted by various State Attorneys General pursuant to state law.

the aftermath of the Enron and Parmalat scandals, the CESR concluded that legislative intervention was not necessary (CESR 2005). The European Commission agreed that the combination of the Market Abuse Directive (Directive 2014/57/EU), that describes extensively "market manipulation" (art. 5 Directive 2014/57/EU), the Capital Requirements Directive (Directive 2000/12/EC) and the Markets in Financial Instruments Directive (Directive 2004/39/EC) with the IOSCO Code of Conduct Fundamentals adequately covered the working of CRAs (De Bruyne and Vanleenhove 2015, 120; European Commission 2006, 2-4).

In 2009, the CRA I Regulation only stated that claims against CRAs in relation to infringements of the Regulation had to be made according to national legislation on liability (recital 69 CRA I Regulation). The liability regimes, however, varied between member states and could lead to forum shopping. In 2010, the European Commission initiated a Consultation with CRAs in order to update the CRA I Regulation (European Commission 2010). The Commission pointed to the diversification of national legislations on the liability of CRAs, which meant that CRAs had the possibility to shop around and choose jurisdictions under which their liability was less likely. Therefore, the Commission asked the respondents whether there was need to include a liability regime in the Regulation on CRAs. The stakeholders favoured the introduction of gross negligence-based liability (European Commission 2010, 24-25). After the consultation, the European Commission issued its proposal with strict provisions, which were amended in many aspects by the Council and the European Parliament.[30]

Article 35a CRA Regulation

Since CRAs assess complex economic factors, art. 35(a) CRA Regulation establishes the liability of CRAs towards both the issuers (contracting parties) and the investors (third parties) under clear rules on conditions and burden of proof, undermined however by the national reference laws for interpreting basic concepts and private national law implications for determining international jurisdiction and applicable law. Art. 35a(1) provides that only when CRAs intentionally or with gross negligence commit "any of the infringements listed in Annex III [of the CRA Regulation], having an impact on a credit rating, an investor or issuer may claim damages from that CRA for damage caused to it due to that

[30] See Procedure 2010/0160/COD Credit rating agencies: Supervision (Legislative Observatory 2010).

infringement". CRAs are exonerated in case of simple negligence for a "wrong" rating, or because of lack of reasonable care.

The burden of proof is a critical issue that was upheld by CRAs in the regulatory discussion, since it is charged to investors and issuers, the two categories involved in civil liability disputes (Cavallaro and Trotta 2019, 223; European Commission 2010). Art. 35a(2) CRA Regulation has a common rule that it is the "responsibility of the investor or issuer to present accurate and detailed information indicating that the credit rating agency has committed an infringement of this Regulation, and that that infringement had an impact on the credit rating issued". What constitutes accurate and detailed information shall be assessed by the competent national court, taking into consideration that the investor or issuer may not have access to information, which is purely within the sphere of the CRA. In such a case, the burden of proof is on the CRA (Veil 2017, 572).

In addition, art. 35a(1) CRA Regulation puts a specific burden of proof to each category: the investor, who is usually a third party to the contract of the issuer and the CRA, must establish that "it has reasonably relied, in accordance with Article 5(a)(1) or otherwise with due care, on a credit rating for a decision to invest into, hold onto or divest from a financial instrument covered by that credit rating". The issuer, who usually has a contract with the CRA, establishes that: a) the issuer himself or his financial instruments are covered by that credit rating, and b) the infringement was not caused by misleading and inaccurate information provided by the issuer to the CRA, directly or through information publicly available. Therefore, the burden of proof is based on a high threshold of proof, especially for investors (third parties to the contract) that must establish reasonable reliance on the rating and the impact on decision-making processes.

Private international law implications

On international jurisdiction, Regulation 1215/2012 (Brussels I Regulation) puts the priority to the place of the domicile of the defendant, i.e., the CRA. After the implementation of CRA Regulation and the establishment and registration of the Big Threes' subsidiaries in many member states thanks to art. 14 CRA Regulation, the rules of Brussels I Regulation will point to a national court of the EU member states. Otherwise, the Brussels I Regulation offers as jurisdiction grounds: a) art. 7(1) in contractual disputes filed by issuers (i.e., for solicited ratings) pointing to the place where the services were provided, except if there is an exclusive jurisdiction clause in favour of a court in US or elsewhere (art. 24 Brussels I Regulation); and b) art. 7(2) in non-contractual disputes filed by investors, the place where the harmful event occurred, i.e., both the place of the damaging event (*locus acti*) and the place of the damage (*locus damni*) (De Bruyne and Vanleenhove 2015, 127). Regulation 864/2007 (Rome II Regulation) provides that the applicable national law will be determined according to the law of the country in which the damage occurred (art. 4(1) Rome II Regulation).

The reference to national law

The EU had two choices: either to include all relevant aspects of civil law damage claims directly in the CRA III Regulation, or to refer to the national laws of the member states; it selected the second option, but with conditions. The first section of art. 35a(4) CRA Regulation specifies that terms such as "damage", "intention", "gross negligence", "reasonably relied", "due care", "impact", "reasonable" and "proportionate", which are referred to in the article but are not defined, shall be interpreted and applied in accordance with the applicable national law as determined by the relevant rules of private international law. This sentence caused many commentators to state that art. 35a was redundant since, in any case, national legislation could provide for civil liability (Nästegård 2015). Indeed, there is a wide diversity of civil liability regimes in the member states, leading to different implementation of art. 35a CRA Regulation. Legal treatment of tort liability and interpretation of concepts like "damage", "causal link", etc., differ greatly among member states. The CRA Regulation should not have left this question open, as harmonisation is needed (Estas 2014, 80). In this way, art. 35a created an "androgynous" liability, since the legal basis and certain prerequisites are found in the CRA Regulation, while other prerequisites are based on national law, which should be determined according to the "law of the country in which the damage occurred" (Veil 2017, 572-573). Though this liability should exist in parallel to contractual claims, it is not clear how effective it will be (Veil 2017, 573).

Disclaimers

Disclaimers may play a huge role. CRAs are able to limit their liability in advance where that limitation is reasonable, proportionate, and allowed by the applicable national law. Any limitation that does not comply with these requirements, or any contractual exclusion of the liability, is deprived of legal effect. The S&P disclaimer states: "Ratings are opinions and not recommendations to purchase, hold or sell securities, and they do not address the market value of securities or their suitability for investment purposes. Ratings should not be relied on as investment advice" (Financial Industry Regulatory Authority 2018).

Towards financial stability

The last sovereign debt crisis revealed the importance of CRAs in the financial system through the performance of information, monitoring and certification services in the context of their role as providers of forward-looking opinions on the probability that the issuer of debt-liability security will default on the due payment (De Pascalis 2012). The regulatory framework of CRAs constitutes a significant first step towards mitigating the adverse influence that they were found to have in terms of favouring mechanical and exclusive reliance on an oligopolistic market of CRAs governed by the Big Three. The CRA Regulation, with all its subsequent amendments, takes into account interdependencies, conflicts of interest, inadequate disclosure practices, asymmetry of information, and over-reliance on mathematical and statistical methodologies based on inadequate data, with the view to reducing uncritical, overestimated, and country-biased credit ratings, which proliferated in the former legal environment. Additionally, the provisions regarding sovereign ratings and conferring supervision of CRAs, at the European level, on ESMA contribute to delinking the activity of credit rating both from self-regulation and from national regulation of CRAs. They thus lessen the incidents of downward price spirals, herd behaviour, and cliff-effects, which emerged during the 2008 financial crisis and have been strongly accused of triggering financial instability in countries with spill-over effects at the European as well as the global level.[31]

However, it needs to be noted that hardly can this regime be considered effective enough to alleviate the regulatory debate on CRAs. The reason is that it is quite difficult to make the activity of rating the debt of the government that partly regulates CRAs, or the activity of the issuer that pays a CRA for its rating, come up to the targets of the European CRA Regulation regarding independent, objective, and of adequate quality ratings. The rating business is also a major contributing factor to informed investment decisions that go along with financial stability. This is mainly

[31] According to de Pascalis (2012), "herd behaviour" represents the systematic and erroneous decision-making by a group, while "cliff-effects" are concerned with the simultaneous sell-off of securities in case of abrupt downgrades.

due to the inherent risk associated since the early 1970s with the still existing issuer-pays model applying to the CRAs, i.e., the issuer pays the CRA for its rating (White 2018), which entails that CRAs have the incentive to favour the issuer's business, ignoring that this actually backfires when the bond market participants realise that the credit ratings are not objective. By the time that the wrong investment decisions have been revealed, the reputation of both the specific credit rating concerned and financial stability have already been irreparably hit. This conflict of interest is conspicuous in the case of significant financial institutions, since a great part of their issues are controlled by a few big investment banks ensuring a significant part of CRAs' income (Rafailov 2011).

The 2008 financial crisis and the subsequent sovereign debt crisis have shown that regarding ratings to sovereign borrowers,[32] the existence of corruption, along with the existing issuer-pays model[33] dominating CRAs, have obscured transparency considerably, and have favoured misleading ratings mainly based on wealth generation and debt sustainability. In this context, the CRAs were accused of giving high-quality credit ratings to debts that later turned out to be high-risk investments, thus failing to identify risks associated with certain types of debts such as CDOs. Additionally, there are other reasons for the inaccuracy of credit ratings, such as the lack of powers to ensure and examine the veracity of the information, lack of competition, lack of alternative assessments, and use of inadequate mathematical models (Rafailov 2011).

Failures of CRAs, and the associated with them information asymmetry and lack of benchmarking with regard to best practices, are mainly due to the large disparity among CRAs that stem from differences in size, scope (both geographical and sectoral), methodologies, and definitions of the default risk. Such differences have strengthened the negative effects of credit ratings on the global financial crisis by generating additional systemic risk. Credit ratings have thus seriously put into question their adequacy regarding financial stability.

Against this background, it is crucial to consider CRAs as part of a broader context in the pursuit of financial stability. The European Banking Union (hereinafter EBU) project refers to shifting banking sector

---

[32] Sovereign borrowers may include national governments, state governments' municipalities, and other sovereign-supported institutions.

[33] According to Lannoo (2015), the "issuer pays model competes for the supply side of the industry (i.e., the issuer) not the demand side (i.e., the investor). The CRA Regulation does not change this situation" (27).

policy instruments from the national to the European level (Véron and Schnabel 2018). It was established to preserve the safety of the banking system and to correct the misalignment between the reality of banks' business and the institutional supervisory structure comprising banking activities both in the home state and those of branches and subsidiaries hosted in other countries (ECB 2019). The European Banking Union project provides for the ECB as the common supranational banking supervisor of the significant euro area banks, the so-called Single Supervisory Mechanism (hereinafter SSM). This is in accordance with the acknowledgment that a fragmented system of national supervisors is not well suited to spot the risks associated with cross-border banking or to act swiftly to deal with them (ECB 2019). The SSM is addressed to all euro area banks, and paves the way for more informed investment decisions, since it provides a solid supervisory base that enables it to gather and share substantial knowledge about the inherent risks of the banking system, which are strongly correlated with sovereign risk, as witnessed in the euro area crisis. This is mainly achieved through the performance of stress tests, which equip the SSM, as well as national banks and investors, with deep insight by comparing banks to one another and by benchmarking their relative performance with the same criteria (ECB 2019). One of the main targets of the stress tests is to establish adaptable levels of resilience to new risks and to shed light on cases that require intensified supervisory scrutiny. In addition to this, financial stability is also favoured by the fact that within the Banking Union, Joint Supervisory Teams (JST) put into consideration national and European perspectives, which provide the basis for a fruitful debate on emerging risks and help insulate stakeholders from political and market pressures (ECB 2019).

On the other hand, the Capital Markets Union (hereinafter CMU) project aims at mobilising capital in Europe and channeling it into companies by fostering a stronger and more resilient financial system that opens up a wider range of funding sources and more long-term investment. The CMU thus ensures that EU citizens and companies have access to a relaunched securitisation market where they are less vulnerable to financial shocks. In this context, financial stability is enhanced by regulation that promotes the introduction of increased transparency, and by the creation of a single online access point for information on national rules related to marketing requirements and applicable fees. This, in turn, promotes vigorous competition and consistency in regulation, as well as in the implementation of agreed standards and principles that are adaptable to changed circumstances, if needed (European Commission 2019b).

It is beyond the scope of this chapter to refer to the EBU and the CMU in greater detail, but it is to be noted that the regulation introduced by these emerging Unions could mitigate the pro-cyclical impact of the credit ratings, while enhancing vigorous competition in a level playing field. This regulatory framework could progressively provide additional approaches to assessing capital requirements, and generally, the factors that are associated with risk in the EU financial acquis and relevant industry practices. Accordingly, single supervision and common regulation of the financial market could provide alternative standards of creditworthiness to investment policies and institutional investors. Such alternative standards could concern determining net and regulatory capital requirements, as well as disclosure requirements or prospectus eligibility.[34] Thus, the dependency of the regulations and supervisory practices on credit ratings could be gradually set on a basis that would favour a more comprehensive and independent credit judgment, as well as chart the way forward for safer investment decisions. To this end, the emerging regime of the EBU and the CMU could gradually establish the co-existence of common regulation, supervision, guidelines, coordination of safety standards, and best practices that could in the long run set a more concrete framework regarding financial stability. In this respect, mechanistic reliance on credit ratings could be mitigated in a framework that would enable investors to deploy the advantages of credit ratings under conditions of greater coherence, consistency, and safeguards.

Conclusions

The 2008 financial crisis put into question the accuracy of the credit ratings, thus triggering various debates regarding the involvement of CRAs in the repercussions on financial stability, since they failed to shed

---

[34] "The Council adopted updated rules on the prospectuses. A prospectus is a legal document that companies issue to potential investors about the securities they are issuing and about themselves. In addition to the information about the securities, the prospectus contains detailed information about the company's business, finances and shareholding structure. Prospectuses are therefore an essential source of information for investors and one of the key tools for companies wishing to raise capital across the EU securities markets. The first prospectus directive was adopted in 2003 and revised in 2009. The updated prospectus rules are in the form of an EU regulation. The Commission issued the proposal for the prospectus regulation on 30 November 2015 as part of the legislative proposals aimed at creating a Capital Markets Union" (Council of the European Union 2019).

light on the solvency problems of big corporations[35] and on the risk associated with RMBSs and CDOs that adversely affected the financial markets as a whole. There were many proposals for regulatory intervention, such as "the creation of government-sponsored CRAs, the dismantling of the CRA oligopoly, [and] tougher controls on sovereign ratings" (Petit 2011, 587-588; Rafailov 2011). The ongoing impact on financial stability paved the way for more regulation, leading to the CRA Regulation, with all its subsequent amendments, with the view to setting the corporate governance of CRAs at the European level, mitigating conflicts of interest, and favouring independent risk assessment and due diligence as a qualified contribution to stabilising the financial system. However, despite these positive steps, the remaining oligopolistic nature of the credit ratings market signals that the inadequacy of competition leaves unaddressed the issues of objectivity and quality associated with credit ratings, as well as the pro-cyclical impact on the financial system as a whole.

Financial stability is a state in which the financial system is resistant to economic shocks and is fit to smoothly fulfil its basic functions: the intermediation of financial funds, management of risks, and the arrangement of payments. In other words, as defined by the World Bank, financial stability is about the absence of system-wide episodes, in which the financial system fails to function (crises). It is also about the resilience of financial systems to stress (World Bank 2020). To this end, multiple contributing factors are essential, and guidance to credit risk for investors is just one of these prerequisites. The combination of credit ratings, along with a broader range of risk indicators, such as capital adequacy, interest payments in financial markets, profitability, and fiscal policy as an indicator of credit quality, could lead to safer investment decisions. Against this background, regulating banks in the context of the EBU and compliance of the financial institutions with the requirements of the CMU could also be a positive step towards decoupling the competition issue from the ratings market and reinforcing more objectivity in decisions, thus averting investors from embarking on time-consuming and risky paths. The inadequacy of credit ratings in terms of financial stability has already been witnessed by the fact that the development of the financial crisis resulted in a reduction of credit ratings on a global scale, affecting issues amounting to USD 3 trillion (Rafailov 2011).

[35] Such as Enron in 2001, Worldcom in 2002, Parmalat in 2003, and Lehman Brothers in 2008.

Additionally, since the onset of the EBU project in November 2014 with the establishment of the Single Supervisory Mechanism, and later with the ongoing developments of the Capital Markets Union Action Plan (European Commission 2015a), financial stability is progressively linked with the overall banking and financial services' legal framework rather than with credit ratings of CRAs alone. This is mainly due to the fact that prudential legislation, centralised supervision and resolution, that are associated with the EBU, on the one hand, and the channelling of capital and investment into a stronger and more resilient financial system that are associated with the CMU, on the other, seem to be paving the way for a level playing field. This, in turn, reinforces the level of resilience to new risks, and builds the adequate consistency and predictability required for safer investment decisions and their gradual delinking from credit ratings, which tend to generate systemic risk in their inherent pursuit of greater profit. This entails that the EBU, in combination with the CMU via regulation, supervisory colleges, and voluntary memoranda of understanding, have the potential to distil the best practices of experts across the euro area and to facilitate information flows across borders among banks, other institutions, and the financial markets that connect them together in the financial system as a whole. This, in turn, could gradually mitigate the negative repercussions of potentially misleading credit ratings on financial stability. It is thus interesting to consider these two policy initiatives as interconnected parts of a complementary and mutually reinforcing basis (Constancio 2017), which along with the credit ratings, could more efficiently meet the lingering structural challenges of the risk environment in the broader euro area financial system. In this context, the market power of CRAs could be tailored to function under circumstances of enhanced financial stability, specifically in financial markets where the existence of centralised EU legislation, along with intensified supervisory scrutiny and common macro-prudential tools, render cross-border investment risks more identifiable and easier to prevent from materialising in the long run.

The CRAs' regulatory role as gatekeepers of the EU capital market and banking finance has been constrained to certain limits in the EU due to the elimination of over-reliance and the gradual loss of regulatory advantages they once enjoyed in the US and the EU. Internal rating procedures was the method chosen, among other alternatives, to limit the reliance on external credit ratings by CRAs, e.g., market-implied ratings, accountancy-based measures, or third-party assessments, like those of the OECD (European Commission 2015b, 82-83). The end of the mechanistic over-reliance on CRAs' ratings stopped on both sides of the Atlantic due to binding legislation and the coordinated work of international fora. Competition infringements due to their significant market power have not yet been confirmed, despite their increasing market shares in the US and the EU. Their oligopoly and eventual arbitrariness could be controlled through new entrants, which already register as CRAs with ESMA. However, their market shares are extremely low in the EU and the US, while they face certain barriers that should be lifted by the proportional application of the legislation. Art. 35(a) CRA Regulation has imposed rules on civil liability, but there are many loopholes that would allow a CRA to escape liability. Despite the fact that the CRAs have settled to pay enormous amounts of money to compensate for the 2008 crisis in the US, it is troubling that their market share and reputation capital are increasing.

The problem with credit ratings may rise again because of the Covid-19 crisis and the fall in oil prices, which led to stress in credit markets. Equity markets "experienced the fastest drop in history… [and] conditions in the corporate credit markets have deteriorated sharply [because] of liquidity risks" (International Monetary Fund 2020, 1-2). For example, S&P Global Ratings affirmed the "BB-" Foreign Currency LT credit rating of ThyssenKrup on March 4, 2020. As the Economist (2020) observes:

> The agencies have rushed to mark down bonds and loans of all types… in cars and entertainment… This bears on the most pressing question facing rating agencies today: what to do about the more than $3trn of corporate debt rated triple-b, on the precipice above junk. In 2010, 45% of all investment-grade debt was in this bottom tier; now it is just shy of 60%" […] "A… challenge will be to get sovereign ratings right as public finances come under heavy strain. What, for instance, to make of America's Treasury borrowing a record $3trn this quarter? […] A decade ago the rating agencies were accused of accelerating the euro-zone sovereign-debt crisis by downgrading some of the bloc's big economies, including France. How the agencies handle these tests will determine whether the crisis brings more calls for root-and-branch reform of the ratings market.

ESMA's supervisory priorities regarding CRAs will include, among others, proactive identification of risks in outstanding credit ratings, and will ensure that CRAs have robust and well-structured rating processes (ESMA 2020a). However, both legislative changes for a CRA IV Regulation and EU coordinated action with the US and international fora seem necessary in order to ease the barriers on new entrants, break the CRAs oligopoly, and harmonise civil liability issues, closing thus all loopholes. The momentum certainly is here in order to stop the "perfect storm" caused by Covid-19 (Roubini 2020).

References

Australia Reserve Bank. 2015. "Bulletin," June, https://www.rba.gov.au/publications/bulletin/2015/jun/pdf/bu-0615.pdf (accessed February 10, 2021).

Basel Committee on Banking Supervision. 2006. "International Convergence of Capital Measurement and Capital Standards – A Revised Framework" (Basel II Accord), June, https://www.bis.org/publ/bcbs128.pdf (accessed February 24, 2021).

Cantor, Richard, and Frank Packer. 1995. The Credit Rating Industry. *The Journal of Fixed Income* 5, no.3: 10–34.

Cavallaro, Giusy, and Annarita Trotta. 2019. Role and Regulation of Credit Rating Agencies: The European Way. *International Journal of Accounting and Financial Reporting* 9, no.1: 209–228.

CJEC. 1988. A. Ahlström Osakeyhtiö and others v Commission of the European Communities (Wood pulp case). 27 September, Joined cases 89, 104, 114, 116, 117 and 125 to 129/85, ECLI:EU:C:1988:447.

CJEC. 1972. Imperial Chemical Industries Ltd. v Commission of the European Communities (ICI case). 14 July. Case 48/69. ECLI:EU: C:1972:70.

Coffee, John C. Jr. 2006. *Gatekeepers: The Role of the Professions and Corporate Governance*. Oxford: Oxford University Press.

CESR. 2005. "CESR's Technical Advice to the European Commission on Possible Measures Concerning Credit Rating Agencies," CESR final report 05-139b, March, https://www.esma.europa.eu/sites/default/files/library/2015/11/05_139b.pdf (accessed February 27, 2021).

Constancio, Vítor. 2017. "Synergies between banking union and capital markets union," Keynote speech by the Vice-President of the ECB at the joint conference of the European Commission and the European Central Bank on European Financial Integration, 19 May, https://www.ecb.europa.eu/press/key/date/2017/html/ecb.sp170519_1.en.html (accessed February 16, 2021).

Council of the European Union. 2019. "New rules on prospectuses: improving access to capital markets for companies," https://www.consilium.europa.eu/en/policies/capital-markets-union/prospectus/ (accessed February 27, 2021).

Craig, Paul, and Gráinne de Burca. 2015. *EU Law: Text, Cases, and Materials*. 5th ed. Oxford: Oxford University Press.

Dashwood, Alan, Michael Dougan, Barry J. Rodger, Eleanor Spaventa, and Derrick Wyatt. 2011. *Wyatt and Dashwood's European Union Law*. Oxford: Hart Publishing.

De Bruyne, Jan, and Cedric Vanleenhove. 2015. Rating the EU Regulatory Framework on the Liability of Credit Rating Agencies – "Triple A or Junk"?, *Edinburgh Student Law Review* 2, no.4: 117–128.

De Pascalis, Francesco. 2017. *Credit Ratings and Market Over-reliance: An International Legal Analysis*, Leiden: Brill Nijhoff.

De Pascalis, Francesco. 2012. Reducing overreliance on credit ratings: failing strategies and the need to start from scratch. *Amicus Curiae* no.91: 17–21.

Deutsche Welle. 2019. "Are ratings agencies hurting Africa's economies?" *Deutsche Welle*, 12 March, https://www.dw.com/en/are-ratings-agencies-hurting-africas-economies/a-47870146 (accessed February 16, 2021).

Directive 2014/57/EU of the European Parliament and of the Council of 16 April 2014 on criminal sanctions for market abuse (market abuse directive). OJ L 173: 179–189.

Directive 2014/51/EU of the European Parliament and of the Council of 16 April 2014 amending Directives 2003/71/EC and 2009/138/EC and Regulations (EC) No 1060/2009, (EU) No 1094/2010 and (EU) No 1095/2010 in respect of the powers of the European Supervisory Authority (European Insurance and Occupational Pensions Authority) and the European Supervisory Authority (European Securities and Markets Authority). OJ L 153: 1–61.

Directive 2013/36/EU of the European Parliament and of the Council of 26 June 2013 on access to the activity of credit institutions and the prudential supervision of credit institutions and investment firms, amending Directive 2002/87/EC and repealing Directives 2006/48/EC and 2006/49/EC. OJ L 176: 338–436.

Directive 2013/14/EU of the European Parliament and of the Council of 21 May 2013 amending Directive 2003/41/EC on the activities and supervision of institutions for occupational retirement provision, Directive 2009/65/EC on the coordination of laws, regulations and administrative provisions relating to undertakings for collective investment in transferable securities (UCITS) and Directive 2011/61/EU on Alternative Investment Funds Managers in respect of over-reliance on credit ratings. OJ L 145: 1–3.

Directive 2011/61/EU of the European Parliament and of the Council of 8 June 2011 on Alternative Investment Fund Managers and amending Directives 2003/41/EC and 2009/65/EC and Regulations (EC)No 1060/2009 and (EU) No 1095/2010. OJ L 174: 1–73.

Directive 2010/78/EU of the European Parliament and of the Council of 24 November 2010 in respect of the powers of the European Supervisory Authority (European Banking Authority), the European Supervisory Authority (European Insurance and Occupational Pensions Authority) and the European Supervisory Authority (European Securities and Markets Authority). 2010. OJ L 331: 120–161.

Directive 2009/138/EC of the European Parliament and of the Council of 25 November 2009 on the taking-up and pursuit of the business of Insurance and Reinsurance (Solvency II). 2009. OJ L 335: 1–155.

Directive 2004/39/EC of the European Parliament and of the Council of 21 April 2004 on markets in financial instruments amending Council Directives 85/611/EEC and 93/6/EEC and Directive 2000/12/EC of the European Parliament and of the Council and repealing Council Directive 93/22/EEC. OJ L 145: 1–44. Consolidated text https://eur-lex.europa.eu/legal-content/EN/TXT/?uri=CELEX%3A02004L0039-20110104 (accessed February 20, 2021).

Directive 2000/12/EC of the European Parliament and of the Council of 20 March 2000 relating to the taking up and pursuit of the business of credit institutions. OJ L 126: 1–59. Consolidated text https://eur-lex.europa.eu/legal-content/EN/TXT/PDF/?uri=CELEX:02000L0012-20060329&from=EN (accessed February 20, 2021).

Economist. 2020. "Markers marked. Credit-rating agencies are back under the spotlight," *Economist*, 7 May, https://www.economist.com/finance-and-economics/2020/05/07/credit-rating-agencies-are-back-under-the-spotlight (accessed February 16, 2021).

Estas, Céline. 2014. "The civil liability of credit rating agencies: A comparative perspective within the European Union," Thesis supervised by Professor Stefan Grundmann, European University Institute, https://cadmus.eui.eu//handle/1814/34557 (accessed February 16, 2021).

ECB. 2019. "The Banking Union Option – observations from my experience," Panel intervention by Pentti Hakkarainen, Member of the Supervisory Board of the ECB, to Session 2 "Banking Union" at the event "A deepening of EMU – where will it leave Sweden and Denmark?," Stockholm, 5 February, https://www.bankingsupervision.europa.eu/press/speeches/date/2019/html/ssm.sp190205~b0b7cdad7c.en.html (accessed February 16, 2021).

ECB. 2004. "Financial Stability Review", December, https://www.ecb.europa.eu/pub/pdf/fsr/financialstabilityreview200412en.pdf (accessed February 16, 2021).

European Commission. 2019a. "Communication on equivalence in the area of financial services," COM(2019) 349 final, 29 July, https://eur-lex.europa.eu/legal-content/EN/TXT/?uri=CELEX%3A52019DC0349 (accessed February 16, 2021).

European Commission. 2019b. "Capital Markets Union: Agreement reached on measures to improve the EU's investment fund market," Press release, 5 February, https://ec.europa.eu/commission/presscorner/detail/en/IP_19_861 (accessed February 16, 2021).

European Commission. 2017. "Capital Markets Union: EU reaches agreement on reviving securitisation market", Press release, 30 May, https://ec.europa.eu/commission/presscorner/detail/en/IP_17_1480 (accessed February 16, 2021).

European Commission. 2016. "Report to the European Parliament and the Council on alternative tools to external credit ratings, the state of the credit rating market, competition and governance in the credit rating industry, the state of the structured finance instruments rating market and on the feasibility of a European Credit Rating Agency," COM(2016) 664 final, 19 October, https://eur-lex.europa.eu/legal-content/en/TXT/?uri=CELEX:52016DC0664 (accessed February 16, 2021).

European Commission. 2015a. "Communication Action Plan on Building a Capital Markets Union," COM(2015) 468 final, 30 September, https://eur-lex.europa.eu/legal-content/EN/TXT/?uri=CELEX%3A52015DC0468 (accessed February 28, 2021).

European Commission. 2015b. "Study on the Feasibility of Alternatives to Credit Ratings: Annexes to Final Report," December, https://ec.europa.eu/info/sites/info/files/alternatives-to-credit-rating-study-01122015_en.pdf (accessed February 17, 2021).

European Commission. 2010. "Public Consultation on Credit Rating Agencies," 5 November, https://ec.europa.eu/finance/consultations/2010/cra/docs/cpaper_en.pdf (accessed January 19, 2021).

European Commission. 2006. "Communication from the Commission on Credit Rating Agencies," OJ C 59: 2–6.

European Court of Auditors. 2015. "EU supervision of credit rating agencies-well established but not yet fully effective," Special Report No 22, https://www.eca.europa.eu/lists/ecadocuments/sr15_22/sr_esma_en.pdf (accessed February 17, 2021).

ESMA. 2021. "CRA authorisation," 4 January, https://www.esma.europa.eu/supervision/credit-rating-agencies/risk (accessed January 17, 2021).

ESMA. 2020a. "ESMA's supervision focuses on outstanding credit ratings, data quality and third country CCPs," Press release, 9 March, https://www.esma.europa.eu/press-news/esma-news/esma%E2%80%99s-supervision-focuses-outstanding-credit-ratings-data-quality-and-third (accessed February 17, 2021).

ESMA. 2020b. "ESMA publishes results of the Annual Transparency Calculations for Non-Equity Instruments", Press release, 15 July, https://www.esma.europa.eu/press-news/esma-news/esma-publishes-results-annual-transparency-calculations-non-equity-instruments (accessed January 18, 2021).

ESMA. 2020c. "ESMA Report on Annual Market Share of Credit Rating Agencies", Press release, 14 December, https://www.esma.europa.eu/press-news/esma-news/esma-reports-annual-market-share-credit-rating-agencies-0 (accessed January 18, 2021).

ESMA. 2019a. "Report on CRA Market Share Calculation", 29.11.2019, ESMA33-9-340. https://www.esma.europa.eu/sites/default/files/library/esma33-9-340_cra_market_share_calculation_2019.pdf (accessed January 18, 2021).

ESMA. 2019b. "Guidelines on the submission of periodic information to ESMA by Credit Rating Agencies – 2nd Edition," Final Report, ESMA33-9-295, 5 February, https://www.esma.europa.eu/sites/default/files/library/esma_33-9-295_final_report_guidelines_on_the_submission_of_periodic_information_to_esma_by_credit_rating_agencies.pdf (accessed February 17, 2021).

ESMA. 2018a. "ESMA fines five banks €2.48 million for issuing credit ratings without authorization," Press release, 23 July, https://www.esma.europa.eu/press-news/esma-news/esma-fines-five-banks-%E2%82%AC248-million-issuing-credit-ratings-without-authorisation (accessed February 17, 2021).

ESMA. 2018b. "Annual Report 2017", ESMA20-95-916, 15 June, https://www.esma.europa.eu/sites/default/files/library/esma20-95-916_2017_annual_report_0.pdf (accessed February 17, 2021).

ESMA. 2015a. "Competition and choice in the credit rating industry: Market share calculation required by Article 8d of Regulation 1060/2009 on Credit Rating Agencies as amended," ESMA/2016/1662, 18 December, https://www.esma.europa.eu/sites/default/files/library/2016-1662_cra_market_share_calculation.pdf (accessed January 20, 2021).

ESMA. 2015b. "Guidelines on periodic information to be submitted to ESMA by Credit Rating Agencies," Final Report, ESMA/2015/609, 19 March, https://www.esma.europa.eu/sites/default/files/library/2015/11/2015-609_cra_guidelines_on_periodic_reporting.pdf (accessed February 17, 2021).

Financial Stability Board. 2018. "History of the FSB," https://www.fsb.org/about/history-of-the-fsb/ (accessed February 24, 2021).

Financial Stability Board. 2010. "Principles for Reducing Reliance on CRA Ratings," 27 October, https://www.fsb.org/wp-content/uploads/r_101027.pdf (accessed February 12, 2021).

Financial Industry Regulatory Authority. 2018. "FINRA Bond Facts Tool Terms and Conditions," 28 August, https://www.finra.org/finra-bond-facts-terms-and-conditions (accessed February 24, 2021).

International Monetary Fund. 2020. "Global Financial Stability Report: Markets in the Time of COVID-19," April, https://www.imf.org/en/Publications/GFSR/Issues/2020/04/14/global-financial-stability-report-april-2020 (accessed February 17, 2021).

IOSCO. 2015. "Code of Conduct Fundamentals for Credit Rating Agencies," Final Report, FR05/2015, March, https://www.iosco.org/library/pubdocs/pdf/IOSCOPD482.pdf (accessed February 28, 2021).

Langohr, Herwig, and Patricia Langohr. 2009. *The Rating Agencies and Their Credit Ratings: What They Are, How They Work, And Why They Are Relevant*, Chichester: John Wiley & Sons Ltd.

Lannoo, Karel. 2015. *The Great Financial Plumbing: From Northern Rock to Banking Union*, Centre for European Policy Studies (CEPS), London: Rowman & Littlefield.

Legislative Observatory. 2010. Credit rating agencics: supervision, Procedure file 2010/0160/COD, https://oeil.secure.europarl.europa.eu/oeil/popups/ficheprocedure.do?reference=2010/0160(COD)&l=en (accessed February 20, 2021).

Levich, Richard M., Giovanni Majnoni, and Carmen Reinhart. 2002. "Ratings, Rating Agencies and the Global Financial System: Summary and Policy Implications". In *Ratings, Rating Agencies and the Global Financial System.* Edited by Richard Levich, Giovanni Majnoni, and Carmen Reinhart, New York: Kluwer Academic Press.

Longstaff, Francis A. and Arvind Rajan. 2008. An Empirical Analysis of the Pricing of Collateralized Debt Obligations. *The Journal of Finance* 63, no.2: 529–563.

Miller, Jennifer. 2016. Ratings. In *The SAGE Encyclopedia of Corporate Reputation*. Edited by Craig E. Carroll. California: SAGE Publications, Inc.

Moloney, Niahm. 2018. *The Age of ESMA: Governing EU Financial Markets*. Oxford: Hart Publishing.

Nästegård, Emil. 2015. Does Member State Law Make Article 35a of the EU Regulation on Credit Rating Agencies Redundant?. University of Oslo Faculty of Law Research Paper No. 2015-04, https://ssrn.com/abstract=2546728 (accessed February 18, 2021).

Neyrinck, Norman, and Nicolas Petit. 2011. "Credit rating agencies and competition law," *Competition Policy International*, 30 August, https://www.competitionpolicyinternational.com/credit-rating-agencies-and-competition-law/ (accessed February 18, 2021).

OECD. 2010. "Competition and Credit Rating Agencies," Hearing, DAF/COMP(2010)29, 5 October, https://www.oecd.org/competition/sectors/46825342.pdf (accessed February 18, 2021).

Partnoy, Frank. 2006. "How and Why Credit Rating Agencies are Not Like Other Gatekeepers," San Diego Legal Studies Paper No. 07-46, https://papers.ssrn.com/sol3/papers.cfm?abstract_id=900257 (accessed February 20, 2021).

Petit, Nicolas. 2011. "Credit Rating Agencies, the Sovereign Debt Crisis and Competition Law," *European Competition Journal* 7, no.3: 587–632.

Pliakos, Asterios. 2018. *Δίκαιο της Ευρωπαϊκής Ένωσης [The Law of the European Union].* Athens: Nomiki Vivliothiki.

Rafailov, Dimitar. 2011. The Failures of Credit Rating Agencies during the Global Financial Crisis – Causes and Possible Solutions, *Economic Alternatives* no.1: 34–45.

Regulation (EU) 2017/2402 of the European Parliament and of the Council of 12 December 2017 laying down a general framework for securitisation and creating a specific framework for simple, transparent and standardised securitisation, and amending Directives 2009/65/EC, 2009/138/EC and 2011/61/EU and Regulations (EC) No 1060/2009 and (EU) No 648/2012. OJ L 347: 35–80.

Regulation (EU) 2017/1131 of the European Parliament and of the Council of 14 June 2017 on money market funds. OJ L 169: 8–45.

Regulation (EU) No 575/2013 of the European Parliament and of the Council of 26 June 2013 on prudential requirements for credit institutions and investment firms and amending Regulation (EU) No 648/2012. 2013. OJ L 176: 1–337.

Regulation (EU) No 462/2013 of the European Parliament and of the Council of 21 May 2013 amending Regulation (EC) No 1060/2009 on credit rating agencies (CRA III). OJ L 146: 1–33.

Regulation (EU) No 1215/2012 of the European Parliament and of the Council of 12 December 2012 on jurisdiction and the recognition and enforcement of judgments in civil and commercial matters (Brussels I Regulation). OJ L 351: 1–32.

Regulation (EU) No 513/2011 of the European Parliament and of the Council of 11 May 2011 amending Regulation (EC) No 1060/2009 on credit rating agencies (CRA II). OJ L 145: 30–56.

Regulation (EU) No 1095/2010 of 24 November 2010 establishing a European Supervisory Authority (European Securities and Markets Authority), amending Decision No 716/2009/EC and repealing Commission Decision 2009/77/EC (ESMA Regulation). OJ L 331: 84–119.

Regulation (EU) No 1094/2010 of the European Parliament and of the Council of 24 November 2010 establishing a European Supervisory Authority (European Insurance and Occupational Pensions Authority), amending Decision No 716/2009/EC and repealing Commission Decision 2009/79/EC. 2010. OJ L 331: 48–83.

Regulation (EU) No 1093/2010 of the European Parliament and of the Council of 24 November 2010 establishing a European Supervisory Authority (European Banking Authority), amending Decision No 716/2009/EC and repealing Commission Decision 2009/78/EC. 2010. OJ L 331: 12–47.

Regulation (EU) No 1092/2010 of the European Parliament and of the Council of 24 November 2010 on European Union macro-prudential oversight of the financial system and establishing a European Systemic Risk Board. 2010. OJ L 331: 1–11.

Regulation (EC) No 1060/2009 of the European Parliament and of the Council of 16 September 2009 on credit rating agencies (CRA I). OJ L 302: 1–31.

Regulation (EC) No 1060/2009 of the European Parliament and of the Council of 16 September 2009 on credit rating agencies. Consolidated text https://eur-lex.europa.eu/legal-content/EN/TXT/?uri=CELEX%3A0 2009R1060-20190101 (accessed February 20, 2021).

Regulation (EC) No 864/2007 of the European Parliament and of the Council of 11 July 2007 on the law applicable to non-contractual obligations (Rome II Regulation). OJ L 199: 40–49.

Reuters. 2015. "S&P reaches $1.5 billion deal with U.S., states over crisis-era ratings," 3 February, https://www.reuters.com/article/us-s-p-settlement-idUSKBN0L71C120150203 (accessed January 20, 2021).

Reuters. 2013. "Settlement cost for Moody's, S&P, Morgan Stanley is $225 million: WSJ," 30 April, https://www.reuters.com/article/us-moodys-sp-settlement-wsj-idUSBRE93S11920130429 (accessed February 18, 2021).

Robinson, David. 2018. "Portugal: from pig to golden child," *International Adviser*, 15 May, https://international-adviser.com/ portugal-from-pig-to-golden-child/ (accessed February 18, 2021).

Roubini, Nouriel, 2020, "Ten reasons why a 'Greater Depression' for the 2020s is inevitable," *The Guardian*, 29 April, https://www.theguardian.com/business/2020/apr/29/ten-reasons-why-greater-depression-for-the-2020s-is-inevitable-covid (accessed February 24, 2021).

Rodemann, Julian. 2017. "Ratingagenturen: Das große Geschäft mit der Unsicherheit" [Big business with uncertainty], *Suddeutsche Zeitung*, 19 February, https://www.sueddeutsche.de/wirtschaft/ratingagenturen-das-grosse-geschaeft-mit-der-unsicherheit-1.3385726 (accessed February 10, 2021).

ThyssenKrupp. 2005. Jahresabschluss und Lagebericht 2004_2005 [Annual financial statements and management report 2004_2005], https://ucpcdn.thyssenkrupp.com/_legacy/UCPthyssenkruppAG/assets.files/media/investoren/berichterstattung-publikationen/archiv/finanzberichte-de/2004-2005/thyssenkrupp_2004_2005_ja.pdf (accessed February 18, 2021).

US Commodity Futures Trading Commission. 2010. "Final Rule Regarding Removal of References to Credit Ratings from Commission Regulations," Office of Public Affairs, 21 July, https://www.cftc.gov/sites/default/files/idc/groups/public/@newsroom/documents/file/rcr_factsheet_final.pdf (accessed February 18, 2021).

US Credit Rating Agency Reform Act. 2006. Public Law 109–291, September 29. 120 Stat. 1327, https://www.sec.gov/ocr/cra-reform-act-2006.pdf (accessed February 28, 2021).

US Department of Justice. 2017. "Justice Department and State Partners Secure Nearly $864 Million Settlement With Moody's Arising From

Conduct in the Lead up to the Financial Crisis, In re: Moody's Investors Service Inc.," Press release, 13 January, https://www.justice.gov/opa/pr/justice-department-and-state-partners-secure-nearly-864-million-settlement-moody-s-arising (accessed February 18, 2021).

US Department of Justice. 2015. "Justice Department and State Partners Secure $1.375 Billion Settlement with S&P for Defrauding Investors in the Lead Up to the Financial Crisis," Press release, 3 February, https://www.justice.gov/opa/pr/justice-department-and-state-partners-secure-1375-billion-settlement-sp-defrauding-investors (accessed February 18, 2021).

US District Court, Southern District of New York. 2013. Abu Dhabi Commercial Bank et al v. Morgan Stanley & Co et al, No. 08 Civ. 7508, https://law.justia.com/cases/federal/district-courts/new-york/nysdce/1:2008cv07508/331416/584/ (accessed January 20, 2021).

US District Court, Southern District of New York. 2010. King County, Washington et al v. IKB Deutsche Industriebank AG et al., No. 09 Civ. 08387, https://law.justia.com/cases/federal/district-courts/new-york/nysdce/1:2009cv08387/352929/162/ (accessed January 20, 2021).

US District Court, Southern District of New York. 2001. U.S. v. Moody's Investors Service Inc., No. 01 Cr. 339, https://www.justice.gov/atr/case-document/information-417 (accessed January 20, 2021).

US Dodd-Frank Wall Street Reform and Consumer Protection Act. 2010. Public Law 111–203, July 21. 124 Stat. 1376, https://www.congress.gov/111/plaws/publ203/PLAW-111publ203.pdf (accessed February 22, 2021).

US Financial Crisis Inquiry Commission. 2011. "The Financial Crisis Inquiry Report," Final Report of the National Commission on the Causes of the Financial and Economic Crisis in the United States, Official Government Report, Submitted by the Financial Crisis Inquiry Commission pursuant to Public Law 111-21, January, https://www.govinfo.gov/content/pkg/GPO-FCIC/pdf/GPO-FCIC.pdf (accessed February 12, 2021).

US Securities Act of 1933, Public Law 73-22, May 27. 48 Stat. 74, https://www.govinfo.gov/content/pkg/COMPS-1884/pdf/COMPS-1884.pdf (accessed February 18, 2021).

US SEC. 2020. "Annual Report on Nationally Recognized Statistical Rating Organizations," As Required by Section 6 of the Credit Rating Agency Reform Act of 2006, January, https://www.sec.gov/files/2019-annual-report-on-nrsros.pdf (accessed February 22, 2021).

US SEC. 2017. "Updated Investor Bulletin: The ABCs of Credit Ratings," 12 October, https://www.sec.gov/oiea/investor-alerts-and-bulletins/ib_creditratings (accessed February 12, 2021).

Veil, Rüdiger. 2017. *European Capital Markets Law*. 2nd ed. Oxford: Hart Publishing.

Véron, Nicolas, and Isabel Schnabel. 2018. "Completing the Banking Union means breaking the vicious circle between banks and sovereigns," Bruegel Blog Post, 17 May, https://www.bruegel.org/2018/05/completing-europes-banking-union-means-breaking-the-bank-sovereign-vicious-circle/ (accessed February 22, 2021).

Whish, Richard, and David Bailey. 2012. *Competition Law*. 7th ed. Oxford: Oxford University Press.

White, Lawrence J. 2018. The Credit Rating Agencies and Their Role in the Financial System. In *The Oxford Handbook on Institutions, International Economic Governance, and Market Regulation.* Edited by Eric Brousseau, Jean-Michel Glachant, and Jérôme Sgard. Oxford: Oxford University Press.

World Bank. 2020. "Financial stability," https://www.worldbank.org/en/publication/gfdr/gfdr-2016/background/financial-stability (accessed February 20, 2021).

CHAPTER 11

DO CREDIT RATES CONTRIBUTE TO MARKET EFFICIENCY AND/OR RESILIENCE?

EMMANOUIL VLACHOGIANNIS*

Introduction

The subject that will be discussed in this chapter is whether credit ratings contribute to market efficiency and/or resilience. Market efficiency in a credit market in which different participants take part, either investors or issuers of bonds, is considered as an outcome that allows a stable relationship between interest rates and inherent (idiosyncratic) risks. Instead, market resilience is seen in a more dynamic, i.e., time-dependent, setting. Narrowly conceived, market resilience allows a smooth convergence to the outcome of an efficient market when market conditions, either in the supply or in the demand side, change. We can hypothesise that oscillation, or even divergence, of prices in markets cannot be attributed to market resilience.

Most economists trained in the 1970s embraced the concept of the so-called Neoclassical Synthesis (Samuelson 2009) and are convinced of the validity of the Efficient Market Hypothesis (Fama 1970). For mainstream economics, market performance is considered optimal under the condition that by establishing the market, sound market principles are not disregarded. An equilibrium is established when markets are cleared; supply and demand define the price and the quantity traded. Fluctuations in prices are rather random, and convergence to the mean is the most probable outcome, unless there is a change in market conditions. Therefore, the classical way of training economists entails the pursuit of equilibria. As the science of economics has become enriched by systems theory, considered one of the major achievements in today's economic

* First Vice-President, Thessaloniki Chamber of Commerce and Industry (TCCI).

theory, a gradual departure from the equilibrium concept has started to occur.

From the point of view of a traditional economist (conventional wisdom), credit ratings enable market transparency because they provide investors with information about the credibility of bonds. Therefore, as is the main belief in equilibrium theory, they improve market efficiency, allowing supply and demand to define interest rates and to incorporate the underlying risks in stable relations. This has to be empirically tested in a very wide time frame. The validity of this assumption shall be investigated with some theoretical considerations throughout this chapter.

Sharp reactions to changes in market conditions have been a usual phenomenon in the past, and even after the late-2000s financial crisis. High vulnerabilities of economies have also been prominent, leading to the question of whether credit ratings are self-fulfilling prophecies. Inevitably, strong political opposition to credit ratings is emerging due to the above. For instance, the president of Turkey Recep Tayyip Erdoğan condemned in May 2017 the three major rating agencies for having portrayed a false picture of the Turkish economy, and attributed their statements to a conspiracy against his country. During the same period (May 2017), Greek politics were extensively affected after having acted on the advice, based on credit ratings, about economic measures that had to be taken by the Greek government in order to improve credit ratings, especially on the question of whether the country needs a precautionary credit line by the European Stability Mechanism (ESM) or not. The agenda of credit ratings of sovereign debt issues can be politicised too easily. This happens because credit ratings take more the form of a political judgment rather than a forecast or information or service of a purely economic nature given to potential investors. It seems that political considerations blur economic information, or at least give the impression of doing so. This effect is compounded when we take a look at the conditions under which credit ratings are produced.

Microeconomics of credit ratings

The conditions under which credit ratings are produced do affect the frame under which their impact on markets is unfolded. Hence, studying the microeconomics of credit ratings can provide us with some considerations about their contribution to market efficiency and/or resilience. We consider credit ratings as a service to market participants. Investors may use this service to adjust their engagement according to the features of issued bonds, and debt issuers may shape the features of bonds according to credit ratings. Credit ratings constitute a service provided by certified agencies, which are in general commercial, for-profit companies, aiming to "condense or compile information" (Migiakis 2018), the content of which should reflect default probabilities or default risks.

The next step is to analyse, at least conceptually, how Credit Rating Agencies (hereinafter CRAs) come up with this kind of service. It is quite clear that considerable resources are required in order to produce a rating. First of all, credit ratings are produced with reference to historical data and their analysis. There is no doubt that this part constitutes a more scientific endeavour, with increasing feasibility as computational power increases. Agencies may fine-tune, with some effort, the underlying analysis in order to harden the evidence gathered by historical data.

Credit ratings are not conceived as a service providing an accurate analysis of the past. Instead, they try to capture information about the future. Hence, CRAs need to construct a framework for representing future developments that, by nature, are contingent. They do so by attempting to forecast the most probable state of affairs for the debt issuer, on the basis of a very complex set of indicators. They can engage in extrapolation of historical data, for instance, in the form of linear regression, assuming that past structures will remain the same for the future. They may fine-tune, and calibrate accordingly, the forecasting model with the implied risk of over-adjustment. Certainly, they have to make decisions on how to proceed, and for that reason, they have to engage in human and computational capacity, which comes with considerable costs. Nevertheless, at that point, a source of a major trade-off emerges: will the agency look for sophisticated forecasts leading to what is perceived as a more accurate prediction, or will it focus on controlling costs? If the agency could be exposed to markets, there would be an answer: expected revenues must cover the costs. In the case of CRAs, this is not so simple.

Even after painfully resolving the issue of selecting a forecasting model, things may still be complicated due to the fact that one has to make assumptions for future events and assign weights in the process of condensing or compiling. In technical terms, a vector consisting of evaluated parameters must be brought down to a single value. Inevitably, subjective valuation has to be engaged, which is, by nature, dependent on personal views. Then the next problem arises, i.e., how to estimate market reactions. Debt issuers may change their policies due to various reasons, including political pressure or in an effort to anticipate a more favourable credit rating. Investors may be affected by some types of emotional reactions, including fear or greed. By and large, CRAs have to come up with ratings by assessing not only the impact of facts and the hard data of the past, but also an array of expectations, including their own.

First of all, this means that, for obtaining credit ratings, resources have to be involved, and these resources vary significantly from one type of rating to another. For corporate credit ratings, the resources needed are probably fewer when forming expectations about future developments depending on market observations, changes in technology, or consumer demographics and preferences. For sovereign credit ratings, with all its complications, forming expectations about future developments might be an intractable act, or at the very least, they imply a need for a considerable amount of resources. The emerging trade-off mentioned earlier becomes more difficult to handle.

There is certainly the need to employ personnel with very high skills from different backgrounds, such as economists, statisticians, forecasters, political analysts, and sociologists, and with assumingly high remuneration packages. By borrowing some of the findings from organisational theory, we may also infer that one of the most important challenges of rating agencies is how to create a mechanism that collects the wisdom generated by people from different backgrounds in order to establish weight between different kinds of data. For instance, is hard data from the past more important than the assumptions leading to an analysis of future political developments, or vice versa? Several malfunctions can occur during this process. Firstly, various group dynamics are observed within each company, leading to differentiation in the collective choice of the appropriate weighting indicators. Secondly, dependence on external views can vary greatly. Thirdly, several other factors can implicitly or explicitly be part of the valuation by the people engaged in this kind of judgment. It seems that there are inherent difficulties in streamlining the process of arriving at a coherent credit rating for sovereign debt; hence the outcome looks a little bit fuzzy, and by any means contestable. Nevertheless, as this short analysis has shown, credit ratings are costly endeavours.

Systemic peculiarities

A credit rating is conceived as a service to investors, presumably to be obtained under the prevalence of high costs. "Normal" private companies seek profit and develop services in order to sell them to customers. Once information is disclosed and made publicly available, there is no longer a price to be charged for this service. For sure, credit ratings are not sold to potential investors, so issuers have to come up with financial compensation for incurring costs. That results in an anomaly often identified by various analysts (Migiakis 2018).

In the case of sovereign debt, the fact that the source of financial compensation is unknown adds to obscurity. In any case, the temptation to manipulate credit rating outcomes is inherent in this system of privately produced, "condensed or compiled" information, which is broadcasted and made available to the general public. Even if regulation attempts to limit temptations by the active supervision of processes, a system of partly adverse incentives is created, with the inherent risk of producing unintended consequences, where investors are misinformed in making their decisions in the aftermath of a credit rating broadcast.

Even in the case of excluding any possibility of intended or unintended misinformation of investors, the outcome of the current credit rating system may have an unforeseen impact. Under normal circumstances, various participants in the market develop patterns of dispersed risk appetite. By providing a credit rating, a homogenisation of investors' expectations takes place. Depending on the degree of homogenisation, positive loops are generated in a dynamic setting amplifying market trends. This is a conclusion provided as a contribution of systems theory to economics. As we will later show once we discuss the application of the cobweb theorem for our case of credit ratings, much will depend on existing elasticities of supply and demand to converge to an equilibrium or to move into an unstable setting. However, at that point of analysis, we may conceive credit ratings not as an instrument of neutral information, and within this framework the impact of politics is unclear. The emerging properties resulting from the entanglement of broadcasted and, to some extent, fuzzy credit ratings may jeopardise market efficiency and resilience.

Inferring assumptions on market efficiency

It is a bold attempt to try to draw conclusions based on formulated assumptions for a dynamic setting of markets under the impact of credit ratings. Of course, any assumptions postulated here have to be empirically tested for their validity. Firstly, we assume that investors form their expectations around a statistical measure of the past that might be a median or an average of default risks. For simplicity, we may choose the median, as this is simple information gathered by past data. Secondly, when credit ratings suggest that the default risk is below the median, then disproportionate funding is attracted, allowing debt with lower interest rates to be issued, even lower than anticipated within an "ignorant" market before any additional information based on credit ratings. Thirdly, when credit ratings suggest that the default risk is above the median, then funding can be attracted under only significantly higher interest rates. Remarkably, interest rates obtained affect the default risk of a debtor, since higher interest for investors increases financial distress, while lower interest reduces it. Bearing this in mind, one can say that credit ratings, which aim to be an instrument of information, transform themselves into instruments of giving bonuses or maluses, and besides, one has to remember that credit ratings inevitably spell a kind of political judgment.

In the next step, we try to visualise all these assumptions in a traditional market setting, with supply and demand curves representing the state of affairs. Let us suppose that the supply curve is constituted by the willingness of investors to engage in funding with varying amounts regarding interest rates. Let us also suppose that the demand curve is constituted by the willingness, or even more so, by the needs of debtors for funds in varying amounts, depending on interest rates. Let us finally suppose that a perceived supply curve intersects with the perceived demand curve in a price/quantity point that corresponds to the median default risk, as perceived by the investors on the basis of past data.

Firstly, let us examine theoretically what the impact of credit ratings on the supply curve will be. If credit ratings suggest a higher default risk, then investors will supply fewer funds for the same level of interest rates. If credit ratings suggest a lower default risk, then investors will supply more funds for the same level of interest rates. The elasticity of the supply curve may thus increase. Secondly, let us examine theoretically what the impact of credit ratings on the demand curve will be. A prudential debtor will take care of the impact of rising interest rates and will alter the pattern of demand. Aware of the credit rating, the debtor will further "squeeze" demand when faced with higher interest rates in case of a higher than the median perceived default risk, and will increase demand in the opposite case. The elasticity of the demand curve may thus increase as well.

Remarkably, on both sides of the market, risk intolerance is admitted to form that pattern of change. Steeper risk curves go hand in hand with increasing elasticities in the underlying bond market. If both elasticities increase due to credit ratings, that might be a problem for market efficiency, as both curves will intersect and create a new equilibrium, where interest rates will reflect increasing risk intolerance as market participants become more informed. However, we have to ask if a smooth transition is always at work, as we have to examine closely not only static patterns, but also their dynamics. It turns out that we may have to pay closer attention to the famous cobweb theorem developed by Nicholas Kaldor (1934). In its simple form, this means that if in the point of intersection, the elasticity of supply is higher than the elasticity of demand, then prices (interest rates) are prone to diverge, putting the Efficient Market Hypothesis under question. If the elasticity of supply is less than the elasticity of demand, then prices (interest rates) might converge to a new equilibrium allowing for the Efficient Market Hypothesis to stay valid.

In the above analysis, we came to the conclusion that both elasticities will likely increase. It is a bold assumption that despite the changes in elasticity, elasticity of supply will stay at a level less than the elasticity of demand. Moreover, we assumed that the debtor acts prudentially, which is not always the case, as political pressure may lead the debtor to exercise non-prudential strategies. In that case, increasing elasticity of supply will not be offset by an increase in the elasticity of demand.

To make a concluding point here: it is likely that credit ratings will have such an impact on debt markets via fuzziness, broadcasting, homogenisation, and elasticities that the wisdom of the crowd will slip into the madness of the mob. It is not a given that interest rates will always correspond to risk, so market efficiency is questioned. Of course, we shall once again mention that the need for empirical data always exists.

Inferring assumptions on market resilience

The main conclusion of the previous section is that credit ratings, due to their determinants, do not always lead to market efficiency, as defined at the beginning of this chapter, i.e., as an outcome that allows a stable relation between interest rates and inherent risks. Applying the cobweb theorem of Nicholas Kaldor, we came to the conclusion that under certain conditions, convergence is not tractable. Following this path of reasoning, we may not expect that credit ratings can lead to more market resilience. However, the case for market resilience is defined by the way markets react to external shocks, and it is eminent that by studying the history of markets, one can identify a high sensitivity of their outcomes concerning liquidity. The correlation between credit ratings and interest rates is becoming not that much expressed after the crisis due to the fact that global liquidity exploded after the crisis because of measures taken by central banks and state authorities in order to fight recession (Migiakis 2018).

Liquidity is subject to monetary supply. By increasing the monetary base and/or relaxing banking regulations, the flow of liquid instruments around the world is expanding. We may examine theoretically how expanding liquidity affects the supply of funds in the bond market. We will hold the assumption that elasticities of supply do not change despite the expansion of liquidity, but that the supply of funds will increase. Technically speaking, the supply curve moves to the right. In the case of a convergent setting, the market is expected to move to a new equilibrium. In the case of a divergent setting, the market is expected to explode.

However, what happens when there is a steady expansion of liquidity, either because of an inflating central bank balance sheet or due to increased leverage? Divergence effects, manifested through a bizarre movement of interest rates, are postponed until liquidity expansion comes to an end. "When the music stops, in terms of liquidity, things will be complicated. As long as the music is playing, you've got to get up and dance. We're still dancing", in the words of Chuck Prince, CEO of Citigroup, in the summer of 2007 (Nakamoto and Wighton 2007). Nevertheless, when the music stopped, the markets burst, liquidity disappeared, and divergence started its play. The records showing the interactions between credit ratings and interest rates and/or spreads for the Greek sovereign debt give us a vivid example of what can happen when bond markets with settings prone to divergence are confronted with contracting, or even disappearing, liquidity.

Based on systems theory, we may also postulate that if the market is overreacting to any changes because of positive loops, then we may also localise and identify conditions inducing a very vicious circle on interest rate developments. Moreover, the fact that credit ratings try to anticipate market reactions aggravates the problem. Overall, credit ratings seem to be contributing to an enhanced instability of financial markets instead of improving market resilience.

Conclusion

Concluding, credit ratings, at least in the way they are formed today, are instruments bearing a high risk for unintended consequences. They do not conform to basic market principles. The fact that something intended for use as a service is not paid for by the person taking advantage of this service leads to a "free lunch", i.e., a situation of costless profit for the beneficiary of the service provided, which is certainly a violation of sound market principles. In fact, this is the way of complacency that may deviate and finally destroy markets. Credit ratings, along with other features of financial markets, underpin the validity of the Financial Market Instability Hypothesis associated with the name of Hyman Minsky (1986). Combined with aggravating effects created by leveraging or deleveraging, expanding or contracting monetary supply seem in fact to induce what Ludwig von Mises (1981) anticipated in the 1920s, when he developed his monetary theory, i.e., that financial markets flooded with created "artificial" money not anchored in the real economy will always provoke damage. Therefore, we come to the conclusion that credit ratings certainly need to be reformed.

References

Fama, Eugene F. 1970. Efficient Capital Markets: A Review of Theory and Empirical Work. *The Journal of Finance* 25, no.2: 383–417.

Kaldor, Nicholas. 1934. A Classificatory Note on the Determinateness of Equilibrium. *The Review of Economic Studies* 1, no.2: 122–136.

Migiakis, Petros M. 2018. "Pricing sovereign credit risk: The impact of credit ratings". Presentation, Jean Monnet Centre of Excellence at the University of Macedonia, International Conference "EU Growth: Credit Rating and Foreign Direct Investment", Thessaloniki, 17 May, https://www.youtube.com/watch?v=yESSwei9U3M (accessed July 8, 2021).

Minsky, Hyman P. 1986. *Stabilizing an Unstable Economy*. New York: McGraw-Hill Professional.

Nakamoto, Michiyo and David Wighton. 2007. Citigroup Chief Stays Bullish on Buy-Outs. *Financial Times*. 10 July. https://www.ft.com/content/80e2987a-2e50-11dc-821c-0000779fd2ac (accessed July 8, 2021).

Samuelson, Paul A. 2009. *Economics: An Introductory Analysis*. 19th ed. New York: Mc Graw Hill Education.

Von Mises, Ludwig. 1981. *The Theory of Money and Credit*. Indianapolis: Liberty Fund.